GENDER POLITICS IN THE EXPANDING EUROPEAN UNION

GENDER POLITICS IN THE EXPANDING EUROPEAN UNION

Mobilization, Inclusion, Exclusion

Edited by Silke Roth

Berghahn Books
New York • Oxford

Published in 2008 by

Berghahn Books

www.berghahnbooks.com

©2008 by Silke Roth

Library of Congress Cataloging-in-Publication Data

Gender politics in the expanding European Union : mobilization, inclusion, exclusion / edited by Silke Roth.

    p. cm.

  Includes index.

  ISBN 978-1-84545-516-3 (hardback : alk. paper) — ISBN 978-1-84545-517-0 (pbk. : alk. paper)

  1. Women—European Union countries—Social conditions. 2. Women's rights—European Union countries. I. Roth, Silke.

  HQ1587.G457 2008

  323.3'4094—dc22   2008020321

British Library Cataloguing in Publication Data

A catalogue record for this book is available from the British Library

Printed in the United States on acid-free paper

ISBN: 978-1-84545-516-3 hardback

5/09

Contents

❦

List of Tables and Figures

Tables

Figures

LIST OF ABBREVIATIONS

ASTRA	Central and Eastern European Women's Network for Sexual and Reproductive Health and Rights
CEDAW	Convention on the Elimination of All Forms of Discrimination
CEE	Central and Eastern Europe
CEECs	Central and Eastern European countries
CIS	Commonwealth of Independent States
CR	Czech Republic
ČSSD	Czech Social Democratic Party
CSW	Commission on the Status of Women
DAPHNE	"Fight Against Violence" Program
EC	European Community
ECJ	European Court of Justice
ECNC	European Community Network on Childcare
ECU	European Currency Unit
EEC	European Economic Community
EES	European Employment Strategy
ENAR	European Network Against Racism
EOCP	Equal Opportunities Childcare Problem
ETA	Equal Treatment Authority
EU	European Union
EWL	European Women's Lobby

GDR	German Democratic Republic
KARAT	Regional Coalition of Women's NGOs in CEE and CIS
KŠCM	Communist Party of Bohemia and Moravia
MFA	Ministry of Foreign Affairs
MLSA	Ministry of Labor and Social Affairs
NDP	National Development Plan
NESC	National Economic and Social Council
NESF	National Economic and Social Forum
NEWW	Network East-West Women
NGO	Nongovernmental organization
NMS-10	New Member States-10
NWCI	National Women's Council of Ireland
OECD	Organization for Economic Cooperation and Development
OMC	Open Method of Coordination
OSKA	Organization of Women's Initiatives (Poland)
OWEN	East-West European Women's Network (Germany)
UFV	Independent Women's Association (Germany)
UK	United Kingdom
UN	United Nations
UNDP	United Nations Development Fund
WIDE	Women in Development Europe

INTRODUCTION

GENDER POLITICS IN THE EXPANDING EUROPEAN UNION

Mobilization, Inclusion, Exclusion

Silke Roth

Since 1957, when Belgium, the Federal Republic of Germany, France, Italy, Luxembourg, and the Netherlands formed the European Economic Community (EEC) later renamed the European Union (EU), this supranational opportunity structure has been an important resource for the promotion of gender equality in member states and candidate countries. At least discursively, the EU endorses gender equality as a fundamental value and demands that its member states embrace this principle. This volume addresses the impact of EU accession on member states as well as the European Union from a gender perspective. Each enlargement—western in the 1970s, southern in the 1980s, northern in the 1990s, and most recently eastern—broadened and deepened gender policies either in the EU or in the member states or in both to various extents. In 1973 Denmark, Ireland, and the United Kingdom joined the European Communities; in 1981 Greece followed; in 1986 Portugal and Spain became members; in 1995 Austria, Finland, and Sweden joined the EU; in 2004 Cyprus, the Czech Republic, Estonia, Hungary, Latvia, Lithuania, Malta, Poland, Slovakia, and Slovenia became part of the EU; and most recently, in 2007 Bulgaria and Romania followed. In contrast to the other former socialist countries, due to German unification, East Germany joined the EU already in 1990. So far, gender equality policies have been neglected in research concerning EU expansion, whereas analyses of European women's movements and gender equality politics tended to concentrate either on the old EU member states or on the experiences of women in the former socialist countries, but rarely brought them together. This book seeks to fill these gaps, by assessing gender equality policies and feminist mobilization in both old and new member states, as well as in a candidate country, Turkey. It needs to be kept in mind that the EU is not identical with Europe, as Switzerland does not belong to the EU whereas the candidacy of Turkey and thus the boundaries of Europe are highly contested.

The contributions in this volume comprise fresh scholarship that challenges previous assessments of the impact of the EU and shows that it is a contradictory process. The successes of women's movements and activists at the EU level are juxtaposed with the lack of clarity, effective implementation, and enforcement of directives—in old and new member states. Furthermore, successful EU integration and economic development might go hand in hand with considerable disadvantages for women. The case studies also address the tensions between top-down reforms and grassroots autonomous movements. And it is also considered that while transnational women's movements provide important networking opportunities, East-West relations have not always been easy. Employing a social constructivist approach, the authors in this volume address the importance of framing and agenda setting at both the EU level and the domestic level. As the contributions to this volume emphasize, the relationship between the EU and its member states is interactive and dynamic. The EU is at the same time shaped by and shaping member states as well as candidate countries, whereas domestic politics remain of crucial importance regarding the adoption and implementation of EU regulations.

In this introduction, firstly, I review the impact of the EU on domestic gender equality policies and conclude that it differs by country as well as by policy area and has changed over time. Secondly, I show how the transformation process and the enlargement process in Central Eastern Europe intersected and how this affected the status of women. Thirdly, I discuss the role of women's networks and feminist mobilization in the EU and the enlargement process. Finally, I give an overview of the book.

The European Union as Political Opportunity Structure for Feminist Mobilization and Gender Equality

The EU is acknowledged as a supranational institution influencing gender equality policy in its member states—as well as in candidate countries—even against their preferences (Ellina 2003). Although the initial gender equality legislation of the EEC was an unintended side effect (e.g., Hoskyns 1996, Berkovitch 1999) and was initially restricted to questions of equal pay, it nevertheless provided the foundation for later gender equality legislation. Because France was at that time the only country with an equal pay provision among the founding members and was concerned that this might be a potential barrier to fair and equal competition among member states, it demanded the inclusion of such a provision (Cichowksi 2002, 222). Article 119 of the Treaty of Rome (1957), guaranteeing equal pay for equal work, could be used for national equal pay campaigns and provided a starting point for further sex equality legislation. Despite its limitations, the EU therefore provided a favorable venue for women's interests—often more open to feminist demands than national governments. Over time, EU policies on women's rights became broader, eventually addressing the reconciliation of employment with family life and, more recently, gender mainstreaming (for overviews see Ellina 2003; Hantrais 2000a; Hoskyns 1996).

In the 1970s and 1980s, in addition to striving for gender equality in terms of equal pay, the European Commission addressed other aspects of gender inequality, which led to the adoption of a number of directives addressing tax and social security measures, child care facilities, education, and training opportunities (see chapters by Wahl, Morgan, and Zippel). These directives were accompanied by positive action programs on behalf of women. However, the member states decide how they allocate the available resources such as structural funds to gender equality.

In the 1980s and 1990s, European women were not only dissatisfied with respect to the achievement of EU women's rights, but they also found favorable opportunity structures to strengthen a broader policy frame. European women's groups became more and more involved in international women's networks, and the UN conferences contributed to the emergence and consolidation of an international network (Keck and Sikkink 1998). At the Fourth World Conference of Women in Beijing in 1995, gender mainstreaming was formally adopted. In the same year, Austria, Finland, and Sweden joined the EU. Finland and Sweden in particular had a strong existing commitment to equal opportunities and considerable experience in mainstreaming gender in their national policies (Pollack and Hafner-Burton 2000; Hellgren and Hobson in this volume).

Due to the northern enlargement of the EU in 1995, the proportion of women in the European parliament increased. Furthermore, within the commission a number of feminists ensured that gender mainstreaming entered and stayed on the agenda of the EU (Mazey 2000). Women's activism and international networks like the European Women's Lobby played a central role in the expansive development of EU sex equality legislation and the introduction of gender mainstreaming (Helferrich and Kolb 2001; Cichowski 2002). The impact on the member states varied, depending on the gender equality policies already in existence. For example, in Ireland and Spain EU membership contributed to strengthening gender equality policy (see chapters by Cullen and Valiente in this volume). In contrast, the Nordic countries (Sweden and Finland) had more to give than to gain from joining the EU. In particular, the euro-skeptic Swedish women feared that joining the EU would have a negative impact on gender equality in their country and therefore successfully sought to "export" Swedish gender equality policies (see Hellgren and Hobson in this volume). Their access to the EU as well as the UN conferences played a crucial role for strengthening the EU's position on women's equality (Ellina 2003).

The impact of EU policies varies not only in member states, but also in different areas (employment, reconciliation of work and family life, sexual harassment, etc.). Due to this variation, it is therefore not surprising that the assessment of the importance of the EU for gender equality policies in the member states also differs. Some see it as extensive, others as limited (for a discussion see Walby 2004, 5ff.). As Elman (1996a) emphasizes, the importance of gender equality in the economic sphere cannot be underestimated, but it is crucial to address issues such as reproductive rights and violence against women in order to overcome women's subordination. Walby (2004, 6–7) distinguishes several major limitations: the primary concern with standard employment; taking the male life course as the norm; the uneven implementation of EU Equality Directives due to national differences; the neglect of key areas of gender inequality such as sexual preference, abortion, and violence against women; soft (i.e., nonbinding) rather than hard law interventions; decreasing support for gender equality; and the underrepresentation of women in the convention.

The inclusion of gender equality in Article 2 of the Treaty of Amsterdam (1997) can be seen as a high point of the gender equality strategy (Walby 2004, 7). Furthermore, the adoption of gender mainstreaming in the Amsterdam treaty represents a new strategy that shifts attention from equality of treatment to equality of impact, and has the potential to transform government and policy making (Beveridge, Nott, and Stephen 2000, 286). In contrast to affirmative action and to singling out women's issues, gender mainstreaming "is the (re)organisation, improvement, development and evaluation of policy processes, so that a gender equality perspective is incorporated in all policies at all levels and at all stages, but the actors normally involved in policy making" (Council of Europe 2000, 15). Gender impact assessment is a tool of mainstreaming. It requires that every planned policy has to be assessed as to what influence it might have on women, men, and gender relations in general. Furthermore, it needs to be emphasized that gender mainstreaming and affirmative action are two complementary strategies. Gender mainstreaming does not replace, but supplements affirmative action.

Gender mainstreaming plays a crucial role in the discourse of transnational European women's organizations (Ferree and Pudrovska 2006), but it is also a controversial strategy. While some argue that it is undermining positive action

(Stratigaki 2005), others suggest that "the combination of gender mainstreaming with policy instruments in the context of the Open Method of Coordination (OMC) could promote the introduction of new proactive gender measures in the CEECs [Central and Eastern European Countries]" (Velluti 2005, 224). The Open Method of Coordination is a new form of nonbinding normative system that employs nonbinding objectives and guidelines to affect change in social policy and other areas (Trubek and Trubek 2005), but it does not put serious pressure on governments (Pascall and Lewis 2004). In order to be successful, gender mainstreaming needs to include activists and experts from a wide range (Van der Molen and Novikova 2005). Furthermore, because of the increased complexity and diversity across the EU due to enlargement, "it [is] increasingly evident that there are problems with the 'one size fits all' approach adopted by the European Council of Ministers in its recommendations to member states" (Fagan et. al 2005, 587). Gender mainstreaming can have negative impacts and contribute to de-gendering, the covering up of gender specific differences (see Stratigaki 2005, Kakucs and Pető in this volume). This means that gender mainstreaming can undermine feminist approaches. In their assessment of the National Reform Programme reports of the twenty-five member states released in 2005, Fagan, Grimshaw, and Rubery (2006) conclude that the removal of the gender equality guideline resulted in less attention to gender. But gender mainstreaming also provides a key step to pursue women's projects and issues and provided women's projects and women's movements in the new member states with legitimacy and international attention. The EU approach to gender equality thus both represents a hybrid model—as Ferree argues in this volume—encompassing principles of liberalism and social democracy as well as innovative ideas of the global women's movements. It encompasses opportunities as well as threats to feminist achievements.

Winners or Losers? The Impact of the Transformation Process and EU Accession on Women

In order to understand the impact of the EU accession process on gender relations in the twelve new member states that have joined the EU since 2004, it is crucial to keep in mind that transformation and EU accession are two intersecting processes. Women have often been labeled "losers" of the transformation process (for a critical discussion of this assessment see Ghodsee 2004). In the first half of the nineties, in almost all transformation countries, employment and revenues declined and the Gross National Product dropped. Unemployment affected women more than men because they were strongly represented in shrinking sectors, in particular the public sector, and many women shifted their work into the informal sector (Einhorn 1993; Domsch, Ladwig, and Tenten 2003). The rise of nationalism was accompanied by a return to traditional roles, and women were directly or indirectly encouraged to return to the role of housewives and full-time caregivers (Pollert 2003). However, there is evidence for a more equal division of care work in the new member states (Pascall and Lewis 2004, 376).

Despite high education and extensive skill training, women faced explicit discrimination in hiring, particularly age discrimination (Heinen and Portet 2002). Pollert (2003, 336) summarizes these developments as follows: "The capitalist transformation not only failed to maximize the female human resource legacy left by the communist regimes, but damaged it." In addition, the transition to democracy also resulted in a decrease in women's political participation. When the parliaments gained real power during the process of democratization of Eastern Europe, the percentage of female members of parliament dropped between 1980 and 1990 on average from 27 percent to 8 percent. However, while the numbers of women in government and parliaments dropped, there was a sharp increase in their participation in civil society. The advocacy of women's groups and networks resulted in some improvement with respect to women's participation (Chołuj and Neusüß 2004) and after the initial drop, the proportion of women in parliaments in the CEE countries started to rise again to an average of 17 percent in 2002 (Sloat 2004).

Before the agreements were signed, the candidate countries had to meet the Copenhagen criteria from 1993 (*acquis communautaire*) requiring political reforms, economic transformations, and social policy changes. The accession countries had to adjust their legal and institutional frameworks to accelerate the transition to a market economy, and strengthen human rights standards as well as democratic, civic, and political policies and practices. Miroiu (2006, 90) refers to the import of EU equality legislation as "costless room-service state feminism"— by this she means "the offer of a gender-sensitive legislation for CEE countries through the authority of international political actors . . . before internal public recognition of such a need." However, gender equality came relatively late onto the agenda of negotiations for entry to the EU. Much greater priority was placed on social and economic reforms based on neoliberal principles that are characterized by an implicit antiequality bias, whereas the mechanisms that are needed to ensure effective implementation of EU gender equality directives were weak (Chołuj and Neusüß 2004).

The candidate countries did not adhere equally to the political, economic, and social EU norms—in particular, gender norms—nor did the EU hold them accountable to each of these aspects to the same degree (Pollert 2003). The EU as well as the governments of the candidate countries did not take active steps to counteract the increasing unemployment of women and the increasing lack of day care facilities. Three years before EU enlargement, gender mainstreaming was still notably absent from policies towards Central and East European countries (Bretherton 2001).

However, even if the EU paid less attention to the adoption of gender mainstreaming and provided fewer resources to women's projects, the fact that gender mainstreaming was a part of the *acquis communautaire* and could be used by activists in the accession countries to demand the establishment of gender offices and the adoption of gender equality legislation (see the contributions by Regulska and Grabowska, Hašková and Křížková, and Kakucs and Pető in this volume). This meant for the activists that gender issues and feminist demands obtained more legitimacy as well as resources, although opportunities to systematically integrate gender during the pre-accession period have been missed (Bretherton 2001).

Thus from a gender perspective, the EU expansion is contradictory. On the one hand, national adaptation to the ostensibly gender-neutral political and economic standards of the EU led to an exclusion of women from labor markets and the public sphere. On the other hand, the (at least formally) explicit commitment to gender mainstreaming as an integral part of the EU policies provided some important policy instruments in the enlargement process for both increasing equality between men and women and fighting against exclusion based on ethnic, geographical, and social origin (see Hellgren and Hobson in this volume).

Due to the fact that some of the new EU members have conservative governments, the EU represents an important ally in the fight for gender equality and antidiscrimination policies in those countries. But it is important to ask not only how the accession has affected women's NGOs and women's movements in the new member states, but also what impact the new member states might have on gender issues in the EU. Will gender equality be strengthened through the Eastern expansion in 2004 because of the high employment orientation in the former socialist countries? Or, due to the conservative governments and attacks on reproductive rights in some of these countries (for example, Poland) should we expect it to result in a backlash? Shortly after Romania and Bulgaria joined the EU in January 2007, a caucus of right-wing parties in the European Parliament was formed. In addition to homophobic and racist attitudes, such parties tend to promote "traditional" gender relations, i.e., women's roles as mothers and caregivers and their exclusion from the public sphere.

Given these developments, how will EU expansion shape gender equality policies in the EU? In a collaborative effort, interventions at different levels—individual, household, civil society, and the state—need to be explored, in order to develop an improved gender regime for combining paid and unpaid care and other work that overcomes the shortcomings of the old regimes of both East and West (Pascall and Lewis 2004). The outcome will depend on the interaction of transnational opportunity structures (EU, UN), domestic politics, and local and transnational feminist mobilization. In order to take advantage of the potential for strengthening workplace gender equality legislation as well as gender equality overall, and to avoid a backlash on sexuality, reproductive rights, and family policies, women's NGOs, networks, and movements from the old and the new member states need to share resources and strategies. Keck and Sikkink (1998, 12) describe a "boomerang pattern" that can be employed when the channels between states and their domestic actors are blocked. Zippel (2004 and in this volume) employs the concept of the "ping-pong effect" and argues that activists not only use supranational opportunity structures in order to influence policies at the national level, but they also shape supranational organizations—like the EU—in member states. Furthermore, it must be kept in mind that state-movement interaction shapes states as well as social movements (Banaszak, Beckwith, and Rucht 2003).

Mobilizing for Gender Equality—Women's Nongovernmental Organizations and Networks

The opportunities and constraints of women's nongovernmental organizations in the accession countries varied in different stages of the European Union expansion process (Roth 2007). During the accession process, women's nongovernmental organizations (NGOs) in the Central and Eastern European (CEE) states were able to use the EU for putting pressure on national governments to introduce gender equality legislation and regulations (see contributions by Regulska and Grabowska, Hašková and Křížková, and Kakucs and Pető in this volume).

The European Women's Lobby (EWL), an umbrella organization of feminist and women's NGOs, has been crucial for bringing women's issues to the EU agenda (Helferrich and Kolb 2001). The EU provides the European Women's Lobby with access, credibility, legitimacy, and resources. Since 2000, the EWL addressed EU enlargement as an area of concern that is reflected in its annual reports. However, since the EWL can spend the funding provided by the European Commission only on behalf of the member states, it lacked funds to support or carry out any activities on enlargement issues. Thus with respect to the new member states, the lobby can be most effective after expansion has occurred, which also changed the composition of the EWL. In 2007, it comprised members from twenty-three EU member states (Poland, Slovenia, Cyprus, and Romania were not regular EWL members) and several EU candidate states (Croatia, Republic of Macedonia, Turkey) as well as associate members from Cyprus, Georgia, Morocco, and Romania.

Women in Central and Eastern Europe also started organizing networks among themselves. The KARAT coalition of women's NGOs in Central and Eastern European countries formed during the Fourth World Conference on Women in Beijing in 1995 in response to the invisibility of the CEE/CIS (Commonwealth of Independent States) region at this international forum

(Marksova-Tominova 2006). The goal of the coalition is to advocate for the regionally specific needs of women. In 1997, the KARAT Coalition was formally established by representatives of ten CEE countries in Warsaw. Since then KARAT has concentrated on monitoring the responses of the CEE/CIS governments to their international commitments, especially those made at the Beijing conference. In 2002, lobbying at the EU level was added to the activities of the coalition. The KARAT coalition decided against joining the EWL because they felt it was important to develop a dialogue and agenda of women in the CEE/CIS countries without the participation of "Western women." However, these two transnational networks collaborate.

Overall, the expectations of activists in the accession countries were modest, and they realized that they needed to use the accession phase in order to put pressure on the governments to introduce gender equality and antidiscrimination legislation (Roth 2007). They saw EU accession as an opportunity to improve national legislation and make governments and the public more gender sensitive. At the same time, activists realized that it was important to defend achievements under the socialist regime—for example, legal, safe, and free abortion; free contraception and reproductive health care; subsidized child care; and extensive family leave—all of which were undermined to a greater or lesser degree by the EU minimal standards on these issues. Variations with regard to women's issues and gender equality among the old member states were noted— for example, the Scandinavian countries were much more advanced than Germany. The employment rates in the former socialist countries resembled the high employment of the Nordic countries much more than the lower overall employment rate and higher rate of part-time employment in other European countries (Fagan et al. 2005). Furthermore, it needs to be emphasized that with each enlargement the EU became more demanding, and that with respect to human rights it does not live up to its own standards (Williams 2004, see also Aldıkaçtı-Marshall in this volume). Since the governments in the candidate countries felt that they needed to address women's issues, the accession process had a positive effect by bringing gender into the public debate in the East and impacting legislation. However, Pollert (2003, 347) warns that gains in equal opportunities achieved in the pursuit of another agenda—EU membership— might weaken the commitment of governments.

The fact that women's issues were seen as "European" improved their standing among those who were pro-EU, and governments felt that they needed to give at least lip service to these standards. The progress in the implementation of gender equality policies is monitored in National Action Plans. The combination of losses in the public sphere (labor market and political participation), contacts with Western feminists, as well as the top-down gender reforms in the context of EU accession all contributed to feminist mobilization. EU membership has resulted in losses of funding, but at the same time gave access to EU funds (Roth

2007). Furthermore, women's organizations from the new members states can now fully participate in the European Women's Lobby and thus attempt to impact EU gender policies, for example, with respect to reproductive rights. In addition, they can use the European Court of Justice to address violations of EU standards in their countries. To what extent a cross-national convergence of feminist mobilization will occur remains to be seen. An analysis of feminist mobilization in old member states indicates that reproductive rights is an area in which convergence can be noted, while prostitution is an area that is characterized by greater diversity, indicating that the national level is an important intervening variable in transnational feminism (McBride and Mazur 2006).

As the chapters in this volume demonstrate, feminist mobilization played a crucial role in shaping gender equality politics at the EU level and domestic level. Activists benefited from a combination of the participation in transnational networks and domestic grassroots mobilization. While the EU offers important political opportunities, the domestic level is a crucial factor for the success (or failure) of feminist mobilization, in particular with respect to the implementation of gender equality policies, in old as well as new member states.

Inclusion and Exclusion in EU Equality Politics

After the losses during the transformation period, the EU accession process has resulted in the adoption of gender equality legislation and the introduction of a women's machinery. Overall, the biggest progress has been made during the accession period. This makes it important to observe (and support) future member states such as Croatia or Turkey. A couple of years after the accession, some activists from the new member states stated that they wished that the pressure in the accession process to adapt to EU standards on their countries had been as strong as it is currently on Turkey, because this is the magic moment when doors did open to them (Roth 2007).

Whereas gender equality policies have been on the agenda of the EU from the beginning and have been broadened during the past fifty years, as the contributions to this volume show, the record of the EU with respect to ethnic minority groups is not as strong (Williams 2004). A comparison of gender and ethnic mobilization shows that the extent the EU represents a source of leverage politics depends on the national context. As Hellgren and Hobson (in this volume) demonstrate, the EU frameworks open new opportunities for leverage politics while closing off others. Class rather than race provides the crucial framework in the European context (Ferree in this volume). Furthermore, the EU must be understood as a hybrid model incorporating two competing orientations—liberalism and social democracy. This hybridity on the one hand offers opportunities—for example, strong antidiscrimination laws and policies—while on the other hand a neoliberal discourse brings risks for vulnerable groups (see Ferree in this volume).

Overview of the Book

The chapters in the first part of the book—*Broadening Gender Equality Policies: The Role of the EU*—discuss the increasing scope of gender equality politics in a comparative perspective. Initially restricted to workplace equality issues such as equal pay, the removal of barriers to employment or careers, and nondiscrimination, over time substantive barriers to women's equality such as the unequal division of labor in care work; lack of childcare, parental leave, or flexible working-time arrangements; and sexual harassment have been acknowledged and addressed. Furthermore, gender mainstreaming has been introduced.

Angelika von Wahl's contribution analyzes the development of a supranational and distinctive EU equal employment regime and notes that equal employment policies developed in response to women's movement organization and that only some EU equality laws are new to the new member states that joined the EU since 2004. She discusses the variety and diffusion of gender policies in three new member states (Poland, Hungary, and the Czech Republic) and the theoretical implications for the study of enlargement or accession.

Kimberly Morgan shows that despite a lack of an EU-wide consensus, the role of the EU in work-family policy has been transformed. Her chapter traces the Europeanization of work and family policy, from the equal opportunity measures of the early 1970s, to the childcare and parental leave directives of the 1990s, to the Open Method of Coordination in more recent years. Morgan concludes that the progress in the area of care policies is due to the work of feminists and other activists at the EU level. However, she also emphasizes that the similar mobilization at the domestic level is critical.

Kathrin Zippel demonstrates how advocates won the discursive struggle over what constitutes sexual harassment at the EU level. Her analysis of framing processes and discursive politics indicates that political actors at the EU as well as at the member state level have used various frames for sexual harassment in order to pursue their aims. Zippel notes a lack of effective implementation and enforcement mechanisms, but also notes that the struggle led to important national debates and awareness of the issue and to the binding EU 2002 Equal Treatment directive.

The second part of the book—*The EU Accession Process: Six Case Studies from West and East*—surveys the effects of EU accession and includes three case studies from old member states (Ireland, Spain, and Germany) and three from new member states (Poland, the Czech Republic, and Hungary). Women's movements and gender equality policies in founding members such as France and Italy, or in member states that joined the EU later, such as Britain, have been extensively studied (see for example Stetson and Mazur 1995; Elman 1996b; Hantrais 2000b; Liebert 2003; Banaszak, Beckwith, and Rucht 2003). The choice of Ireland, Spain, and Germany seems particularly instructive for a comparison with the new member states. Like Poland, Spain and Ireland are Catholic countries, which is of high significance with respect to reproductive rights in particular, as well as gender relations overall. Furthermore, Spain shares with the former socialist countries an undemocratic past. EU accession and the democratization process in Spain were closely related. It should also be kept in mind that EU membership of Spain, Portugal, and Greece was encouraged in order to support democratization processes—whereas the new member states faced much closer scrutiny until accession was granted, and Turkey is still denied membership (see Aldıkaçtı-Marshall in this volume). Germany represents a special case, since through unification the East German state ceased to exist while its former citizens became EU members.

Pauline P. Cullen shows that although the impact of EU membership on Ireland's economic development cannot be underestimated, the same is not the case for gender equality politics. In the fourth richest country of the world women suffer from significant pay reduction for motherhood, and the childcare costs are the highest in Europe. Ireland—together with Sweden and Great Britain—was one of the few old EU member states that invited free movement of labor from the new member states. Women constitute almost half of these migrants and are filling the gap that the care deficit produced. Cullen's chapter analyzes to what extent the National Women's Council of Ireland is able to effectively represent the diversity of women in Ireland.

Celia Valiente's chapter describes how Spain—once a laggard—has become a vanguard in European gender equality policies, due to the influence of the EU as well as favorable domestic developments such as secularization, the increasing strength of the women's movement and the activities of gender equality institutions, and the support of the social democratic government formed in 2004. However, Valiente points out that despite these impressive achievements, the deficit of implementation is a pending problem.

The chapter by Ingrid Miethe differs in several respects from the other contributions in this volume: it provides an analysis of the relationship between the feminists from West and East Germany, it focuses on the academic sphere, and it concentrates on the time prior to EU enlargement. However, these aspects are well chosen, because German unification represents an informal and precocious eastern EU enlargement and because the institutionalized framework of academia represents an important context of contemporary women's movements, not only in Germany. In addition to presenting a unique case, Miethe's chapter analyzes the tensions between Eastern and Western feminists and therefore also serves as an introduction to the following chapters that survey the mobilization for gender equality in some of the new member states. Poland, the Czech Republic, and Hungary were chosen because they represent some of the most advanced of the new member states.

Joanna Regulska and Madga Grabowska analyze how the accession process affected the mobilization of Polish women's and feminist NGOs and the construction of new political spaces. Transnational cooperation enabled Polish activists to create new political spaces and to resist the state at home. As the chapter shows, the greatest gains with respect to gender equality legislation were made prior to accession.

Similarly, the chapter by Hana Hašková and Alena Křížková indicates that the preparation for EU accession was the most important legitimizing force to promote gender equality in the Czech Republic, while the Beijing World Women's Conference provided crucial networking opportunities. The accession process resulted in the professionalization of women's civic groups, and gender mainstreaming offers the potential to promote gender and women's equality, although it needs to be activated.

In their analysis of the impact of EU Accession, Noémi Kakucs and Andrea Pető address the paradoxes of the institutionalization of gender equality in Hungary. Gender mainstreaming was introduced through top-down reforms in order for Hungary to be eligible for EU accession. Although equal opportunity policies were introduced, positive action was missing, and regardless of the institutionalization of a women's machinery, a gender perspective was subordinated to presumably more important social and economic concerns. Kakucs and Pető conclude that without high-level mobilization and strong pressure from women's organizations, little change can be expected.

The third and last part of the book—*Inclusion and Exclusion in EU Equality Politics*—goes beyond the boundaries of the EU as well as gender issues. Gül Aldıkaçtı-Marshall analyzes the impact of the EU candidacy on women's mobilization in Turkey. She points out that the EU has increased the demands on candidate countries over time, that the application of a democratic threshold has been inconsistent, and that the extent to which directives have been implemented varied among member states. However, Turkey's goal to join the EU has provided Turkish feminists with important political opportunities, tracking and demanding the implementation of amended laws as well as putting new issues on the agenda.

Framing processes play a crucial role in the chapter by Zenia Hellgren and Barbara Hobson who analyze the gender and ethnic minority claims in Swedish and EU frames. They point to the hierarchies of equality in EU law regarding discrimination with respect to gender and ethnicity. As Hellgren and Hobson show, although the EU provides legal and discursive resources, how these resources are employed depends on the position of actors within the national policy. This means that in the Swedish case the opening of new opportunities was accompanied by the closing off of other opportunities for leverage politics.

In the final and concluding chapter, Myra Marx Ferree assesses the problems and chances that the hybrid model of the EU offers for gender equality politics in the member states. The hybridity of the EU model encompasses two orientations—liberalism and social democracy—that are in tension with each other. Comparing the United States, representing the liberal model, and Germany, representing the European social model, Ferree indicates the strengths and weaknesses of both approaches. She concludes that the future of gender equality in the hybrid model of the EU suggests caution, since it opens up new discursive spaces as well as dangers. In order to take advantage of the opportunities that the hybrid EU model offers, it is thus necessary that feminist advocacy networks engage in framing and discursive politics, and thus shape gender politics at the EU as well as at the domestic level.

Acknowledgements

My gratitude belongs first and foremost to the authors who made this volume possible through their contributions. The collaboration was delightful! The collection is grounded in a conference of the same title that took place in Philadelphia in February 2005. Two of the speakers—Claudia Neusüß and Eva Fodor—unfortunately are not represented in the volume, while the papers of Pauline P. Cullen, Celia Valiente, Hana Hašková and Alena Křížková, as well as Noémi Kakucs and Andrea Pető, were not part of the conference. Demie Kurz, Janice Madden, and Robin Leidner served as discussants during the conference and provided valuable comments. The conference would not have been possible without the financial support of the German Academic Exchange Service and the University of Pennsylvania, in particular the Sociology Department, the Women's Studies Center, the School of Arts and Social Sciences, and the Department of Germanic Languages and Literature. I am very grateful for the support of Frank Trommler, Demie Kurz, and Paul Allison.

The manuscript has greatly benefited from the comments of Amy Elman and three further anonymous reviewers. I am grateful to Marion Berghahn for her support of this volume. The Division of Sociology and Social Policy at the University of Southampton provided excellent working conditions for the completion of the manuscript. Milena Büchs, Myra Marx Ferree, Athina Vlachantoni and Kathrin Zippel provided support and advice.

References

Banaszak, Lee Ann, Karen Beckwith, and Dieter Rucht, eds. 2003. *Women's Movements Facing the Reconfigured State*. Cambridge: Cambridge University Press.

Berkovitch, Nitza. 1999. The Emergence and Transformation of the International Women's Movement. In *Constructing World Culture. International Nongovernmental Organizations since 1975*, ed. John Boli and George M. Thomas, 100–126. Stanford: Stanford University Press.

Beveridge, Fiona, Sue Nott, and Kylie Stephen. 2000. Mainstreaming and the Engendering of Policymaking: A Means to an End? Special Issue, *Journal of European Public Policy* 7 (3): 385–405.

Bretherton, Charlotte. 2001. Gender Mainstreaming and EU Enlargement: Swimming Against the Tide? *Journal of European Public Policy* 8 (1): 60–81.

Chołuj, Bozena and Claudia Neusüß. 2004. *EU Enlargement in 2004. East-West Priorities and Perspectives from Women Inside and Outside the EU.* Discussion paper written with support from the United Nations Development Fund for Women. New York: UNIFEM.

Cichowski, Rachel A. 2002. 'No Discrimination Whatsoever'. Women's Transnational Activism and the Evolution of EU Sex Equality Policy. In *Women's Activism and Globalization. Linking Local Struggles and Transnational Politics*, ed. Nancy A. Naples and Manisha Desai, 220–38. London: Routledge.

Council of Europe. 2000. Gender Mainstreaming: Conceptual Framework, Methodology and Presentation of Good Practices. Final Report of the Activities of the Group of Specialists on Mainstreaming. EG-S-MS(98) 2rev. Strasbourg: Council of Europe. At http://www.humanrights.coe.int/equality/Eng/WordDocs/EGSMS(98)%202%20rev%20-%20Final%20report%20mainstreaming%20May%202000.doc.

Domsch, Michel E., Desiree H. Ladwig, and Eliane Tenten, eds. 2003. *Gender Equality in Central and Eastern European Countries*. Frankfurt: Peter Lang.

Einhorn, Barbara. 1993. *Cinderella Goes to Market: Citizenship, Gender, and Women's Movements in East Central Europe*. London: Verso.

Ellina, Chrystalla A. 2003. *Promoting Women's Rights: The Politics of Gender in the European Union*. New York: Routledge.

Elman, Amy. 1996a. Introduction: The EU from Feminist Perspectives. In *Sexual Politics and the European Union: The New Feminist Challenge*, ed. Amy Elman, 1–12. Providence and Oxford: Berghahn Books.

Elman, Amy, ed. 1996b. *Sexual Politics and the European Union: The New Feminist Challenge*. Providence and Oxford: Berghahn Books.

Fagan, Colette, Jill Rubery, Damian Grimshaw, Mark Smith, Gail Hebson, and Hugo Figueiredo. 2005. Gender Mainstreaming in the Enlarged European Union: Recent Development in the European Employment Strategy and Social Inclusion Process. *Industrial Relations Journal* 36 (6): 568–91.

Fagan, Colette, Damian Grimshaw, and Jill Rubery. 2006. The Subordination of the Gender Equality Objective: The National Reform Programmes and 'Making Work Pay' Policies. *Industrial Relations Journal* 37 (6): 571–92.

Ferree, Myra Marx, and Tetyana Pudrovska (2006). Transnational Feminist NGOs on the Web: Networks and Identities in the Global North and South. In *Global Feminism: Transnational Women's Activism, Organizing and Human Rights*, ed. Myra Marx Ferree and Aili Mari Tripp, 247–72. New York: New York University Press.

Ghodsee, Kristen. 2004. Feminism-by-Design: Emerging Capitalism, Cultural Feminism, and Women's Nongovernmental Organizations in Post-socialist Eastern Europe. *Signs* 29 (3): 727–53.

Hantrais, Linda. 2000a. From Equal Pay to Reconciliation of Employment and Family Life. In *Gendered Policies in Europe. Reconciling Employment and Family Life*, ed. Linda Hantrais, 1–26. Basingstoke and London: Macmillan.

Hantrais, Linda, ed. 2000b. *Gendered Policies in Europe. Reconciling Employment and Family Life*. Basingstoke and London: Macmillan.

Heinen, Jacqueline, and Stéphane Portet. 2002. Political and Social Citizenship: An Examination of the Case of Poland. In *Gender Justice, Development, and Rights*, ed. Maxine Molyneux and Shahra Razavi, 141–69. Oxford: Oxford University Press.

Helferrich, Barbara, and Felix Kolb. 2001. Multilevel Action Coordination in European Contentious Politics: The Case of the European Women's Lobby. In *Contentious Europeans: Protest and Politics in an Emerging Polity*, ed. Doug Imig and Sidney Tarrow, 143–61. Lanham, MD: Rowman & Littlefield.

Hoskyns, Catherine. 1996. *Integrating Gender: Women, Law and Politics in the European Union*. London: Verso.

Keck, Margaret E. and Kathryn Sikkink. 1998. *Activists beyond Borders: Advocacy Networks in International Politics*. Ithaca, NY: Cornell University Press.

Liebert, Ulrike, ed. 2003. *Gendering Europeanisation*. Brussels: Peter Lang.

Marksova-Tominova, Michaela. 2006. Die Koalition Karat: Ein Zusammenschluss von Frauenorganisationen der ehemaligen sozialistischen Länder. *Femina politica* 15 (1): 115–17.

Mazey, Sonia. 2000. *Gender Mainstreaming in the EU: Principles and Practice*. European Dossier Series. London: Kogan Page.

McBride, Dorothy E. and Mazur, Amy G. 2006. Measuring Feminist Mobilization: Cross-National Convergences and Transnational Networks in Western Europe. In: Global Feminism. Transnational Women's Activism, Organizing and Human Rights, ed. Myra Marx Fewee and Aili Mari Tripp, 219–46. New York: New York University Press.

Miroiu, Mihaela. 2006: A Mayflower Turned Titanic: The Metamorphosis of Political Patriarchy in Romania. *Femina politica* 15 (1): 84–98.

Pascall, Gillian, and Jane Lewis. 2004. Emerging Gender Regimes and Policies for Gender Equality in a Wider Europe. *Journal of Social Policy* 33 (3): 373–94.

Pollack, Mark A. and Emilie Hafner-Burton. 2000. Mainstreaming Gender in European Union Policymaking. *Journal of European Public Policy* 7 (1): 432–56.

Pollert, Anna. 2003. Women, Work and Equal Opportunities in Post-Communist Transition. *Work, Employment and Society* 17 (2): 331–57.

Roth, Silke. 2007. Sisterhood and Solidarity? Women's Organizations in the Expanded European Union. *Social Politics. International Studies in Gender, State & Society* 14 (4): 460–87.

Sloat, Amanda. 2004. Where are the Women? Female Political Visibility in EU Accession States. *Transitions* 46 (1): 45–58.

Stetson, Dorothy McBride and Amy G. Mazur, eds.1995. *Comparative State Feminism*. Thousand Oaks, CA: Sage.

Stragitaki, Maria. 2005. Gender Mainstreaming vs. Positive Action: An Ongoing Conflict in EU Gender Equality Policy. *European Journal of Women's Studies* 12 (2): 165–86.

Trubek, David M. and Louise G. Trubek. 2005. "Hard and Soft Law in the Construction of Social Europe: The Role of the Open Method of Co-ordination." *European Law Journal* 11, no. 3 (May 2005): 343–64.

Van der Molen, Irna, and Irina Novikova. 2005. Mainstreaming Gender in the EU-accession Process: The Case of the Baltic Republics. *Journal of European Social Policy* 15 (2): 139–56.

Velluti, Samantha. 2005. Implementing Gender Equality and Mainstreaming in an Enlarged European Union—Some Thoughts on Prospects and Challenges for Central Eastern Europe. *Journal of Social Welfare and Family Law* 27 (2): 213–25.

Walby, Sylvia. 2004. The European Union and Gender Equality: Emergent Varieties of Gender Regime. *Social Politics* 11 (1): 4–29.

Williams, Andrew. 2004. *EU Human Rights Policies: A Study in Irony*. Oxford: Oxford University Press.

Zippel, Kathrin. 2004. Transnational Advocacy Networks and Policy Cycles in the European Union: The Case of Sexual Harassment. *Social Politics* 11 (1): 57–85.

Part I

Broadening Gender Equality Policies

The Role of the EU

I

THE EU AND ENLARGEMENT

Conceptualizing Beyond "East" and "West"

Angelika von Wahl

European integration has opened the door for the formulation and development of a variety of equal opportunity and equal treatment laws for women. An extensive body of norms and policies, including nine directives, has been passed over the last thirty years to foster gender equality and end discrimination, particularly in employment related areas. The European Court of Justice (ECJ) has granted direct effect status to gender equality directives and has supported equal treatment on many occasions. The dense and complex web of legislation, institutions, court decisions, programs, and interaction with privileged interest groups that emerged in Brussels over the last three decades can be conceptualized as a *supranational* equal employment regime (Wahl 2005). The EU combines liberal market-related notions with social concerns and has been described as "hybrid" (Ferree, this collection). The goal of this chapter is to further analyze the process of the Europeanization of gender policy, especially in regards to the accession of the new Central European members since 2004 using the concept of an equal employment regime. I address the *variety* of equal employment regimes in Europe and the *diffusion* of gender policies through recent EU enlargement to Central and Eastern Europe (CEE) in the accession process.

I posit that postsocialist states entering the European Union find themselves at the crossroads of four distinct paths: their own socialist legacy, the transition to capitalist economy, the states' desires to reinvent and invigorate their own national heritage, and the EU. In terms of gender policy, states can take one of several directions: moving towards a liberal, market-oriented model, a conservative national project, or to some extent staying put and supporting the evolution of a social democratic model combining the equality approach of the communist legacy with pluralist democracy. However, the EU accession process pushes *all* applicant countries into the direction of a hybrid regime, i.e., a regulatory and supranational nonstate regime combining a market-driven core with social concerns. I argue that whatever the exact results of the enlargement process will be, it is clear that regarding gender equality, the EU equal employment regime is a future standard—albeit ambivalent and highly debatable—for the new and old members of the EU. It constitutes the dense policy framework that national and local political actors must deal with in some form or other, whether that is to implement, reframe, call upon, contend, compromise with, support, get around or evade it.

To understand what patterns emerge in accession states with regard to the institutionalization of equal employment policies, I *first* elaborate the concept of a supranational equal employment regime and spell out its effects on the different national level regimes. *Second*, the chapter presents an outline of the theoretical approaches to the study of the EU and transition research. A central question in transition research asks if a common postcommunist path dependency exists, or if divergence among states dominates. Three empirical cases—the Czech Republic, Hungary, and Poland—are briefly examined to ascertain what patterns of adjustment, implementation, or opposition have emerged in these three states and how they can be explained. *Third*, I will conclude with some remarks on the variety and diffusion of gender policies in these states and the theoretical implications for the study of EU enlargement.

National-level Equal Employment Regimes

Esping-Andersen's comparative studies firmly established the concept of welfare state regimes (1990; 1999).[1] He identifies three class-based dimensions that enable the analytical development of ideal types: *decommodification, stratification,* and *state-market relations.* He then identifies three relatively coherent clusters of nations where conservative, liberal, or social-democratic welfare policies dominate, calling each a "regime" type. Feminists quickly recognized the analytical potential of this regime typology, but also criticized an implicit tendency to base welfare regime analysis on several erroneous assumptions: that the worker is male, that lifelong employment is a universal experience, and that the head of a household is by definition a male with certain needs (Langan and Ostner 1991; O'Connor 1993; Orloff 1993). Three significant suggestions for additional dimensions have been made by feminists to move beyond this implicitly andro-centric view of the welfare state: *access to the labor market* is often a problem for women, which should be included in the analysis (O'Connor 1993; Orloff 1993). Furthermore, we must also take into account the *ability to establish an autonomous household* and *personal autonomy* as additional dimensions.

These six dimensions produce an expanded analytical framework that can productively be applied to the study of equal employment policies (Wahl 1999). I demonstrate that equal employment policies correspond closely with the structures of national welfare and labor market regimes. Of considerable significance also, however, are the actions of social movements that are trying to improve women's position in the labor market and welfare state by articulat-ing gender-sensitive concerns and formulating new demands towards the state. In that way feminist mobilization has triggered policy change and has affected the outline and content of the specific equal employment regime. As a result, states cluster according to the equal employment policies they introduce, im-plement, and enforce.

However, welfare state regimes and equal employment regimes differ in several important regards. First, unlike welfare policies, equal employment policies do not involve direct transfer payments. These latter policies are thus non-redistributive. Second, many equal employment policies focus on creating a level playing field, opening opportunities, and expanding labor market participation. A third differ-ence lies in the current climate of welfare state retrenchment. In postindustrial-ized states, social policies of all kinds are being scaled back to reduce labor costs, while equal employment policies are simultaneously expanding and are often dis-cursively legitimated as assets to market competitiveness. All three characteris-tics are especially relevant for the development of EU gender policies, because first, the EU is mainly a system of regulation, not redistribution; second, the EU is concerned with the realization of fair competition and an equal playing field; and third, in the EU these policies are not negatively effected by welfare state retrenchment because the EU is not a welfare state (Walby 1999a; 1999b). On the contrary, an expansion of "low-cost equality" policies will be likely. I define an equal employment regime as the combined, interdependent ways in which equal opportunity, nondiscrimination, and policies supporting women's care work and employment are produced and allocated among state, market, and family (com-pare Esping Andersen 1999, 34–35). As such, an equal employment regime is a more focused concept than a "gender regime" and particularly useful when inves-tigating the employment nexus (Walby 2004). Equal employment policy models cluster to an extensive degree into liberal, conservative, and social-democratic equal employment regimes. Two questions emerge: First, what happens to these distinct regimes in Western Europe in the case of European integration? And sec-ond, is there a common postsocialist regime type in Eastern Europe?

The Emerging EU Equal Employment Regime

Over the last thirty years, partial convergence among different regime types in the West has developed through European integration. I hypothesize that these steps are leading in a nonlinear fashion towards the development of a supranational and distinctive equal employment regime. However, some aspects of national-level equal employment regimes persist because they are deeply entrenched in the welfare state, the labor market, and national ideologies. They can find themselves at odds with the policies being developed at the EU level because of the persistent importance of national politics and institutions. As a result, the new, integrating EU regime only develops slowly and against a background of more or less contradictory national policies and nations' powerful "exit-options."

The slowly integrating, common aspects of the new European equal employment regime were formed at the intersection of all three nation level regime types. The common, central area of this EU regime is responsible for activities related to the market, and is dominated by economic and paid employment issues. The national and nonintegrated areas include social policy, such as childcare services (see Morgan, in this volume). Equal employment policies are generally non-redistributing and civil rights oriented, while welfare is redistributive and social rights oriented. Women's needs, however, include *both* aspects.

The assessment that "the position of women in the labor market (the central concern of EC sex equality policies) is linked to and mirrors to a considerable degree their status within national family and welfare regimes" is very convincing (Mazey 1998, 134). Thus one can conceptualize the system of EU gender equality measures as a new kind of "regime" (Walby 2004; see also Jacobsson on EU employment policy as a system, 2004). In contrast to the national level, the EU equal employment regime has not emerged amidst the market-state-family triad but amidst *markets, nations, and supranational forces.* This changes the functions and influence of this kind of "regime," because, for example, traditional corporatist pressures and implementation are rather weak.

It is well established that early EEC policies, such as equal pay and equal treatment, are based on a *liberal* interpretation of equality: the emphasis lies on equal pay, on removing barriers to employment or careers, and on nondiscrimination (Lewis and Ostner 1998). The main directives relating to employment and gender equality are equal pay and equal treatment directives. In order to clarify the complex institutional and policy-related processes and changes taking place, I have developed a list of testable hypotheses. The institutional, ideological, and regulatory changes in the EU since 1975 are extremely relevant for the implementation process in the new member states, and can be summarized as follows:

1. The "reach and spread" of equal employment policies has moved *from* narrow (economic: equal pay and equal treatment) *to* broad (social and economic: pregnant worker directive, parental leave, sexual harassment, indirect discrimination, gender mainstreaming, nondiscrimination for lesbians and gays).

2. The number and kind of players involved in this policy area has increased (*from* strictly EU institutions *to* additional committees on gender equality and women's rights) and broadened (*from* experts-only *to* civil society/social mobilization).

3. The implementation of equal employment policies in the EU has moved *from* hard law (directives and regulations) and a clear level of coercion *to* soft law and policy learning.

4. The process of policy making has shifted institutionally *from* the classic community method *to* the open method of coordination, i.e., *from* harmonization and mutual recognition *to* self-regulation and semivoluntarism, giving nation-states more freedom to implement policies as they see fit.

5. While *earlier* policies originated from member states primarily, *later* policies can be formulated and developed on the supranational level (mainstreaming and OMC).

6. Earlier policies reflect a more hierarchical style of governance, while the latest policy reflects a network style of governance.

7. The logic of the emerging EU equal employment regime expands *from* a limited sameness approach *to* the inclusion of women's difference (care responsibilities, sexual harassment/violence, and sexuality), thus expanding the definition of gendered justice.

Institutional and regulatory changes include the dynamics of intergovernmental negotiations, supranational policy-making, and the open method of coordination. Distinctive policy innovations, such as gender mainstreaming, add another layer to the emerging EU equal employment regime. These changes are leading to a new equal employment regime that is shared at the core by all members of the EU, but Europeanization plays out differently in the various member states (Caporaso and Jupille 2001).

One further comment is in order about the new EU regime type: it is not the result of one regime type (i.e., the liberal) simply dominating the others, although liberal policies are at the core of the EU. Instead one can apply the idea of a "hybrid" model that combines various and sometimes competing and/or contradictory frames of gender equality, as is visible in the simultaneity of market orientation and the European social model. Overall, the new EU level regime

type is an outcome of the complex interplay among intergovernmental negotiation, supranational policy-making, and recent innovations in governance,
revealing a wide variety of possible paths and levels of implementation at the
national level.

Theorizing the Effects of the EU on Nation-States and Vice Versa

Much has been written on the relationship of the EU to the nation-state and the
process of European integration (Haas 1958; Hoffmann 1966; Moravcsik 1993;
Scharpf 1988; Streeck 1996; Pierson 1996). The following section will provide
a brief sketch of this literature and focus on some ideas that seem relevant for
the analysis of EU enlargement. The European Union has been characterized
by "rapid institutional evolution and a . . . complex policymaking process," with
the result that many EU observers accept that "there is no single theoretical
framework for the study of the EU" (Ellina 2003, 3; Pollack 2001). The theoretical sources of the literature on the EU originated with International Relations
(IR). Realists analyzed the EEC as an outcome of international bargains among
competing nation-states (Grieco 1988). Intergovernmentalists overtook and expanded the realist perspective by introducing domestic politics and negotiations
into the equation of international relations (Moravcsik 1993). Neofunctional-
ists, on the other hand, tried to explain why nation-states were indeed giving
up some attributes of sovereignty in the process of European integration, and
developed the concept of "spillover." A review of the recent literature shows,
however, that liberalism and institutionalism seem to be more frequently utilized
when analyzing gender politics and European integration. The liberal paradigm,
which is generally more optimistic about international cooperation and peaceful
conflict resolution, is more easily adapted to analyze European integration and
supranational policy-making through trade and communication (Russett et al.
1993). The process of policy formulation and diffusion of gender equality policies
within the EC becomes clearer when paying close attention to supranational organizations and nonstate actors. The variety of implementations during enlargement can very well be addressed by the insights of institutionalists: Mazey argues
that "national political traditions and ideology have been influential 'filters' in
the sense that they have determined the manner in which national governments
have complied with EC legislation and, by implication, its impact" (1998, 133).
One can discern two basic notions about enlargement in the literature: one perspective views enlargement as an *internal* process of the EU, while another frames
EU extension as the *external* process of accession. Accordingly, enlargement/ac-
cession is either understood from a "domestic" Comparative Politics perspective,
or from a foreign policy IR perspective. Both views are useful when studying
EU politics, as it is likely that accession states will perceive EU policy largely

as foreign policy, while old member states will understand the process more in domestic terms.

The institutional translation process of EU gender equality policy is incomplete or even incomprehensible without taking into account "civil society," especially women's movements pushing for gender equality. Feminist ideas, such as questioning and critiquing traditional female roles, repressive reproductive policies, violence against women, and the exclusion of women from politics and from many profitable and interesting occupations, spread during the 1960s and 1970s, especially among younger and better-educated women in Western Europe and other pluralist democracies. Local and national social movements emerged that later also organized on the EU level. The European Women's Lobby (EWL), the European Network of Women (ENOW), and the Committee for Women's Rights in the European Parliament formed during this time (Hoskyns 1996; 1999). These and other groups have been part of an "advocacy coalition" that has successfully lobbied for improvements for women (Sabatier 1988). Over the last thirty-five years, the EU Commission and Parliament have generated what is not only their own feminist constituency, but a constituency that has itself become savvy in using the supranational level to pressure reluctant nation-states through the so-called boomerang (Keck and Sikkink 1998) and ping-pong effects (Zippel 2004). This influence is also observable in regards to the creation of EU-friendly feminist discourses and networks in CEE states after 1989 (Chołuj 2003), while marginalizing others (Hašková and Křížková in this volume). If or to what extent women in general should expect lasting and fundamental redress from the EU for the manifold aspects of continuing sex inequality they experience in daily life is another question, and one that I judge with some pessimism.

Transition and EU Enlargement of the CEE States: Is There a Postcommunist Regime Type?

In terms of an ideological legacy in accession states, one first thinks of the existence of socialist values, but it is just as important to note the absence of forty years of Western feminism and social mobilization, with its discourses on autonomy, difference, and sexual politics. Reemerging national traditions relating to religion, especially Catholicism, and ethnic divides also influence the construction of a "new" national identity for Central European states, undermining commonalities of the communist legacy. Emerging ideological and institutional differences among postcommunist states result in a diversity of adaptations of EU legislation on the national level as pertains to the *speed, extent,* and *depth of implementation.*

After 1989, the direction of policy development in the CEE states has been vigorously debated (for example, in the special edition of *East European Politics and Societies* [15 (2), 2001] and the special issue of *West European Politics* [25 (2), 2002] (for an overview see also: Manning 2004). At the center of the discussion stands the question of whether common postcommunist legacies will keep CEE states together in a sort of postcommunist regime type based on their former common political and economic path, or if the end of communism will lead to clear divergence among CEE states or, perhaps, to the emergence of new regimes. The literature on the socioeconomic development of Central and Eastern Europe shows a broad array of assessments on where these countries are heading. Some interpret the last decade and a half of transition as the end of the common Soviet and post-Soviet legacy, while others see only limited divergence with a lot of persistent overlap (Manning 2004). Of course, CEE states share similarities, such as the legacy of Soviet ideology, centralized politics and economies, political oppression, and the economic shock of reduced revenues after 1989 that brought many social services to a halt and lead to unemployment and increasing social inequality. Communist states also experienced dramatic political change in the form of the emergence of vibrant civil societies and the freedom to organize. Additionally, suppressed religious, cultural, and ethnic identities are resurgent. But, does that conclusively mean that there is no "postcommunist regime type," and that all the CEE countries are following unique or divergent paths? And if they were diverging, is there a resemblance between some of them and the social democratic, liberal, or conservative regime types existent in the West? Does Scandinavia's embrace of Estonia as part of the Baltic and Nordic region influence the gender politics of this postcommunist state in the direction of a social democratic gender regime, for example?

As an alternative to the discourse of similarity and divergence, Pascall and Lewis describe the emergence of *new* gender regimes in the East *and* West due to the demise of the male breadwinner model in the West and the crisis of the dual worker model in the East. They make the interesting argument that European "[e]nlargement brings new challenges as it draws together gender regimes with contrasting histories and trajectories" (2004, 373). This would mean that differentiation between Western and Eastern models are becoming a thing of the past.

It is important to remember that the notions of *West* and *East* are discursive constructs that have changed according to historic events over the last centuries. The current notion of the West is heavily influenced by the Cold War. This view implicitly (and sometimes explicitly) makes references to *freedom* and *liberty* as its core values. Watson argues that this definition of the West is a type of "imagined community" (B. Anderson 1983) that has become the "unspoken point of reference for the representation of Eastern Europe, a 'westerncentredness' analogous to whiteness" (Watson 2001, 38). Taking the West as an unspoken point of reference has troubling effects for a more nuanced study of the new EU member states, because this perspective undermines the ability to understand their complex and contradictory developments and can bias interpretation towards the view of the East as primarily *lacking* attributes of the West. As a result, the analysis of women's position and mobilization during and after transition can suffer. Since many Eastern European countries instituted equal pay, public day care, abortion rights, and so forth *before* Western states, this outcome would be particularly ironic.

"Westerncentredness" also presents the West as a unified group of countries with the same standards, institutions, and ideologies—an assumption not supported by evidence, as comparative research among older EU member states and regime typologies show. Thus, it is important to keep in mind the relativity of the political-geographical East-West category so often employed, as Roth and Miethe (2003) underscore.

In the last fifteen years, differences among the CEE states have come to the fore. Domsch, Ladwig, and Tenten (2003) divide the countries of the former communist bloc into three groups: the first group includes the most advanced eight Central European states called "transition countries," basically the East European newcomers to the EU. Manning describes them as a "recovery group," in which economic growth has returned and governments have the capacity to tax and spend funding on social programs (Manning 2004, 219). The second group comprises Bulgaria and Romania, which are labeled "evolving or reforming hybrid transitional states." Russia fits into the last category, characterized as "hybrid transitional states, in which transition is stalled or in reversal" (Domsch, Ladwig, and Tenten 2003, 11).

This chapter focuses on the "transitional countries" as a good test case because they were early and directly confronted with the "collision" of Western and Eastern notions of gender relations. In addition, they were also the most advanced economically. In 1991, the political leaders of Czechoslovakia, Hungary, and Poland met with the goal to eliminate remnants of communism in Central Europe and to join efforts to accomplish successful transition and EU accession.[2] Their advanced economic and political positions mean that, we can assume that first, they have the actual capacity to implement EU gender equity policy and second, that if any number of states among the CEE countries forms a somewhat coherent postcommunist group, it would be these three. In the following section I will focus on women's access to the labor market and the issue of equal pay.

Interests and Identities

Economically, CEE countries were dependent upon full female labor market participation and accommodated the labor demands and women's needs through the establishment of a well-developed network of nurseries and kindergarten facilities. Work has been central to communist ideology and to the practical underpinnings of "real existing socialism." Employment was seen as the way towards women's liberation from familial dependency (Engels) and was embedded in an effective—if also sometimes tiring—rhetoric of class equality and solidarity. Accordingly one can argue, as Pascall and Lewis have done, that "gender equality in CEE countries has been contaminated by communism (2004, 388)." As such, pretransition women's employment was not questioned by state ideology and practice, nor by the population. Instead, popular disagreement and resistance was felt by men *and* women on a variety of other political and social issues towards the ever-encroaching state and its apparatus (Watson 2000; 2001). As a result, basic freedoms for everyone stood at the forefront of concerns, not "special interests" of women.

In addition, the level of equality between men and women in CEE states was comparatively high—and it still is when measured in employment, education, and wage differentials. While many Western feminists have described women as the "losers" of the transition process (Young 1999, 2000; Einhorn 1993), this argument refers mostly to reproductive rights—rights that Western feminists fought for long and hard (see chapters on struggles over reproduction in CEE countries in Gal and Kligman 2000). However, Eastern women are also seen as the economic losers of transition where the loss of employment, declining labor market participation, weakened political representation, and increased income inequality is criticized (Steinhilber 2001).

In contrast to these rather gloomy interpretations of women's lives after 1989, Lippe and Fodor (1998) argue that for the first five years of transition, women in CEE states have not been the losers in the economic realm in terms of labor force participation, unemployment, occupational status, and income. Instead, the numbers have been surprisingly stable considering the extent of turmoil. According to these authors, the fact that women have not been the sole or predominant losers of transition is partly due to the legacy of state socialism with its very high employment rates for women, and to women's earlier dominance in the underappreciated service sectors, which have become more important under capitalism (Lippe and Fodor 1998). Others show that labor force participation has declined somewhat from the very high levels under state socialism, but remains more or

Table 1.1. Female Labor Force Participation in Czech Republic, Hungary, and Poland, 1980s, 1998, 2000

Percentage of overall labor female force participation	Czech Republic	Hungary	Poland
(1980s)[a]	59.3 (1985)	50.2 (1980)	54.9 (1985)
(1998)[a]	52.0	45.4 (1999)	50.0
(2000)[c]	57	49	49

Sources: (c) Domsch, Ladewig & Tenten, 2003, 22 (a): Nagy, 2003 154.

less on the level of Scandinavian states (Pascall and Manning 2000). Overall, female labor force participation in East European states is still higher than in the old EU member states.

The data shows, first, the very high rates of female labor force participation in the three states during the period of state socialism and, second, a decline during early transition and the relative recovery soon after. In comparison, in the Western states during the 1980s, only Denmark with 57.5 percent and Finland with 57.1 percent score comparatively high, while the other EC member states range between 24.6 percent in Spain and 44.5 percent in the UK. The EU average percentage of women in the labor force in the West was about 32 percent (Pascall and Manning 2000, 245). The 2000 labor force participation numbers for all accession countries are still somewhat higher than the EU15 average, but not in Poland and Hungary (Source for c is figure 3 in Domsch, Ladwig, and Tenten 2003: 22). Interesting is also the development of the gender pay gap, which does *not* point in the direction of overall loss.

The data on equal pay seem to indicate relative stability; however, the numbers are somewhat contradictory (see b and c for the same year).[3] What stands out is that the overall trend is a slightly *decreasing* pay gap in CEE countries since 1989 despite the turbulent transition. In addition, the overall gender pay gap is not as high as in the West. Both findings contradict the view that women are the economic losers of transition. But the decreasing pay gap is difficult to explain because little data exist on the causes. Due to women's high education levels, human capital differences are only a small amount of the pay gap, according to the World Bank study *Making the Transition Work for Women in Europe and Central Asia* (2000), while the unexplained gap is rather large. This could indicate unequal treatment and discrimination. The decrease in the pay gap could be the result of additional legislative equality measures that have been enacted during

Table 1.2. Equal Pay Gap in Czech Republic, Hungary, and Poland (1987–1999)

Equal pay gap[a]	Czech Republic	Hungary	Poland
1987[b]	66.1	74.3	73.7 (1985)
1992[b]	73.0	80.8	79.0
1992[a, c]	70.2	79.4	67.7
1996[b]	81.3	78.1 (1997)	79.0
1999[d]	73.2	n/a	n/a

Notes: [a] Income of full-time employed women as percentage of full-time employed men of the same age group 20–64.

[d] Other studies have found a lower pay gap in East Germany than in West Germany (Trappe and Rosenfeld 1998).

Sources: [b] Pascall and Manning, 2000, 249; [c] Lippe and Fodor 1998, 21, table 7; [d] Maříková 2003, 115.

the accession process, but could also be the effect of male job loss and men's pay cuts (Pollert 2005).

From the legacy of state-sponsored inclusion in the labor market, it makes sense that feminist mobilization seemed *less* urgent in CEE states than it did it the West. Mobilization for gender equality is weaker overall in CEE countries. This probably has a variety of reasons, one of them being the legacy of state-supported class and gender equality. Nagy sees another cause at work: "After 40 years of socialism people are not enthusiastic about emancipation or even positive discrimination" (2003, 164). As a result, the existing feminist mobilization has taken a different turn by focusing on different issues and working in differently organized movements (Roth 2003; see Regulska and also Hašková in this volume).

Legislating Equality in the Accession Process

The Czech Republic, Hungary, and Poland entered the EU as members simultaneously in 2004, having fulfilled their side of the negotiations and legislative adjustments. How did these states proceed during the accession process in regards to the implementation of EU gender equality measures? The governmental approach towards EU notions of gender equality can be measured in the speed and extent of adjustment of national laws to the hefty 80,000-page *acquis communautaire* containing all EU laws. Lange (2003) has measured the implementation of nine gender-related directives according to a scale from zero to two. Zero indicates no compatibility with the *acquis* in national legislation, while one means partial compatibility and two full compatibility of national law with the EU requirements. According to Lange (2003), the CEE countries studied have performed quite differently in the nine gender-related directives. My secondary analysis shows that, taken together, each of the CEE countries could reach a maximum summary score of eighteen. For 2001–2002, the Czech Republic and Hungary score the highest with thirteen points each and constitute the vanguard of transition countries, while Poland scores the lowest of the three with only eight points. Poland even lags behind Russia (12), Lithuania (13), Latvia (10), Slovenia (9), and Slovakia (9); only Estonia (6) and Bulgaria (5) score lower. Poland is a laggard among the three states in the implementation of EU gender equality directives. This finding corresponds to L. Anderson's (2006) research on EU gender regulations during the Czech and Polish accession, where Poland lagged during formulation and implementation of gender equality due to strong domestic resistance. In a detailed and current CEE ten-country study, Pollert also finds that "there is no evidence of any conception of 'positive action' programs, either in training or recruitment" (Pollert 2005, 228).

L. Anderson (2006) argues that the *external* pressure of the EU lies at the core of the legislative adjustments in CEE states, as opposed to national or local pro-equality pressure. Anderson convincingly demonstrates that during early transition Poland and the Czech Republic had abandoned their former gender equality-friendly constitutions from communist times for a loosely worded and less-committed stance on equality. Following 1989, a general disinterest for gender equality in politics and civil society pervaded the Czech Republic, while in Poland a strong antifeminist opposition emerged in the form of a coalition of conservative parties and the Catholic Church. The behavior of the Catholic Church in Poland during accession talks has been one indicator of its power in regard to gender politics: while the Catholic Church supported EU accession, it did so in return for the government's acquiescence to limiting access to abortion (Chołuj 2003).

With disinterest or opposition to gender equality dominating, one would not expect a slate of antidiscrimination and equality measures to pass the legislatures in these three states. However, in 1998, with the beginning of accession talks the Czech government abruptly shifted gears and passed the first regulations that intended to facilitate the future creation of equal treatment laws and their enforcement (L. Anderson 2006, 110). By 2000, the Czech Republic had met the majority of the criteria of the EU equal employment regime, while the Polish government had only begun to deal with the issue because of the imminent closure of EU accession negotiations. In Poland, EU accession and gender equality laws became politically contested among active feminist movements on one side and conservative parties and the powerful Catholic Church on the other. Abortion rights and what became characterized as an "objectionable sameness" approach towards gender were especially resisted by conservative and religious forces. Given such resistance, it is remarkable that any important gender equality legislation was passed at all in 2000 and 2001. It is clear that these adjustments were not undertaken because of powerful internal demands for gender equality in Poland, but as part of international negotiating and with the goal of EU accession.

The same seems to be true for Hungary. Women in Hungary were, for example, in a comparatively advantageous position compared to those in Austria in regards to employment rate, promotions, wage differentials, and education (Fodor 2004). Today unemployment levels for women in Hungary are still lower than for men (Nagy 2003, 155). Nevertheless the main parties were set against EU equal opportunity laws and instituted them only "under strong EU pressure" and with a narrow focus on equal treatment (Kakucs and Pető in this volume). The recent inclusion of other forms of inequality seems to have led to a further watering down of a gender focus.

The Catholic Church is weaker in Hungary and the Czech Republic than it is in Poland. Thus Catholicism alone can not explain the current weakness of pressure for gender equality. In terms of the Czech implementation process, "many legislative and institutional measures adopted . . . were not an expression of society examining itself, but were instead realized as a result of external pressures—the pressure of the EU accession process—and not from an 'inner' need of women or society as a whole" (Maříková 2003, 107). Nevertheless, a *Department for Equality of Men and Women* in the *Ministry of Labour and Social Affairs* was established in 1998. The task of this commission was to cooperate with NGOs and women's groups, something that proved to be quite difficult. But these small women's groups and organizations are "negligible" and "even . . . marginal," according to Maříková (2003, 109). Lendvai describes the situation of civil society in postcommunist societies thus: "Social movements, civil organizations, and the institutional channels of interest representation in the region are weak. Local and regional self-governments are passive and voiceless" (2004, 329). Pollert states similarly that neither men nor women seem to be concerned with sex equality and that trade unions are weak (Pollert 2005, 228). It is then no wonder that feminist movements and their demands are marginal in Eastern European accession countries.

The Diffusion and Variety of Equal Employment Regimes

After the fall of the Berlin Wall, the question of how CEE states would adapt to market economies, as well as to the EU and to new domestic interests has been the focus of much research. This chapter has tried to assess how three CEE states have developed in regards to labor market participation and equal pay. The extent of *diffusion* and *variety* in gender policies—with the response to external pressure to the supranational equal employment regime of the EU and the domestic formulation of preferences—lay at the center of this essay. The outcome is that (similar to many of the old member states) the governments of the three accession countries studied here do *not* formulate and implement gender equality policies because of a broad domestic discourse supporting expanded women's rights, but rather to gain access to the otherwise advantageous domain of the EU and comply to its standards. The accession talks spurred CEE states on to put forward and reintroduce a number of sex equality laws for women. These laws are circumscribed and predefined by the framework of the increasingly relevant EU equal employment regime, its emphasis on paid work, and its hybrid nature.

The main reasons for the *disinterest* in or *opposition* to gender equality in the three accession states seems to be that these states—and most of society—either perceive women's rights as already long established and achieved or see equal opportunity legislation as negative in three ways: either as an unsavory reminder of communism, a hindrance in the development of a market economy, or as the symbol of a new and quasi-"colonial" encroachment of the EU undermining religious values or cherished national sovereignty and distinctness.

The implications of these findings are fourfold: *first*, the traditional separation between International Relations and Comparative Politics seems to be at odds with what is happening in and during EU enlargement and accession. The expansion of the EU equal employment regime through the "enlargement process" needs to be investigated as both a *domestic* policy of old (and dominant) member states towards the new and weaker applicants and as an "accession" process through the lens of a *foreign* policy of the CEE States. *Second*, the boomerang and ping-pong effects will increase in importance for some social movements who will take advantage of the permeability between domestic and foreign policy to receive financing from the EU and lobby on the supranational level, while pressuring national governments to comply with the laws that they support. *Third*, more empirical research is needed to assess women's gains and losses in the accession process. So far the findings are contradictory, but in regards to labor market participation and equal pay they do not indicate a serious decline compared to the old EU member states. *Forth*, because of the divergent paths that CEE countries have taken over the last fifteen years, I agree with Pascall and Manning (2000, 262) that the construction of CEE countries into an overarching postcommunist regime type is a flawed approach. Even the three transition states discussed here diverge on a variety of levels. To ascertain the CEE states' development of gender-sensitive policies and identities, much research has to be kept focused on national politics and on the developing (or not) affinity to existing types of national equal employment regimes. With its emphasis on religious values, Poland shows, for example, a variety of overlaps with social and employment policies in the conservative state cluster of the old member states such as Italy. Following this trend and as time passes, a variety of new regimes and constellations might emerge, challenging also the perceived and historically bound differences between "East" and "West."

Notes

I thank the editor Silke Roth, my colleague James Martel, and the anonymous reviewer for their helpful feedback and editorial advice.

1. In this section I draw on Wahl 2005.
2. Czechoslovakia separated peacefully into two states, and the Czech Republic and Slovakia formed in 1993. The focus is here on the Czech Republic.
3. Although similar overall, Pascall and Manning's study shows a smaller pay gap than Lippe and Fodor's (differences C: 2.8%, H: 1.4%), but the difference is most extreme in the case of Poland in the year 1992 (P: 11.3%). Reports by the World Bank and UNICEF are discussing the difficulty of obtaining exact data on this issue (Fajth 2000)

References

Anderson, Benedict. 1983. *Imagined Communities, Reflections on the Origin and Spread of Nationalism.* London: Verso.

Anderson, Leah Seppanen. 2006. European Union Gender Regulations in the East: The Czech and Polish Accession Process. *East European Politics and Societies* 20 (1): 101–125.

Caporaso, James and Joseph Jupille. 2001. The Europeanization of Gender Equality Policy and Domestic Structural Change. In *Transforming Europe: Europeanization and Domestic Change*, eds. Maria Green Cowles, James A. Caporaso, and Thomas Risse-Kappen, 21–43. Ithaca, NY: Cornell University Press.

Chołuj, Bożena. 2003. Die Situation der Frauen-NGOs in Polen an der Schwelle zum EU-Beitritt. In *Europas Töchter. Traditionen, Erwartungen und Strategien von Frauenbewegungen in Europa*, eds. Ingrid Miethe and Silke Roth, 203–24. Opladen, Germany: Leske + Budrich.

Domsch, Michel, Désirée Ladwig, and Eliane Tenten. 2003. General Overview of the Larger Economic and Social Context behind the Changes in Women's Lives in Russia and 10 Central and Eastern European Countries. In *Gender Equality in Central and Eastern European Countries*, eds. Michel Domsch, Désirée Ladwig, and Eliane Tenten, 11–36. New York: Peter Lang.

Einhorn, Barbara. 1993. *Cinderella Goes to Market. Citizenship, Gender, and Women's Movements in East Central Europe*. London: Verso.

Ellina, Chrystalla. 2003. *Promoting Women's Rights: The Politics of Gender in the European Union*. New York: Routledge.

Esping-Andersen, Gøsta. 1990. *The Three Worlds of Welfare Capitalism*. Princeton, NJ: Princeton University Press.

———. 1999. *Social Foundations of Postindustrial Economies*. Oxford: Oxford University Press.

Fajth, Gáspár. 2000. Regional Monitoring of Child and Family Well-Being: UNICEF's MONEE project in CEE and CIS in a Comparative Perspective. Innocenti Working Paper, no 72. Florence: UNICEF Innocenti Research Center.

Fodor, Eva. 2004. The State Socialist Emancipation Project: Gender Inequality in Workplace Authority in Hungary and Austria. *Signs: Journal of Women in Culture and Society* 29 (3): 783–813.

Gal, Susan and Gail Kligman, eds. 2000. *Reproducing Gender: Politics, Public, and Everyday Life After Socialism*. Princeton, NJ: Princeton University Press.

Grieco, Joseph. 1988. Anarchy and the Limits of Cooperation: A Realist Critique of the Newest Liberal Institutionalism. *International Organization* 42 (3): 486–507.

Haas, Ernst. 1958. *The Uniting of Europe: Political, Social, and Economic Forces*. Palo Alto, CA: Stanford University Press.

Hix, Simon. 1994. The Study of the European Community: The Challenge to Comparative Politics. *West European Politics* 17 (1): 1–30.

Hoffmann, Stanley. 1966. Obstinate or Obsolete? The Fate of the Nation-State and the Case of Western Europe. *Daedalus* 95 (3): 862–915.

Hoskyns, Catherine. 1996. *Integrating Gender. Women, Law and Politics in the European Union*. London, New York: Verso.

———. 1999. Then and Now: Equal Pay in the European Union. In *Women, Work, and Inequality*, eds. Jeanne Gregory, Ariane Hegewisch and Rosemary Sales, 27–43. Houndmills, UK: Macmillan.

Jacobsson, Kerstin. 2004. Soft Regulation and the Subtle Transformation of States: A Case of EU Employment Policy. *Journal of European Social Policy* 14 (4): 355–70.

Keck, Margaret and Kathryn Sikkink. 1998. *Activists beyond Borders: Advocacy Networks in International Politics*. Ithaca, NY: Cornell University Press.

Langan, Mary and Ilona Ostner. 1991. Geschlechterpolitik im Wohlfahrtsstaat: Aspekt im internationalen Vergleich. *Kritische Justiz* 24: 302–17.

Lange, Gisela. 2003. Gender Equality in Central and Eastern European Candidate Countries—An ILO Perspective. In *Gender Equality in Central and Eastern European Countries*, eds. Michel Domsch, Désirée Ladwig, and Eliane Tenten, 37–56. Frankfurt: Peter Lang.

Lendvai, Noémi. 2004. The Weakest Link? EU Accession and Enlargement: Dialoguing EU and Post-communist Social Policy. *Journal of European Social Policy* 14 (3): 319–33.

Lewis, Jane and Ilona Ostner. 1998. Geschlechterpolitik zwischen europäischer und nationalstaatlicher Regelung. In *Standort Europa, Europäische Sozialpolitik*, eds. Stephan Leibfried and Paul Pierson. Frankfurt am Main: Suhrkamp.

Lippe, Tanja van der and Eva Fodor. 1998. Changes in Gender Inequality in Six Eastern European Countries. *Acta Sociologica* 41 (2): 131–50.

Manning, Nick. 2004. Diversity and Change in Pre-accession Central and Eastern Europe since 1989. *Journal of European Social Policy* 14 (3): 211–232.

Maříková, Hana. 2003. Gender Equality in the Czech Republic—The Position of Highly Qualified Women in the Transforming Society. In *Gender Equality in Central and Eastern European Countries*, eds. Michel Domsch, Désirée Ladwig, and Eliane Tenten, 103–121. Frankfurt: Peter Lang.

Mazey, Sonia. 1998. The EU and Women's Rights. From Europeanization of National Agendas to the Nationalization of a European Agenda?" *Journal of European Public Policy* 5 (1): 131–52.

Moravcsik, Andrew. 1993. Preferences and Power in the European Community: A Liberal Intergovernmentalist Approach. *Journal of Common Market Studies* 31 (4): 473–524.

Nagy, Beáta. 2003. Women in the Economic Elite in Hungary. In *Gender Equality in Central and Eastern European Countries*, eds. Michel Domsch, Désirée Ladwig, and Eliane Tenten, 151–68. New York: Peter Lang.

O'Connor, Julia. 1993. Gender, Class and Citizenship in the Comparative Analysis of Welfare State Regimes: Theoretical and Methodological Issues. *British Journal of Sociology* 44 (3): 501–18.

Orloff, Ann. 1993. Gender and the Social Rights of Citizenship: The Comparative Analysis of Gender Relations and Welfare States. *American Sociological Review* 58 (3): 303–328.

Pascall, Gillian and Nick Manning. 2000. Gender and Social Policy: Comparing Welfare States in Central and Eastern Europe and the Former Soviet Union. *Journal of European Social Policy* 10 (3): 240–66.

Pascall, Gillian and Jane Lewis. 2004. Emerging Gender Regimes and Policies for Gender Equality in a Wider Europe. *Journal of Social Policy* 33 (3): 373–94.

Pierson, Paul. 1996. The Path to European Integration: A Historical Institutionalist Analysis. *Comparative Political Studies* 29 (2): 123–63.

Pollack, Mark. 2001. International Relations Theory and European Integration. *Journal of Common Market Studies* 39 (2): 221–44.

Pollert, Anne. 2005. Gender, Transformation and Employment in Central Eastern Europe. *European Journal of Industrial Relations* 11 (2): 213–30.

Roth, Silke. 2003. Nationale und Internationale Einflüsse—Ein Vergleich europäischer Frauenbewegungen. In *Europas Töchter. Traditionen, Erwartungen und Strategien von Frauenbewegungen in Europa*, eds. Ingrid Miethe and Silke Roth, 275–85. Opladen, Germany: Leske + Budrich.

Roth, Silke and Ingrid Miethe. 2003. Die EU als Chance und Herausforderung für Frauenbewegungen. In *Europas Töchter, Traditionen, Erwartungen und Strategien von Frauenbewegungen in Europa*, eds. Ingrid Miethe and Silke Roth, 9–20. Opladen, Germany: Leske + Budrich.

Russett, Bruce with the collaboration of William Antholis, Carol Ember, Melvin Ember, and Zeev Maoz. 1993. *Grasping the Democratic Peace*, Princeton, NJ: Princeton University Press.

Sabatier, Paul. 1988. An Advocacy Coalition Framework of Policy Change and the Role of Policy-oriented Learning Therein. *Policy Sciences* 21 (2–3): 128–68.

Scharpf, Fritz. 1988. The Joint-Decision Trap: Lessons from German Federalism and European Integration. *Public Administration* 66 (3): 239–78.

Steinhilber, Silke. 2001. Gender Relations and Labour Market Transformation: Status Quo and Policy Responses in Central and Eastern Europe. In *Gender in Transition in Eastern and Central Europe*

Proceedings, eds. Gabriele Jähnert, Jana Gohrisch, Daphne Hahn, Hildegard Nickel, Iris Peinl, and Katrin Schäfgen, 201–13. Berlin: Trafo-Verlag.

Streeck, Wolfgang. 1996. Neo-Voluntarism: A New European Social Policy Regime. In *Governance in the European Union*, eds. Gary Marks, Fritz W. Scharpf, Philippe C. Schmitter, and Wolfgang Streeck, 64–94. London: Sage.

Trappe, Heike and Rachel Rosenfeld. 1998. A Comparison in Job-Shifting Patterns in the Former East Germany and the Former West Germany. *European Sociological Review* 14 (4): 343–68.

Wahl, Angelika von. 1999. *Gleichstellungsregime: Beruflichche Gleichstellung von Frauen in der Bundesrepublik und den USA*. Leverkusen: Leske + Budrich.

———. 2005. Liberal, Conservative, Social Democratic or . . . European? The European Union as Equal Employment Regime. *Social Politics* 12 (1): 67–95.

Walby, Sylvia. 1999a. The EU and Equality Opportunities Policies. *European Societies* 1: 59–80.

———. 1999b. The New Regulatory State: The Social Powers of the European Union. *British Journal of Sociology* 50 (1): 118–40.

———. 2004. The European Union and Gender Equality: Emergent Varieties of Gender Regime. *Social Politics* 11 (1): 4–29.

Watson, Peggy. 2000. Politics, Policy and Identity: EU Eastern Enlargement and East-West Differences. *Journal of European Public Policy* 7 (3): 369–84.

———. 2001. Gender and Politics in Postcommunism. In *Gender in Transition in Eastern and Central Europe Proceedings*, eds. Gabriele Jähnert, Jana Gohrisch, Daphne Hahn, Hildegard Nickel, Iris Peinl, and Katrin Schäfgen, 37–48. Berlin: Trafo-Verlag.

Young, Brigitte. 1999. *Triumph of the Fatherland: German Unification and the Marginalization of Women*. Ann Arbor, MI: University of Michigan Press.

———. 2000. Disciplinary Neoliberalism in the European Union and Gender Politics. *New Political Economy* 5 (1): 77–98.

Zippel, Kathrin. 2004. Transnational Advocacy Networks and Policy Cycles in the European Union: The Case of Sexual Harassment. *Social Politics* 11 (1): 57–85.

2

Toward the Europeanization of Work-Family Policies?

The Impact of the EU on Policies for Working Parents

Kimberly J. Morgan

The issue of how to help parents balance work and family has gained increasing prominence at the EU level in the past ten to fifteen years. The EU has a long history of promoting gender equality, yet most initiatives in the past were antidiscrimination measures that could not address the substantive barriers to women's equal integration into paid work. Since the 1990s, however, EU directives on maternity protection, parental leave, part-time work, and atypical employment have sought to do so by recognizing that women's labor force patterns often differ from those of men due to childbirth and childcare. The EU's "open method of coordination"—a system of voluntary cooperation among the member states on sensitive areas such as social and employment policy—has produced voluntary targets for childcare provision by 2010 and highlighted the need for the member states to tackle gender gaps in employment, pay, and occupational segregation. In short, the role of the EU in work-family policy has been transformed.

What accounts for the increasing Europeanization of these issues and what are the implications for the new member states? The long evolution towards contemporary EU policies in this area was marked by fits and starts. Transnational networks of feminists long pushed the EU to tackle the root causes of gendered employment patterns, and they often have had allies in the European

Commission and Parliament on this issue. Their efforts have been hemmed in by the member states, however, many of which were unwilling to cede control over social and employment policy to the EU. By the early 1990s, however, there was growing agreement among the member states that Europe should develop its social agenda, while fertility and employment fears spurred domestic discussions about the barriers to mothers' employment. This created an opening for EU-level initiatives on childcare, parental leave, and working time.

To evaluate the potential impact of these measures on the new member states, it is worth looking at their effects so far on the old. These policies have brought important changes to the EU-15, particularly through the binding directives passed in the 1990s. As a voluntary system of social policy harmonization, the open method of coordination has had less impact so far, although it has raised the profile of work-family issues and may ultimately promote policy learning among elites. Fundamentally, however, large-scale reforms in policies for working parents are most likely to originate at the national level, and it is there that the main battles must be fought. This is particularly the case given continuing ambiguities in EU-level statements about what a gender-egalitarian model of work-family policy would look like, which leaves much room for the individual member states to fashion their own interpretations. The same is true in the new member states, which face similar issues regarding women's employment and the gendered division of care. Thus, while this chapter argues that much of the progress made on this issue at the EU level has been due to the work of feminists and other activists at the EU level, without a similar mobilization by groups in domestic politics, the transformative potential offered by EU policies and discourses for policy change will not be realized.

This chapter will first discuss the long road toward the Europeanization of work and family policy, from the equal opportunity measures of the early 1970s, to the childcare and parental leave directives of the 1990s, to the Open Method of Coordination in more recent years. The chapter then evaluates the impact of these diverse measures on work-family policies in the old member states. The final section discusses some implications for the countries that have more recently acceded to the EU.

The Expanding Role of the EU in Work-Family Policies

The EU has come a long way on the issue of work and family. Originally, the EU had no competence over family policy, and the idea that gender equality should fall within the purview of the EU was based on a slender reed. The sole reference to gender equality in the 1957 Treaty of Rome was Article 119, which asserted that men and women should receive equal pay for equal work, yet this was largely ignored by the member states. It took a series of European Court of Justice (ECJ) rulings in the 1970s to establish that this treaty article took "direct effect" in the member states and should therefore be enforced (Warner 1984). At the same time, the European Commission began taking a more active role in gender equality policies, and throughout the 1970s and 1980s it oversaw the passage of a number of equality directives on equal pay, working conditions, and social security rights (for a summary, see Hantrais 2000, 14–15). ECJ rulings backed up and expanded the scope of these directives, and infringement proceedings brought against many of the member states helped ensure legislative changes were concordant with the equal pay directive (Mazey 1995, 598–99; Walby 1999, 131–32).

Feminist activism was critical to the growing European Community (EC) role in promoting gender equality. For example, feminist lawyer Eliane Vogel-Polsky brought the first case on equal pay to the ECJ. The resulting 1976 *Defrenne* ruling established that EC treaty articles applied immediately to the member states and created the right for women to receive equal pay for equal work based on article 119 of the Treaty of Rome (Warner 1984, 148–49).[1] In general, however, the greatest influence of women's movements came less from direct lobbying of the EC than from the development of these movements at the domestic level, which moved the commission to adopt gender equality as one of its objectives (Hoskyns 1994, 232; Stratigaki 2004, 36). The spurt of commission-driven activity in the 1970s was also part of a larger campaign by the commission to broaden its support by appealing to disaffected constituencies in the member states (Warner 1984, 161–62).

Although EC directives and court rulings helped promote women's formal equality on the labor market, the member states still controlled those areas of policy that could address the deeper causes of gender inequality in paid work. EC policies were rooted in a liberal view of equality, one that sought to remove overt barriers to women's employment (Wahl, this volume). Such equal opportunity measures are of great importance, yet women's social citizenship claims ultimately require the redistributive allocation of resources, namely through spreading the costs of children and parenting across the broader society (Hoskyns 1996, 199). The EC, and later the EU, has had the power to enforce directives through the ECJ, but the member states have jealously guarded their responsibility for redistributive policy (Walby 1999). Without the political capacity for substantive social welfare or family policies, the EC could do little to address the substantive barriers to women's equality—such as the unequal division of labor in care work and lack of childcare, parental leave, or flexible working-time arrangements.

Given these limitations, some within the European Commission sought to use "soft" measures—such as opinions, recommendations, or action programs— that could at least raise the profile of the work-family issue. Already in 1974, the Council of the European Communities agreed to a Social Action Program that not only supported equal opportunity measures in employment and paid work, but also called for efforts "to ensure that the family responsibilities of all concerned may be reconciled with their job aspirations."[2] During the 1980s, the commission developed two equal opportunity programs that highlighted the need for childcare, parental leave, and a redistribution of caring responsibilities in the home as prerequisites for women's equal chances on the labor market (Stratigaki 2000, 31–32).

The emerging gender egalitarian discourse reflected the increasing activism of feminist groups at the European level, as well as the efforts of individual women working within European institutions (Hoskyns 1996; Stratigaki 2000). A women's policy network began developing in the 1970s and 1980s and included the Advisory Committee on Equal Opportunities, expert committees established by the commission's Women's Bureau, the Women's Committee of the European Parliament, and various women's and feminist organizations. To some degree, the commission shaped this policy community as it actively fostered transnational networks in a number of policy areas to build up its own legitimacy and create a constituency for its reforms. Attention to women's issues also was institutionalized through the Equal Opportunities Unit in the Directorate-General V, which was established in 1976 and given responsibility for the development and implementation of equality policies (Mazey 1995, 604).

This unit created a number of networks to address various equality issues, including the European Community Network on Childcare (ECNC) that was active from 1986 to 1996. The ECNC collected and compiled information about childcare policy in the member states and offered some of the first and best comparative data available on the subject (Ross 1998, 236–37).[3] Their efforts culminated in the 1992 Council of Ministers Recommendation on Childcare, which called upon the member states to take steps to "enable women and men to reconcile their occupational, family and upbringing responsibilities arising from the care of children," with particular emphasis on childcare services, parental leave, the organization of work, and improving men's participation in childcare responsibilities (Bleijenbergh 2004, ch. 5). While this was an important milestone, it was nonbinding and thus depended entirely on the will of the member states for its implementation. Even with this nonbinding measure, however, some countries perceived that the EU was beginning to impinge on their prerogatives in social policy, which was one reason why the ECNC was eliminated in 1996. Another motivation was the desire of some member states to reduce commission spending. The Equal Opportunities Unit also lost half its funding in 1995, and nearly all of its networks were closed (Ross 1998, 256–57).

Several of the member states also blocked attempts by the commission to use the EC's regulatory authority over labor markets to improve parents' working conditions. The demand for a parental leave directive originated in the European Parliament's Ad Hoc Committee on Women's Rights and the European Commission. The proposed measure required a minimum leave of three months per worker, per child (giving a total entitlement of six months for one child with two parents, as long as they equally split the leave); an optional allowance paid by the state; and a part-time option for taking the leave (Rutherford 1989, 301, 303). When considered in 1982, the proposed directive met with considerable opposition in the Council of Ministers, as most of the 10 countries that were members of the EC would have to make substantial legislative changes to meet the requirements of the parental leave directive (Rutherford 1989, 305). By 1986 the initiative had died, and the hostility of the UK to any initiatives imposing costs upon employers barred consideration of the directive throughout the rest of the 1980s (Treib and Falkner 2004). Efforts to get a part-time work directive also fell victim to a UK veto, although a 1986 ECJ ruling held that part-time workers should have the same benefits and working conditions as those working full-time (Bleijenbergh 2004, 86).

By the 1990s, however, a number of developments at both the EU level and in the member states increased the prospects for an EU role in family-related policies. By now, the women's lobby at the EU level was well institutionalized, with the European Parliament's Standing Committee for Women's Rights playing an active role on gender equality issues, the creation of the European Women's Lobby in 1990, and a host of women's organizations being regularly consulted by the European Commission for advice. Transnational networks of gender equality activists and experts took advantage of EU institutional changes in the 1990s to push gender equality onto the agenda, with a particular focus on gender mainstreaming—the idea that gender issues should be incorporated into all areas of policymaking (Pollack and Hafner-Burton 2000). The 1995 Beijing summit on women also furthered the cause of gender mainstreaming, as the European Commission played a critical role in negotiating the platform for this meeting and embraced the concept of gender mainstreaming (Rubery 2005, 392; Pollack and Hafner-Burton 2000, 435). At least at the supranational level, the stage was set for a renewed commitment to gender equality goals, one that went beyond the earlier, narrower focus on antidiscrimination policy (Pollack and Hafner-Burton 2000).

The ambition to develop a social dimension to European integration also led to important institutional reforms. The 1987 Single European Act established the possibility of using qualified majority voting in the council for questions concerning minimum workplace standards. This opened the door to the 1992 directive on pregnant workers, once the commission repackaged a gender equality measure into one about health and safety at work (Heide 1999). The directive banned discrimination against pregnant workers and created a right to fourteen weeks of maternity leave paid at the level workers would normally receive for absences due to illness. The new voting rules also enabled passage of the 1993 Working Time Directive, over the UK's objections. The measure sought to limit maximum working hours and assure minimum periods of rest and paid annual leave (Heide 1999).

Another key development was the 1992 Maastricht Treaty, which empowered the European-level social partners to negotiate agreements that could then be translated into directives.[4] Thus, when faced with continued UK opposition to a parental leave directive, the issue was referred to the European social partners, who concluded an agreement that later became the 1996 Parental Leave Directive (Falkner 1998).[5] Additional negotiations between the social partners led to the Part-Time Work Directive of 1997, which required that part-time and full-time workers be treated equally in matters of pay and working conditions, and the 1999 Fixed-Term Work Directive that aims to prevent discrimination against temporary workers.

Political shifts within the member states also enabled a more active EU role on work-family issues. Given the ability of member states to block gender equality measures in the Council of Ministers, both policy shifts within the member states and the accession of states that prioritize egalitarian work-life policies (e.g., Sweden and Finland) spurred greater attention to work-life issues at the EU level (Stratigaki 2000). By the 1990s, the question of women's employment was increasingly prominent on the domestic agendas of many European countries. The seemingly inexorable rise in women's employment, and the decline of the male breadwinner model, highlighted the mismatch between existing welfare state arrangements and social realities (Esping-Andersen 1999). While some countries in Europe have extensive public childcare systems and generous parental leave options, many lack policies that address the needs of wage-earning mothers (see table 2.1). In addition, concerns about social exclusion led to an increased focus on the situation faced by solo mothers, and thus calls for improved childcare and other policies that would enable (or compel) these mothers to be in paid work (Lewis 1997). Women were at the center of another set of concerns: chronically high unemployment, yet also fears of future labor shortages given the imminent retirement of the baby boom generation and low fertility rates. Active and flexible labor market policies increasingly were seen as the answer—policies that would stimulate women's employment and enable mothers to better combine paid work and childbearing (Mahon 2002).

Thus, by the 1990s, EU discourse had shifted from a focus on equal opportunities in paid work to an agenda that targeted the deeper sources of gender inequality—namely, the division of labor at home (Hantrais 2000). Symptomatic of this ideational shift was the nonbinding Community Charter of the Fundamental Social Rights of Workers (1989), which all member states signed except for the UK. The charter included a commitment by the member states to adopt measures helping parents "reconcile" work and family as a way to promote equal treatment of men and women. Similar language and commitments were included in the Third Action Program on Equal Opportunities between Women and Men (1991–95), the Agreement on Social Policy that was annexed to the Maastricht Treaty (1992), a 1994 White Paper on European Social Policy, and the Fourth

Table 2.1. Percentage of Children in Childcare up to Thirty Hours per Week

	0–2 year olds	3–5 year olds (or until school age)
Austria	13	85
Belgium	31	100
Czech Republic	1	77
Cyprus	12	82
Denmark	68	92
Estonia	34	86
Finland	28	77
France	41	100
Germany	9	90
Western Länder	3	88
Eastern Länder	37	105
Greece	5	55
Hungary	10	88
Italy	23	94
Latvia	16	81
Lithuania	21	70
Luxembourg	11	n/a
Netherlands	26	91
Poland	2	60
Portugal	24	70
Slovak Republic	19	45
Slovenia	37	77
Spain	37	95
Sweden	75*	96
United Kingdom**	35	86

Data unavailable for Malta and Ireland. Figures mostly from 2004–05.

* For children aged 1–3 only.

** UK data is for England only and includes child-minders, nannies, au pairs, crèches, nursery schools and reception classes in primary school, day nurseries, playgroups, preschools, family centers, out of school clubs and holiday clubs.

Sources: Figures are the reports of member states in their National Reform Programs, as compiled by the European Commission, Employment and Social Affairs DG, *Indicators for Monitoring the Employment Guidelines, 2006 Compendium* (Brussels: November 30, 2006). On the sub-national breakdown in Germany, see *National Action Plan for Employment Policy* (2004: 91).

Action Program for Equal Opportunities between Women and Men (1996–2000) (for details, see Hantrais 2000, 16–17; Stratigaki 2000, 36–39).

These ideas also have been important in the Open Method of Coordination (OMC), a new policy instrument for the voluntary coordination of social policy among the member states (Zeitlin 2005). The OMC expands the influence of the EU over sensitive policy areas, while preserving autonomy for the member states. Thus, there are no directives or ECJ rulings that compel states to adopt particular policies, as competence over policy is left at the national or lower levels of government. Instead, the OMC relies on benchmarking and peer review processes to move the member states closer to objectives that they themselves have agreed on. States submit regular reports ("national reform programs") about their progress in meeting these goals, and receive recommendations from the Council about where they can improve. Lacking hard sanctions for the failure to meet specified targets, policy change is to happen through learning on the part of policy makers and some amount of international shaming (Borrás and Jacobsson 2004; Trubek and Mosher 2003, 39).

Gender equality and questions of work and family have had a prominent place in the most developed form of the OMC, the European Employment Strategy (EES).[6] When the EES emerged out of an intergovernmental conference in Amsterdam in 1997, equality was one of four pillars of employment guidelines adopted by the member states at the Luxembourg European Council meeting in November of that year (Trubek and Mosher 2003, 37–38). Within that pillar, there were specific recommendations about reducing gender gaps in employment; combating occupational segregation; improving parental leave, part-time work, and childcare provision, with a particular emphasis on the latter; and facilitating the reintegration of workers back into the labor market after an absence from paid work. Over time, these goals have become more concrete through specific targets. At the March 2000 European Council meeting in Lisbon, the member states agreed that they should work to increase the female labor force participation rate from an EU average of 51 percent to 60 percent by 2010.[7] They then decided at the Stockholm European Council meeting to create intermediary targets, with 57 percent of women employed by 2005. Then, at the Barcelona European Council of 2002, they set concrete targets for childcare provision: by 2010, the member states agreed to make sure there was childcare for at least 90 percent of children aged three to the mandatory school age, and 33 percent of children below the age of three.

A number of recent developments confirm the commitment of the EU to improving the situation of working mothers. There now is greater emphasis in the EES on reducing gender gaps, such as the gender gap in pay and occupational segregation (Rubery et al. 2004, 605). As both reflect the societal distribution of care work, reducing gendered patterns of employment and pay will require more attention to the work-family nexus. More recently, the European Commission has begun doing annual reports on gender equality, the most recent of which gives a prominent place to work and family issues (Commission of the European Communities 2005). Not only does the report emphasize the need for improved care facilities for children and other dependents, but it also calls for measures that target men as well, such as incentives to take parental leave. More generally, as Rubery et al. (2004) report, gender equality has become such a regular feature of European policy debates that few employment reports or speeches neglect any mention of gender. While the depth of the commitment to gender equality may not match the rhetorical attention it now receives, the shift in discourse is a significant change (Rubery et al. 2004, 604).

In short, the EU has become an important actor in the area of work and family due to the lobbying of feminist groups, the continuing efforts of the commission to expand the competence of the EU, and changes within the member states that made them more amenable to these ideas. What have been the concrete effects of these various measures? As the succeeding section will show, there have been some policy shifts in the EU-15, but there remain obstacles to more fundamental reforms in national work-family policies.

Impacts and Limitations of EU-Level Work-Family Policies in the EU-15

The EU directives on parental leave and working time have produced some important changes in the domestic policies of the member states. Although some did not expect the parental leave directive to have much impact (Stratigaki 2000, 43), one study shows that six member states (Austria, Germany, Greece, Italy, the Netherlands, and Portugal) had to make minor changes to their existing parental leave systems, while four more (Belgium, Ireland, Luxembourg, and the UK) had to make more fundamental reforms.[8] In the UK, Luxembourg, and Ireland, for example, because there was no previous entitlement to parental leave, the directive produced a significant change in domestic policy (Treib and Falkner 2004). In Belgium, there also was no legal entitlement of all workers to parental leave prior to this directive, although public sector workers did have that right and there was a career breaks system that provided a de facto leave. Still, the directive required that leave rights be extended to all workers (Treib and Falkner 2004). A study of the part-time work directive also finds that nearly all of the member states had to make changes to their domestic laws—some relatively minor, while others were more significant—and that part-time workers gained improved legal protections as a result (Clauwaert 2002).[9] Walby (2003) argues more generally that the EU was crucial to the adoption of equal opportunity laws in the UK, and that without the EU such measures never would have been adopted prior to the change in government in 1997.

These directives also were important in that they went beyond the "sameness" perspective characteristic of antidiscrimination measures and recognized that the distinctive patterns of women's employment reflect the gendered division of labor in the home (Walby 2004). For example, while the part-time work directive was shaped in part by the goal of increasing labor market flexibility, it also sought to improve the working conditions of part-time workers—the majority of whom are female—and it reflected the idea that access to such jobs would enable or encourage mothers to be in paid work (Bleijenbergh et al. 2004). The 1996 parental leave directive also moved beyond a view that childcare is solely an issue for women, as it requires the member states to make a *parental* leave available to all parents, beyond the mandatory maternity leave justified by reasons of health. As Walby has argued, these directives are starting to implant the concept of the "worker-parent" in employment law (Walby 2004, 6).

One limit to these directives lies in the continuing lack of agreement among the member states on the reach of the EU in social affairs. For example, the directive on part-time work does not mandate equal treatment of part-time and full-time workers in social security systems, as that was seen as an intrusion into a domain of national authority (Bleijenbergh et al. 2004).[10] In addition, the parental leave directive lacks any requirement of a *paid* leave, leaving such decisions entirely to the member states. As table 2.2 shows, entitlement to paid parental leave varies considerably across the EU, with entirely unpaid leaves in Greece, Ireland, the Netherlands, Portugal, Spain, and the UK, and leaves paid at varying levels of compensation in other countries. The low level or lack of pay ensures that women are far more likely to take these leaves than men, as women often earn less than men and are therefore more likely to sacrifice their salary during an unpaid leave. It also limits the usefulness of these minimum leave requirements for low-income or impoverished families.

As for the OMC, at the very least it has helped put the work-family issue on the political agenda, raising its profile among the member states and requiring them to be publicly accountable for the progress they have made on reducing gender gaps in employment and pay, combating occupational segregation, and building up the supply of public childcare (Rubery 2005; Plantenga 2004). One important achievement of the EES has been that it requires member states to collect and report data on childcare, which could make them more accountable on this issue. A Eurostat study has laid the foundations for the collection of comparable childcare data so that since 2006 the commission has had data that it can use to evaluate the progress of the member states on meeting the Barcelona childcare targets (Eurostat 2004; *Childcare in a Changing World* 2004). The potential for policy learning and exchange also follows from the peer review sessions that are a regular part of the OMC. In recent years, EES peer reviews have covered such topics as "parental insurance and childcare," "increasing the employment of women through flexible work arrangements," and "gender mainstreaming in

Table 2.2. Compensation for Statutory Parental Leave, 2003

	Compensation	Country
None		Greece, Ireland, Netherlands, Portugal, Spain, UK
Flat-rate	Means-tested	Poland
	Lower for higher-income claimants	Germany
	Not means-tested	Austria, Belgium, France, Finland*, Luxembourg, Slovakia
Proportional to pay	Below 80% of pay	Finland*, Hungary, Italy
	80–90% of pay	Denmark, Sweden
	100% of pay	Norway, Slovenia

* In Finland, the first twenty-six weeks are not means-tested but paid at a flat-rate, and the second twenty-six weeks are proportional to pay.

Source: European Foundation for the Improvement of Living and Working Conditions, *Family-Related Leave and Industrial Relations* (September 2004).

the public employment service." In general, government officials in the member states say that they value the peer-review session and other opportunities for cross-national policy learning (Govecor 2004a). Finally, Rubery (2005) argues that the larger push for gender mainstreaming has helped forge a more holistic view of employment issues by linking different strands of economic and social policy that affect gender equality.

The EES also has its limits, however, given that it relies on the states for implementation. As the member states could make inflated claims about the progress they are making, domestic pressure is necessary to make sure these states do what they say they are doing. Yet, the fundamental problem facing the EES is that it is not yet embedded in the domestic decision-making processes of the member states. As a recent study by the EU-funded Govecor project[11] concluded, the EES process is largely a transnational dialogue between a small number of actors within domestic bureaucracies, their counterparts in other states, and EU-level actors (Govecor 2004a; Jacobsson and Vifell 2007). National action plans and EU-level targets do not appear much in national parliamentary debates, nor has there been much domestic media attention given to the EES (de la Porte and Nanz 2004, 277–78). As a result, key interest groups such as labor unions and business associations are not fully engaged in the EES, although the degree of involvement of the social partners does vary by country (Govecor 2004b). Jacobsson and Vifell (2005) point out that many member states have resisted allowing civil society groups to become more involved in the OMC, while also opposing the idea of EU-run information campaigns to raise the visibility of the EES.

The lack of embeddedness in national policy-making reduces the potential impact of the OMC. Of course, measuring the effects of the OMC is fraught with methodological difficulties, which makes it tempting to simply claim that it has not mattered in domestic policy-making (Trubek and Trubek 2005, 350). Interpreting the consequences of the OMC also depends on one's views of what counts as significant change. Here, Peter Hall's typology of policy change is useful, as he distinguishes between changes in the levels or settings of policy instruments, changes in the hierarchy of objectives, and more fundamental paradigm shifts (Hall 1993). He locates the source of the first two forms of change in the realm of bureaucratic elites who, through policy learning, decide to adjust current instruments or modify the priorities attached to different goals. Paradigm shifts are more political processes, potentially involving a greater degree of social and political mobilization and politicized debates.

In the immediate term, the OMC is perhaps best suited to achieve the first two forms of change. While intergovernmental exchanges and peer review sessions are conducive to policy learning among bureaucrats, these transnational bureaucratic networks are unlikely to be powerful enough to bring paradigmatic shifts in policy unless they spark debates at the domestic level about the need for wide-ranging reforms. This is all the more reason why the disconnect between the EES and national parliaments or interest groups is so problematic. For the OMC to effect more fundamental change, domestic actors have to use the OMC targets as leverage in domestic political debates. If this generates some policy shifts at the national level, this has the potential to feed back into the OMC process, as support for a particular set of objectives grows among the member states and then Europe-wide targets become more ambitious and detailed.

The childcare targets in the EES reveal the limits of the OMC thus far. Some have argued that childcare is an example of success by the EES, as there has been some increase in the services available in recent years (Rubery et al. 2004, 616). The pace of change has been fairly incremental, however, and so far there is little evidence of more fundamental shifts in policy-making priorities on work and family. Countries with the highest supply of public childcare—Sweden, Denmark, France, and Belgium—remain countries that are near to or already meet the EU targets (table 2.1). By contrast, in countries that have traditionally been reluctant to encourage or support mothers' employment, such as Austria or Germany, there have been no dramatic shifts in policy. In Germany, data from 2004 show that only 2.7 percent of children under the age of three had access to day care in the western *Länder*—virtually no change from the late 1990s (Federal Republic of Germany 2004, 91). Perhaps a paradigm shift in work-family policy is forthcoming, but it has not manifested itself in concrete policy changes, as of yet.[12]

Achieving more significant policy changes requires that domestic-level actors take advantage of the EU targets to push reform from below. Thus far, however, there is little evidence that the national interest groups that care about work-and-family issues have become very engaged in the EES process. The social partners have become less interested in participating in the EES process because they do not believe it to be the key decision-making site for government policy. It therefore appears that a small number of bureaucratic actors dominate the process of drafting the national reports to the EU (Govecor 2004b, 12; de la Porte and Nanz 2004, 279–80). Richardt's study of childcare politics in the UK and Germany (2005) finds that, in both cases, domestic women's groups have not tried to use the EES as a source of leverage in pushing for expanding childcare availability, although she does find that the German government's justification of its labor market reforms by EES requirements created a window of opportunity for feminists within the government to push for improved childcare. Zeitlin (2005, 465–66) notes that there has been greater participation of civil society thus far in the area of social inclusion, with antipoverty groups increasingly engaged and involved in the OMC, but that if women's groups have been involved in the EES process, they have done so behind the scenes and thus escaped the notice of scholars. In short, the work of activists at the EU level can only go so far in pushing for change; domestic-level activism is now critical for ensuring that the member states meet the goals they have formally agreed to.

Another reason why action from below is so important is that current EES targets, recommendations, and other statements do not provide a coherent and fully articulated vision of gender egalitarian policies for balancing work and family. As Mahon's analysis shows (2002), some EU statements and measures appear to endorse egalitarian, Scandinavian-style policies that emphasize public childcare and women's employment, while others favor "neo-familialist" policies of lengthy parental leaves and part-time work for mothers. This leaves considerable room for interpretation on the part of the member states on the kinds of policies needed to meet the EES targets. For example, the Barcelona childcare targets do not differentiate between part-time and full-time care services, even though this difference has significant implications for the ability of parents to work full time. Thus, a country such as Germany currently meets the childcare targets for three-to-six-year-olds even though the short opening hours of preschools in the western *Länder* are a major obstacle to mothers' employment (Hank and Kreyenfeld 2002). The targets also do not distinguish between public and private care services. Although the private childcare market is quite significant in some countries (Ireland, the Netherlands, and the UK), the low level or lack of public subsidies for these programs often keeps these services prohibitively expensive for lower-income parents (OECD 2002). However, governments can point to this market as evidence that childcare needs are being met, masking the "care deficit" experienced by many parents (Cullen, this volume).

The EES process also has not dealt with the issue of whether or not part-time work is to be encouraged. On the one hand, the EES has often called on member states to encourage part-time and flexible work options as a way to encourage mothers' employment, but council recommendations also emphasize the need to fight occupational segregation and the gender pay gap. Yet, encouraging states to develop flexible forms of employment, which usually are taken up disproportionately by women, contributes to the diminished place of women in the hierarchy of paid work. It appears that the council has not systematically addressed the question of whether the ongoing focus on labor market flexibility promoted through the EES might be incompatible with gender equality goals (Rubery 2005; Ayad and Masselot 2004).

We can see this in the example of the Netherlands, where a rapid rise in women's workforce participation since the 1980s came largely through the spread of part-time work. This is especially true for mothers; currently, nearly 80 percent of employed mothers with a child under age six work part-time, and nearly no young children attend childcare more than two or three days a week (OECD 2005, 41). Is the Dutch model an example of the successful "reconciliation" of work and family? The Netherlands now meets both the formal employment targets and is close to meeting the childcare goals, but this is because of the prevalence of part-time work and part-time childcare. Interpretations of Dutch policies hinge on one's views about the merits of part-time work, yet EU actors have hardly been clear on this. In its recommendations to the Netherlands, the Council of the European Union has sent some mixed signals on the Dutch "one-and-a-half-worker" model, as it first lauded the Netherlands for having achieved the employment targets, and more recently has remarked that the high rate of part-time work among women is a concern.[13] There are similar ambiguities on the question of parental and longer care leave policies. In France, for example, rates of women's labor force participation are fairly high, and France offers a good supply of childcare, yet many women leave the labor market for three years after the birth of a child owing to a lengthy paid leave that is available (Morgan and Zippel 2003). Measured through EES targets, it might appear that France is meeting the EU's equality goals, yet some might argue that this model is reinforcing the traditional division of labor rather than challenging it, while generating occupational segregation of the workforce. Thus far, the council has said nothing to France about its parental leave policy in the recommendations it has issued, nor has it really grappled with the question of just how long a parental leave should be. This has wider significance in the EU, as several other member states also offer either paid or unpaid leaves for two or three years after the birth of a child. The lack of clarity on this issue allows the member states to determine their own policies in this area. This is evident in their National Action Plans, which often contain widely varying views on what counts as gender egalitarian policy (Rubery 2005).

This lack of clarity reflects the fact that there is no widely agreed-upon vision at the EU level of what constitutes a gender egalitarian set of policies for working parents. One dilemma facing decision-makers is how to adopt policies that recognize the social realities that produce gendered employment patterns without reinforcing these realities. Whether by choice, compulsion, or some mix of the two, mothers often reduce their working time during the period of child-rearing, and this creates a demand for lengthy parental leaves, part-time jobs, and flexible working arrangements. Making such possibilities available will increase the attachment of mothers to the workforce but risks reinforcing the gendered division of labor, with lasting consequences for occupational segregation and the gender pay gap. Yet another dilemma stems from the calls by some feminists for a "right to care" that recognizes the importance of caring activities and does not subordinate them to the imperatives of the labor market (Knijn and Kremer 1997). Part-time work options and parental leave can provide those rights, but risk reproducing existing gendered patterns of work and care.

Another reason for the lack of clarity is that it would be difficult to spell out one model of family policy that would appeal across the European continent. The welfare regimes of the member states are historical constructions that reflect specific political, social, and cultural conditions. Such is the case with their policies for working parents, as paid leave, childcare, and working time policies differs markedly by country (Lokhamp-Himmighofen and Dienel 2000; Randall 2000; Haas 2003). Some countries (e.g., Denmark) support mothers' paid work through public childcare and parental leaves that are generous but not too long, whereas others subsidize mothers' retreat from paid work for an extended period of time after the birth of a child (e.g., France, Austria). Still others offer neither public care services nor extensive benefits for mothers who care for their children at home (UK). Such policy differences may or may not be congruent with the wishes of the population, but figure 2.1 gives a sense of the widely varying perspectives on mothers' employment that can be found across Europe. The figure shows vast differences in the proportion of people who believe preschool children suffer if their mother works, and thus gives some perspective on preferences for leave time or part-time work versus greater care facilities. It also shows differences in the intensity with which these views are felt, with people in some countries holding strongly to the view that mothers' employment is harmful to young children (Morgan 2006).

Finally, it is essential to note that the European discourse on work and family is composed of diverse and often competing strands. As the previous section noted, anxieties over unemployment and declining fertility rates created an opening for greater attention to work-family issues, but these concerns have left their mark on EU policies and recommendations. This is evident in the European Commission's annual report on gender equality (2005), which repeatedly

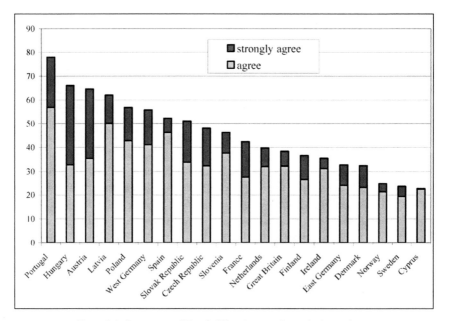

Figure 2.1. Percentage of People Who Agree or Strongly Agree that a
Preschool Child Will Suffer If His/Her Mother Works.
Source: ISSP, *Family and Changing Gender Roles III* (2002).
Data unavailable for Belgium, Estonia, Greece, Italy, Lithuania, and Malta.

uses demographic concerns to justify the need to be more attentive to work and
family issues. It is not coincidental that the EES childcare and labor force targets
are set for 2010, the year that the labor supply in Europe will peak and then start
to decline (Ingham and Ingham 2003, 384). While this potentially dire labor
market situation has created a window of opportunity for a discussion of work
and family, Stratigaki (2004) argues that feminists have had difficulty maintain-
ing control over these debates and keeping gender equality goals at the center of
the discussion. As a result, employment motivations often have superseded those
of gender equality in EU measures for working parents.

Implications for the New Member States

What are the implications of the expanded EU role in work-family policies
for the new member states (NMS-10)? While many of these countries have
distinct historical legacies regarding women's employment, they face many of
the same challenges as the EU-15. In most of the countries of Central Eastern
Europe (CEECs) and the former Soviet Union, there were high rates of female

workforce participation under state socialism, enabled by systems of family benefits, paid leaves from work, and childcare services that were provided at workplaces. The collapse of communism and the difficult economic transitions that followed produced sharply higher unemployment among men and women, yet generally higher risks of unemployment for women and greater declines in women's activity rates (Pollert 2005). The infrastructure of childcare for under-threes also deteriorated in many of these countries, although preschool provision has remained reasonably stable (European Foundation for the Improvement of Living and Working Conditions 2005, 40). A recent survey of the situation of women in the former communist countries finds an overall decline in women's place in paid work since the 1990s, with continued occupational segregation and a higher pay gap than in the West (European Foundation for the Improvement of Living and Working Conditions 2005).

As a result, overall rates of women's employment are lower in the new member states, although there is considerable variation within the NMS-10 (figure 2.2). In 2004, employment rates in the EU-15 were just shy of the 57 percent target for 2005 (56.8 percent), but a little over 50 percent in the NMS-10 (Commission of the European Communities 2006). Although childcare data is not yet fully available for all of these states, table 2.1 shows that provision varies by country and by age group, with relatively higher provision in some of the former Soviet republics, but lower availability of services in the Czech Republic and Hungary, particularly for the under-threes. In fact, in many CEECs, it is common for mothers to leave work for several years following child birth, and in most of these states, mothers can be absent from the labor market for two to four years and receive some kind of benefit and job protection during that time (European Foundation for the Improvement of Living and Working Conditions 2005, 41).

It will be some time before we can appreciate the full effects of EU accession on gender equality and work-family policies in the new member states. An early analysis found that gender mainstreaming was downplayed by the EU during the accession process for the CEECs (Bretherton 2001). A more recent study (European Foundation for the Improvement of Living and Working Conditions 2005) finds that the new member states have formally adopted the various directives on parental and maternity leave, as well as the many EU requirements on equal opportunities in paid work. However, Kakucs and Pető (in this volume) argue that in Hungary, the government adopted the minimal measures necessary to pass muster with the EU but has not really integrated gender equality goals into its policy-making. Moreover, in many of the new member states the formal adoption of these laws has not necessarily led to changes in practices on the ground, as it is still common for employers to discriminate against female workers based on the belief that they are less committed to employment because of their child-rearing propensities (European Foundation for the Improvement of Living and

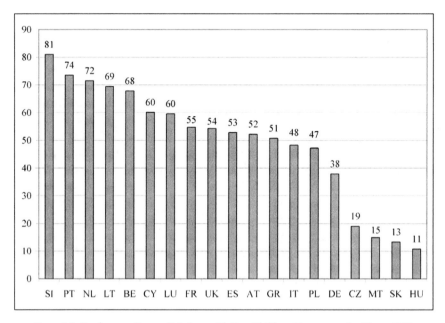

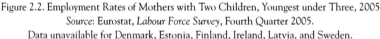

Figure 2.2. Employment Rates of Mothers with Two Children, Youngest under Three, 2005
Source: Eurostat, *Labour Force Survey*, Fourth Quarter 2005.
Data unavailable for Denmark, Estonia, Finland, Ireland, Latvia, and Sweden.

Working Conditions 2005). Thus, one problem facing mothers in paid work may be the outright discrimination and nonimplementation of EU equality measures in many of these countries.

As for the impact of the EES on the new member states, so far these countries have received different messages from the council than have the EU-15. Although the council has highlighted the importance of childcare in the old member states, in the new member states the council emphasizes the need for greater labor market flexibility, including the development of part-time work (Kirton and Greene 2005, 114). Indeed, the first council recommendations to the NMS-10 mention the need for care services only to Cyprus and Malta, and the council holds up part-time work as the main remedy for gender gaps in employment to virtually all the new member states. This is so despite the fact that many of the CEECs could improve their supply of childcare (see table 2.1), and that in their first national action plans submitted for the EES, states such as the Czech Republic and Poland made virtually no mention of the need to improve their childcare, while the plans of the Slovak Republic, Hungary, and Lithuania had only vague references to it.[14] Only Estonia, Latvia, and Malta offered detailed discussion of childcare, and these states expressed the strongest commitment to improving the supply of services.

Thus, in the new member states, as in the old, EU actors have inadequately addressed the question of whether flexible labor markets are congruent with a gender egalitarian model of work-family policy. There also is no reflection on the question of parental leave time, which has particular resonance in the NMS-10 given that so many of these states provide lengthy care leaves for mothers of young children. Such leaves may be particularly detrimental to the place of women in paid work given that firms collapse or are restructured with greater frequency in many of these states, thereby diminishing the value of the job protection that often accompanies these leaves (European Foundation for the Improvement of Living and Working Conditions 2005, 39).

These ambiguities and problems highlight the need for a mobilization from below to ensure that the NMS-10 are implementing the formal equality measures required by the EU and are meaningfully grappling with the question of how to ensure parents truly can balance their work and family lives. As Regulska and Grabowska (this volume) point out, although the EU may create opportunities for women's empowerment, authority for many critical policy areas remains at the national level, and so this should be the target of collective mobilization. In addition, there is no EU-wide consensus about the best policy in this area: as figure 2.1 shows, stated views on the acceptability of mothers' workforce participation vary markedly between countries, with people in many of the NMS-10 expressing opposition to mothers' employment while their children are young. Given the latitude afforded to these states by the EES, it will be up to domestic actors to initiate debate about these issues and to guide government policy in the area of work and family.

Conclusion

The EU has embraced the cause of helping parents balance their lives in paid work and care, and this represents a major achievement for the advocates who have pushed this issue for decades. The opening for an increased EU role came with growing concerns among EU and member-state officials about fertility and employment in a rapidly ageing Europe. These concerns and a continuing lack of agreement about what gender-egalitarian work-family policies look like have produced many ambiguities in EU policies and pronouncements in this area. This leaves considerable room to the member states to define their own models, which perhaps makes sense given the widely different traditions and values in the member states—both new and old—with regard to mothers' employment. Thus, while the EU has become an important actor in putting this issue on the agenda and prodding the member states to action, what is most needed now is a mobilization of domestic actors to shape the concrete measures that states develop for working parents.

Notes

The author gratefully acknowledges Silke Roth and Kathrin Zippel for their very helpful comments on this chapter.

1. Case 43/75 Defrenne v. Sabena, 1976, E.C.R. 455.
2. "Council Resolution of 21 January 1974 concerning a social action programme," *Official Journal* C 013, December 2, 1974, p. 0001–0004.
3. Some examples of its reports include *Childcare in the European Communities 1985–1990* (1990); *Men as Carers: Towards a Culture of Responsibility, Sharing and Reciprocity between Women and Men in the Care and Upbringing of Children—A Seminar Report* (1994); *Costs and Funding of Services for Young Children* (September 1995); *School-Age Childcare in the European Union* (1996).
4. Labor unions and employers are represented at the European level by organizations such as the European Trade Union Confederation, the Union of Industrial and Employers' Confederations of Europe, and the European Center of Enterprises with Public Participation.
5. The directive required that all states offer a minimum of three months of unpaid parental leave that parents can take at any time until the child's eighth birthday, and that the states must allow a part-time option for taking the leave.
6. The OMC also has spread to the areas of social inclusion and pensions.
7. The member states also agreed to raise overall employment rates from 61 percent to 70 percent by 2010.
8. These countries had to make changes to their leave policies so that they were in line with the gender egalitarian principles of the directive. In Austria and Italy, for example, the existing leave system was more generous than that required by the directive, but fathers could only take the leave if the mother did not. The parental leave directive, by contrast, required that men and women be equally entitled to take three months of unpaid leave, and thus required this change in the Austrian and Italian laws. In Austria, Germany, Greece, and Portugal, the main breadwinner (usually male) could not take the leave if the partner was a housewife or at school, a policy that again was barred by the parental leave directive. See Treib and Falkner 2004.
9. The measures adopted are too diverse to comprehensively describe in this paper. Some countries made only incremental changes to existing law, whereas others opted to entirely rewrite their laws on part-time work so as to meet the directive's requirements and other policy-making goals. In some countries, implementation came through collective agreements, whereas legislatures and/or courts shaped implementation in others. For details, see Clauwaert 2002.
10. The directive does require equal treatment of part-time workers in occupational benefits, such as supplemental pensions, but not in public social security programs.
11. The purpose of the Govecor research project was to study changing governance patterns in the EU member states under the Stability and Growth Pact and the Open Method of Coordination in employment policy. The project ran from ran from 2001 to 2004. Final reports of the project are available at http://www.govecor.org.
12. Germany's 2006 National Reform Program discusses the 2004 Day Care Expansion Act, which obliges municipalities to offer adequate childcare for under-threes by 2010 and is backed up by monetary transfers from the federal government. Germany has held this law up to the Council in response to questions about its commitment to public childcare. The reform program is available at http://ec.europa.eu/employment_social/employment_strategy/national_en.htm.
13. Council of the European Union, *Council Recommendation of 18 February 2004 on the implementation of Member States' employment policies* (2002/178/EC); Council of the European Union, *Council Recommendation of 14 October 2004 on the implementation of Member States' employment policies* (2004/741/EC).

14. The national action plans (now called "national reform programs") and European Council recommendations are available through the European Employment Strategy website, http://europa.eu.int/comm/employment_social/employment_strategy/index_en.htm.

References

Ayad, Sonia Hadj and Annick Masselot. 2004. Reconciliation between Work and Family Life in the EU: Reshaping Gendered Structures? *Journal of Social Welfare and Law* 26 (3): 325–38.

Bleijenbergh, Inge. 2004. *Citizens Who Care: European Social Citizenship in EU Debates on Childcare and Part-time Work.* Amsterdam: Dutch University Press.

Bleijenbergh, Inge, Jeanne de Bruijn, and Jet Bussemaker. 2004. European Social Citizenship and Gender: The Part-time Work Directive. *European Journal of Industrial Relations* 10 (3): 309–28.

Borrás, Suzanne and Kerstin Jacobsson. 2004. The Open Method of Coordination and New Governance Patterns in the EU. *Journal of European Public Policy* 11 (2): 185–208.

Bretherton, Charlotte. 2001. Gender Mainstreaming and EU Enlargement: Swimming Against the Tide? *Journal of European Public Policy* 8 (1): 60–81.

Childcare in a Changing World: Conference Report. 2004. http://www.childcareinachangingworld.nl/downloads/conference_report.pdf Accessed 15 December 2005.

Clauwaert, Stefan. 2002. *Survey on the Implementation of the Part-Time Work Directive/Agreement in the EU Member States and Selected Applicant Countries.* Brussels: European Trade Union Institute.

Commission of the European Communities. 2005. *Report on Equality between Women and Men* (COM(2005) 44 final). Report from the Commission to the Council, the European Parliament, the European Economic and Social Committee, and the Committee of the Regions.

———. 2006. *Indicators for Monitoring the Employment Guidelines, 2005 Compendium.* http://europa.eu.int/comm/employment_social/ employment_strategy/compendium_en.pdf. Accessed 7 April 2006.

de la Porte, Caroline and Patrizia Nanz. 2004. The OMC: A Deliberative-Democratic Mode of Governance? The Cases of Employment and Pensions. *Journal of European Public Policy* 11 (2): 267–88.

Esping-Andersen, Gøsta. 1999. *The Social Foundations of Postindustrial Economies.* Oxford: Oxford University Press.

European Foundation for the Improvement of Living and Working Conditions. 2005. *Working Conditions and Gender in an Enlarged Europe.* Dublin.

Eurostat. 2004. *Development of a Methodology for the Collection of Harmonized Statistics on Childcare.* Luxembourg: European Commission.

Falkner, Gerda. 1998. *EU Social Policy in the 1990s: Towards a Corporatist Policy Community.* London: Routledge.

Federal Republic of Germany. 2004. *National Action Plan for Employment Policy.* http://europa.eu.int/comm/employment_social/employment_strategy/nap_2004/nap2004de_en.pdf. Accessed 14 December 2005.

Govecor 2004a. *EU Governance by Self Co-ordination? Towards a Collective "gouvernement économique."* Cologne: Govecor. http://www.govecor.org/intro/ GOVECOR_Final_report.pdf. Accessed 14 December 2005.

———. 2004b. *Self-Coordination at the National Level: Towards a Collective "governement économique?" Final National Reports.* Cologne: Govecor.

Haas, Linda. 2003. Parental Leave and Gender Equality: Lessons from the European Union. *Review of Policy Research* 20 (1): 89–114.

Hall, Peter A. 1993. Policy Paradigms, Social Learning and the State: The Case of Economic Policy-making in Britain. *Comparative Politics* 25 (3): 275–96.

Hank, Karsten and Michaela Kreyenfeld. 2002. *A Multilevel Analysis of Childcare and the Transition to Motherhood in Western Germany*. Berlin: German Institute for Economic Research Discussion Paper 290.

Hantrais, Linda. 2000. From Equal Pay to Reconciliation of Employment and Family Life. In *Gendered Policies in Europe: Reconciling Employment and Family Life*, ed. Linda Hantrais, 1–26. Houndmills, UK: Macmillan Press Ltd.

Heide, Ingeborg. 1999. Supranational Action against Sex Discrimination: Equal Pay and Equal Treatment in the European Union. *International Labor Review* 138 (4): 381–410.

Hoskyns, Catherine. 1994. Gender Issues in International Relations: The Case of the European Community. *Review of International Studies* 20 (3): 225–39.

———. 1996. *Integrating Gender: Women, Law and Politics in the European Union*. London: Verso.

Ingham, Mike and Hilary Ingham. 2003. Enlargement and the European Employment Strategy: Turbulent Times Ahead? *Industrial Relations Journal* 34 (5): 379–95.

Jacobsson, Kerstin and Åsa Vifell. 2005. Soft Governance, Employment Policy and Committee Deliberation. In *Making the European Polity—Reflexive Integration in the EU*, ed. Erik O Eriksen, 214–36. London: Routledge

Jacobsson, Kerstin and Åsa Vifell. 2007. New Governance Structures in Employment Policy-making? Taking Stock of the European Employment Strategy. In *Economic Government of the EU: A Balance Sheet of New Modes of Policy Coordination*, eds. Ingo Linsenmann, Christoph Meyer, and Wolfgang Wessels, 53–71. Basingstoke: Palgrave.

Kirton, Gill and Anne-Marie Greene. 2005. Gender, Equality and Industrial Relations in the "New Europe": An Introduction. *European Journal of Industrial Relations* 11 (2): 141–9.

Knijn, Trudie and Monique Kremer. 1997. Gender and the Caring Dimension of Welfare States: Toward Inclusive Citizenship. *Social Politics: International Studies in Gender, State & Society* 4 (3): 328–61.

Lewis, Jane, ed. 1997. *Lone Mothers in European Welfare Regimes: Shifting Policy Logics*. London: Kingsley Publishers.

Lohkamp-Himmighofen, Marlene and Christiane Dienel. 2000. Reconciliation Policies from a Comparative Perspective. In *Gendered Policies in Europe: Reconciling Employment and Family Life*, ed. Linda Hantrais, 49–67. Houndmills, UK: Macmillan Press Ltd.

Mahon, Rianne. 2002. Childcare: Toward What Kind of Social Europe? *Social Politics: International Studies in Gender, State & Society* 9 (3): 343–79.

Mazey, Sonia. 1995. The Development of EU Equality Policies: Bureaucratic Expansion on Behalf of Women? *Public Administration* 73 (Winter): 591–609.

Morgan, Kimberly J. 2006. *Working Mothers and the Welfare State: Religion and the Politics of Work-Family Policies in Western Europe and the United States*. Palo Alto, CA: Stanford University Press.

Morgan, Kimberly J. and Kathrin Zippel. 2003. Paid to Care: The Origins and Effects of Care Leave Policies in Western Europe. *Social Politics: International Studies in Gender, State & Society* 10 (1): 49–85.

Organization for Economic Cooperation and Development. 2002. *Babies and Bosses: Reconciling Work and Family Life. Volume 1: Australia, Denmark and the Netherlands*. Paris: OECD.

———. 2005. *Society at a Glance: OECD Social Indicator*. Paris: OECD.

Plantenga, Janneke. 2004. Investing in Childcare: The Barcelona Childcare Targets and the European Social Model. Paper presented at Childcare in a Changing World, 21–23 October 2004, Groningen, Netherlands.

Pollack Mark A. and Emilie Hafner-Burton. 2000. Mainstreaming Gender in the European Union. *Journal of European Public Policy* 7 (3): 432–56.

Pollert, Anna. 2005. Gender, Transformation and Employment in Central Eastern Europe. *European Journal of Industrial Relations* 11 (2): 213–30.

Randall, Vicky. 2000. Childcare Policy in the European States: Limits to Convergence. *Journal of European Public Policy* 7 (3): 346–68.

Richardt, Nicole. 2005. Europeanization of Childcare Policy: Divergent Paths towards a Common Goal? Paper prepared for the American Political Science Association's Annual Meeting, Washington, DC, 1–4 September.

Ross, George. 1998. L'union européenne: La performance d'un acteur sans rôle. In *Qui doit garder le jeune enfant? Modes d'accueil et travail des mères dans l'Europe en crise*, eds. Jane Jenson and Mariette Sineau, 227–57. Paris: Librairie Générale de Droit et de Jurisprudence.

Rubery, Jill. 2005. Gender Mainstreaming and the OMC: Is the Open Method Too Open for Gender Equality Policy? In *The Open Method of Co-ordination in Action: The European Employment and Social Inclusion Strategies*, eds. Jonathan Zeitlin and Philippe Pochet, 391–415. Brussels: Peter Lang S.A.

Rubery, Jill et al. 2004. The Ups and Downs of European Gender Equality Policy. *Industrial Relations Journal* 35 (6): 603–28.

Rutherford, Françoise. 1989. The Proposal for a European Directive on Parental Leave: Some Reasons Why it Failed. *Policy and Politics* 17 (4): 301–310.

Stratigaki, Maria. 2000. The European Union and the Equal Opportunities Process. In *Gendered Policies in Europe: Reconciling Employment and Family Life*, ed. Linda Hantrais, 27–48. Houndmills, UK: Macmillan Press Ltd.

———. 2004. The Cooptation of Gender Concepts in EU Policies: The Case of "Reconciliation of Work and Family." *Social Politics: International Studies in Gender, State & Society* 11 (1): 30–56.

Treib, Oliver and Gerda Falkner. 2004. The EU and New Social Risks: The Need for a Differentiated Evaluation. Paper prepared for the Conference of Europeanists, Chicago, 11–13 March.

Trubek, David M. and James S. Mosher. 2003. New Governance, Employment Policy, and the European Social Model. In *Governing Work and Welfare in a New Economy: European and American Experiments*, eds. Jonathan Zeitlin and David Trubek, 33–58. Oxford: Oxford University Press.

Trubek, David M. and Louise G. Trubek. 2005. Hard and Soft Law in the Construction of Social Europe: The Role of the Open Method of Co-ordination. *European Law Journal* (3): 343–64.

Walby, Sylvia. 1999. The New Regulatory State: The Social Powers of the European Union. *British Journal of Sociology* 50 (1): 118–40.

———. 2003. Policy Developments for Workplace Gender Equity in a Global Era: The Importance of the EU in the UK. *Review of Policy Research* 20 (1): 45–64.

———. 2004. The European Union and Gender Equality: Emergent Varieties of Gender Regime. *Social Politics: International Studies in Gender, State & Society* 11, (1): 4–29.

Warner, Harriet. 1984. EC Social Policy in Practice: Community Action on Behalf of Women and Its Impact in the Member States. *Journal of Common Market Studies* 23 (2): 141–67.

Zeitlin, Jonathan. 2005. The Open Method of Co-ordination in Action: Theoretical Promise, Empirical Realities, Reform Strategies. In *The Open Method of Co-ordination in Action: The European Employment and Social Inclusion Strategies*, eds. Jonathan Zeitlin and Philippe Pochet, 447–503. Brussels: Peter Lang S.A.

3

Violence at Work?

Framing Sexual Harassment in the European Union

✒

Kathrin Zippel

This chapter addresses the question of how feminists and advocates made a successful case for European Union intervention on sexual harassment. What used to be considered a moral, deeply private, and personal issue has in the EU context increasingly been depicted as a deeply cultural, nationally specific one. Given that in the 1980s the European Community (EC) had little authority to intervene in any social issues, including violence against women, getting sexual harassment on the agenda of EU institutions and promoting legal changes in member states through supranational intervention was a major accomplishment (Carter 1992; Gregory 1995, 2000). I argue that advocates succeeded by winning the discursive struggle over what constitutes sexual harassment at the EU level. They expanded the narrow paragraph on equal pay for equal work for women in the 1957 Treaty of Rome to equal treatment of working conditions in the 1976 Equal Treatment Directive and prohibition of sexual harassment in the amended 2002 Directive on Equal Treatment of Women and Men.

As a result of this advocacy, the EU has been an innovator in this policy field, ahead of most member states in developing policy measures against sexual harassment. The development of sexual harassment policy and the complex interaction among advocates, member states, and supranational levels constitute what I call the "ping-pong effect" (Zippel 2003). Tracing these discursive struggles highlights both the limitations and opportunities for finding universally applicable frames to combat gender inequality, especially in the face of reconfigurations of gender equality politics in the enlargement process in the European Union.

This chapter compares the frames that advocates and opponents of European Community intervention have used since the mid-1980s in the struggle over bringing sexual harassment onto the EC agenda. The final section examines the policy reforms in member states triggered by the 2002 directive. Generally speaking, these laws have lacked effective implementation and enforcement mechanisms, though their adoption has led to important national debates and generated some awareness on the issue.

Sexual Harassment as a Social Problem

Researchers have persistently found that sexual harassment constitutes a serious problem across the EU member states: a comparative study of the prevalence of sexual harassment, commissioned by the European Commission, revealed that 30 to 50 percent of women experience sexual harassment (European Commission 1999; Timmerman and Bajema 1999). According to these surveys, sexual harassment is a problem primarily for women (although about 10 percent of men report such harassment) and the perpetrators are most often men. Hence, the majority of victims are women who are sexually harassed by male perpetrators. Researchers in these studies have also documented its psychologically and physically harmful effects on victims. Workplace effects include victims losing jobs because they get fired when they complain about or do not go along with jokes, teasing, or demands for sexual favors. Victims also leave when they cannot endure the harassment any longer.

Research is lacking for most member states that have joined the EU in 2004, but sexual harassment cases are slowly getting into the news and courts. For example, in Hungary, a case of sexual harassment between employees in the Government Office for Equal Opportunities went to court, and the alleged victim was sentenced to pay financial compensation to the man she had accused (Kakucs and Pető in this volume). In another example, an international news service reported that 45 percent of Czech women reported sexual harassment (Rybarova 2000).

Despite opponents' claims that sexual harassment is a culturally specific issue and should therefore be dealt with at the national, not the supranational level, the Council of the European Union and the European Parliament did adopt a binding directive in 2002 after almost twenty years of demands for EU intervention. Directive 2002/73/EC of the European Parliament and of the Council of 23 September 2002 amended Council Directive 76/207/EEC on the implementation of the principle of equal treatment for men and women "as regards access to employment, vocational training and promotion, and working conditions" (OJ

L269, 5 October 2002, p.17). All member states were required to comply by October 2005. This directive, referred to in the following as the 2002 directive, sets forth a new "European model" to prohibit sexual harassment at work and provides a universal definition for sexual harassment as the violation of dignity. Sexual harassment is there defined as "any form of unwanted verbal, non-verbal or physical conduct of a sexual nature [that] occurs, with the purpose or effect of violating the dignity of a person, in particular when creating an intimidating, hostile, degrading, humiliating or offensive environment." The 2002 directive also prohibits nonsexual sex-based harassment and defines gender harassment as "unwanted conduct related to the sex of a person [that] occurs with the purpose or effect of violating the dignity of a person, and of creating an intimidating, hostile, degrading, humiliating or offensive environment."

Whereas the notion that sexual harassment is sex discrimination has been controversial in many member states, the 2002 directive states clearly that both sex-based and sexual harassment constitute sex discrimination. Hence, the enforcement and implementation mechanisms the broader 2002 directive developed for sex discrimination measures in general now also apply to both sexual and nonsexual harassment. This means that member states need to have equality bodies to monitor the implementation of these laws, damages awarded by courts cannot have upper limits, and the burden of proof lies with the employer. The European model seeks to combine strengthening the rights of individuals to complain with involving employers and unions in creating policies and internal grievance procedures through collective agreements.

Social movement theorists have developed the concept of the "frame" with which activists interpret problems in order to identify grievances, mobilize activists, or attract resources or allies (for an overview, see Snow 2004). Advocates used strategically interpretive frames to define sexual harassment as an injustice and as harmful to victims. When activists created the term *sexual harassment,* the frames they used gave specific cultural meanings to the concept. Defining the phenomenon radically changed the interpretation of everyday behavior: behavior previously considered private became politicized and redefined as injustice done to women. Behavior that women had felt they needed to put up with became an injustice.

These interpretive frames are crucial, because much of the political struggle in new policy fields concerns defining concepts and determining which existing laws can be applied. These struggles over meaning and interpretive frameworks are "discursive politics." Social movements engage in these struggles by conceptualizing a problem in new ways and creating alternative discourses (Eyerman and Jamison 1991). When activists seek to establish sexual harassment as a legitimate field of policy intervention, they frame the issue in ways that resonate with particular gender ideologies, cultural and legal traditions, and national or supranational debates, as well as existing laws.

Movements use frames strategically to convince employers, courts, states, or supranational institutions to take the issue seriously by invoking legal rights. In this case, advocates connected their notion of sexual harassment strategically to established community laws in order to bolster their demands and to justify Community intervention. Within the EU system of multilevel governance, advocates have different discursive opportunities—what Ferree (2003) defines as institutional anchors that connect institutional contexts to the cultural frames movements use. Depending on the policy level (regional, national, or supranational), advocates were able to draw on different existing laws to make a case for sexual harassment law given the diverse range of antidiscrimination, violence against women, and labor, civil, and criminal laws. The frames used by advocates and opponents on European Community intervention in sexual harassment allow us to examine the discursive struggles about whether sexual harassment warrants intervention at all, by whom, and what should be done about it.

Framing Sexual Harassment in the European Union

In the 1980s, none of the EU member states had taken steps to legally define sexual harassment. The concept was first introduced in the European Community in debates in the European Parliament by French socialist parliamentarian Yvette Fuillet and her colleague Maria-Lisa Cinciari-Rodano from the Communist Party of Italy, who initiated the first resolution in the European Parliament in 1983 (*Tageszeitung* 2 February 1983; *Frankfurter Rundschau* 8 February 1983). These feminist socialists established the link between inequality at work and inequality through sexuality by using the discourse of "worker exploitation" and framing sexual harassment as the "sexual exploitation of women in companies." The official response was the 1984 resolution by the Council which mentioned sexual harassment as relating to the dignity of women in the context of positive measures for women at work.[1]

A 1987 community-wide research study triggered further studies of sexual harassment and created professionalized expertise and knowledge about the issue in several member states and at the EC level. Its report, *The Dignity of Women at Work* by Michael Rubenstein (1987), became an influential tool at both the EU and national levels. Rubenstein, a legal expert on industrial relations, reported that consciousness about the issue varied greatly from state to state. Empirical studies (Rubenstein 1987) showed that such workplace harassment did indeed affect many women and some men throughout the EC, but that only a few member states, including the United Kingdom, Ireland, and Belgium, had laws providing adequate legal redress for victims. Rubenstein made several suggestions for directives and a code of practice. The study was widely cited because of the expertise it offered: a professional, transnational examination of sexual harassment. In subsequent years the study provided legitimacy for national and EU advocacy groups because it provided models for a "European way" to address the issue. It also provided the impetus for national governmental action to acquire more expertise.

In addition, proponents of legal measures against sexual harassment at the national level in France, the United Kingdom, and the Netherlands saw the EU as an opportunity to push for changes at the supranational level when they found their own governments not very responsive. By the 1990s, a consensus had been reached among employer associations, trade unions, and the European Commission that sexual harassment is a serious issue for women and men in the EU member states, yet the member states could not agree on a binding tool, such as a directive. Instead, several soft-law resolutions and recommendations in the early 1990s encouraged member states to adopt meaningful measures against sexual harassment in the context of equal treatment of women and men, including a Code of Practice that drew on several models to legally define sexual harassment.

In these debates about European Community measures, advocates and opponents used different frames to argue for or against community intervention. Feminists used the feminist discourse of sexual harassment as male abuse of power over women, and violence against women more generally, to frame sexual harassment as an injustice. In order to justify European Community intervention, advocates for legally binding instruments framed sexual harassment as a workplace issue, including both the frame of equality for women and equal opportunities for women and men at work and the gender-neutral issue of health and safety. By contrast, opponents defined sexual harassment as a moral, individual problem and used arguments of cultural diversity as a reason why EU-wide legal measures would be inadequate or inappropriate.

The Violence Against Women Frame

Feminist advocates frequently framed sexual harassment as a form of violence against women, explicitly arguing that the latter constitutes a serious threat to sex equality (Baer 1996, 53). This discourse was promoted by nonprofit feminist organizations, such as the Association européenne contre les Violences faites aux Femmes au Travail (AVFT), which lobbied in the European Commission and Parliament for community-level measures against sexual harassment. Women from the socialist party promoted a brochure entitled *Sexual Violence against Women* in 1987. Within the parliament, this discourse was successful already in the mid-1980s; in 1986, it passed a resolution that used the notion "sexual harassment" explicitly as one form of "violence against women." At this point, the European Community had no authority to take measures on violence against women (Hanmer 1996). Because of the strong mandate for economic integration, focusing on creation of a single market, community measures were limited to the workplace domain. Social and cultural domains were left entirely to the member states, with the understanding that national-level politicians were best able to take action against unemployment, poverty, and other social and cultural issues (Hoskyns 2000).

During the 1990s, however, support grew to address violence against women within the European Parliament and Commission.[2] On the one hand, member states had begun to address "domestic violence," for example by national legal reforms that made rape in marriage illegal. Since the 1980s, the member states began slowly to respond to demands of the autonomous antiviolence feminist movements, though the activists themselves had been ambivalent about state intervention (Weldon 2002; Elman 2005).

In the 1990s, public awareness grew around the broader phenomenon of violence against women, in part a response to the international women's movement that also used the UN to draw attention to the transnational/international dimensions of the issue (Keck and Sikkink 1998). Throughout Europe, the media reported on highly publicized cases of the political scandal of a serial rapist, the murder of children and young women in Belgium, and the mass rapes of women and girls during the wars in the former Yugoslavia. With the fall of the Berlin Wall of 1989, member states increasingly became concerned about how to deal with trafficking in children and women, especially from the Central and Eastern European countries.

Sweden, which had just joined the EU in 1995, sent Anita Gradin, as EU Commissioner for immigration, home affairs, and justice to Brussels. Commissioner Gradin used this window of opportunity to mainstream "violence against women" and put trafficking in women and children onto the agenda of the European Union while she was in office from 1995–1999. This meant that "violence against women" was addressed primarily as a crime, but it was also framed as a common issue, because the member states were called upon to cooperate on border control and prosecution. Commissioner Gradin, for example, initiated the program STOP (Sexual Trafficking of Persons).

The parliament passed another resolution in 1997, for an EU-wide campaign for "zero tolerance of violence against women" (OJ C304, 6 October 1997, p. 55). This resolution listed sexual harassment among other forms of violence against women, including "ill-treatment, battering, genital and sexual mutilation, incest, sexual harassment, sexual abuse, trafficking in women and rape." Referring explicitly to feminist frameworks that define sexual harassment as an abuse of power based on gender, the resolution pointed out that sexual harassment is not limited to abuse of hierarchical power between superiors and subordinates, but can occur between colleagues and clients as well. Despite this early and continued framing of sexual harassment as a form of violence against women, however,

EU antiviolence discourses have increasingly focused on gendered and sexual violence against women and children, while excluding sexual harassment at work. For example, sexual harassment at work has remained marginal in the main EU program that addresses violence against women.

The Daphne project, designed to support member state actions to combat violence against children, young persons, and women, began funding projects in 1997. Daphne has had several goals, including helping to form coordination and information networks at the European level, and it has explicitly sought to further cooperation between nongovernmental organizations (NGOs) and voluntary organizations and authorities in these areas. While the calls for applications for research, training, and awareness have included forms of violence at work in principle, they do not mention the term *sexual harassment*. For example, the breadth of forms of violence is explained in this way: "all types of violence and all aspects of this phenomenon are concerned, whether occurring in public or in private. It includes violence in the family, in schools and other educational institutions or in the *workplace*, commercial sexual exploitation, genital mutilation and human trafficking" (emphasis added, see http://ec.europa.eu/justice_home/funding/daphne/funding_daphne_en.htm). Most of the EUR 20 million budget for the period 2000–2003 was spent on projects related to sexual violence, gender-family related violence, and Internet and child pornography (European Commission 2004). Only 6 out of over 300 projects focused on workplace harassment (see http://www.daphne-toolkit.org/).

Hence, while feminist advocates have formulated sexual harassment at work as a problem of gender violence against women, the problem of sexual harassment at work remains marginal in EU anti-violence campaigns. When we think of sexual harassment as "violence," the implicit claim is that state laws need to protect victims from the violence and punish perpetrators with penal and criminal codes. Hence, the primary responsibility lies with states to take action.

Those who contested European Community action on sexual harassment at first were hesitant to acknowledge that sexual harassment constituted a problem at all. The initial response was similar to national-level debates that ridiculed and trivialized the problem. Opponents have primarily used two intertwined frames to argue against community intervention.

First, they framed sexual harassment as a moral problem and one that is culturally too specific to be addressed at the supranational level. When asked to respond to the European Commission's fourth medium-term Community action program on "equal opportunities for women and men," the Committee of the Regions, which represents local and regional authorities, made a statement against Community intervention on sexual harassment. The argument was that "policing measures" on the EU level would be inadequate because they would not eliminate sexual harassment (OJ CC 034, 2 March 1997, p. 39). Instead of legally binding measures, the committee favored European Community action to emphasize training, information, and cooperation with NGOs. They found no reason why unions and employers should be involved. Strikingly, the committee defined sexual harassment as "behavior among colleagues that is not conducted in a 'proper manner.'" This behavioral definition of sexual harassment individualizes the problem and frames it as one of "morality." Depicting sexual harassment as a problem of moral standards raises questions of what constitutes acceptable or proper behavior. The responsibility to uphold and protect society's norms and standards then can easily fall on the victim, a connection feminists have identified as "victim blaming." Furthermore, since these sensibilities towards sexual or nonsexual behaviors vary from country to country because of different cultural norms, sexual harassment becomes a cultural problem and out of the reach of the European Union.

The national specificity of the phenomenon of sexual harassment based on *cultural differences* was the most widely used argument against community action. In this understanding, sexual harassment is profoundly shaped by cultural norms of gender relations and sexuality, and common definition is seen as impossible. Thus, in the draft of the European Commission's recommendation, a list of behaviors that would constitute sexual harassment could not be agreed on. Northern Europeans did not necessarily object to pornographic images; southern Europeans did not object to kissing, touching, and hugging. Kisses on the cheek are common greeting practices for women and men in many southern European countries, including France and Italy (Collins 1996). In the mid-1990s, therefore, the Union of Industrial and Employers' Confederations of Europe (UNICE), broke up the negotiations with the European Trade Union Association (ETUC) on sexual harassment, using the argument that attitudes toward it are culturally too diverse, and that action would be better taken on the national level.

Arguments about cultural diversity were predominantly used to make a case against EU-wide definitions, policies, and measures. Cultural diversity could have been used as an argument *for* Europe-wide standards in the frame of the mobility—the free movement—of workers, the foundation of the EU. Whose cultural standards are supposed to be applied when employees from different countries work together in companies and on the shop floor? The questions brought about by cultural "diversity" of workers in a single workplace are left out of discussions around sexual harassment. Nevertheless, cross-cultural conflicts around it are an underlying current in discussions. In Germany, cultural differences in negotiations around gender and sexual norms in the workplace have gone to the courts. In a labor court case, a migrant man from Turkey filed suit against his employer after being dismissed on the grounds of sexually harassing German women colleagues (LAG Hamm 6 Sa 730/96, 22 October 1996). A group of English dancers and models complained about being sexually harassed while they were working in Greece (OJ C 112, 17 April 1996, p. 47). Diverse cultural standards for "appropriate behaviors in the workplace" between women and men could be seen as standing in stark opposition to the EU primary intention—furthering the internal market by allowing the free movement of workers—especially if women feel more harassed by behaviors and actions of those who are culturally different. Instead, references to cultural heterogeneity in the EU have been used to argue that uniform policies against sexual harassment would not be appropriate.

In a similar vein, in several countries critics of the very concept of sexual harassment in have framed it as a "foreign," "Western," or "American" problem (Zippel 2006). While they emphasize the positive value of nationally specific gender and sexual cultures, they argue that attention to and measures against sexual harassment will destroy national, natural, and healthy gender relations by stifling flirtation and eroticism at work. In France, even politicians argued that the Mediterranean culture of seduction between women and men (also at work) should be protected (Saguy 2003; Mazur 1994; Louis 1994). Skepticism about sexual harassment as an American concept was also prevalent in Germany. The German media found more problems with the American concept of "sexual correctness" than with the difficulties sexual harassment poses for victims (Zippel 2006). In the countries that joined the European Union in 2004, in particular in the Czech Republic, Hungary, and Poland, journalists and researchers have pointed out that sexuality was taboo under the former socialist rule, and that women do not dare to speak up against sexual harassment because they fear stigmatization as victims (Minnesota Advocates for Human Rights et al. 2002; Bauerova 2000; Perlez 1996).

Hence, with the cultural frame, the main issues in debates are national differences in societal, moral, and cultural standards. By contrast, feminists brought up sexual harassment as a sociocultural problem women face particularly at work when they venture into male-dominated fields such as construction, mining, police, or the military, or encounter as an abuse of hierarchical power of men in supervisory positions. The cultural discourses that emphasize national specificity of socio-sexual cultures and value these differences do not address the core issue for feminists, that is, unequal gender culture at work.

Sexual Harassment as a Workplace Problem

In order to avoid these cultural debates and the weak legal base for rights concerning the body, advocates for EU intervention strategically framed sexual harassment as a gendered workplace issue, arguing that it was an impediment to women's integration into the workplace. As already noted, French and Italian feminist socialist parliamentarians had argued in 1983 that sexual harassment affected women as workers and as sexual beings. Hence, they established a double exploitation of women employees as workers and as sexual beings. The 1976 Equal Treatment Directive provided an important legal frame for advocates to claim European Community intervention by focusing on the "workplace" dimension of sexual harassment. Originally focused only on equal pay, the 1976 directive provided the basis for equal opportunities for women and men in regard to hiring, promotion, and conditions of work.

Advocates for EU measures against sexual harassment argued that sexual harassment impinges on equal opportunities for women and men in the workplace because it constitutes inequality of working conditions: a barrier for women entering male-dominated jobs and unequal, unfair conditions of work. American feminists had helped with these arguments by linking sexual harassment to problems of vertical sex segregation, lack of equal respect for women and men at work, and abuse of power by supervisors due to horizontal sex segregation.

A prominent US feminist legal scholar, Catherine MacKinnon (1979), aided European feminist discourse to establish this link between gender inequality at work and sexuality by making a case that sexual harassment should be considered sex discrimination. Familiar with the US debates, Rubenstein (1987) later made a strong case for this. The Council resolution and the committee recommendation both refer to the 1976 Equal Treatment Directive as the legal basis to legitimize EU action. The 2002 directive defines sexual harassment as a violation of equal treatment of women and men in the workplace with regard to working conditions, and sees it as warranting positive action for women. However, even though the Council uses this legal reference and the European Commission had promoted the framework of antidiscrimination law to be applied to sexual harassment, there had been resistance within the Council to defining it as sex discrimination. In the debates about the 2002 directive, the Union of Industrial and Employers' Confederation of Europe (UNICE) insisted that sexual harassment had nothing to do with sex discrimination, thus questioning the legitimacy of EU intervention in this new field of workplace policy (eironline 2000).

The important discursive move to frame sexual harassment as a workplace issue allowed feminists to call on the European Community to promote legal and policy measures that would hold employers responsible and demand legal regulation to hold them accountable. This frame also fitted most closely the legacy of EU sex equality law and workplace policies, which can be best characterized as neoliberal and market oriented. Because of the EU focus on paid labor, advocates needed to find frames to define sexual harassment as a gender "workplace issue" to justify EC action.

Sexual Harassment as a Health and Safety Issue

Alternatively, advocates who "mainstreamed" sexual harassment framed it as a workplace issue, but as a non-gender-specific frame of health and safety conditions. In this organizational and sociopsychological discourse, the rationale is that sexual harassment can be understood as a form of stress in the workplace and thus a hazard to working. Rubenstein (1987) reported that sexual harassment produces anxiety and stress in victims, and can be defined as individual harm and an issue of health and safety in the workplace. Advocates called on the European Union to prohibit "unsafe working conditions." The Economic and Social Committee (OJ C039, 1 February 1996, p. 26) identified sexual harassment as a problem of occupational health and safety.

These advocates also framed sexual harassment in terms of non-gender-specific (psychological) violence, attempting to expand the directive on health and safety from exclusively physical to nonphysical threats to health and safety in workplaces. This frame allows stronger attention to state intervention and enforcement to prevent harassment as a collective hazard from occurring, rather than using a confrontational focus to remedy individual cases based on claims of individual rights. Rubenstein (1987) argued, for example, that employers were responsible for preventing sexual harassment from occurring, as for other workplace hazards. In this regulatory approach, states can sanction employers if they fail to comply with the regulations, rather than relying on individuals to claim damages in confrontational legal action. The health and safety frame emphasizes the harm done to individuals by sexual harassment, but does not address *why* these victims face the stresses at work. Individual or groups of perpetrators who create these hazards are not the target of measures, nor can they be clearly held accountable; the focus is on the responsibilities of employers. Though the legal basis for EU policy measures in the area of health and safety was during the 1990s the strongest area of social policy, stronger than the sex equality policy, the commission did not propose anti–sexual harassment with this frame. Based on EEC Treaty Art. 118a, the harmonization of health and safety standards in the workplace has been one key element in European integration (Bernstein 1994, 1256).

Sexual Harassment as Violation of Dignity

Proponents for EU measures first brought sexual harassment forward in the context of personal rights and freedoms. In particular, they framed it as a violation of human dignity and personal integrity. The first report for the European Commission (Rubenstein 1987) was entitled *The Dignity of Women at Work*. Since then, the violation of dignity frame has become the universal European approach to defining sexual harassment. This frame draws on international human rights tradition of "human dignity" and the labor tradition of "workers' dignity." The rationale is that sexual harassment is wrong or is an injustice if the perpetrator violates a person's dignity. The dignity frame sets an absolute standard of respectful, dignified treatment.

By contrast, the equal treatment or sex discrimination frame uses a comparability standard. For example, the question is whether a man in the same situation would have been treated the same; only if the woman was treated differently or had different working conditions imposed on her would a judge rule that she was indeed discriminated against based on her sex. In practice, the dignity frame resonates with victims more than does the concept of sex discrimination, in part because it is less abstract. Women experience sexual harassment as overstepping their personal, intimate space, as intrusion into their privacy, as intimidation, debasement, humiliation, and so on.

This concept of dignity has raised much controversy among feminists in Europe and the United States. Some US legal scholars, unsatisfied with the limitations of the frame *sex discrimination*, endorse the frame *violation of dignity* (Ehrenreich 1999; Husbands 1992). Ehrenreich, for example, argues, "Workplace harassment of women is wrong not because women are women, but because women are human beings and share with all other human beings the right to be treated with respect and concern" (1999, 1). Other feminist legal scholars, including MacKinnon (1979) and European scholars Susanne Baer (2004), and DeSacco (1996), are opposed to this frame or cautious, arguing that legal definitions of sexual harassment as sex discrimination are stronger formulations and reflect more clearly the problem of sexual harassment as an injustice to women and a contribution to gender inequality. Frames that are not gender specific do not make the causes of harassment visible; they do not ask why these women experienced sexual harassment. Nor do they link it to the societal or workplace structures that perpetuate abuses of power by men over women in the form of sexism or sexuality. The frame of human dignity is silent about gender inequality as the cause of sexual harassment.

The advantage of the concept of human dignity is that it resonates with various gender cultures. The sex discrimination frame relies on an understanding of gender equality as *sameness*; that is, equality means equal treatment for everyone, a notion of justice that is most prevalent in the United States, based on the history of racial segregation. In gender ideologies where gender differences are taken for granted, as in France, Italy, Spain, or Germany, the concept of dignity is more easily applicable because it sets absolute and not comparable standards of respectful treatment. The fact that women and men treat each other in different ways and flirtation between the sexes is a "natural" component of interactions in the workplace resonates with cultural understandings of gender relations and is affirmed and justified, for example, by the German Federal Ministry for Women and Youth (Bundesministerium für Frauen und Jugend 1993).

Because the European dignity frame sets an absolute standard of respectful, dignified treatment, it has been broadly applied not only to sexual or gender harassment, but to harassment of people in general. The European Commission's 1991 Code of Practice already included men and specific vulnerable groups based on sexual orientation and race. Evelyn Collins (1996) attributes this inclusion of harassment based on sexual orientation to the successful lobbying activities of the International Lesbian and Gay Association and the organization Stonewall, who met with Commissioner Papandreou in 1990. The code of practice recommended that policies against sexual harassment should take into account that it occurs not only between women and men, but also as same-sex harassment. In addition, it recognized the diversity of women and discussed how sexual harassment affects women in a complex interplay of sexism and racism. Because the definition is not gender specific, it allows for recognition of multiple causes of harassment. Thus, even though the legal foundation for EU action in the early 1990s was restricted to unequal treatment of women and men, the code of practice pointed to conceptualizations of sexual harassment in the broader framework of antiharassment policy in workplaces.

Finally, with framing sexual harassment as the violation of dignity, sexualized behaviors that are experienced as a humiliation, degradation, and devaluation of the person are seen as an injustice per se, not as linked to the sex of the person. Due to this broad applicability of the dignity frame, sexual harassment has been mainstreamed. In the EU, the feminist project to combat "women's victimization by men" has been reformulated to the broader notion of the right not to be harassed. By 2000, three equal treatment/antidiscrimination directives for race/ethnicity, sexual orientation, age, disability, and so forth had used the dignity frame to define harassment of individuals. In several member states, governments and unions have gone farther to draw attention to or even outlaw harassment of every worker. These campaigns for fairness in the workplace and against violations of dignity of all workers tend to emphasize the *exclusionary* aspects of harassing practices, such as bullying, mobbing, and moral harassment.

To summarize, political actors in the EU have defined sexual harassment in various ways in the discussions about adequate measures. These different concepts emerged in the political struggle to justify EU action or to conceptualize the issue as outside the reach of EU institutions. Opponents emphasized the cultural embeddedness of sexual harassment, and argued that the EU cannot devise adequate measures because of the cultural diversity among member states. Since EU regulations and interventions have only restricted legitimacy in the realm of economic and social issues but lack justification on "cultural" issues, the reference to sexual harassment as culturally embedded delegitimized EU action in this field. With the reference to cultural difference, sexual harassment becomes an individual, moral, and psychological issue rather than one of systematic economic and structural discrimination against women. Most importantly, stressing the cultural aspect of sexual harassment supports the argument that the EU interference in sexual harassment would be against the principle of subsidiarity of the member states. Because the issue warrants specific member states' action, the EU should merely support action on the national level rather than aim to devise legally binding instruments.

By contrast, proponents of legally binding measures from the EU link sexual harassment to existing legitimate fields of EU intervention. Thus, those favoring EU measures frame sexual harassment as an issue of equal opportunities for women and men and as an issue of health and safety. Different conceptions of sexual harassment have important consequences for the legitimacy of EU action, but also for questions about the responsibility of employers, trade unions, and states. And the implementation and enforcement mechanisms available depend to a large extent on the institutional realm in which sexual harassment occurs.

Developments in Member States since the 2002 Equal Treatment Directive

Which of these frames have prevailed in member states' laws? Not until 2002 did the European Union have a binding tool to prohibit sexual harassment. Given the various gender regimes, legal traditions, labor relations, and gender ideologies in the member states, these different frames of sexual harassment competed with each other both in the member states and in European Union institutions during the 1990s. Because member states had not been able to reach a consensus about how to combat sexual harassment, the European Commission had promoted a variety of ways to frame sexual harassment. Experts and activists recommended several ways to combat it; the commission used the best-practice approach and several "soft law" tools, including the Council resolution and the commission's recommendations and code of practice, to encourage member states to take action. Without supranational pressure, however, member states adopted various laws against sexual harassment, ranging from labor and civil laws to reforming their criminal and penal codes to prohibit sexual harassment throughout the 1990s.

In 2002, the new commissioner for Employment, Social Affairs, and Equal Opportunities, Anna Diamantopoulou, successfully pushed through a binding tool to force the member states to take the issue of sexual harassment seriously. The EU Directive of 2002, which revised the 1976 Equal Treatment Directive, prohibits both aspects of sexual harassment. It clearly frames sexual harassment as a workplace issue of equal treatment of women and men, and follows the US model to define sexual harassment as sex discrimination. In contrast to the US model, however, the European version adds that sexual harassment constitutes a violation of dignity. More explicitly than the US law, the directive also defines gender harassment as sex discrimination. It calls on member states to better protect the rights of victims of sexual harassment and to ensure the integrity, dignity, and equality of women and men at work. In addition, it establishes general guidelines for sanctions, legal action, and potentially unlimited compensation for victims for all sex discrimination issues. Member states are also required to establish agencies to promote equality and enforce antidiscrimination laws. The most important strength here is that this binding directive defines sexual and gender harassment as forms of sex discrimination and required member states to adopt or modify national laws against sexual harassment by October 2005.

Sexual harassment as a workplace issue has become the dominant frame in the member states. Since 2002, most member states have been implementing the 2002 directive to modify their equal opportunity laws in general and improve the legal situation of victims of sexual harassment in particular (see table 3.1). A 2004 report showed that most of the twenty-five member states outlaw sexual harassment (Government of Ireland 2004). Focusing on employer liabilities, most countries have amended their labor law or equal opportunity laws for women and men. A few countries have taken their time to comply and are still in the process of revising older laws to bring them into line. In 2004, twenty of the twenty-five countries had laws that allow victims to hold their employers liable when supervisors or peers harass an employee (Government of Ireland 2004).

The violence frame is less pronounced, though sixteen of the twenty-five member states do have laws, usually criminal or civil codes that allow a victim to hold the perpetrator liable as an individual harasser (Government of Ireland 2004). These laws cover sexual coercion, stalking, and sexual intimidation or insult. For instance, the Hungarian criminal code outlaws constraining a person "with violence or menace to do, not to do, or to endure something" (Government of Ireland 2004, 22).

The dignity frame is the most widespread legal definition; nineteen out of twenty-five member states have adopted sexual harassment laws and define sexual harassment as the violation of dignity. Four countries have not explicitly outlawed sexual harassment, but other laws (for example, gender equality laws) implicitly prohibit sexual harassment. Denmark and Latvia did not have specific laws against sexual harassment as of 2004 (Government of Ireland 2004, 22). The dignity frame varies a bit: for example, Swedish law considers sexual harassment a violation of "integrity," and the Spanish penal code defines it in the context of the right to respect of privacy in the human rights terminology.

Because of the broader conception of sexual harassment as the violation of dignity, the laws in member states are not limited to sexual harassment between women and men and some include nonsexual as well as sexual harassment. Feminists have long argued that nonsexual harassment based on sex as well as sexual harassment should be illegal. Such harassment includes nonsexual intimidation and derogatory words against women without sexual connotations, which nonetheless can create debasing, denigrating workplace environments. Even though the 2002 directive clearly specifies gender harassment, more than half the member states did not have laws against sex-based conduct by 2004 (Government of Ireland 2004, 20). Member states' laws were more inclusive regarding same-sex and transgender harassment: in twenty-one countries sexual harassment laws cover also same-sex harassment, and in nineteen countries transsexual or

Table 3.1. Laws against Sexual Harassment and/or Relevant Court Decisions

	Sexual Harassment Laws	Name of Sexual Harassment Law	Explicit Definition	Dignity Frame
United States	1980	EEOC Guidelines/ Supreme Court Decision	Explicit	No
EC/EU	1990	EC Recommendations	Explicit	Yes
	2002	EU Directive one Equal Treatment	Explicit	Yes
Austria	1992	Federal Equal Treatment Act	Explicit	Yes
	2004	Criminal Law Amendment	Explicit	
Belgium	1992	Royal Decree	Explicit	
	2002	Protection against Violence and Moral and Sexual Harassment	Explicit	Yes
	2003	Form of Sex Discrimination	Explicit	Yes
Cyprus	2002	Equal Treatment for Men and Women in Employment and Vocational Training Law	Explicit	Yes
Czech Republic	2004	Labor Code	Explicit	Yes
Denmark	1978/2002	Gender Equality Act (sexual harassment not specified)	—	—
Estonia	2004	Gender Equality Act	Implicit	Yes
Finland	1995	Act on Equality between Women and Men	Explicit	
France	1992	Penal Code Reform	Explicit	
	1992	Law on sexually oriented abuse of power within working relationships	Explicit	Yes
	2002	Law on Social Modernization	Explicit	Yes
Germany	1994	Law to Employee Protection Law	Explicit	Yes
	2006	General Anti-discrimination law	Explicit	Yes
Greece	2006	Equal Treatment Law	Explicit	Yes
Hungary	1992	Labor Code	Explicit	
	2003	Act on Equal Treatment & Equal Opportunities	Explicit	Yes
Ireland	1998	Employment Equality Act	Explicit	Yes
Italy	2000	Act No. 9039 12/77, Act No. 125, and Legislative Decree 196	Implicit	

(continued)

Table 3.1. *(continued)*

	Sexual Harassment Laws	Name of Sexual Harassment Law	Explicit Definition	Dignity Frame
Latvia	2004	Proposed	—	
Lithuania	1998	Law on Equal Opportunities	Explicit	
Luxembourg	2000	Law on Protection Against Sexual Harassment within the Relationships	Explicit	Yes
Malta	2002	Employment and Industrial Act	Explicit	
Netherlands	1994	Regulation on Sexual Harassment of Civil Servants	Explicit	
	1998	Working Conditions Act	Explicit	
Poland	2004	Labor Code (Article 18 3a)	Explicit	Yes
Portugal	2003	Labor Code No. 88/2003	Explicit	Yes
Slovakia	2004	Equal Treatment Law	Explicit	Yes
Slovenia	2002	Employment Legislation	Explicit	Yes
Spain	1989	Working Standards Act Act on Labor Infringements and Penalties	Implicit	Yes
Sweden	1991	Equal Opportunities Act	Explicit (integrity)	Yes
	1998	Reform		
United Kingdom	1996	Employment Rights Act	Implicit	No
	2005	Regulations to amend Sex Discrimination Act	Explicit	Yes

Sources: Because of these availability and translation issues I relied primarily on the report of the Government of Ireland covering legal developments until 2004. For the time since 2004, when available, I used various sources, including governmental websites to update the information for 2005 and 2006.

transgender harassment was also included in the anti–sexual harassment laws (Government of Ireland 2004, 19). This might be because the member states were supposed to implement the 2002 directive only by 2005, while member states needed to comply with the directive prohibiting discrimination on sexual orientation by 2003.

Hence, the dominant legal definition of sexual harassment in the European Union is *violation of dignity in combination with sex discrimination.* Beyond this convergence, member states laws are likely to range widely in their implementation. This is because the 2002 directive has given member states much leeway to deal with the most difficult aspects, including prevention and enforcement of these laws. The 2002 directive merely requires member states to set up equality bodies within state agencies; though their enforcement powers, resources, etc. are left up to the member states. Possible sanctions for employers vary greatly between the member states. The compensation ranges between a few months of the victim's salary to awards for injury to feelings, with a £25,000 limit set by the Court of Appeals guidance in *Vento (No.2)* in Great Britain.[3] The overall compensation that judges of tribunals have awarded to victims can be several hundred thousand pounds. Out-of-court settlements in the United Kingdom are probably even higher. By contrast, German labor court judges have awarded only a few thousand Euros compensation even when they found that sexual harassment had occurred (Pflüger and Baer 2005). Criminal sanctions against harassers also vary greatly. In France, perpetrators face a maximum fine of EUR 15,000 and/or one year imprisonment. In Belgium, judges of criminal courts can impose up to two years imprisonment (Government of Ireland 2004).

The Future of Sexual Harassment in the Enlarged European Union

Political actors both at the EU and at the member state level have used various frames for sexual harassment to pursue their agendas. The discourses are most visibly differentiated among opponents of and advocates for legally binding EU measures. While feminists introduced the issue in the context of violence against women and as sexual exploitation at work, promoters of legally binding instruments framed it strategically as a workplace issue, of equal opportunities for women and men and of health and safety. Opponents defined sexual harassment as a moral, individual problem and used arguments of cultural diversity to make a case for or against EU intervention.

With the binding 2002 Equal Treatment Directive, the member states have been converging on the frame of sex discrimination and violation of dignity, and most member states now have laws to hold employers responsible for sexual harassment. The EU subjective definition of sexual harassment as unwanted behaviors can be applied in diverse cultural settings. The challenges now lie in the member states that need to implement and enforce these laws. In order for sexual harassment laws to be successful to prevent harassment from occurring, awareness of both discrimination at work and violence against women across the member states needs to be raised and the rights of victims de facto strengthened through effective implementation mechanisms. In order for sexual harassment laws to work to protect employed women and men from becoming victims, employers need incentives to take these laws seriously and to work on preventing sexual harassment from occurring. Potential perpetrators need to be informed that behaviors they believed were acceptable are now illegal, supervisors need to be informed about their obligations, and victims who took for granted that they needed to put up with certain behaviors have to be aware of their legal rights. Employers, furthermore, need to take preventive steps, including awareness campaigns and creating internal policies and complaint procedures.

Raising awareness around sexual harassment and bringing the issue onto the national agenda in many countries is currently tempered with the harsh economic and social context throughout Europe. On the one hand, in the face of declining fertility, governments have become ever more concerned with the employment of younger women—trying to help women to reconcile family and work and to focus on women's rights at work as mothers, but not necessarily on rights of women as individuals. On the other hand, many "old" member states are dealing with long-term unemployment and marginal or precarious employment of women as main political concerns.

The rapid transformation processes in Central and Eastern European countries have fundamentally changed the political, economic, and social situation of women. On the one hand, violence against women issues have only recently been discussed in public, pushed onto the agenda by the nonprofit organizations sponsored in part by Western donors and European Union projects like Daphne. On the other hand, historically women's employment in these countries has been higher than in many other EU member states. Despite horizontal and vertical sex segregation, it used to be taken for granted that women did paid work and had access to male-dominated work. The reality or the threat of unemployment, however, now creates new vulnerabilities: as one woman in East Germany, for example, stated: "I would rather have a job where I get harassed than have no job" (Interview 2000). These circumstances make it difficult to resist sexual harassment individually or collectively, and working women continue to take for granted sexually harassing behaviors at work.

EU funding is aiding activists in Central and Eastern European member states to organize campaigns to create awareness. For example, one of the sexual harassment projects funded through Daphne in 2004 focused on a one-month campaign in Poland, Lithuania, Latvia, Bulgaria, Greece, and Finland. Because member states have to implement and enforce EU laws, the ultimate test for EU measures against sexual harassment is the local level: how they achieve changes in gender culture at the workplace level, where they have the potential to improve the everyday lives of working woman and men. Perhaps the universal European frame of sexual harassment as the violation of dignity can provide a counterbalance against the frames of sexual harassment as an American problem or a Western plague.

Notes

1. See for the history of policy measures against sexual harassment in the EU Gregory 2000, Collins 1996, Zippel 2006.

2. See R. Amy Elman for a pointed critique of the EU's approach to addressing violence against women (Elman forthcoming).

3. *Chief Constable of West Yorkshire v Vento* (No.1) [2001] IRLR 124 EAT (No.2) [2002] IRLR 177 EAT, [2003] IRLR 102 Court of Appeal.

References

Baer, Susanne. 2004. Dignity or Equality? Responses to Workplace Harassment in European, German, and U.S. Law. In *Directions in Sexual Harassment Law*, eds. Catharine A. MacKinnon and Reva B. Siegel, 581–601. New Haven, CT: Yale University Press.

3Bauerova, Ladka. 2000. Sexual Harassment at Work Widespread in Europe. *New York Times*, 9 January, National, page 7A.

Bernstein, Anita. 1994. Law, Culture, and Harassment. *University of Pennsylvania Law Review* 142 (4): 1227–311.

Bundesministerium für Frauen und Jugend. 1993. *(K)ein Kavaliersdelikt? Ein Kavaliersdelikt? Sexuelle Belästigung im Arbeitsleben*. Bonn, Germany: Bundesministerium für Frauen und Jugend.

Carter, Victoria A. 1992. Working on Dignity: EC Initiatives on Sexual Harassment in the Workplace. *Northwestern Journal of International Law and Business* 12: 431–53.

Collins, Evelyn. 1996. European Union Sexual Harassment Policy. In *Sexual Politics and the European Union: The New Feminist Challenge*, ed. R. Amy Elman, 23–34. Providence, RI: Berghahn Books.

DeSacco, Dena. 1996. *Sexual Harassment in the European Union: A Post-Maastricht Analysis*. Brussels: European Interuniversity Press and College of Europe.

Ehrenreich, Rosa. 1999. Dignity and Discrimination: Toward a Pluralistic Understanding of Workplace Harassment. *Georgetown Law Journal* 88: 1.

eironline. 2000. Commission Proposes Amendments to 1976 Equal Treatment Directive. http://www.eiro.eurofound.eu.int/2000/06/feature/eu0006255f.html (downloaded 19 March 2006).

Elman, Amy. Forthcoming. *Sexual Equality in an Integrated Europe*. New York: Palgrave.

European Commission. 2004. Commission Final Report to the European Parliament and the Council on The Daphne Programme (2000–2003). http://ec.europa.eu/justice_home/funding/2004_2007/daphne/doc/daphne_final_report01_2004_en.pdf accessed December 10, 2007

European Commission. 1999. *Sexual Harassment at the Workplace in the European Union*. Luxembourg: Office for Official Publications of the European Communities.

Eyerman, Ron and Andrew Jamison. 1991. *Social Movements: A Cognitive Approach*. University Park, PA: Pennsylvania State University Press.

Ferree, Myra M. 2003. Resonance and Radicalism: Feminist Framing in the Abortion Debates of the United States and Germany. *American Journal of Sociology* 109 (2): 304–44.

Government of Ireland. 2004. Report on Sexual Harassment in the Workplace in EU Member States. The Irish Presidency of the European Union in association with FGS Consulting and Professor Aileen McGolgan. http://www.justice.ie/80256E010039C5AF/vWeb/pcJUSQ63QLTX-en.

Gregory, Jeanne. 1995. Making the Best Use of European Law. *European Journal of Women's Studies* 2: 421–40.

———. 2000. Sexual Harassment: The Impact of EU Law in the Member States. In *Gender Policies in the European Union*, ed. Mariagrazia Rossilli, 175–92. New York: Peter Lang.

Hanmer, Jalna. 1996. The Common Market of Violence. In *Sexual Politics and European Union: The New Feminist Challenge*, ed. R. Amy Elman, 131–45. Oxford: Berghahn.

Hoskyns, Catherine. 2000. A Study of Four Action Programmes on Equal Opportunities. In *Gender Policies in the European Union*, ed. Mariagrazia Rossilli, 43–60. New York: Peter Lang.

Husbands, Robert. 1992. Sexual Harassment Law in Employment: An International Perspective. *International Labour Review* 131 (6): 535–59.

Interview. 2000. With anonymous woman from East German. Berlin.

Keck, Margaret, and Kathryn Sikkink. 1998. *Activists Beyond Borders: Advocacy Networks in International Politics.* Ithaca, NY: Cornell University Press.

Louis, Marie-Victoire. 1994. Sexual Harassment at Work in France: What Stakes for Feminists? In *Women and Violence*, ed. Miranda Davies, 85–96. London: Zed Books Ltd.

MacKinnon, Catharine. 1979. *Sexual Harassment of Working Women: A Case of Sex Discrimination.* New Haven, CT: Yale University Press.

Mazur, Amy G. 1994. The Formation of Sexual Harassment Policies in France: Another Case of French Exceptionalism? *French Politics and Society* 11 (2):11–32.

Minnesota Advocates for Human Rights, Women's Rights Center, International Women's Human Rights Clinic. 2002. Employment Discrimination and Sexual Harassment in Poland. http://www.mnadvocates.org (downloaded 19 March 2006).

Perlez, Jane. 1996. Central Europe Learns About Sex Harassment. *New York Times* 3 October, section A, 3.

Pflüger, Almut and Susanne Baer. 2005. *Beschäftigtenschutzgesetz in der Praxis. Bericht.* Berlin: Bundesministerium für Familie, Senioren, Frauen und Jugend. www.bmfsfj.de.

Rubenstein, Michael. 1987. *The Dignity of Women at Work: A Report on the Problem of Sexual Harassment in the Member States of the European Communities.* Brussels/Luxembourg: Office for Official Publications of the European Communities.

Rybarova, Nadia. 2000. Sexual Harassment Widespread among Czechs—But Many May Not Be Aware. *Associated Press*, 13 January, International News.

Saguy, Abigail. 2003. *What Is Sexual Harassment? From Capitol Hill to the Sorbonne.* Berkeley, CA: University of California Press.

Snow, David A. 2004. Framing Processes, Ideology, and Discursive Fields. In *The Blackwell Companion to Social Movements*, eds. David A. Snow, Sarah A. Soule, and Hanspeter Kriesi, 380–412. Oxford: Blackwell.

Timmerman, Greetje and Cristien Bajema. 1999. Sexual Harassment in Northwest Europe. *European Journal of Women's Studies* 6: 419–39.

Weldon, S. Laurel. 2002. *Protest, Policy, and the Problem of Violence Against Women: A Cross-National Comparison.* Pittsburgh, PA: University of Pittsburgh Press.

Zippel, Kathrin. 2003. Practices of Implementation of Sexual Harassment Policies: Individual vs. Collective Strategies. *Review of Policy Research* 20 (1): 175–97.

———. 2006. *The Politics of Sexual Harassment: A Comparative Study of the United States, the European Union, and Germany.* Cambridge: Cambridge University Press.

Part II

THE EU ACCESSION PROCESS

Six Case Studies from West and East

4

IRISH WOMEN'S ORGANIZATIONS IN AN ENLARGED EUROPE

Pauline P. Cullen

Ireland,[1] long the recipient of significant EU regional development and agricultural and structural funding, has since the mid-1990s experienced unprecedented economic growth and has been hailed as the success story of EU membership and neoliberal economic policy making. While EU enlargement has increased in-migration across Western Europe, Ireland has, in contrast to other countries, attracted a considerable number of migrants. In the twelve months prior to April 2006, the highest levels of immigration since records on in-migration began in 1987 were recorded, with 86,900 immigrants entering the state (Central Statistics Office 2006a). Nearly half (43 percent) were nationals of the ten new EU accession states. A preliminary analysis of the 2006 census suggests that the number of non-Irish nationals in Ireland increased from 222,000 in 2002 (equivalent to 5.8 percent of the population) to around 400,000 in 2006 (about 9.4 percent of the population) (Central Statistics Office 2006a).

Citizens from accession states and non-EU nationals face considerable challenges in their efforts to integrate into Irish society. Ireland's decision to open its labor market to citizens of accession states has revealed gender- and race-based divisions within a society that has prided itself on its pro-European spirit and its sensitivity to the immigration experience. Ireland, the UK, and Sweden were the only three EU member states to accept free movement of labor from new countries entering the EU on 1 May 2004. Ireland's decision to remove restrictions on workers coming from new EU member states was motivated in part by the need for an increased work force to fuel economic growth. However, the Irish government, reacting to perceived concerns about the level of in-migration and social problems associated with the integration of "non-nationals," shifted its position with regard to the most recent phase of enlargement. Workers from Bulgaria and Romania, countries that joined the EU in January 2007, face restrictions that include a system of limited work permits, quotas, and green cards (*The Irish Times* 2006).[2]

Migrant women in particular are concentrated in low-paying service employment and are subject to multiple discriminations based on gender, race, and ethnicity. Despite economic prosperity, Irish women also continue to face pervasive structural inequalities. Narrowly focused on economic growth, government policy has shown a weak commitment to gender equality and a preliminary effort to acknowledge pervasive racism as a significant issue. Gender mainstreaming, a potentially transformative policy tool, is (as I will argue in this chapter) poorly understood and lacks political support. The Celtic Tiger in an enlarged Europe has brought affluence to some, but marginalization for many women in Irish society. This chapter examines the efforts of the Irish women's movement to mobilize in a political context indifferent to the multiple discriminations facing diverse women in an increasingly unequal society. I begin with a brief review of the situation of women in Irish society. I detail the Irish state's response to gender inequality, the "equality machinery" in place, and progress made on gender mainstreaming. I continue with a consideration of the efforts of the largest women's organization in Ireland—the National Women's Council of Ireland (NWCI)—to articulate a common platform amid rising levels of gender and racial/ethnic stratification.

This chapter examines how women's rights organizations are negotiating the changing nature of Irish society within an enlarged Europe. Specifically, this chapter investigates the challenges confronting the central official representation of the Irish women's movement, the National Women's Council of Ireland. The NWCI represents a combination of statutory linked and service organizations for women with a predominantly reformist agenda, it is engaged in "collective action through established means" (Connolly 2003, 110). The organization has wrestled with its ability to build a cohesive and representative membership of Irish women from different classes and across the urban/rural divide. However, with enlargement the diversification of the Irish population to include immigrants from the accession states and other economic migrants and political refugees from non-accession countries has created additional cleavages and issues for the organization.

The Celtic Tiger and Gender Inequality

Clearly Irish society has changed tremendously since joining the European Union. Ranking twenty-second in the world in terms of income per capita in

1975, Ireland is per capita now the fourth richest country in the world and has been heralded as a highly globalized nation, with low levels of unemployment, declining rates of poverty, and a vibrant, cosmopolitan, and inclusive population. Empirically it is clear that although some sectors of Irish society have experienced relative prosperity, for many this has not been the case. In February 2006 an independent think tank ranked Ireland fifty-one out of fifty-six countries in terms of equality of economic opportunity for women, with one of the highest penalties in pay reduction associated with motherhood—with working mothers having lower earnings than women without children (National Economic and Social Forum 2006). Furthermore, the proportion of women at risk of poverty was 19.9 percent (Central Statistics Office of Ireland 2006a, 10).

Certainly, rising levels of female labor force participation, particularly of women with children, which have taken place in the context of a severe scarcity of childcare, have fueled economic growth (Kennedy 2003, 96–97). Women do experience the "double burden" of the Celtic Tiger as they struggle to reconcile work and family life. Despite a vigorous debate on the issue and the production of a state-sponsored national childcare strategy, childcare provision remains a privatized system where working-class women are priced out of childcare and about 50 percent of single female parents experience high rates of poverty (Central Statistics Office 2006c, 9). Recent reports comparing EU member states estimate that Irish parents spend the most of their income on childcare, while the Irish government spends the lowest percentage of GDP (0.2%) in investment in public childcare. Childcare costs in Ireland are the highest in Europe.[3] At an average of EUR 180 a week for one child, they are three times the European Union average and equal to 38 percent of an average Irish worker's take-home pay (ISME 2005, 20).

Women in Irish Society

Before 1970, the position of women in Irish society was circumscribed by Catholic ideology and restrictive public policies. The pervasive influence of the Catholic Church on Irish society and politics is illustrated in the 1937 constitution, which formally inscribed women's role as predominantly that of wives and mothers. Hobson's (2003) work on gender and recognition in Ireland notes that gender difference is imprinted in the constitution in the construction of familialism and nationalism. This has resulted in a gender policy logic that revolves around a strong male breadwinner model (ibid. 79). Two specific articles detail the constitutional "protection" of women as homemakers and spouses: "In particular the state recognises that by her life within the home the woman gives to the state a support without which the common good cannot be achieved," and "The state shall therefore endeavor to ensure that mothers shall not be obliged by economic necessity to engage in labor to the neglect of their duties in the home" (Bunreacht NA Heireann, 1937, Articles 40.1 and 41.2).[4] Women's place is understood to be within the home, while participation in the labor market is discouraged.[5] These principles shaped subsequent public policy and legislation that subjugated women's rights to those of men.

The 1990s were a decade of change, marking significant changes in legislative and policy frameworks that served to promote gender equality. Some of these changes were indeed in response to EU legislation, but other changes came from internal domestic pressure, including the Second Commission on the Status of Women in 1993. This government-appointed commission reviewed the position of women in Ireland and made recommendations on actions needed to achieve women's rights. By 2000 over 75 percent of these recommendations had been implemented. These include the introduction of divorce, employment equality legislation and equal status legislation, outlawing of sexual harassment, changes in family law, and changes in legislation to counter domestic violence. Other developments included the introduction of unpaid parental leave, the introduction of a national minimum wage, an increase in maternity leave (most recently in 2006 to 26 weeks paid), individualization of income tax for married couples, EU and state funding for positive action for women and some investment in childcare, and the publication of a National Plan for women in 2002 (McGauran 2005, 15). Recent shifts in reproductive rights and marriage suggest a move towards a less traditional and conservative political culture and societal milieu. However, Irish women still experience a significant pay gap with their male counterparts. Women are paid 14 percent less than men in Ireland (Central Statistics Office 2006b, 17). In 2006, a mere 14 percent of politicians were women (Central Statistics Office 2006b, 10).

The Irish political system can be characterized as conservative with centralized bureaucracies and most recently a system of social partnership (Carney 2003). Galligan (1998) argues that the male-dominated political culture has ensured that the EU and the UN have been favored contexts for the promotion of gender equality in Ireland. Initiated by the women's movement and facilitated by the EEC, the development of equality policies in the 1970s laid the groundwork for the pursuit of a liberal conception of equality in political institutions in the 1980s (Galligan 1998). By the mid 1990s, gender mainstreaming became a priority across many policy areas (Carney 2003).

Irish governments have also acceded to international gender equality commitments including the 1995 UN Beijing Platform for Action and the UN Convention on the Elimination of All Forms of Discrimination Against Women (Connolly 2003). However, women's organizations suggest that the Beijing Platform for Action is not taken seriously by the Irish Government (NWCI 2000). National-level equality legislation has also been initiated, including the Equal Status Act 2000 and the Employment Equality Act 1998, and most recently the Equality Act 2004. Equality legislation has significantly changed the framework for equality in the Republic of Ireland, because these acts are informed by a differentiated notion of equality—especially the Equal Status Act, which extends the remit for equality beyond labor market concerns for the first time (Carney 2003).

Gender mainstreaming,[6] implemented in Ireland through the National Development Plan (NDP) (2000–2006) an investment and development program promoting human resources development, peace in Northern Ireland, and regional development, and partly funded by EU structural funds, has been the main official response of the Irish state to profound and persistent gender inequalities. However, as Carney (2003) and most recently McGauran (2005) have argued, there is no foundation for the integration of gender mainstreaming into Irish bureaucratic and political culture.

McGauran's analysis suggests an incompatibility between the center-right government's neoliberal policy framework and the social justice objectives of gender mainstreaming. Furthermore, local politicians are disinterested or unaware of gender mainstreaming priorities. Policy makers see gender mainstreaming as an imposition and have little incentive to embrace the concept or practice (McGauran 2005, 87–89). The absence of internal champions for the gender mainstreaming agenda within state bureaucracies has also rendered the initiative impotent. Her report suggested that without political will and resources, gender mainstreaming will remain a marginal element in Irish policy making.

The economic imperative of successive Irish governments means that policies related to the labor market (parental leave, maternity leave, equal pay, and childcare) have been favored as gender mainstreaming priorities (Carney 2003). Childcare and benefits for children, both hotly contested political issues, have in many regards become the central state initiative in the arena of gender equality. Childcare became a political issue because policy makers identified it as having a negative impact on economic growth and on Ireland's competitiveness in comparison to the rest of the EU. The establishment of the Equal Opportunities Childcare Programme (EOCP) in 2000, the first and only significant government investment in childcare, was achieved in the clear economic context of facilitating women's return to education and training fields. However, the strength of the prevailing ideology regarding childcare severely restrained any political action to seriously address the issue. All political parties have resisted the establishment of a strong childcare infrastructure, sensitive to the traditional view that children should be cared for by their mothers in the home (O'Connor 2005, 2–3). Coakley (2005, 20) argues that the government, in line with EU doctrine[7], frames childcare in an "economistic" mode: as the responsibility of women and as a labor market equality strategy to move women into paid work. A review of the current government's EOCP suggests that childcare is indeed framed as a labor market equality strategy. This is due principally to the activation model being promoted by the EU, which includes funding for childcare as part of an equality strategy (O'Connor 2005).

A number of pieces of legislation designed to keep women in the labor force have also been passed: the Maternity Protection Act (1994), the Adoptive Leave Act (1995), and the Parental Leave Act (1998). In short, as Carney (2004) argues, gender policy has always been subject to more dominant mainstream policy concerns, particularly employment, labor market supply, and general economic growth. For this reason, feminist organizations including the NWCI have long argued that political priorities will not alter until women are equally represented at the decision-making level.

The Irish government has made a formal commitment to achieving the EU target of a 60 percent female employment rate by 2010. In addition, the government is committed to developing strategies to expand the labor force. The Department of Justice Equality and Law Reform (DJELR), the central site of state engagement on equality issues, argues that women returnees, in particular those who have been outside the labor market as mothers and carers, are seen as a potential group on which to capitalize (Coakley 2005, 7). However, ideologically the role of mothers as carers continues to be underwritten by the Irish constitution. The state recognizes that it has to tread a careful path due to constitutional restraints. It has opted to substantially increase child benefits rather than provide a childcare benefit and, for pension purposes, has introduced a home carers tax allowance that gives credit for a number of years to mothers who are caring full-time (Mahon 2004).

The Irish Women's Movement

Building on the political work, networks, and strategies developed by traditional women's groups between 1922 and 1969, the Irish women's movement reemerged in the 1970s and was dominated by two main styles of activism: equal rights and radicalism. Both styles of activism possessed their own ideological, tactical, and organizational diversity but shared common themes, concepts, and goals. This loose form of collaboration helped create cohesion rather than a unity, and ensured the continuance of a collective vibrant women's movement in the 1980s and 1990s (Connolly 2003).

The first Commission on the Status of Women (CSW) was formed in 1970 after intense lobbying by women's organizations, and challenged discriminatory legislation that had been progressively institutionalized since the founding of the Free State in 1922. The CSW was tasked with monitoring the European Commission's recommendations and acting as an umbrella organization coordinating women's organizations and claims making (Hobson 2003, 83). The CSW gained regular funding in 1978, and by the 1980s formed a national executive with headquarters and a regular staff. By 1992 the CSW, now renamed as the National Women's Council of Ireland (NWCI), had become a formal negotiating member within state policy setting forums.

The NWCI has 165 affiliated member organizations comprised of women's groups, women's sections or committees of larger national organizations such as trade unions and political parties, and organizations where women comprise a majority of members. The organization claimed in 2006 to represent 300,000 women in Ireland. Their mission statement states: "Working together as the national representative organization of women in Ireland, our mission is to achieve women's equality, empowering women to work together, while recognizing and mobilizing difference, in order to remove structural political, economic, social/cultural and affective inequalities" (Brown 2004, 1). The NWCI represents the most institutionalized form of feminist mobilization, but has been recognized as unique in combining a broad representation of different groups and diversity in feminist claims (Hobson 2003). Working-class women and women from the ethnic minority indigenous population the Travellers[8] have had in the past a contentious relationship with the NWCI. However, this relationship has in recent years become more formalized as these constituents occupy discrete positions within an organizational field with its own specific division of labor.

For Connolly (2003), while the 1970s were dominated by autonomous, direct action tactics of radical social movement organizations, the early 1980s emerged as a period of strategic and legally astute mobilization around European Court of Justice legislative opportunities. By the end of the 1980's a combination of general movement gains were important symbolically, including the election of Mary Robinson, the first female president and a feminist activist, in 1990; the application of international legal pressure through European courts ruling in favor of access to information on abortion in 1992; the election of twenty women to political service in 1992; and the publication of the Report of a Second Commission on the Status of Women in 1993. The 1990s also marked a professionalization of the movement, alongside an increase in working-class women's activism particularly in the community sector. This formalization that had begun in the 1980s directed coalitions towards narrower, institutionalized strategies that opened up a divide between the NWCI and newer grassroots activists in the community sector.

The National Women's Council of Ireland (NWCI): Difference, Diversity and Consensus?

In the early 1990s, the NWCI was rebuilt and radicalized with the adoption of its work plan around four intersective and dynamic "equality spheres." Each of the four spheres—Affective, Social/Cultural, Economic, and Political Equality—was linked with its own rights-based goal. Underlying these intersective spheres is the stated aim of "building the base as a means to regenerate the organization and rebuild its representational capacity" (Brown 2004, 2).

Diversity among women is listed as a key goal of the organization and antiracism is considered since the late 1990s a key policy priority. In its submission to the government's 2002 National Plan for Women (now defunct), the organization was clear to frame its critique of state policy in terms of diversity. Up to the late 1990s, the term *diversity* was used in NWCI documents to refer to lone parents and disabled women, but particularly with reference to the indigenous ethnic minority of Traveller women. By 2001 the organization's documents extended this framing to include minority ethnic women, asylum seekers, and refugees. The organization also sits on the board and the Women's Sub-committee of the National Consultative Committee on Racism and Interculturalism and works with the Immigrant Council of Ireland. Ten organizations that deal with ethnic minority, asylum, immigrant, or migrant issues are listed as affiliates of the NWCI. The NWCI also campaigned vigorously against the Citizenship 2004 amendment that removed the automatic right of citizenship for children born on Irish soil (NWCI 2004).

Social Partnership and Gender Equality: The Limits of "Partnership"

In 1996 the government invited the NWCI, alongside seven other community and voluntary organizations, to join unions and employers in negotiations on the national public policy program. The NWCI also advises a variety of state-appointed committees dealing with women's health, maternity services, and violence against women. The most detailed submission prepared each year is the NWCI's pre–budget submission, which makes specific recommendations calling on the government to allocate resources to areas such as childcare, pensions, unemployment payments, or violence against women.

Social partnership has been credited with a key role in Ireland's recent economic success. It has also influenced the gender equality agenda (Carney 2003). As a social partner,[9] the NWCI is represented on the National Economic and Social Council (NESC), which determines the overall strategy and context for the national agreements, as well as on the National Economic and Social Forum (NESF), which focuses on the implementation of specific measures and programs, especially those concerned with the achievement of equality and social inclusion.

The structures of social partnership exert a strong pressure against dissent. Furthermore, both economic and social policy is effectively ring-fenced from significant influence from dissenting forces—a way of ensuring that it is functional to the needs of capital accumulation by economic elites (Kirby 2002, 32; Meade 2005).

Successive cutbacks in social expenditure and a set of toothless proposals for the proposed National Plan for Women had emboldened the NWCI to reject the 2003 partnership agreement (NWCI 2005b). However, the NWCI decision to pull out of partnership negotiations was highly controversial. After the pullout there were no women's rights organizations represented in these policy-setting contexts (McGauran 2005, 73). The government in turn excluded the NWCI from the monitoring committees of the National Development Plan (NDP), the program through which gender mainstreaming is implemented. These committees were not part of the social partnership framework and the organization saw this exclusion as evidence of punitive actions taken by the state to police the NWCI. With no group representing women's issues, the NWCI no longer received progress reports that would allow the council to identify areas where gender inequalities arise in the implementation of the NDP. The consequence for the NWCI is their inability to raise issues in the context of the implementing committees. From the other side of the equation, the NDP Gender Equality Unit can also no longer rely on the support from the NWCI representatives, which in turn reduces the focus and level of debate occurring in relation to gender inequalities (McGauran 2005, 74).

On leaving social partnership the NWCI did embark on a national program of outreach to its members aimed at strengthening their lobbying capacity at local and regional levels. Simultaneously, the NWCI embarked on a political lobbying campaign aimed at building their relationship with both the incumbent and opposition political parties. In concrete terms, the organization claims that the shift in its strategy and tactics has enabled it to provide a clearer and more consistent message from local and national level for consumption by policy makers.

Despite losing their formal footing in the state policy-making machinery, there is evidence of the council's continuing discursive power. The 2005 "Brown Envelope Campaign" aimed at social welfare reform included poor and immigrant women to help orient the campaign. Despite their official exclusion from policy-setting contexts, the council did gain access to the minister for Social Welfare, who suggested that their report has influenced debates at ministerial level. Their second significant policy submission in the period provided a comprehensive assessment of childcare provision and recommendations for a subsidized day care, an early childcare education system, and the extension of maternity and parental leave options (NWCI 2005c).

The disadvantage of staying outside of the social partnership process can be evidenced in the perceived hollowing out of the government's commitment to a National Women's Strategy. In 2006, the organization contemplated re-entering the next round of social partnership negotiations as the National Women's Strategy, delayed once again, was to be included in those discussions. For the NWCI this was a difficult choice; they feared losing legitimacy if the strategy were agreed to without their input, but remained wary of providing political cover for an administration less than sympathetic to their agenda. Analyses of the latest round of social partnership "Towards 2016" concluded in late 2006 suggest that the process has become a repackaging of existing government policy, with little real negotiation and therefore increasingly irrelevant to civil society organizations (Connolly 2006, 33–35). The National Women's Strategy finally launched in May 2007 without NWCI input acknowledges the breadth of women's inequality but mechanisms, targets and timescales to remove these inequalities are largely absent. Unhappy with the Strategy but concerned to influence its implementation, the NWCI opted to re-engage formally with the state by joining a monitoring committee for the implementation of the social partnership agreement.

Multilevel Activism

Assessing the organization's relationship to the EU and the implications of EU gender policy for Irish women, the NWCI director stated, "Generally any progress that comes, comes from the EU."[11] The NWCI is a member of the European Women's Lobby (EWL) and maintains a "steady level of investment on the Brussels level." For the NWCI, the EWL was an important source of information and expertise on EU gender policy and initiatives. The organization applies EWL toolkits to its campaigns during general and European Parliamentary elections. On more than one occasion when the policy officers or the director were to be interviewed on national media, the Dublin-based staff had called the Brussels office looking for relevant information on the implications of European directives. Policy submissions also make direct reference to EU policy commitments. The EWL also provided the NWCI with resources to build relations with women from the accession countries, particularly on the issue of prostitution and trafficking areas within which the EWL has had significant investment since 2003. The EWL network of Observatories on Violence against Women was also perceived as a valuable resource. Another aspect of the NWCI's EU strategy is their use of connections with left-wing members of the European Parliament (MEPs). The organization had on occasion provided MEPs with questions to pose during European Parliamentary debates. The Irish presidency of the EU (January–June 2004) also provided some important opportunities—in particular, a conference held in May 2004 on violence against women, where women from accession countries were invited to participate.

Overall, NWCI efforts to "shame" the government to maintain its international commitments have had mixed results. Ten years after the Beijing Conference for Women, the Irish government had still not drafted a National Plan for Women. A "National Women's Strategy" was promised for the end of 2004 by Willie O'Dea, minister of State at the Department of Justice, Equality and Law

Reform (O'Dea 2004). Instead, preparation began in February 2005 on a National Women's Strategy, which had not been completed in 2007. Gender mainstreaming remains a formal state policy objective and may, under a different political administration, yield a more fruitful outcome to counter gender inequality. However, as Roth (2004) argues, for gender mainstreaming to be transformative it requires a strong civil society. Lacking this, in Ireland gender inequality is rendered invisible, erased by economic prosperity, left in the realm of institutional consciousness-raising and potentially used to undermine positive action.

However, some progress can be acknowledged. Between March 2006 and March 2007, a key demand of the NWCI was realized when maternity leave was extended to 26 weeks of paid leave with the option of 16 additional weeks of unpaid leave. In 2006, EU law obliged Ireland to make an Early Childcare Allowance available to all EU citizens working in the country, as well as to children not living in Ireland. However, this policy change immediately became subject to a racialized discourse as the media seized upon the policy to point out its implications for the 166,000 workers from accession states working in Ireland. In theory, parents from accession states can claim the child benefit for children living in their home country. Opposition political parties also seized on the issue as "a ridiculous situation that Irish tax payers would be funding childcare for children not resident in Ireland" (O'Regan 2006, 8).

Consequences of EU Enlargement:
Migrant Care Workers and Irish Women

Women account for almost half the migrants moving into the fifteen countries of the EU (Thorogood and Winqvist 2003). Common demographic trends across EU countries, particularly aging populations, are coupled in the Irish case with an increase in female labor force participation. The European economy is dependent on female labor, which is often underpaid and undervalued. Ireland and its Celtic Tiger prosperity have been facilitated by similar dynamics surrounding female labor. Since the 1990s, thousands of Irish women have taken up employment. However, the Irish gender regime is defined in part by the ideological construct that childcare is a private concern of families and predominately the responsibility of women. Ireland sits near the bottom of the EU league tables when considering childcare provision. Despite a vigorous public debate on the issue and some efforts to channel EU funds towards public provision of care, there remains a critical scarcity of affordable services. The result has been the opening up of what Conroy refers to as a "care deficit" (Conroy 2003, 18). Migrant women are filling this gap. Between 1999 and 2002, the numbers of migrant domestic workers increased tenfold (Conroy 2003, 21). At the same time, early childhood care and education in Central and Eastern Europe has been experiencing its own crisis. EU enlargement has brought with it the pressure to disinvest from the social infrastructure, and consequently services for women and children have been significantly reduced. Conroy (2003, 23) cites a significant reduction in the availability of formal childcare in Latvia, Lithuania, Romania, and Poland. The implications of this scenario are that working mothers from these countries that migrate but are unable to bring their children face their own care crisis at home (Conroy 2003).

Migration in the Irish context is part of broader trends acknowledged in the globalization of women's work in caring, cleaning, and prostitution (Ehrenreich and Hochschild 2003; Yeates 2006). Conroy (2003) argues that the back-story of the Celtic Tiger phenomenon is a story of unpaid or cheap female labor increasingly supplied by migrant women. The mass entry of Irish women into the paid labor force has been paralleled by the outsourcing and commodification of a range of social reproductive labor (Yeates 2006). Occupational gender segregation as an entrenched feature of the Irish labor market is consequently broadly reproduced among the migrant workforce. This combination of unpaid care work and poorly paid "feminized" labor has fuelled Irish economic growth and created a situation where the relationship between Irish women and migrant women is in part shaped by the "transfer of the domestic burden." In particular, for many middle-class Irish women, migrant women become the Other as they fulfill roles as domestic workers, childcare providers, and sex workers (Conroy 2003). These processes are understood to occur thusly: "In the context of a generally unchanging sexual division of labor at individual household and institutional levels (as evidenced by poor public care service provision), this outsourcing (in principle) enables the avoidance of gender conflicts among couples, at least, that is, in those households able to purchase domestic services" (Yeates 2006, 9).

The Migrants Rights Center of Ireland has recorded substantial evidence that many migrants are receiving wages below the minimum wage level, and have documented several incidents of migrants being forced to work hours in the region of twelve–fourteen a day, seven days per week, without any holidays. Those most vulnerable are migrant women employed as domestic workers (O'Donoghue 2004). Interviews conducted as part of a report for the Equality Authority examining the situation of women migrant workers suggests that women migrants experience gender and ethnic inequalities supported by negative stereotypes (Pillinger 2006).

While the EU has been an important resource for Irish feminist activists and has provided for the strengthening of protections and equal treatment for women in full time paid employment, working-class women and, most recently, migrant women employed in part-time and insecure work have been less well serviced. Feminist mobilization up to the late 1990s has been characterized by those working in the community sector as dominated by individual middle-class women "who have used it for their personal advancement and for launching themselves

politically," and thus "the Council (NWCI) has not in the past reflected the realities of women who are poor, women who experience racism and women who
are parenting alone" (Cochrane 2004/2005, 64–65). However, a shift towards a
more inclusive strategy has been recognized. The coordinator of the Migrants
Rights Center Ireland stated, "There has been a remarkable shift in the last seven
years. The Women's Council has become more focused on solidarity with all
women, prioritizing agendas addressing poor women and women experiencing
racism and inequality. There has been an outreach to migrant women employed
as domestic workers and childcare workers. This is important because economic
progress for some women has been on the backs of other women" (Cochrane
2004/2005). Although the Irish women's movement has not yet fully included
women from minority ethnicities in all feminist projects, the NWCI, in an effort
to reach women from racialized minority ethnic groups, had published an antiracism handbook in November 2000, undertook a submission on recent Irish legislation amending rules for immigration and residency and organized a conference
on migrant women in Ireland in September 2007 (Lentin and McVeigh 2006,
11; NWCI 2005a; 2007). Importantly, migrant women are also beginning to organize their own advocacy networks. Lentin (2006) suggests that emerging migrant women's networks, although seriously underfunded and underrepresented,
are beginning to take part in new conversations on needs, discrimination, rights,
and entitlements. An example of such an organization is the NGO Ruhama,
which works with women who engage in prostitution, including trafficked migrant women, providing support, advocacy, and training.[11]

EU Enlargement: Commonalities and
Cooperation among Women East and West

Although long held up as the poster child of gender regime change as a result of
EU membership, as this chapter has outlined, women in Irish society continue
to face considerable disadvantages. Ireland often ranks at the low end of the EU
league tables when it comes to the application of gender equality policies. Perhaps the Irish experience can also be understood as a cautionary tale for women's
organizations in the newest member states on the limits of EU membership in
challenging patriarchal and increasingly neoliberal policy-making contexts. Poland in particular offers an interesting comparative case, as in both countries
Catholicism has been a mechanism for preserving the nation-state and forging
the contemporary national identities of both populaces.

Women from the new member states have experienced a narrowing of their
political, economic, and social rights. Gender inequality came relatively late on
the agenda for negotiations for entry into the EU (Roth 2004). In the Irish case,
and now reflected in particular in the Polish experience, while upon entry to

what was then the EEC the state formally accepted the bulk of gender equality legislation, it has been slow to comply with many issues. Irish women did mobilize around EU membership negotiations in the early 1970s, and in a similar vein to women in the newest member states found that the EEC provided an alternative frame for gender equality claims making and later as a "source of leverage politics for bodily rights" (Hobson 2003, 84). For example, Irish feminists in coalition with trade unionists lobbied in Strasbourg to ensure that the Irish government abandoned its efforts to delay acceptance of EEC equal pay directives. Polish women have reacted in similar fashion to Irish feminists decades earlier—supplying information, engaging in public debates, and building alliances. For these organizations the EU has acted as a mediator and a catalyst, allowing them to build capacity and gain official recognition (see Regulska and Grabowska in this volume).

However, on the issue of reproductive rights, recourse to a market-derived claim structure has been less successful (Hobson 2003, 86). In this regard there are similarities between the Irish and Polish experiences, where the EU has enabled the Irish and Polish states to retain their abortion restrictions on grounds of cultural and moral distinctiveness (Cap 2004; Roth 2004). Irish feminists have always attempted to move beyond the constraints of this particularistic cultural discourse responding to the government's refusal to legislate on the issue, by supporting individual litigants and employing a human rights frame at UN and EU level (Mullally 2005, 15). Irish women, and most recently a Polish woman, continue to employ legal strategies, with two cases contesting abortion restrictions currently pending before the European Court of Human Rights (Center for Reproductive Rights 2006).

There are fledgling attempts to craft sustained cooperation between Western feminists and their "sisters" in the newest member states. International NGOs have been active in providing information and legal support and facilitating exchanges between women from older and newer member states. Examples include European Parliamentary hearings on sexual and reproductive health and rights where Irish and Polish women provided testimony of their experiences.[12] Another area for transnational cooperation is the issue of trafficking and sexual exploitation. The issue of migrants' rights also provides a possible area for collaboration.

Gender equality advocates, both in the West and in the East, are hopeful that processes of accession and integration into the EU will translate into positive change for women in the region (Choluj and Neusüß 2004, 10). As the Irish case attests, where collaboration occurs, it seems to originate at the European level and is initiated by EU-level networks like the EWL or international NGOs working in the Central and Eastern EU member states. Western women's groups may yet have to realize the importance of connections between their struggles and those of their counterparts in the newest EU member states.

Conclusion

Hobson (2003) argues that the main challenge for Irish feminists remains their weak base in political parties and unions, and that their dependence on transnational lobbies in the absence of strong national-level political representation renders the Irish women's movement weak in comparison to the other social partners (ibid. 91). Certainly, the weak representation of women in decision making inhibits the mobilization of feminist activists in Irish society. It has been suggested that the established women's movement has been most successful in areas that closely complied with the state's agenda of modernization (Connolly 2006, 225).

The NWCI faces considerable challenges in its efforts to effectively represent the diversity of women in Irish society. Recent efforts to build relationships with transnational feminist organizations from Eastern and Central Europe, including the organization the Network of East-West Women (NEWW), indicate that the organization is investing in diversifying its alliances. The focus on intersective equality spheres and the rationalization of the organization's work-plan has enabled the organization to stay focused and invest in transversal policy objectives including women in decision making, social welfare, and childcare. The current director, a core feminist and movement entrepreneur, has brought a combination of sensitivity to both community-based participative dynamics and professionalized movement activity to the organization. An increasing focus on affiliate-led policy initiatives and the involvement of migrant women, coupled with the resources available from the EWL, have enabled the NWCI to begin to respond to new constituencies accompanying an enlarged Europe.

The NWCI faces considerable obstacles in sustaining a focus on gender inequality in general, and in particular the interplay between gender oppression and racism in migrants' lives. These include a multilevel political opportunity structure that considers gender inequality a labor market issue and adopts a defensive posture towards migrants. As the contributors to this volume suggest (see Morgan, and Hellgren and Hobson) there are domestic-level factors that may be essential for capturing the transformative potential of the EU as a site for pursuing gender equality—including increasing the numbers of women in decision making, mobilizing grassroots constituents in campaigns and at the ballot box, and finally, illustrated in the Irish case and more recently for Polish feminist organizations, resisting the potential for demobilization that comes from entering into formal relations with the state.

Notes

This work was supported by a research and development grant from Dickinson College and included data from interviews with the director of the National Women's Council of Ireland in 2004 and 2007.

1. Ireland and Irish refers to the Republic of Ireland.
2. British policy on EU enlargement is used as the official rationale for Ireland's approach to workers from the newest EU member states. Ireland and Britain are bound by an agreement formalized in 1961, which created a common labor market between the two countries. Those who enter the labor force in either state effectively have access to the other one. The Irish decision to opt for a distinct approach from Britain would, it is argued, endanger free movement between the two jurisdictions.
3. For a comparison of childcare provisions in Europe, see Morgan in this volume.
4. An all-party body has been periodically tasked with a review of the constitution, which has resulted in a repeal of some legislation. However, the articles on the family have for the most part remained unchanged. Contradictions now arise between these principles and the neoliberal project embraced by the late modern Irish state, fuelled in part by increasing rates of gender, class, and, increasingly, race/ethnic-segregated female labor market participation.
5. Of course, Irish working-class women have always worked outside of the home in the absence of state supports for combining their familial and labor market roles.
6. Gender mainstreaming suggests that policies should be analyzed for their gender impact. This approach requires incorporating a gender equality perspective into mainstream policies as these are developed, implemented, and evaluated. The aim is to alter mainstream institutions to ensure that women and men derive equally beneficial outcomes from them. Originating at the United Nations Fourth World Conference in Women in Beijing in 1995, it has subsequently been adopted by the European Commission and by the EU member states.
7. Within the EU policy framework, individualization is cast in terms of self-sufficiency and independence, and coupled to the market activation of all individuals. Women's labor market activity is center stage in this policy discourse. How to integrate women into an individualized worker model is the challenge faced by EU member states (Hobson 2003).
8. Travellers are a Roma nomadic indigenous minority, documented as being part of Irish society for centuries. They experience significant racism, and social and cultural exclusion.
9. Social partnership involves the partnership of the government, employers, trade unions, and the Community and Voluntary Pillar to agree on national economic and social policy priorities and measures. Its role as a social partner is to represent women's interests in the negotiation and monitoring of national agreements. There are four pillars in social partnership: Trades Unions, Employers, Farmers, and the Community and Voluntary Pillar. The NWCI is part of the Community and Voluntary Pillar.
10. This and the following quotes are based on interviews with the Director of the NWCI, 25 July 2003 and 17 August 2005.
11. For more detail see Lentin 2006.
12. European Parliament hearing on Women's Right to Self-Determination and Adequate Sex Education and abortion rights as a public health, gender equality and human rights issue. 18 October 2005 and 9 February 2006.

References

Bunreacht NA Heireann [Constitution of Ireland]. 1937. Dublin: Government Publication Office.
Brown, Imelda. 2004. *A History of the National Women's Council of Ireland 1973–2003*. Dublin: National Women's Council of Ireland.
Cap, Krystyna. 2004. The Roman Catholic Church and the Democratic Process: A Comparative Analysis of Abortion Policies in Ireland and Poland. In *Critique: A World Wide Journal of Politics*.

Illinois State University Department of Politics and Government. www//lilt.ilstu.edu/critique/archives/FALL2004.htm. Accessed 12 May 2006.

Carney, Gemma. 2003. Communicating or Just Talking? Gender Mainstreaming and the Politics of Global Feminism. *Women and Language* 23 (23): 1–52.

———. 2004. Gender and Childcare: Creating a Space for Women and Children in Irish Policy Making. Paper presented at the Irish Social Policy Association Conference, Dublin, September.

Center for Reproductive Rights. 2006. *Women of the World: Laws and Policies Affecting Their Reproductive Lives, East Central Europe.* http://www.crlp.org/ pub_bo_wowece.html. Accessed 12 May 2006.

Central Statistics Office. 2006a. *Population and Migration Estimates. April 2003, April 2005 and Sept 2006.* Dublin: Stationery Office.

———. 2006b. *Women and Men in Ireland.* Dublin: Stationery Office.

———. 2006c. *EU Survey on Income and Living Conditions.* Dublin: Stationery Office.

Chołuj Bożena and Neusüß Claudia. 2004. *EU Enlargement in 2004: East–West Priorities and Perspectives from Women Inside and Outside the EU.* Discussion Paper, UNIFEM.

Coakley, Anne. 2005. *Mothers, Welfare and Labour Market Activation.* Working Paper 05/04 Combat Poverty Agency Research Paper Series. www.combatpoverty.ie. Accessed 2 March 2006.

Cochrane, Regina. 2004/2005. In the Field Women and Globalization in Ireland: Interview with Siobhan O'Donoghue Coordinator of the Migrants Rights Center Ireland. *Women and Environments International Magazine,* Fall/Winter: 64–5.

Conroy, Pauline. 2003. Migrant Women—Ireland in the International Division of Care. Paper presented at the Women's Movement: Migrant Women Transforming Ireland Conference, Trinity College, Dublin, 21 March.

Connolly, Eileen. 2006. The Institutionalisation of Anti-Poverty and Social Exclusion Policy in Irish Social Partnership. Working Paper No. 1, Working Papers in International Studies. Centre for International Studies School of Law and Government, Dublin City University.

Connolly, Linda. 2003. *The Irish Women's Movement: From Revolution to Devolution.* Dublin: The Lilliput Press.

The Irish Times. Migrant Workers. 25 October 2006, 17.

Ehrenreich, Barbara and Hochschild Russell Arlie. 2003. *Global Women: Nannies, Maids and Sex Workers in the New Economy.* London: Metropolitan Books.

Galligan, Yvonne. 1998. *Women and Contemporary Politics in Ireland: From the Margins to the Mainstream.* London: Pinter.

Hobson, Barbara. 2003. Recognition Struggles in Universalistic and Gender Distinctive Frames: Sweden and Ireland. In *Recognition Struggles and Social Movements,* ed. Barbara Hobson, 64–92. Cambridge: Cambridge University Press.

Irish Small and Medium Enterprises Association. 2005. Pre-Budget Submission 2006. Getting the Competitive Balance Right. www.isme.ie/press-page27406.html. Accessed 10 May 2006.

Kennedy, Sinead. 2003. Irish Women and the Celtic Tiger. In *The End of Irish History? Critical Reflections on the Celtic Tiger,* ed. Colin Coulter and Steve Coleman, 95–109. Manchester, UK: Manchester University Press.

Kirby, Peadar. 2002. Contested Pedigrees of the Celtic Tiger. In *Reinventing Ireland: Culture, Society and the Global Economy,* eds. Kirby, Peadar, Luke Gibbons, and Michael Cronin, 21–37. London: Pluto.

Lentin, Ronit. 2006. Migrant Women's Networks and Intercultural Ireland. Discussion Paper, no 148. Dublin: Institute of International Integration Studies, Trinity College.

Lentin, Ronit, and Robbie McVeigh. 2006. Irishness and Racism—Towards an E-Reader. *Translocations: The Irish Migration, Race and Social Transformation Review.* http://www.imrstr.dcu.ie. Accessed 23 November 2006.

Mahon, Elizabeth. 2004. Reconciling Work and Family Lives. Paper presented at the Irish Social Policy Association Conference, Dublin, September.

McGauran, Anne. 2005. *Plus Ca Change. .? Gender Mainstreaming of the Irish National Development Plan*. Studies in Public Policy. Dublin: The Policy Institute at Trinity College.

Meade, Rosie. 2005. We Hate it Here, Please Let Us Stay! Irish Social Partnership and the Community/Voluntary Sector's Conflicted Experiences of Recognition. *Critical Social Policy* 25 (3), 349–73.

Mullally, Siobhan. 2005 Debating Reproductive Rights in Ireland. *Human Rights Quarterly* 27 (1): 78–104.

National Economic and Social Forum. 2006. *Report No. 33, Creating a More Inclusive Labour Market*. Dublin: NESF Executive Summary, page xi and paragraphs 2.27 and 2.28.

NWCI. 2000. *Beijing + 5 Alternative Report for Ireland*. Dublin: NWCI.

———. 2004. The National Women's Council of Ireland Urges Women to Vote No in the Citizenship Referendum. Press Release 1 June 2004. Dublin: NWCI.

———. 2005a. *Submission by the National Women's Council of Ireland on the Irish Government's Discussion Document on Immigration and Residence in Ireland*. Dublin: NWCI.

———. 2005b. National Women's Council of Ireland Does Not Endorse New National Agreement. Press Release 6 March 2005.

———. 2005c. *An Accessible Childcare Model*. Dublin: NWCI.

———. 2007. *ENews Letter September 2007*. Dublin: NWCI.

O'Connor, Orla. 2005. *Building Working Relationships with Decision Makers*. Dublin: NWCI.

O' Dea, Willie. 2004. T.D. Minister of State Department of Justice, Equality and Law Reform. Address at the New Horizons for Gender Equality Conference. Limerick, Ireland, 6 May 2004.

O' Donoghue, Siobhan. 2004. *Migration: The Experience of Migrating to Ireland and the Challenge Facing Community Work*. www.cwc.ie/nws/artic.html. Accessed 10 March 2006.

O' Regan, Michael. 2006. Taoiseach Defends Child Benefit for Migrants. *The Irish Times*. 6 February 2006, 8.

Pillinger, Jane. 2006. *An Introduction to the Situation and Experience of Women Migrant Workers in Ireland*. Dublin: The Equality Authority.

Roth, Silke. 2004. One Step Forwards, One Step Backwards, One Step Forwards: The Impact of EU Policy on Gender Relations in Central and Eastern Europe. *Transitions* 46 (1), 15–28.

Thorogood, David and Karen Winqvist. 2003. *Women and Men Migrating to and from the European Union*. Statistics in Focus: Populations and Social Conditions (2) Eurostat, European Communities.

Yeates, Nicola 2006. Changing Places: Ireland in the International Division of Reproductive Labour. *Translocations: The Irish Migration, Race and Social Transformation Review*. http://www.imrstr.dcu.ie. Accessed 23 November 2006.

5

Spain at the Vanguard in European Gender Equality Policies

Celia Valiente

Introduction

In Spain, progressive measures at the central state level, such as an ambitious Act on Gender Violence, have been recently passed under a social democratic government formed in spring 2004, when the Spanish Socialist Workers' Party (Partido Socialista Obrero Español, PSOE) reached power.[1] In early 2007 other progressive gender equality measures were seriously considered, such as the approval of a comprehensive (Gender) Equality Act. In the first part of this chapter, I succinctly describe the main Spanish gender equality policies. How had the socialist government arrived at this point at the beginning of the twenty-first century, given the fact that, at least up to the 1970s, Spain was a backward country regarding gender equality? In the second part of this chapter, I argue that the European Union (EU) acted as a source of inspiration as well as resources for both politicians and the women's movement in the policy area of gender equality.[2] The influence of the EU took place in a favorable political and social context characterized by four factors: secularism and the (imperfect) separation of church and state; the high presence of women in civil society, and the increasing strength of the women's movement; the support of some demands of the feminist movement by the PSOE, and the partial convergence of the conservative People's Party (Partido Popular, PP) towards the positions on gender equality of the Socialist Party; and the policy impact of the main gender equality institution of the central state, the Women's Institute (Instituto de la Mujer, IM), which was created in 1983, one year after the Socialist Party first came to power.

Central State Gender Equality Policies

After the spring 2004 election, socialist Prime Minister José Luis Rodríguez Zapatero formed a government with an equal number of female and male ministers. One of the two vice-presidents was a woman: María Teresa Fernández de la Vega. She also happened to be a well-known feminist. The socialist government quickly initiated a series of proactive gender equality policies. These (partly or totally) coincided with demands advanced by the explicitly feminist branch of the women's movement (in what follows, "the feminist movement"). A highly ranked position on gender equality was created in the Ministry of Labor and Social Affairs: the General Secretariat on [Gender] Equality Policies (Secretaría General de Políticas de Igualdad). A prominent feminist was appointed to the position: Soledad Murillo de la Vega, an associate professor of sociology in the university with expertise on gender research. Her appointment was backed by most individuals and organizations of the feminist movement. In 2004, a comprehensive Act on Integral Protection Against Gender Violence was passed with the support of all parliamentary groups (Ley Orgánica 1/2004, de 28 de diciembre, de medidas de protección integral contra la violencia de género, hereafter the "Gender Violence Act"). It contained a full package of prevention, protection, and punishment of violence against women. One of the main innovations of this act was that the punishment of domestic violence is more strict when committed by men than by women. The fight against violence against women has been a priority and a unifying battle for the Spanish feminist movement in the last two decades. Since 2005, article 68 of the Civil Code mandates that both spouses perform household chores and caring tasks (although it is difficult to enforce this). The feminist movement has tirelessly argued that the participation of men in household and caring duties is a prerequisite for an equal society. A comprehensive act to promote the personal autonomy and care of dependent people was approved by parliament on 30 November 2006 (Ley de promoción de la autonomía personal y atención a las personas en situación de dependencia, hereafter "Dependency Act"). It established the universal right of dependent people to receive care partly or completely financed by the state. For decades, the feminist movement has denounced that dependent people were cared for mainly by female relatives on an unpaid basis. The feminist movement had demanded some state responsibility in the provision of this care.

In the past decades, part of the feminist movement had denounced that gender equality measures were a set of dispersed legal provisions, and recommended the adoption of a general equality act. The feminist movement in general fa-vored that the state forces private companies to be active in the pursuit of equal-ity between female and male workers, and that political parties adopt women's quotas. In fall 2006, several gender equality measures were prepared by the cabi-net or discussed in parliament. On 3 March 2006, the Council of Ministers ap-proved a bill of a Comprehensive Gender Equality Act (*Anteproyecto de Ley Orgánica de Igualdad entre Mujeres y Hombres*, hereafter "Gender Equality Act"), which made mandatory that all companies of more than 250 workers negotiate firm-level equality plans. In addition, the bill required a quota of 40 percent for women in all electoral lists. Furthermore, the bill increased the length of the period for working men who become fathers of days off work at full pay from two to eight days. The government was also working on the establishment of a fund to guarantee child support (*Fondo de garantía para los impagos de pensiones de divorcio*). In divorce cases, if the person legally obliged to pay child support fails to do so, the state will grant advance child support with the money from this fund (*El País* 18 March 2006, 17). Since the 1980s, the feminist movement had denounced that after many divorce cases delinquent fathers do not pay child support, and as a result, children and women suffered acute economic problems, if not plain poverty.

Gender equality was not only a target of policy making at the central state level, but also became a salient topic in political discourse. For instance, in spring 2005, Prime Minister José Luis Rodríguez Zapatero declared that gender equality was one of the priorities of his mandate, and that his government would not only attempt to change laws, but also lead a progressive public debate on the issue. He added that "the most developed, free and cultivated societies are those where there is equality between women and men" (*El País* 24 April 2005, 25).[3] On more concrete terms, in January 2006, he declared that two of his political priorities for 2006 were the Gender Equality Act and the Dependency Act (*El País* 11 January 2006, 15). After the approval by the cabinet of the bill of the Gender Equality Act, Minister of Labor and Social Affairs Jesús Caldera exultantly affirmed that the bill was the beginning of a "social revolution" (*El País* 5 March 2006, 54).

It is impossible to overestimate the sharp contrast between these socialist measures on gender equality and the policies towards women of predemocratic Spain. From the mid-1930s until 1975, Spain was governed by a right-wing au-thoritarian regime headed by General Francisco Franco that actively opposed the advancement of women's rights and status. The ideal family was a hierar-chical unit, and it was assumed that authority rested with the father, who was supposed to be its sole (or, at least, its main) supporter. Motherhood was defined not only as the main family duty of women, but also as women's main obliga-tion toward state and society. The role of mothering was perceived as incompat-ible with other activities, such as waged work. During the first Francoism (from the second part of the 1930s until the late 1950s to early 1960s), the state took measures to prevent women's labor outside the home. An example of this was the requirement that a married woman had to obtain her husband's permission before signing a labor contract and engaging in trade. Sex-segregated schools were the norm, and boys and girls not only attended different schools but also had different curricula. Divorce was abolished, and the selling and advertising of contraceptives was criminalized. Abortion was defined as a crime punished with prison. During the second Francoism (from the late 1950s-early 1960s to 1975), policy makers approved some liberalization measures related to women's status, such as the abolition of some obstacles regarding paid employment (for instance, marriage bars, or the prohibition to perform some professions in the field of law). Liberalization, however, did not take place regarding the regulation of sexuality and reproduction (Gallego Méndez 1983; Morcillo 2000; Nash 1991).

After 1975, policy makers began to dismantle the discriminatory legislation inherited from Franco's time and to promote women's rights and status. As explained below, part of the drive towards policy reform on gender equality was the desire to emulate EU member states and join the EU. The 1978 constitution explicitly states that women and men are equal before the law, and sex discrimination is prohibited. Due to space constraints, even a mere enumeration of the main gender equality policies in postauthoritarian Spain is an impossible task. I would like to illustrate this change with the following examples: The selling and advertising of contraceptives was decriminalized in 1978. Divorce for civil marriages was permitted in 1981. Whereas the Franco regime actively promoted sex-segregated schooling, the post-Franco governments encouraged girls and boys to go to school together. In 2007, this was the norm (with very few exceptions). A partial decriminalization of abortion took place in 1985. Since then, abortion has been a crime punishable by the Penal Code except on three grounds: when the woman had been raped, when pregnancy seriously endangered the physical and mental health of the mother, and when the fetus was deformed. However, in practice, the mental health clause was used as an (imperfect) proxy for abortion on demand (Blofield 2006, 92). As for childcare, since 1975 the main central state policy has been to supply an ever-increasing number of free educational preschool programs for children between the ages of three and five (mandatory schooling starts at six). In part as a result of this policy, in the academic year 2006/7, school attendance rates for three-, four-, and five-year-olds were comparatively high in Spain, at 96, 100, and 100 percent respectively (Ministerio de Educación y Ciencia 2006a, provisional data).[4] In respect to political representation, since the transition to democracy, the proportion of women in political decision-making positions did increase almost continuously. In the legislative term 2004–2007, the proportion of women among members of the lower chamber of parliament (the Congress of Deputies) was 36 percent. With this number, Spain was ahead of most EU member states, since the proportion of women in the lower chamber of parliament was higher only in Sweden (47 percent), Finland (38 percent), Denmark (37 percent), and the Netherlands (37 percent) (Interparliamentary Union 2006). The increased presence of women in political decision making in Spain has been caused mainly by women's quotas in left-wing political parties (Astelarra 2005, 272–73; Threlfall et al. 2005, 125, 148–49).

In sum, in postauthoritarian Spain, policy makers at the central state level were advocating gender equality policies in line with the policies of other EU member states. Some of these policies were advocated by a coalition of center-right parties—the Unión de Centro Democrático, which governed the country between 1977 and 1982. Although many gender equality policies were installed under the first period of social democratic government (1982–1996), some of them were sustained by conservative governments (1996–2004). Gender equality was firmly on the political agenda regardless of the ideological color of the party in office. Gender equality policy making received an additional push after the electoral victory of the Social Democratic Party in spring 2004.

I next argue that since the transition, the EU has been a positive force for gender equality policy making in Spain. During the last two or three decades, the EU has made some politicians more favorable to gender equality policies. The EU has also given opportunities for mobilization to activists of the women's movement. But the impact of the EU took place in a favorable domestic context characterized by four decisive features. First, the influence of the Catholic Church on politics and private mores declined severely since the transition. Second, the marked presence of women in civil society and the vibrancy of the women's movement meant that female Spaniards formed a women's public that politicians tended to keep in mind. Third, since the transition, the PSOE had backed some demands of the feminist movement due to the increasing mobilization of feminists within the party. Due to increasing electoral competition, since the 1990s, the Conservative Party had converged towards the Socialist Party regarding views on gender equality and actual policy making. Finally, since 1983 the Women's Institute has continuously demanded state interventions aiming at the erosion of gender hierarchies.

The European Union

Feminist scholarship has increasingly recognized the importance of the EU as a promoter of equal pay and equal treatment of working women and men of EU member states. EU gender equality directives and treaty provisions have set in motion a process of revision of discriminatory domestic legislation in some EU member states. As a result, some national laws became more egalitarian and can be used to fight effectively against discrimination in the labor market (Elman 1996; Hoskyns 1996; Liebert 2003).

As explained above, a traditional gender order (male breadwinner/female homemaker division of labor) was promoted by the right-wing authoritarian regime that governed Spain from the mid-1930s to 1975. In 1977, the first democratic elections were held, and Spain applied for EU membership. The Spanish central state adapted part of its legislation to the principle of equality between women and men in the labor market before its accession to the EU (1986). During all those years, both politicians and public opinion viewed the EU as a very positive point of reference. It was perceived as a group of economically developed and democratic member states to which Spain wanted to belong. The EU advocated to some degree equal opportunity for women and men in labor matters (see Wahl in this volume). In Spain, equality of people of both sexes before the law was identified as a leading principle of modern, Western, civilized, and democratic polities.

Legal reforms continued after 1986 in order to make working women and men equal before the law. In some cases, Spanish law included gender equality stipulations even before the adoption of EU directives. For example, the reversal of the burden of proof was established in Spain in 1989–1990[5] and at the EU level in 1997 (Burden of Proof Directive 97/80/EC). The EU sets only minimum criteria, to be improved by member states if they wish. In a number of relevant cases, Spanish legislation related to gender equality in labor matters has established provisions above the minimum level set by EU directives. This was especially so regarding pregnant workers' rights and parental leave (Lombardo 2004; Threlfall 1997; Valiente 2003c, 196–97).

The EU has served as a source of inspiration for policy makers to reform labor laws regarding gender equality. This has been especially the case for some politicians of the Conservative Party. The Socialist Party included a powerful lobby of feminist activists and leaders who endlessly demanded gender equality policies (see below). But the Conservative Party had no such lobby. Therefore, the pressure on conservative leaders to elaborate gender equality policies usually came from outside their party organization. Let me illustrate this point with the example of sexual harassment policy. Under socialist governments, sexual harassment perpetrated by superiors in the workplace was well established as a serious offence in labor law (1989) and penal law (1995). Contrary to expectations, the following conservative government not only did not abolish the measures on sexual harassment undertaken by the previous Socialist Party, but actually extended their scope. In 1999, unwanted sexual harassment perpetrated by co-workers and subordinates was explicitly prohibited by penal law. This 1999 reform reflected the change of position on sexual harassment of certain conservative policy makers. In the 1980s, the Conservative Party frontally opposed any regulation on sexual harassment. In the late 1990s, some conservative politicians accepted and even promoted a broad state regulation on sexual harassment that included unwanted sexual moves perpetrated by co-workers and subordinates. Such a change of views was due to EU influences. Some Spanish conservative policy makers had become increasingly aware that in other EU member states sexual harassment perpetrated by co-workers was already explicitly unlawful, and that this type of legal reform was strongly supported by conservative politicians in other countries (Threlfall et al. 2005, 85–90).[6]

The EU has also influenced the Spanish women's movement by providing various incentives for mobilization (for a similar case, see the chapter on Ireland by Cullen in this volume). The example of political representation is pertinent here. On 22 September 1990, the European Women's Lobby was established, which includes Europe-wide women's groups and women's umbrella organizations from each EU member state. The purpose of this lobby is to promote women's interests at the level of the EU (Hoskyns 1996, 185–86). The Spanish Association to Support the European Women's Lobby was founded in March 1993. It is an umbrella association of nationally based Spanish feminist groups, funded mainly with European money and with close ties to the Spanish Socialist Party. Feminists active in left-wing parties with parliamentary representation have increasingly mobilized through this association in the battle for higher numbers of women in political decision-making positions (Jenson and Valiente 2003).

Secularism and the (Imperfect) Separation of Church and State

Despite the strong influence of the Catholic Church in politics in the past, Spain belongs at least since the 1980s to the group of Western countries with secularized societies and polities. Regarding society, it is true that in 2006 the Catholic Church had an important presence in the education system: approximately one-third of children and youngsters enrolled in preschool, primary, and secondary education attend a center administered by the Catholic Church (Ministerio de Educación y Ciencia 2006a). The majority of adult Spaniards considered themselves Catholic (76.4 percent in October 2006).[7] Although the number of practicing Catholics was much lower than the number of self-declared Catholics, this is significant. In October 2006, 17 percent of self-declared Catholics or believers of other religions affirmed that they attend religious services (excluding social events such as weddings, first communions, or funerals) almost every Sunday or religious festivity, and around 2 percent attend on various days per week (Centro de Investigaciones Sociológicas 2006).

To suspect that the teachings of the Catholic Church influence the ideas and behaviors of the population is reasonable. Nevertheless, this is true only to a certain point. Those required to pay income tax (*Impuesto sobre la Renta de las Personas Físicas*, IRPF) had the option of giving 0.5 percent of their tax either to the Catholic Church or to other social causes, or to both, but in 2003, only 22 percent of IRPF tax payers chose the option of the Catholic Church (Ministerio de

Economía y Hacienda 2006).[8] Examples of disconnection between official Catholic doctrines and societal views and behaviors abound. The Catholic Church mandates that couples marry in the church. In the beginning of the twenty-first century, the acceptance of Catholic marriage was high in Spain, but not overwhelming. In 2002, civil marriages accounted for 30 percent of all marriages in Spain. In 2004, civil marriages outnumbered Catholic marriages in two regions: Catalonia and Balearic Islands (El País 24 November 2005, 27). Although the Catholic Church urges married women to have as many children as possible, in the beginning of the twenty-first century, Spain had one of the lowest fertility rates in the world. While the Catholic Church prohibits homosexual sex, in June 2004, four-fifths (79 percent) of the Spanish adult population agreed with the statement, "Homosexuality is a personal option as respectable as heterosexuality" (Centro de Investigaciones Sociológicas 2004). As José Casanova (1993, 118) rightly points out, "not only can the church no longer control the public morality of the Spaniards, it can no longer take for granted the control of the private morality of the Catholic faithful."

As for the political arena, since the transition to democracy the church had no large direct representation in the political space, because no Christian Democratic party or trade union exists (Casanova 1993). The separation of church and the Spanish state is reflected in the constitution. According to Article 16, Spain is a nondenominational state based on religious freedom. Nevertheless, this very same article also states that "public authorities will take in mind the religious beliefs of the Spanish society" (that is, Catholicism). Article 16 also refers to the desirability of the cooperation between the state and the Catholic Church and other denominations. The especial treatment to the Catholic Church by the state is mainly reflected in important state transfers, tax exemptions, and financial support to most Catholic schools, hospitals, centers of social action, and artistic patrimony. Thus the Spanish Catholic Church was not a self-supporting organization, but one that relied on state money for its economic survival. The Catholic Church accepted the principle of nonconfessionality of the Spanish state, and the constitutional regulation of state-church relations (Bedoya 2006; Casanova 1993, 117; Linz 1993, 35).

The Catholic Church did not agree with some laws regulating moral matters, such as the laws that legalized divorce (1981), liberalized abortion (1985), or permitted gay marriage (2005), but it did not make a big effort to revert them. Resistance by Catholics to these public policies has been more moderate in Spain than in other Western countries. The Catholic Church was not involved in the main political controversies of the country (with the possible exception of the nationalist question in the Basque country) and did not control the agenda of government, but certainly was not silent regarding the matters that the church considers important (education and moral issues such as abortion and sexuality, among others). The church did not explicitly support a political party and did not ask Catholics to vote for any given party. Nevertheless, the Catholic Church sometimes transmitted a sense of preference when speaking about its position regarding certain issues. At times, this coincided with the position of specific parties (Linz 1993, 32–48).[9]

Church-state relations in democratic and predemocratic Spain could not be more different. During the first Francoism, the church and the political regime supported each other. Catholicism was the official religion of the country. Freedom of worship was abolished. The state gave the church the prerogative of managing all matters regarding marriage and the separation of married couples. Catholic marriage was mandatory, with very few exceptions (Pérez-Díaz 1987). The state allowed the Catholic Church to control part of the education system—an important number of primary and secondary schools—but not most universities, which had been under state control at least since the mid-nineteenth century (McNair 1984, 18–19). In all primary and secondary schools, the state made religious teaching and religious practices mandatory, and education had to conform to the teachings of the Catholic Church. The church was given the right to inspect private and public centers (McNair 1984, 28–29). The state economically supported the Catholic Church, which was exempted from taxation. In turn, the church supported the authoritarian regime, provided it with legitimation, and declared the civil war (1936–1939) a crusade, that is, a fight, between supporters of Christianity (Franco's followers) and the unfaithful and immoral (the Republicans). Some of the administrative cadres of the Francoist state came from Catholic lay organizations such as the Asociación Católica Nacional de Propagandistas, and later the Opus Dei. Catholic hierarchies occupied a salient place in official governmental acts. State authorities ex officio attended religious ceremonies (Casanova 1993, 107–08; Linz 1993, 9–25).

In the second Francoism, a small part of the church distanced itself from the regime, self-criticized the position and actions of the church in the civil war, and even gave protection and support to political dissidents. Catholics became members of groups and parties of all ideological colors in opposition to the dictatorship. Due to this progressive distancing of a part of the church from the political regime, when Franco died in 1975 the church could align itself with other political and social forces in the building of a new democratic regime (Casanova 1993, 114–17; Linz 1993, 25–32).

Women in Civil Society and the Women's Movement

Women are increasingly present in organizations of civil society whether in women-only groups or in mixed associations. For example, on average, women outnumber men in the so-called third sector dedicated to social causes (Observatorio Ocupacional and INMARK Estudios y Estrategias 2000, 114–16, 129–31;

Pérez-Díaz and López Novo 2003, 214–17, 231–33, 241–42). The branch of the women's movement that is not explicitly feminist is formed by housewives' organizations, widows' associations, mothers' movements, and cultural and religious associations, among others. This branch is currently blooming in terms of number of members and degree of activity (Ortbals 2004; Radcliff 2002; Valiente 2003b). Thus, women now constitute a visible mass public that politicians often take in mind when calculating what policies they support or oppose.

As for the explicitly feminist branch of the women's movement, its first groups were set up in the late 1960s and early 1970s in a period of liberalization of the authoritarian political regime. Many of the first feminists were active in the opposition to the dictatorship, where they encountered illegal left-wing political parties and trade unions. These have been the (uneasy) allies of the feminist movement ever since (Jones 1997; Threlfall 1985).

The feminist movement has influenced gender equality policy making, mainly due to its imbrication with left-wing political parties. In the last three decades, many feminists mobilized within both feminist groups of civil society and left-wing political parties. When these reached power, some of their feminist activists and leaders occupied decision-making positions in the state. From these positions, they could advance claims on gender equality (see below) (Threlfall 1996; Threlfall et al. 2005).

The feminist movement has also intervened in the gender equality policy area, mobilizing public opinion in favor of the need to improve women's status. The case of abortion liberalization is useful to illustrate this point. In the 1970s and 1980s, the Spanish feminist movement was the only actor that systematically and endlessly demanded abortion liberalization. The feminist movement contributed to the creation of a climate of opinion in civil society favorable to the acceptance of abortion reform. Conducive climates of this type permit politicians to make decisions around very conflictual issues such as abortion (Sundman 1999; Trujillo Barbadillo 1999).

The Socialist and Conservative Parties on Gender Equality

Research on gender equality policy making in Western countries suggests that conservative parties facilitate the elaboration of gender equality policies to a significantly lower extent than social democratic parties (Bashevkin 1998; Lovenduski and Norris 1993, 1996; Lovenduski, Norris, and Burness 1994; among others). This is so at least for six reasons. In comparison with social democratic parties, conservative parties (1) tend to be less prone to establish policies in favor of disadvantaged groups of society, including affirmative action, in an attempt to achieve not only that people compete on the same terms, but also that citizens obtain the same results (Lovenduski, Norris, and Burness 1994, 612). (2)

Conservative parties advocate limited state interventions in economic as well as social affairs (Bosanquet 1994; Ruiz Jiménez 1997). (3) Conservative parties support a traditional agenda regarding both sexes (Lovenduski, Norris, and Burness 1994, 611, 630–31), and (4) are supposed to avoid policies that increase public spending.[10] (5) Feminist activism has been less intense within conservative parties. (6) Finally, the proportion of women (whether self-declared feminists or not) among the political elite (not among the rank and file) is usually lower in conservative than in social democratic parties, notwithstanding world-known conservative women leaders such as Condoleezza Rice, Angela Merkel, or Margaret Thatcher.

In Spain, since the transition, some PSOE women have made considerable efforts to force their party to adopt some of the demands of the feminist movement. That the voices of PSOE feminists could be heard was partly because they previously gained organizational status within the party. In 1976, a women's caucus, Woman and Socialism (Mujer y Socialismo), was formed in the PSOE and in 1981, a member of the caucus was elected to the PSOE's executive committee, with others following her in successive years. In December 1984, party leaders decided to institutionalize the women's caucus at the federal executive level, whereupon it became the women's secretariat. The feminists in the secretariat successfully added clauses involving women's issues to PSOE congress resolutions, electoral programs, and other documents. In Spain, at the central state level, both in general and with exceptions, the initiative on gender equality policy making has corresponded with the Socialist Party (Astelarra 2005; Threlfall et al. 2005; Verge 2006).

Studies on gender and politics in the Western part of the world have also acknowledged that conservative parties have at times responded to the demands of the women's movement (Lovenduski and Norris 1993, 6–7, 13; 1996, 9; Lovenduski, Norris, and Burness 1994, 611–12). Thus conservative parties have to a limited extent converged towards socialist parties. Women within conservative parties have pressed claims to be fairly treated as party members, activists, and leaders. Conservative parties have included women's issues in their agendas and made some efforts to present a higher number of female candidates in elections. Once in office, conservative parties have been more willing than in the past to appoint women to governing positions, establish some gender equality policies (especially those that do not contradict the free market logic), and set up or maintain gender equality institutions (see below). Nevertheless, the general conclusion of the literature on gender and politics in postindustrial societies is that parties matter and that social democratic parties are usually more active than conservative parties in the search for gender equality.

In Spain, since the early and mid-1990s, gender equality has increasingly become an area of electoral competition (Ruiz Jiménez 2006). If in the 1980s the Conservative Party paid little attention to the issue of inequalities between women and men, in the 1990s the Conservative Party was trying to convince the electorate that it could elaborate gender equality policy as the Socialist Party had done, or even better. This new political choice of the Conservative Party was reflected in a convergence of its discourses to the discourses elaborated by the Socialist Party in some policy areas, for instance, regarding women's waged employment (Ruiz Jiménez 1999), and in actual policy making once in office, for example, with respect to sexual harassment (Threlfall et al. 2005, 88–90) and childcare (Valiente 2003a).

Two factors are important here: chronology, and the order at which conservative and social democratic parties reach office (Ruiz Jiménez 2002). The Socialist Party was in power for fourteen years (1982–1996). This was a period long enough to set the agenda in government with respect to gender equality. Socialists were able to set targets, values, and staff in government departments and civil service (Astelarra 2005). Between 1996 and 2004, conservative governments preserved most existing gender equality policies established by preceding administrations. Perhaps dismantling existing programs requires too high an electoral cost for any party to pay. This is especially so in Spain, where society is quite secular and women actively participate in civil society (see above). The preservation of previous policies by the Conservative Party initiated a virtuous circle.[11] When the Socialist Party reached power again in spring 2004, it promised to put in place an ambitious electoral platform on gender equality. The PSOE tried to convince the electorate that it is still the vanguard regarding gender equality policy making.

Gender Equality Institutions

Institutions whose purpose is the advancement of women's rights and status have been established in all Western countries since the 1970s. These institutions are called women's policy machineries (or bureaucracies) or state feminist institutions (Stetson and Mazur 1995). Regarding the Spanish central state, the main state feminist institution, the Women's Institute (*Instituto de la Mujer*, IM) was established thanks to the efforts of feminists within the PSOE, many of whom were (or had been) members of feminist groups in civil society as well (Threlfall 1998).

The major IM objective is to promote policy initiatives for women. The IM is an administrative unit that was first attached to the Ministry of Culture and then moved to the Ministry of Social Affairs created in 1988.[12] In spite of its late establishment in comparison with feminist machineries in other Western countries, the IM is now comparable to those institutions in terms of personnel, budget, and the extent of its functions (Threlfall 1996, 124; 1998). The IM has its own director, staff (around 170 members), facilities, and independent budget. The staff and resources of the IM have constantly increased. In 2006, the IM had an annual budget of 26.25 million euros (*El País* 28 September 2005, 67).

Elsewhere (Valiente 2006), I have shown that between 1983 and 2003, the policy impact of the IM was high under two circumstances: when the issue under political discussion and negotiation was a priority for both the IM and the feminist movement, and when the policy area was open to the intervention of social and political actors different from the usual participants. Three other factors facilitated a high impact of the IM but were not strictly necessary: the cohesion of the feminist movement around certain demands, an IM leadership close to the feminist movement, and the left in power. The policy impact of the IM has also depended on the issue itself. The IM has advanced gender equality provisions in the policy area of political representation, violence against women, sexual harassment in the work place, and abortion. The policy impact of the IM has been modest but nonetheless relevant on prostitution, and negligible regarding job training, childcare, and unemployment protection (Threlfall et al. 2005, 81–124; Valiente 2006, 2003a).

Even if the impact of the IM on gender equality policy has been mixed, its impact has taken place continuously for more than two decades and under governments of different ideologies. The IM has provided all governments with ideas, demands, and expert knowledge on gender equality policy making.

Conclusion

In Spain, the current socialist government at the central state level has promoted progressive gender equality policies, such as a cabinet formed by an equal number of male and female ministers and a comprehensive Gender Violence Act. Other gender equality measures were seriously considered in 2007, such as a bill of an encompassing Gender Equality Act.

How has the current government arrived at this point, given the fact that thirty years ago Spain was a laggard regarding both gender equality and gender equality measures? In this paper, I have argued that since the transition, the EU has functioned as a positive background for gender equality policy making. But the influence of the EU has taken place in a conducive domestic environment due to the interplay of four societal and political factors in the last three decades: secularization and the (imperfect) separation of church and state, the growing presence of women in civil society, the increasing support of gender equality policy making by both the Socialist and (to a lesser extent) the Conservative Party, and the activities of gender equality institutions.

A deficit of implementation is the pending problem of Spanish central state policies on gender equality. For instance, a report by Amnesty International (2005) denounced that the Gender Violence Act has been put in practice with grave irregularities. This means that the state often failed to protect some victims, who were murdered by the perpetrators they accused. The inadequate application of policies in favor of women is a very serious problem that should not be underemphasized. However, the weak execution of gender equality measures did not invalidate the intrinsic worth of the measures themselves. Moreover, policies towards women were also badly implemented under Franco, but scholars unanimously disregard this fact while asserting that Francoist policies severely curtailed women's rights (Gallego Méndez 1983; Morcillo 2000; Nash 1991).

The acceptance of current central-state gender equality policies is widespread but not unanimous. Several judges lodged appeals to the Constitutional Court on the grounds that the Gender Violence Act is unconstitutional. The main employers' organization frontally opposed the Gender Equality Act and conceptualized it as a "death wound to social dialogue" (*El País* 4 March 2006, 1). A part of the feminist movement acknowledged the push towards gender equality given by the present socialist government, but criticized the conception of women and men inserted in these policies. According to these feminists, the government often portrays women as intrinsically weak and in permanent need of state protection, and men as inherently mean and needing state repression (*El País* 18 March 2006, 17).

Current Spanish gender equality measures have yet to produce societal change regarding enormous unsolved problems. For instance, in the month of August 2005 alone, seven women were killed by their spouses or partners (*El País* 30 August 2005, 29). In international assessments on gender equality by country, Spain does not still occupy a good position. According to the assessment made by the World Economic Forum (2005), Spain ranks at number twenty two among the thirty OECD countries regarding gender equality.[13] Given the marked gender inequalities that still characterize the Spanish society, the last thirty years of gender equality policy making, and the progressive features of the last gender equality measures, it is time to ask whether the solution to the problem of gender hierarchies lies in gender equality policies, in public policies in general, or in other realms.

Notes

1. In this chapter, the words "social democratic" and "socialist" are used as synonymous. Given space constraints, this chapter only deals with policies elaborated by the central state. For policies at the regional level, see Bustelo and Ortbals (2007).
2. In the past, the EU had other names. For the sake of brevity, only the EU is used in this chapter.
3. In this chapter, the translation from Spanish to English has been made by Celia Valiente.
4. In contrast, the proportion of Spanish children aged two or younger cared for in public or private centers was comparatively low: 4 percent for children younger than one year, 14 percent of children aged one year, and 28 percent for those two years old (academic year 2004/5: Ministerio de Educación y Ciencia 2006b). For more on work-family policies in EU member states, see the chapter by Morgan in this volume.
5. Basis 19.4 of Act 7/1989 of 12 April, and Article 96 of Royal-Decree Law 521/1990 of 27 April.

6. On the EU politics on sexual harassment, see the chapter by Zippel in this volume.

7. In the same opinion poll, 2 percent of the interviewed considered themselves believers of other religions, 13 percent not believers, 6 percent atheist and 2 percent did not answer.

8. Also in 2003, 32 percent of IRPF taxpayers chose the option "other social causes," 12 percent chose both options, and the remaining 34 percent chose none of the three.

9. on a contrasting case of a much less secularized polity, see the chapter on Poland by Regulska and Grabowska in this volume.

10. A mild variant of this agenda would emphasize that the family is the basic cell of the social fabric. Historically, the family has been the sphere where women dedicate more efforts than men. Some (or many) women may also want (or have to) work for wages. Nevertheless, society has to be organized to support family and caring tasks. The main family function of most men (economic provision) and most women (the management of the intimate sphere in combination or not with bread-winning) are different but complementary, and of equal worth for the development of society and its weakest members (children). Then, conservative governments would try to facilitate that women perform their family responsibilities. Conservative administrations would be less active in making the labor market an equally attractive and rewarding place for women and men.

11. The metaphor of the virtuous circle has been used by other analysts of gender and politics in Spain, including Verge (2006).

12. In 1996, the Ministry of Labor and Social Security and the Ministry of Social Affairs were merged into the Ministry of Labor and Social Affairs, upon which the IM depends.

13. This study measures the extent to which women have achieved full equality with men in five areas: economic participation, economic opportunity, political empowerment, educational attainment, and health and well-being.

References

Amnesty International. 2005. *España: Más allá del papel*. Madrid: Amnesty International.

Astelarra, Judith. 2005. *Veinte años de políticas de igualdad*. Madrid: Cátedra.

Bashevin, Sylvia. 1998. *Women on the Defensive: Living Through Conservative Times*. Chicago: University of Chicago Press.

Bedoya, Juan G. 2006. Las cuentas del catolicismo español. *El País*. 30 September, 43.

Blofield, Merike. 2006. *The Politics of Moral Sin: Abortion and Divorce in Spain, Chile and Argentina*. London and New York: Routledge.

Bosanquet, Nicholas. 1994. *After the New Right*. Chippenham, UK: Dartmouth.

Bustelo, María, and Candice D. Ortbals. 2007. The Evolution of Spanish State Feminism: A Fragmented Landscape. In *Changing State Feminism: Women's Policy Agencies Confront Shifting Institutional Terrain*, eds. Joyce Outshoorn and Johanna Kantola, 201–33. New York: Palgrave.

Casanova, José. 1993. Church, State, Nation, and Civil Society in Spain and Poland. In *The Political Dimensions of Religion*, ed. Said Amir Arjomand, 101–53. Albany, NY: State University of New York Press.

Centro de Investigaciones Sociológicas. 2004. Study Number 2,568, June. www.cis.es. Accessed 12 December 2006.

———. 2006. Study Number 2,657, October. www.cis.es. Accessed 12 December 2006.

El País 2005–2006.

Elman, R. Amy, ed. 1996. *Sexual Politics and the European Union: The New Feminist Challenge*. Providence, RI and Oxford: Berghahn.

Gallego Méndez, María T. 1983. *Mujer, falange y franquismo*. Madrid: Taurus.

Hoskyns, Catherine. 1996. *Integrating Gender: Women, Law and Politics in the European Union*. London: Verso.

Interparliamentary Union. 2006. Women in National Parliaments: Situation as of 31 October 2006. www.ipu.org. Accessed 12 December 2006.

Jenson, Jane, and Celia Valiente. 2003. Comparing Two Movements for Gender Parity: France and Spain. In *Women's Movements Facing the Reconfigured State*, eds. Lee Ann Banaszak, Karen Beckwith, and Dieter Rucht, 69–93. New York: Cambridge University Press.

Jones, Anny Brooksbank. 1997. *Women in Contemporary Spain*. Manchester, UK: Manchester University Press.

Liebert, Ulrike, ed. 2003. *Gendering Europeanisation*. Brussels: Peter Lang.

Linz, Juan José. 1993. Religión y política en España. In *Religión y sociedad en España*, eds. Rafael Díaz-Salazar, and Salvador Giner, 1–50. Madrid: Centro de Investigaciones Sociológicas.

Lombardo, Emanuela. 2004. *La europeización de la política española de igualdad de género*. Valencia: Tirant lo Blanch.

Lovenduski, Joni, and Pippa Norris. eds. 1993. *Gender and Party Politics*. London: Sage.

———. eds. 1996. *Women in Politics*. Oxford: Oxford University Press and The Hansard Society Series in Politics and Government.

Lovenduski, Joni, Pippa Norris, and Catriona Burness. 1994. The Party and Women. In *Conservative Century: The Conservative Party since 1900*, eds. Anthony Seldon and Stuart Ball, 611–35. Oxford: Oxford University Press.

McNair, John M. 1984. *Education for a Changing Spain*. Manchester, UK: Manchester University Press.

Ministerio de Economía y Hacienda. 2006. *Memoria de la administración tributaria 2004*. www.meh.es. Accessed 24 October 2006.

Ministerio de Educación y Ciencia. 2006a. *Datos y cifras, curso escolar 2006/2007*. www.mec.es. Accessed 24 October 2006.

———. 2006b. *Estadística de las enseñanzas no universitarias: Resultados detallados del curso 2004–2005*. www.mec.es. Accessed 24 October 2006.

Morcillo, Aurora G. 2000. *True Catholic Womanhood: Gender Ideology in Franco's Spain*. Dekalb, IL: Northern Illinois University Press.

Nash, Mary. 1991. Pronatalism and Motherhood in Franco's Spain. In *Maternity and Gender Policies: Women and the Rise of the European Welfare States, 1880s–1950s*, eds. Gisela Bock and Pat Thane, 160–77. London: Routledge.

Observatorio Ocupacional, and INMARK Estudios y Estrategias. 2000. *Las ONG's y las fundaciones y su contribución al empleo*. Madrid: Instituto Nacional de Empleo.

Ortbals, Candice D. 2004. Embedded Institutions, Activisms, and Discourses: Untangling the Intersections of Women's Civil Society and Women's Policy Agencies in Spain. Ph.D. dissertation. Indiana University.

Pérez-Díaz, Víctor. 1987. *El retorno de la sociedad civil*. Madrid: Instituto de Estudios Económicos.

Pérez-Díaz, Víctor, and Joaquín P. López Novo. 2003. *El tercer sector social en España*. Madrid: Ministerio de Trabajo y Asuntos Sociales.

Radcliff, Pamela. 2002. Citizenship and Housewives: The Problem of Female Citizenship in Spain's Transition to Democracy. *Journal of Social History* Fall: 77–100.

Ruiz Jiménez, Antonia María. 1997. Reshaping the Welfare State: New Right's Moral Arguments in Southern European Conservative Parties, the Spanish *Partido Popular*. Unpublished paper, Instituto Juan March.

———. 1999. Evolución y actitudes de AP-PP hacia la participación femenina en el mercado de trabajo: Discusión de algunas hipótesis explicativas. In *Género y ciudadanía: Revisiones desde el ámbito privado*, eds. Margarita Ortega, Cristina Sánchez, and Celia Valiente, 449–68. Madrid: Universidad Autónoma de Madrid.

———. 2002. *Mecanismos de cambio ideológico en introducción de políticas de género en partidos conservadores: El caso de AP-PP en España en perspectiva comparada.* Madrid: Instituto Juan March.

———. 2006. *De la necesidad, virtud: La transformación 'feminista' del Partido Popular en perspectiva comparada.* Madrid: Centro de Estudios Políticos y Constitucionales.

Stetson, Dorothy McBride and Amy G. Mazur, eds. 1995. *Comparative State Feminism.* Thousand Oaks, CA: Sage.

Sundman, Kerstin. 1999. *Between the Home and the Institutions: The Feminist Movement in Madrid, Spain.* Gothenburg, Sweden: Acta Universitatis Gothoburgensis.

Threlfall, Monica. 1985. The Women's Movement in Spain. *New Left Review* 151: 44–73.

———. 1996. Feminist Politics and Social Change in Spain. In *Mapping the Women's Movement: Feminist Politics and Social Transformation in the North*, ed. Monica Threlfall, 115–51. London: Verso.

———. 1997. Spain in a Social Europe: A Laggard or Compliant Member State? *South European Society & Politics* 2 (2): 1–33.

———. 1998. State Feminism or Party Feminism? Feminist Politics and the Spanish Institute of Women. *The European Journal of Women's Studies* 5 (1): 69–93.

Threlfall, Monica, Christine Cousins, and Celia Valiente. 2005. *Gendering Spanish Democracy.* London and New York: Routledge.

Trujillo Barbadillo, Gracia. 1999. El movimiento feminista como actor político en España: El caso de la aprobación de la Ley de despenalización del aborto de 1985. Paper presented at the Annual Meeting of the Spanish Association of Political Science and Public Administration, Granada, Spain.

Valiente, Celia. 2003a. Central State Child Care Policies in Postauthoritarian Spain: Implications for Gender and Carework Arrangements. *Gender & Society* 17 (2): 287–92.

———. 2003b. Mobilizing for Recognition and Redistribution on Behalf of Others? The Case of Mothers Against Drugs in Spain. In *Recognition Struggles and Social Movements: Contested Identities, Agency and Power*, ed. Barbara Hobson, 239–59. Cambridge: Cambridge University Press.

———. 2003c. Pushing for Equality Reforms: The European Union and Gender Discourse in Postauthoritarian Spain. In *Gendering Europeanisation*, ed. Ulrike Liebert, 187–222. Brussels: Peter Lang.

———. 2006. *El feminismo de Estado en España: El Instituto de la Mujer (1983–2003).* Valencia: Institut Universitari d'Estudis de la Dona of the Universitat de València.

Verge, Tania. 2006. Mujer y partidos políticos en España: Las estrategias de los partidos y su impacto institucional, 1978–2004. *Revista Española de Investigaciones Sociológicas.* 115: 165–96.

World Economic Forum. 2005. *Women's Empowerment: Measuring the Global Gender Gap.* Geneva: World Economic Forum.

6

From "Strange Sisters" to "Europe's Daughters"?

European Enlargement as a Chance for Women's Movements in East and West Germany

Ingrid Miethe

Due to Germany's specific history, the country's position in the European integration process is special, cast as it is in the middle between Eastern and Western Europe. Western Germany belongs to the very first founding members of the European Union. Eastern Germany, on the other hand, was until 1989 a fixture in the socialist block, and as a member country of the Warsaw treaty was firmly embedded in that system. Come German reunification, Eastern Germany automatically became a member of the European Union and East Germans "overnight" turned into Europeans. Many of the preparatory processes towards a European Union that other former Eastern block countries needed and were able to undergo in good time and speed—which involved getting acquainted with the new legal regulations, leading public debates on a political Europe, and especially mentally coming to grips with the unification process—could not take place in East Germany due to the speed at which reunification as such was pushed through.

Hence, it is hardly astonishing that the EU membership of East Germany was at first barely acknowledged. Much more important in contrast was the by no means simple and uncontroversial reunification process of the former two Germanys, a process that dominated public discourse in Germany itself for a long time. The EU's "first, indirect enlargement to the East," that of the accession of the former GDR to the Federal Republic of Germany and with it to the EU, was hardly defined as the accession of an Eastern European country to the EU, mostly due to the massive German domestic dynamics that took place in the accession process. The women's movements in Germany were no exception to the rule.

As this paper will show in detail, the specifics of the German domestic developments will always stand out when discussing the European unification process. On the other hand, the "premature" EU membership of East Germany also anticipated processes that may depict the chances, as well as the dangers, of the EU's eastward enlargement that has in the meantime begun to take place.

Before entering the discussion, however, it is necessary to define "Eastern Europe" and "Western Europe" as they are used in this chapter. The separation into Eastern and Western Europe (which is also reflected in the term *eastward enlargement of the EU*) refers to the political division of Europe as a result of the Cold War. In this classification of Eastern and Western that forms the basis of the EU perspective, large parts of Western Europe, Northern Europe (for example, the Scandinavian countries), and large areas of Southern Europe belong to the West. In this regard, East Germany (the GDR) belonged to the East (Breckner, Kalekin-Fishmann, and Miethe 2000). The continuation of this political East-West separation from the Cold War era becomes obvious when countries like Poland or Hungary, which are historically considered Western (for example, as part of the Habsburg Monarchy), are today part of the eastward enlargement of the EU. Therefore, when using the term *Eastern Europe* or *eastward enlargement*, it is important to emphasize that the subject is exclusively the political confederation of the former socialist countries, with the exception of East Germany. In this process, East Germany takes a position between "East" and "West." On the one hand, the GDR shares the experience of state feminism with today's Eastern European membership states, as until 1989 it formed an unquestioned part of the policies of the socialist Eastern Block countries. Many aspects of the East German women's stance have to be analyzed with this background firmly in mind. For example, these traditions affected the founding of the East-West-European Women's Network (Ost-West-Europäisches Frauen-Netzwerk, OWEN, www.owen-frauennetzwerk.de). Founded by East German women who had been active in the independent women's movement of the GDR before 1989, this network aims at supporting especially grassroots women's initiatives and local self-help groups by implementing education and networking projects.

On the other hand, due to German reunification, the development that has taken place in Germany since 1989 is very different from that of other former socialist countries. Thus, an issue like "traffic in women" that is central to feminist concern in Eastern European countries hardly features on East German feminist agenda at all, though it is addressed on the agenda of the (West) German women's movement. Instead, the question of "Western" domination is more heavily discussed here than in the other former Eastern Bloc countries. However, after German reunification in October 1990, East Germany automatically became part of West Germany (the Federal Republic of Germany) and as a result became part of the EU in a kind of "piggyback procedure." Due to this special situation in Germany, the processes of European unification and of the reunification of the two Germanys may not be looked at separately. Not only were a large part of the economic decisions in East Germany taken with a European perspective in mind, but also the EU right from the start granted subsidies for structural development to East Germany. Although the reunification of East and West Germany thus may not be separated from the integration process into the EU that took place at the same time, many East Germans hardly took note of the latter, at least not until the late 1990s (see Toepel and Weise 2000).

This lack of conscious perusal of the importance of the European Union might stem not the least from the fact that the EU membership of the East German *Bundesländer* was not publicly discussed, but was seen simply as the natural consequence of German reunification. Public interest and especially East German interest continued to concentrate on this reunification process of East and West Germany for a long time.

Nor was the women's movement any exception. As this paper will show in more detail, the women's debates in Germany were dominated until the 1990s by the debates between East and West German women. A European perspective remained as marginal within this discourse as the controversy about the relationship between "white" German feminists and feminists of other ethnic backgrounds. Equally, ideas of "Western" and "Eastern" feminism were unduly generalized in the shadow of this polarized German domestic East-West perspective. The differences between "Western" and "Eastern" feminism were in consequence mostly ignored for many years. In order to comprehend the current positions of East or West German women regarding the EU, the discourse that took place under the setup of German reunification therefore needs to be addressed first.

An analysis of the Western European countries reveals a significant gap between Scandinavian and other states with regard to their expectations of the EU. Although women in the Eastern countries had an advantage over Western countries in many of these areas—such as employment or political representation—some Western feminists either viewed the eastward enlargement of the EU with skepticism or chose to completely ignore it (see contributions in Miethe and Roth 2003). They feared a backlash in the feminist movement, since Eastern European women were seen as conservative and rejected feminism, perceiving it as "Western" (e.g., Abels and Bongert 1998). The initial euroscepticism of Scandinavian countries promoted the anxiety that the male breadwinner model of dominant EU countries such as Germany would have an impact on Swedish society. In fact, developments have pointed to the exact opposite: the Swedish model has been exported and is increasingly and successfully taking hold in other European countries (see Hellgren and Hobson in this volume). Thus the process of unifying Europe has so far been a rather inconsistent process influenced by a broad spectrum of feminist politics and feminist attitudes, and has at times led to quite unexpected results (see Roth and Miethe 2003).

What are the experiences that have in recent years led to a shift in feminist attitudes in Eastern and Western Germany? And what changes does the eastward enlargement of the EU offer? In this chapter I address these questions focusing on women's movements in East and West Germany. Since 1989, an extremely controversial and sometimes unproductive discussion took place between East and West German women in unified Germany. I argue that the process of European unification presents an opportunity to renegotiate this relationship on an equal footing, and to make progress in developing standpoints on both sides. To this extent, European unification, and the eastward enlargement of the EU in particular, have triggered a new phase in the relationship between East and West German women's movements.

In this chapter, I describe four different phases in the development of the relationship between East and West German women's movements since 1989, each characterized by different treatment of East-West issues at the individual, academic, and public levels. I designate these four phases as follows:

1. Expectations of equality turn to experiences of difference

2. Research and project boom and "Western" dominance

3. Withdrawal on both sides and partly integration

4. Renegotiation in a European context

In keeping with the emphasis of my own research, I will focus closely on the academic sphere. Because women's movements are now strongly concentrated in this institutionalized framework, the academic focus represents a certain current within these movements (see Hark 2005). Since East-West issues were primarily in the public spotlight during the time immediately after 1989, the academic discourse cannot always be separated from the interpretations and debates from and about East and West that have taken place in the media and on the political stage. A certain overlap of the public and academic levels in the descriptions of the individual phases that follow is therefore unavoidable, and, as I suggest, symptomatic of the process itself.

We do not yet have the necessary historical distance from the events, and there is as yet no generation that has not been involved in the East-West-debate; all of the actors are themselves in one way or another part of the process being analyzed. Therefore, I will base my description of the phases on scientific research as well as on my own observations and experiences, having followed the discussion right from the beginning. I made my observations mainly in Berlin, a city with a unique experience of East-West collision that no other place in the world could claim. Having grown up and lived in the GDR up to the age of twenty-eight, I continued to study and work in West Berlin after 1989 and since 2002 have been living and teaching in West Germany. Thus, my personal history has taught me to "commute," if you like, between the East and the West. At least I have had plenty of opportunities to be able to (and to be forced to) study both sides well.

First Phase: Expectations of Equality Turn to Experiences of Difference (1989–1993)

This phase was characterized by a relatively rapid and open interaction between East and West Germany. The expectations of the time were expressed in the slogan "What belongs together shall now grow together" (*Nun wächst zusammen, was zusammen gehört*). This expectation was not only shared by a majority of the population in East and West Germany but the sentiment was adopted especially by the women's movement. Was it not inevitable that women's solidarity would transcend the borders of political systems and add its sisterly support to the assumption of brotherly closeness between the two German states?

Expectations were great on both sides, and so were the disappointments as the actual people encountered often did not meet those expectations. This is not surprising. One reason for the disappointment lay in the fact that, although the notion of a shared language suggested a common culture, the vast majority of the population on either side knew little about the other Germany. The first East-West women's conferences were held shortly after the GDR had ceased to exist, yet instead of celebrating nationwide sisterhood, the women attendees merely brought to light the significant differences between Eastern and Western feminist women, and their difficulties in understanding one another. Catchwords about "strange" or "unequal sisters" or "stepsisters" circulated (see Rosenberg 1995). Women's East-West political conferences started out with efforts to reach understanding after all, and often ended—in spite of good intentions on both sides—more or less in an exchange of accusations about Western "know-it-alls" and Eastern "complainers." The expectations of equality thus turned to experiences of difference.

The positions presented in this chapter form a summary of the research results of various empirical studies (for an overview see Miethe 2006). Those results are depicted in a generalized way. However, beyond this depiction it should not be forgotten that there are social groups in both the East and West German societies who would not totally agree with the opinions presented in this paper. The positions presented actually form a rather dominant and influential discourse, though, within the respective Eastern or Western society. The dispute between Eastern and Western feminists arose over issues such as these:

1. *Motherhood:* Eastern feminists, who were generally mothers, felt that the compatibility of career and family was a central issue. But for West German feminists who generally had no children and in many cases had consciously chosen not to have any in order to pursue a professional career, it was not an important issue.

2. *Men:* While many Eastern feminists often advocated cooperating with men to advance feminist interests, Western feminists regarded the idea with extreme skepticism or even disapproval.

3. *Employment:* East German women valued paid labor and the financial independence from their husbands that it offered as an essential, if not the most important, prerequisite for their own emancipation, and kept the notion throughout the process of transformation. In contrast, the West German feminist movement for a long time marginalized the question.

4. *Abortion rights:* To Western feminists, the right to abortion formed one of the central issues that initiated the women's movement in West Germany and provided the identification to a cause, while in the GDR and most other former socialist countries the right to abortion was long a fact and therefore was no longer an issue for feminist activities or discussions.

5. *The state:* Whereas Eastern feminists held the opinion that the state has a responsibility to address women's issues, Western feminists tended to take the position that women's issues need to be addressed at the grassroots level, some of them even refusing to accept state funding.

6. *Theory:* Western feminists attached crucial importance to symbolic power, such as that of gendered language, and to the formulation of feminist theory. For Eastern feminists, such discussions carried negative connotations per se, and were considered no better than ideology and dogmatism.

7. *Private-public distinction:* Western feminism focused on the definition of the private sphere as a place of violence and moved it to the public-political stage. In contrast, women in socialist societies cherished the private sphere as protecting them from public (i.e., the state's) authority (though violence at home was known there, too), even though a "public" in the sense of Western democracies did not exist. Western feminist concepts that were normally based on an interaction between a private and a public sphere as is indicative of Western democratic societies therefore were repeatedly rebuked as difficult to adopt by Eastern European experiences.

8. *Dominance*: For a long time, Western feminists understood their society as patriarchal, and assumed that the key dividing line was that between men and women. Eastern feminists on the other hand felt that the dominance of West over East was often more crucial than—or at least equivalent with—the dominance of one sex by the other. Thus Western women, much to their disappointment, were seen primarily not as women, but as representatives of the dominant West German society.

In particular the last issue overshadowed many East-West debates, and continued to do so in the following years. Repeated attempts by East German women to address the unequal distribution of power between East and West were only reluctantly acknowledged by West German women, if at all. Because at the time there were hardly any scientific studies available, the discussions in this phase were on a very personal level, based on subjective experiences and biographies.

Second Phase: The Research and Project Boom and "Western" Dominance (1992–1997)

The principal characteristic of the second phase was an enormous boom in research on topics concerning East Germany (see Berth and Brähler 2000; Aleksander 2005). Although this boom began immediately after 1989, its results were not outwardly visible until about 1994–95, due to the time required to conduct research and publish results. New empirical studies led to a certain tendency toward scientific objectivity in the discussions, since now the participants were able to refer to concrete findings rather than to personal opinions and states of mind.

However, this phase also saw an increasing displacement of East German academics, male and female (see Adler 1997; Bimmler 1997). East German academics were forced out of higher education en masse from 1992 on. At colleges and universities in East Berlin, for example, 60 percent of all East German academic staff had been replaced by West Germans by the end of 1992. This replacement of the elite took place in very different ways in the various disciplines and departments, and was without a doubt necessary to a certain extent in order to remove old SED[1] cadres. Indeed, the process was initially welcomed by many East Germans for this reason. It very soon became apparent, however, that the displacement was not being used to integrate politically unobjectionable East Germans in the new elite, but rather—especially in the social sciences—to establish an exclusive West German dominance. East German men were subjected to this process of displacement just as East German women were. As a result, it is not surprising that East German women academics were initially reluctant to perceive this process as having a gendered structure. Nor is it surprising that the few

West German women involved were viewed by East Germans as acting in much the same way as their male colleagues (see Petruschka 1994, 33f.).

The result of this process of displacement is apparent in a representative study on the elite replacement in Germany, which found that the proportion of East Germans among the academic elite in united Germany had fallen to 7 percent by 1995 (Bürklin and Rebenstorf 1997, 67). Compared with the proportions of the East and West German populations, this means that East Germans have a three times smaller chance of advancing to elite academic positions than West Germans (Miethe 2002, 53). Moreover, this structural problem is always linked with the question of who has power to define the terms of discourse in a united Germany: this power increasingly shifted away from Easterners. Although both sides were still engaged in the discourse, "the East" often acted from a more defensive position, not least because Western concepts and ideas were applied to the East with relatively little thought.

"The West" increasingly became the unquestioned norm; "the East" became the deviation from the norm, and required interpretation. Thus a so-called culture of dominance developed in Germany between the Eastern and the Western part of the country (Rommelspacher 1995; Miethe 2002, 2005). Culture of dominance is not a conscious process—neither on the part of the dominant group, nor on the part of those discriminated against. But, as Rommelspacher (1995, 186) points out, "The person's self-image is decisively marked by his or her position in the power structure of society as a whole. Powerlessness is also expressed in the denial of an identity that adequately expresses one's own experiences and life context. . . . The denial of identity is thus a characteristic of cultural dominance." Even more than fifteen years after reunification, speaking of *Germany* still implies addressing *West* Germany. This is also evident in the one-sided orientation of research. Thus, German reunification was not at all taken as an opportunity to examine and question Western *and* Eastern premises and assumptions, much less their interdependencies (Braun 2000). Rather, the object of new research was simply "the East."

The problem of West German dominance in the discourses between East and West German women was, however, not reduced to academia. In East Germany, women's projects abounded in the period of the early to the mid-1990s, and this was one movement sector that expanded most. The women's movement, like any popular movement, is difficult to put into numbers. Rucht et al. (1997, 82) estimate that the number of women's projects increased from about 28 groups in 1989 to some 123 groups in 1993 in the four different (eastern) German cities they investigated (Berlin, Leipzig, Halle, and Dresden). The largest feminist protagonist, the Independent Women's Association (Unabhängige Frauenverband, UFV) founded in 1989, lost its central role in the movement and became just one project of many (see Hampele 2000). The women's initiatives and projects that were formed from the early 1990s on took on topics that were central to the West

German debate, too—for example, violence against women, self-help initiatives, health, child-raising, women's history, as well as feminism. Despite discussing similar topics, the East German projects nevertheless always also addressed specifics. For example, the question of the compatibility of having a family and working, or the various options of re-entering working life have until today taken more space in the discussion among East German women, and women's projects themselves often contain opportunities for (paid) work. The women's initiatives and projects obtained a significant proportion of their resources through job creation measures in eastern Germany, which were funded by the government as a means to combat the rapidly rising unemployment following the collapse of the socialist state and the introduction of the market economy. The fact that they form a segment of the job market therefore characterizes the structures of the women's projects to a much greater extent than in western Germany. Many women earned their living in such projects as long as the public funds were available (until about 1994). At the same time many women's institutes and projects in western Germany were closed, creating a situation of competition for scarce resources, which, understandably, does not further a closer association between eastern and western feminists (see Miethe and Ulrich-Hampele 2001, 29ff).

In summary, we can assess this phase as one marked by a new tendency toward objectivity in dialogue between East and West, thanks to the ability to draw on empirical studies, and at the same time as one in which the dominance of the West German side was institutionalized, and so made manifest. The encompassing and diverse women's projects that developed in this period led on the one hand to feminist concerns being discussed more widely in public and to a stronger institutionalization of the East German women's movement. On the other hand, the competition between women's projects in the East and in the West grew as public means continued to shrink.

Third Phase: Withdrawal on Both Sides and Partly Integration (1997–2002)

This phase is characterized by stagnating public and academic interest in East-West issues, which was replaced by "globalization." This silence was to some extent predictable, because—in the academic context, for example, and primarily in the humanities and social sciences—East German women had been reduced to such small numbers that many conferences and seminars were overwhelmingly Western, and East German objections were very unlikely.

In contrast, the range of feminist projects was comparatively more diverse. On the one hand there were many projects that had been initiated by West German women; on the other hand a number of East German projects had been established independently, too. Here we have to note, however, that many women's initiatives, projects, and publications evaded the simple label of "Western" or "Eastern," since their personnel and range of concerns included both. This applies most of all to East Berlin, where the mixture is the strongest due to the closeness to West Berlin. Most often, however, women from the western side of the city work in women's projects of women's houses in East Berlin. Only in single cases may we observe the opposite movement of East German women to the western side (see Miethe and Ulrich-Hampele 2001, 28). It is then especially within Berlin that an increasing process of integration may be determined. Integration very strongly means, though, an adjustment of the East to West German conditions—which is nothing unusual, as today real life in East Germany is determined by West German ways. A debate on the movement's own East German past and on an independent East German female identity has become the exception to the rule.

When looking at the structure of the projects that have been established in this period in all of Germany, it becomes clear that the differences between the East and the West are more and more diluted with respect to the quantitative existence of women's projects. Moreover, one can determine a north-south divide in East as well as West Germany, in the sense that women's projects are scarcer in the conservative, family-oriented *Länder* where the Christian Democratic Party is the governing majority party than in the *Länder* governed by the Social Democrats. The farther south we go, the fewer women's projects we find. The eastern states conform to this pattern as well (see Miethe 2002, 48ff). The figures support the statement that East Germans are neither more nor less feminist than West Germans. But, since East Germany constitutes only 20 percent of the total population of unified Germany, the East German projects are always in the minority compared with West German projects. However, this means that East German women and projects will always be a minority in the discussion taking place at the national level in Germany, both quantitatively and structurally.

At the same time, however, it was hard to overlook the fact that the East-West discourse itself had reached an impasse. The arguments and positions were clear, and no real progress toward reconciliation had been made. Equally hard to overlook was a certain ritualization of the victim's role on the Eastern side. Although it had been absolutely necessary for Easterners in the first phase of the encounter with the West to refer to their own life histories and disappointments—simply in order to understand the extent of their differences—they could have assumed some awareness of this situation by the mid-1990s at the latest. The continuing reference by East Germans to their biographical involvement became increasingly unproductive. In this situation Western women had almost no chance of getting it right in the eyes of East German women. If they tried to address East German interests, they were accused of interference and exercising dominance; if they withdrew, they were accused of ignoring East German problems. The discourse between Eastern and Western women had gradually come to a dead end.

It was deadlocked, and yielded few new insights. Women in East and West became increasingly aware that instead of homogeneity, the common goal must be a conscious and productive way of dealing with their differences. However, both sides were quite at a loss to imagine how that might be achieved. As a result, both sides increasingly withdrew to themselves.

Of course there continued to be working contacts and personal friendships among East and West, and these may even have grown in numbers; but they were also characterized by a certain caution. The potential faux pas were well known and carefully sidestepped. However, women also avoided addressing differences that arose. Even this silence, though, was "unequally distributed" as Esther Hoffmann (1995, 51) pointed out. In the West it did "not by far reach the existential format" as it did in the East.

Such a phase of retreat can be the prerequisite for a very productive process. However, this requires that in retreat, the phase serves to reassure one's own attitudes in order to renew the process of approaching a discourse with the other side on the basis of the existing distribution of power. However if the silence endures and the East-West issue is simply filed away, this will mean especially for the subordinate East German side that their concerns will continue to be excluded from the unified German agenda for discussions, while the West German side can move on "unconcerned" and unfettered to determine their own agenda.

Sabine Hark's recent book (2005), which claims to constitute a "history of discourse of feminism," is one to confirm the anxiety of the above-mentioned exclusion. In it, Hark points out that German feminist theory—which automatically implies *West German* feminist theory—has after 1989 to the largest extent been influenced by Judith Butler's book *Gender Trouble*. There is no mention of any influence of the East-West dialogue of attitudes and discourse, neither the East German-West German nor the Eastern European-Western European ones, neither does the intercultural discourse (e.g., between black women and white women) feature in Hark's book as having had any major impact on German feminist theory. This book therefore contributes mainly to canonizing a rather biased, though probably still dominant, West German feminist theoretical discourse that ignores its own hegemony against discriminated-against groups. Turning away from the East-West-German confrontations slowly gives way to the option of viewing the wider European perspective, an aspect that has long been neglected in the German discourse.

Fourth Phase: Renegotiation in a European Context (since 2002)

The beginning of the fourth phase coincides with the introduction of the Euro in 2002, which brought the process of European unification much more strongly into the public consciousness than ever before. The eastward enlargement of the EU has now extended this process of European unification to countries once ruled by state socialism, such as Hungary, Poland, and the Czech Republic. As a result, it offers an opportunity to see the German unification from a broader point of view, and puts old East-West dichotomies into a new perspective (see Roth and Miethe 2003). These new perspectives offer a chance to renegotiate the stale debate between East and West Germany. Three different developments further this opportunity:

1. East and West German experiences can be compared and contrasted with other European countries.

From a European point of view, it becomes apparent that many positions that were termed "East German" in the German East-West discussion—for example, the compatibility of family and career or the responsibility of the state to address women's issues—are not specifically "Eastern" at all, but are held in other Western European countries, such as Sweden, as well (see Hellgren and Hobson in this volume). And at the same time, many of the positions that had previously inflamed the debate between East and West German women appear on the European scale as merely West German characteristics, and not typical of "Western" feminism as a whole.

One example of the changing feminist values in a European context is the issue of the compatibility of family and career. In spite of an undeniably high rate of unemployment among East German women, East-West comparisons show again and again that East German women continue to place a high value on their working life (Statistisches Bundesamt 2004, 503). Yet the ability to pursue an occupation is tied to the availability of childcare, which is neither sufficiently provided in West Germany, nor compatible with the West German notion of motherhood. This discrepancy between Eastern and Western women in years past has been repeatedly discussed as an East-West German difference. Yet in the European context we see that the East German concept of combining motherhood and a career, with recourse to publicly organized childcare, is not at all a uniquely East German position, but one that is favored and enjoyed by women elsewhere in Western Europe—as in France and the Scandinavian countries, for example. In addition, European unification has initiated further feminist policies such as gender mainstreaming. Unlike affirmative action and singling out women's issues, gender mainstreaming means the improvement and development of gender balance in all policies at all levels, by the actors normally involved in policy making, and "openly taking into account at the planning stage their possible effect on the respective situation of men and women" (see Commission of the European Union 2000, 5). Concerning the evaluation of gender mainstreaming, a rather controversial discussion has sprung up, especially from an Eastern European and Eastern German perspective. The idea is put into practice with varying results in different states (see Roth 2006). In particular, the discussion is rather complex as to whether the experiences made under state socialism and the processes of transformation that followed further or hinder the introduction of gender mainstreaming. Discussing the Hungarian case, Noemi Kakucs and Andrea Pető (in this volume) put forward the argument that it is exactly the strong orientation of gender mainstreaming towards a working life that provokes an immediate association with the state feminism of the socialist period, which results in the tendency to reject the idea. In addition, the demand linked to gender mainstreaming of changing the traditional role of men presents a clear change of direction even for the former state socialist societies, as even they did not amend the classic gender roles and stereotypes (Einhorn 1993). Thus, there is no final answer to the question of how important gender mainstreaming is in Eastern Germany. In any case, this new development has led to a discourse on an issue in the whole of Germany, where East German women have the advantage of a previous experience of state-enforced women's politics.

Thus the broadening of narrow East and West German horizons in the European context gradually dissolves unproductive dichotomies, and reinforces the position of East German women by reducing and qualifying West German dominance. This makes it more likely that the two sides will be able to resume the discourse on a more equal footing.

2. Generational change accompanies social change and vice versa.

The process of renegotiation in the European context is also supported by two developments within Germany. For one, a new generation of East Germans has grown up since 1989. This means a new generation of East German feminist academics has taken its place, relatively unobtrusively at first—a generation who has undergone most or all of their academic socialization in a united Germany. Women of this generation, for whom the end of the GDR was an opportunity, are perfectly familiar with the Western (and often international) discourse and do not consider themselves outsiders like their older East German colleagues do (see Stenger 1998). Hence they are less susceptible to assumptions of a more "advanced West," and less biographically vulnerable. This generation, quite familiar with Western standards, is at the same time able to look back on East German socialization and experience, and so contributes not only a new self-confidence, but also a new vantage point to the debate. Indeed, the dichotomy of "East" and "West" is gradually dissolving, not least due to the coming of age of a generation who have undergone most of their socialization in a united Germany, who remember East or West Germany only as part of their childhood, and who sometimes have difficulty in identifying themselves with one or the other (see Simon et al. 2000). As women's studies have shown, the deconstruction of categories can pave the way for new discussions and perspectives that can carry the dialog forward.

Another German development that supports the process of renegotiation is one that can no longer be ignored: the fact that the processes of transformation have finally reached West Germany as well, and are beginning—although slowly and subtly—to change Western assumptions. Such transformations are due not only to German reunification, but in equal measure to the process of European unification. For example, there are recent developments in family policy in Germany, such as the government's decision in September 2006 to implement the so-called *Elterngeld* (parents' benefits) (www.elterngeld.net). In addition, public discourse in Germany increasingly puts the compatibility of having a family and having a job against the traditional model of a (paternal) sole earner. A more positive view on public childcare goes hand in hand with this development.

It is ironic (to say the least), and perhaps historic justice, that such new family policies are developed and implemented by a woman chancellor and her government and by a woman minister of family affairs, both of whom are members of exactly that conservative and family-oriented Christian Democratic Party that over long years promoted as only option the (paternal) sole earner model and knew how to prevent any modern alternatives.

These new developments in Germany may be fully explained only with the European unification process in mind, within which the backwards change of (West) German women with respect to compatible family life and working life stands out negatively and is negatively exposed to the norms of gender mainstreaming. Even though the recent developments lean directly on the Scandinavian model, they nevertheless present discussions and positions that are closer to East German women's life experience, in their continuous attempts of making a family and a job compatible, than to the West German phase model of a succession of a job and a family leading to an exclusion of women from the labor market that had long been propagated as dominant. For this reason, we can expect the changes taking place today in the western German states to have a destabilizing effect on positions and attitudes there. Furthermore, the dissolution of Western assumptions is a necessary condition in order to advance the dialog between East and West.

3. The European enlargement into Eastern Europe opens the possibility to renegotiate feminist terms.

Furthermore, this process is reinforced by the eastward enlargement of the EU. The acceptance of several formerly state-socialist countries into the EU means that the EU membership now includes people from countries with whom East Germans share forty years of history. This common root of state socialism may very well be the reason for the more positive outlook that the East German population confesses in view of the eastward expansion of the EU, in contrast to the more negative opinion in the West (Toepel and Weise 2000, 191).

In contrast to all other Eastern Bloc countries, a non-state-organized feminist movement was in place in the GDR. For this reason a strong and publicly visible women's organization, the UFV, could be formed with extraordinary speed during the period of change around reunification (Hampele 2000; Miethe and Ulrich-Hampele 2001). Certain differences to other Eastern Bloc countries are the result. For example, an East German feminist identity emerged prior to 1989—on the one hand inspired through West German feminism (for example through literature or personal encounters), and on the other hand transferred originally and independently from western discussion on their own situation. Therefore, while the Eastern European side only today expresses the hope that EU enlargement might strengthen the cause of a feminist identity in the former state-socialist countries (Pető 2003), the process towards a feminist identity had begun in the GDR even before reunification with West Germany and therefore indirectly even before any EU membership.

However, East Germany before 1989 is only understandable in the context of Eastern Europe. because the GDR's membership in the Eastern Bloc brought with it not only political, but also cultural ties. Not surprisingly, many political positions similar to those described as typical for East Germans are also found among Eastern European women. Hence the eastward enlargement of the EU strengthened East German women's interests. This does not mean that these positions automatically can or must be reflected in their original form in EU policy. But it does improve the extremely unequal position that East German women have faced up to now in dealing with their West German counterparts. Political positions held by a larger group have a better chance of being noticed and discussed at all than those held by a smaller group.

The EU enlargement once more put issues on the public agenda that had long fallen victim to general silence in the discourse between Eastern and Western Germany, and thus opened a chance to discuss the issues in a wider context. The skepticism remains that even in this wider context the chances to promote independent Eastern European ideas in the discourse will remain as futile as it proved to be in the framework of German reunification. So Joanna Regulska (2001, 88) pointed out that "the relationship between states rarely are seen as of equal power." More often these relationships are characterized as asymmetrical and uneven, strong states dominating weaker states. According to Regulska (2001, 93), due to the fact that the gender discourse within the EU has always been connected to the economic sphere and the market, the new EU members will be shaped by these inequalities.

In her discussion of the issue, Peggy Watson (2000) points out that the transfer of EU policies to the accession countries assumes that gender identities and interests in the East and the West are the same. "The history of EU gender policy has been closely related to the rise of second-wave feminism in the West" (Watson 2000, 381). These opinions can be carried over to the situation in Eastern Europe only to a limited extent, as the basic concept of public versus private, for example, as well as the priority ranking of a working life or of the newly formed dominant ranking of the category of "class" are insufficient to grasp the situation in the former state-socialist societies. But EU policy, which disregards the characteristics of the former state socialist countries, "risks not only ineffectiveness, but a loss of EU credibility in its eastward move" (Watson 2000, 381).

Thus, the process of EU eastward enlargement does not present itself as a process involving two equal partners, similar to the process taking place in Germany after reunification. Rather, the process is shaped by hierarchy and dominance. This is where the feminist movements in East and West face the enormous challenge to establish independent feminist political structures despite the dominance of state-imposed structures. This opposition to the patriarchal state structures of power is actually equal to the self-image of the movement. However, so far the self-image has not been put into feminist practice with confidence:

> The more successful it [Western feminism] it becomes, the more it is hegemonically oriented. The more women establish themselves, the more they also participate in the dominant value system, which excludes women and men from discriminated-against groups. Autonomy in the sense of self-determination always includes the determination of others. If these others belong to a discriminated-against group, the probability is high that autonomy will coincide with the oppression of others. This means that it is no longer enough for feminists to look ahead in their fight for emancipation and to concentrate on the oppression which they are fighting. Rather, they must also look back, in order to see whom they are leaving behind." (Rommelspacher 1999, 63)

The process of European unification therefore opens the doors in both directions. On the one hand, the process of European unification presents an opportunity to renegotiate on an equal footing the extremely controversial and sometimes unproductive debate that has taken place in unified Germany since 1989 among Eastern and Western women, and to make new progress in the development of positions on both sides. As can be observed in the increasing number of transnational women's networks and co-operations, the EU is indeed increasing women's activities in Europe, even beyond former East-West borders. The eastward enlargement of the EU therefore offers the opportunity for both sides to break down polarities created during Cold War period. For women's movements in Europe, this means that there is a real opportunity today to revive the high level of internationalization of the women's movement that existed at the end of the nineteenth and the beginning of the twentieth century and had disappeared to a great extent (at least in Europe) due to the Cold War (see Ferree 2004). From this perspective, the eastward enlargement of the EU is not only a regional process, but an aspect of women's increasing global cooperation.

On the other hand, there is the danger of exactly repeating the process of marginalizing the subordinate side on the European level that hampered the efforts on the East-West German level. To prevent or at least minimize this process requires a high degree of reflection on both the "dominant" as well as on the "nondominant" side. In the end, the experiences of the East-West German unification process provide only *one* example for the interaction taking place between groups of different hierarchical power, be it on an individual, state, or international level where the relation of influence is reproduced consciously or subconsciously again and again. The feminist movement, too, falls prey to these dynamics, the more so the less the dynamics are reflected and acknowledged.

Up to now, the European Union has been an open-ended project, and it is difficult to predict how it will develop. However, we have seen so far that this development leads to the dissolution of standpoints and attitudes that had appeared quite entrenched on both the Eastern and Western sides. What the concrete results of this process will be remains to be seen. Even today, however, we can anticipate that future developments in women's policy will not be framed in terms of East and West, and that changes will occur on all sides. And ultimately the question must be raised whether it isn't time to examine the content of the term *feminism* itself, and to rethink it from a broadened point of view.

Notes

1. SED stands for Sozialistische Einheitspartei Deutschlands, the Socialist Party in the GDR.

References

Abels, Gabriele and Elisabeth Bongert. 1998. Quo vadis Europa? Einleitung: Stand und Perspektiven feministischer Europaforschung. *Femina Politica* 7 (2): 9–18.

Adler, Helga. 1997. Gleichstellungspolitik. Ein nachgeordnetes Problem im Umstrukturierungsprozeß ostdeutscher Hochschulen? In *Wissenschaft als Arbeit—Arbeit als Wissenschaft*, eds. Sabine Lang and Birgit Sauer, 67–74. Frankfurt/New York: Campus.

Aleksander, Karin. 2005. *Frauen und Geschlechterverhältnisse in der DDR und in den neuen Bundesländern. Bibliographie von DDR- und BRD-Publikationen ab 1989*. Berlin: Trafo-Verlag.

Berth, Hendrik, and Elmar Brähler. 2000. *Zehn Jahre deutsche Einheit. Eine Bibliographie*. Berlin: Verlag für Wissenschaft und Forschung.

Bimmler, Marion. 1997. Die Situation von Wissenschaftlerinnen in außeruniversitären Forschungseinrichtungen in den neuen Bundesländern. In *Wissenschaft als Arbeit—Arbeit als Wissenschaft*, eds. Sabine Lang and Birgit Sauer, 174–87. Frankfurt/New York: Campus.

Braun, Anneliese. 2000. Ost-West-Kontakte der eher (noch) seltenen Art. Feministische Denkweisen als Klammer und als Überlebenshilfe. *Beiträge zur feministischen Theorie und Praxis* 23 (54): 23–36.

Breckner, Roswitha, Devorah Kalekin-Fischmann, and Ingrid Miethe. 2000. The Construction of Experience, Action and Change in the East. In *Biographies and the Division of Europe*, eds. Roswitha Breckner, Devorah Kalekin-Fischmann, and Ingrid Miethe, 7–20. Opladen, Germany: Leske + Budrich.

Bürklin, Wilhelm and Hilke Rebenstorf. 1997. *Eliten in Deutschland: Rekrutierung und Interpretation*. Opladen, Germany: Leske + Budrich.

Einhorn, Barbara. 1993. *Cinderella Goes to Market. Citizenship, Gender and Women's Movements in East Central Europe*. London, New York: Verso.

EU Commission. 2000. Commission of the European Communities. Equal Opportunities for Women and Men in the European Union 1999. {COM 2000}. Brussels, 8 March 2000.

Ferree, Myra Marx. 2004. "Global denken, lokal handeln!": Deutscher und amerikanischer Feminismus im Weltmaßstab. In *Geschlechterkonstruktionen in Ost und West*, eds. Ingrid Miethe, Claudia Kajatin, and Jana Pohl, 299–324. Münster: LIT-Verlag.

Hampele Ulrich, Anne. 2000. *Der Unabhängige Frauenverband. Ein frauenpolitisches Experiment im deutschen Vereinigungsprozeß*. Berlin: Berliner Debatte Initial.

Hark, Sabine. 2005. *Dissidente Partizipation. Eine Diskursgeschichte des Feminismus*. Frankfurt am Main: Suhrkamp.

Hoffmann, Esther. 1995. "Wenn zwei das Gleiche lesen". Eine Rezeptionsanalyse. In *Spiegelbilder. Was Ost- und Westdeutsche übereinander erzählen*, ed. Ludwig-Uhland-Institut für Empirische Kulturwissenschaft, 25–52. Tübingen: Tübinger Verlag für Volkskunde e.V.

Miethe, Ingrid. 2002. Women's Movements in Unified Germany: Experiences and Expectations of East German Women. In *Feminist Movements in a Globalization World: German and American Perspectives*, eds. Silke Roth and Sara Lennox, 43–59. AICGS Humanities Volume 11, Washington DC: AICGS.

———. 2005. Dominanz und Differenz. Verständigungsprozesse zwischen feministischen Akteurinnen aus Ost- und Westdeutschland. In *Irritation Ostdeutschland. Geschlechterverhältnisse in Deutschland 13 Jahre nach der Wende*, eds. Eva Schäfer, Ina Dietzsch, Petra Drauschke, Iris Peinl, and Virginia Penrose, 218–234. Münster, Germany: Westphälisches Dampfboot.

———. 2006. Eine Frage der Perspektive . . . Ostdeutsche Frauenbewegungen in der Theoriediskussion Sozialer Bewegunge. In *Das Jahrhundert des Feminismus. Streifzüge durch nationale und internationale Bewegungen und Theorien*, eds. Anja Weckwert and Ulla Wischermann, 61–75. Frankfurt: Ulrike Helmer Verlag.

Miethe, Ingrid, and Silke Roth, eds. 2003. *Europas Töchter. Traditionen, Erwartungen und Strategien von Frauenbewegungen in Europa*. Opladen, Germany: Leske + Budrich.

Miethe, Ingrid and Anne Ulrich-Hampele. 2001. Preference for Informal Democracy—the East(ern) German case. In *Pink, Purple, Green: Women's Religious, Environmental, and Gay/Lesbian Movements in Central Europe Today*, ed. Helena Flam, 23–32. New York: Columbia University Press.

Pető, Andrea. 2003. "Angebot ohne Nachfrage" Ungarische Frauen als Bürgerinnen eines EU-Beitrittslandes. In *Europas Töchter. Traditionen, Erwartungen und Strategien von Frauenbewegungen in Europa*, eds. Ingrid Miethe and Silke Roth, 183–202. Opladen. Germany: Leske + Budrich.

Petruschka, Gisela. 1994. Ost- und Westwissenschaftlerinnen im kritischen Vergleich. *Utopie Kreativ* 43 (4): 31–43.

Regulska, Joanna. 2001. Gendered Integration of Europe: New Boundaries of Exclusion. In *Gender in Transition in Eastern and Central Europe. Proceedings*, eds. Gabriele Jähnert, Jana Gorisch, Daphne Hahn, Hildegard Maria Nickel, Iris Peinl, and Katrin Schäfgen, 84–96. Berlin: Trafo-Verlag.

Rommelspacher, Birgit. 1995. *Dominanzkultur: Texte zu Fremdheit und Macht*. Berlin: Orlanda Frauenverlag.

———. 1999. Right Wing "Feminism": A Challenge to Feminism as an Emancipatory Movement. In *Women, Citizenship and Difference*, eds. Nira Yuval-Davis and Pnina Werbner, 54–64. London/New York: Zed Books.

Rosenberg, Dorothy. 1995. Stepsisters: On the Difficulties of German-German Feminist Cooperation. In *Communication in Eastern Europe: The Role of History, Culture and Media in Contemporary
Conflicts*, ed. Fred Casmir, 81–109. Mahwah, NJ: Lawrence Erlbaum Associates Publishers.

Roth, Silke. 2006. Sisterhood and Solidarity? Organizing for Gender Issues and Women's Equality in
the European Union. Paper presented at the Gender, Citizenship and Participation Conference,
23–24 March 2005 at the London School of Economics.

Roth, Silke, and Ingrid Miethe. 2003. Die EU als Chance und Herausforderung für Frauenbewegungen Einleitung. In *Europas Töchter. Traditionen, Erwartungen und Strategien von Frauenbewegungen
in Europa*, eds. Ingrid Miethe and Silke Roth, 9–20. Opladen, Germany: Leske + Budrich.

Rucht, Dieter, Barbara Blattert, and Dieter Rink. 1997. *Soziale Bewegungen auf dem Weg zur Institu-
tionalisierung? Zum Strukturwandel 'alternativer' Gruppen in beiden Teilen Deutschlands*. Frankfurt am
Main: Campus.

Simon, Jana, Frank Rothe, and Wiete Andrasch, ed. 2000. *Das Buch der Unterschiede. Warum die
Einheit keine ist*. Berlin: Aufbau Verlag.

Statistisches Bundesamt, ed. 2004. *Datenreport 2004. Zahlen und Fakten über die Bundesrepublik
Deutschland*. Bonn: Bundeszentrale.

Stenger, Horst. 1998. "Deshalb müssen wir uns fremd bleiben". Fremdheitserfahrungen ostdeutscher
Wissenschaftler. In *Die Herausforderung durch das Fremde*, ed. Herfried Münkler, 305–400. Berlin:
Akademie-Verlag.

Toepel, Kathleen, and Christian Weise. 2000. Die Integration Ostdeutschlands in die Europäische
Union: eine Erfolgsgeschichte? *Vierteljahreszeitschrift zur Wirtschaftsforschung*, 69 (2): 178–93.
http://www.diw.de/deutsch/produkte/publikationen/vierteljahrshefte/docs/papers/v_00_2_4.pdf.

Watson, Peggy. 2000. Politics, Policy and Identity: EU Eastern Enlargement and East-West Differences. *Journal of European Public Policy* 7 (3): 369–84.

7

WILL IT MAKE A DIFFERENCE?

EU Enlargement and Women's Public Discourse in Poland

Joanna Regulska and Magda Grabowska

In this chapter, we examine how the accession process affected the abilities of Polish women and feminist NGOs to mobilize and organize collective responses when confronted with both new possibilities and new threats. We argue that the process of the eastern enlargement, the years of the Polish government's anti-women stance (albeit, of varying strength depending on the political orientation of the regime in power), but also certain ambiguity of the European Union (EU) toward the full support of women's rights in the accession countries, have all contributed to a stronger women's collective agency and their ability to engage politically. At the same time, however, the ultimate power to shape institutional standards and public discourse on women's position and status continues to rest with the national institutions that determine the degree to which women's agendas are recognized and women's rights are respected by the state.

We begin by drawing from different bodies of scholarship to emphasize the role of women's collective agency and that of space and scale in transforming and creating new political subjects. We place this discussion within the contexts of the debates on European integration and the resulting new power relations between the EU and member states. We also acknowledge the emergence of the women's movement as a site of knowledge production, and adopt Star and Griesemer's (1989) concept of the *boundary object* in order to demonstrate how women's groups engage in knowledge-based communication strategies to become active political agents. In the latter part of this work, based on research conducted, we examine how Polish women's nongovernmental organizations (NGOs) construct new political spaces of empowerment, and claim their political subjecthood in response to the new opportunities and challenges provided by the EU eastern enlargement and generated by the Polish state.[1]

Women's Collective Agency, Transnational Activism, and European Integration

The rapid growth of NGOs, networks, alliances, and formal and informal groups run by women and for women indicates the increased focus on women's collective agency and on women's efforts to redefine the meaning of the political (Alvarez 2000; Desai 2005; Ghodsee 2004). These groups are seen as the new entry points that have expanded the political space from which political actions can originate and through which access to policy decision making can be attained across geographical scales (Keck and Sikkink 1998; Pudrovska and Ferree 2004; Regulska 2000). Indeed women's NGOs have gained the ability to influence policy making, as exemplified by successful lobbying efforts to include women's rights issues into the mainstream of the United Nations institutional structures (Fried 1994) or to amend the 1976 EU Equal Treatment Directive (Zippel 2004). Feminist scholars have repeatedly argued that women's agency is critical for social change to emerge (Siim and Marques-Pereira 2002) and that the mere existence of laws and institutions without agents to utilize them is insufficient for political action to take place. In the context of the EU, Hoskyns explicitly pointed out that women's collective mobilization in the 1970s was critical for "the expansion of the EC level women's policy" (Hoskyns 1996, 97).[2]

Parallel to feminist scholarship's greater engagement within the transnational context, geographers have increasingly focused their attention on the ways through which scale is produced (Herod and Wright 2002; Marston, Paul Jones III, and Woodward 2005; Swyngedouw 2000). While initial materialist approaches saw scales as fixed, nested levels and hierarchies connected with the process of capital accumulation, the so-called cultural turn resulted in the need to focus on localism, specificity, and diversity as well as the inclusion of experiences, reality, ideology, culture, and social reproduction. The shift towards the relational approach to scale included an emphasis on global and local connections, questioned the privileging of the global, and focused on the use of networks as a way to expand scale horizontally and destabilize fixity. It also focused on social relations as an element of scale, and emphasized the politics of scale (Howitt 2003; Massey 2004; Merrill 2004). This paper builds on these conceptualizations and suggests that the analysis of women's roles in shaping public discourse has to encompass the recognition of the spatiality of their actions as the critical aspect of women's political subjecthood.

In this context, scale is seen as a web of diverse spaces, flexible and fluctuating, which are characterized by porous boundaries that permit constant overlapping and interactions between people, institutions, and ideas, but can have a distinctive geographical focus (supranational, local, or national). Women's groups engage in the production of new scalar arrangements and strategies when they interact with the UN, the EU, or other global or local institutions. Through these engagements women build new partnerships, alliances, and networks; they gain new knowledge and skills and produce actions that have political meaning. These forms of interactions include, but are not limited to, attending regional and international gatherings; forming new local, transnational, and/or regional advocacy groups or gathering new data and resources; and subsequently, bringing them "home." This process of moving across scale facilitates women's political mobilization locally as well as transnationally, and affords the possibility to bypass the obstructive national state institutions so groups can pursue their agendas (for different explanations of this phenomenon see Keck and Sikkink 1998; Zippel 2004). In short, through what we call *the process of jumping scale*, women produce new political spaces and knowledge that is critical to the formation of their political agency.

These processes also have to be located within the framework of the competing debates on European integration and on the ways in which national policies are subject to the European Union's influence. The ongoing discussions on the merits of intergovernmentalist and institutionalist approaches have been augmented by the additions of the studies of collaborative networks, the significance of national cultures, and formal and informal rules (Walters and Haahr 2005). Thus the values, beliefs, and cultural practices, as well as the national culture and traditions are seen as equally critical to the understanding of how EU policies are ultimately produced. The process of negotiations and bargaining is then molded through the plurality of experiences represented by the multiplicity of actors—states, markets, EU institutions, but also citizens and especially social groups that have been historically excluded.

The most recent case of the EU enlargement has generated further shifts and major challenges for the EU's relations with the states and has altered power relationships (Berger and Moutos 2004; and see also in this volume contributions by Křížková and Hašková, and Kakucs and Pető). As most of the new member states are recently re-established democracies, they struggle with internal conflicts between social groups. Thus, they often do not represent cohesive political positions in their relations with the EU. Conflicted political, social, and economic forces within the nation-states could potentially translate into disordered relations between the EU and nation-states, where different social groups will reach out to the EU level and bypass the national state (Marks and Steenbergen 2004). Further, as a result of the recent enlargement and the admission of countries with very different political traditions, the EU policy-making process will have to evolve (Berger and Moutos 2004).

In this context, we aim to explore to what degree EU gender discourses and EU-generated gender focus policies have affected the actions of national state institutions in Poland and implicated women's political mobilization: How have women's groups responded to these new opportunities and challenges created by the EU and the Polish state? We argue that these new cartographies of power relationships have opened up spaces for Polish feminists and women's groups to be influenced by the EU institutions and their practices. Yet, despite the EU's pressures for change, national institutions not only have retained, but also visibly strengthened their power and their ability to forge patriarchal discourses within the nation-state boundaries—a point made by several contributors to this volume, especially by Roth, Hobson and Hellgren, as well as Morgan.

Transposing and Producing New Knowledge: The Boundary Object Concept

With the impending enlargement of the EU, the task for women's groups in Poland was to acquire, transport, and create new knowledge and information about the EU that would address women's concerns. With the progression of the accession negotiations, most avenues were opened by new legal measures. Yet, legal measures alone are insufficient to achieve desired changes in practice. Ellina (2003) showed the significance of the policy-making context and of the role that social partners played in the process of introducing, in the EU, a variety of gender policies. Woodward (2001) pointed to the need to build and increase gender expertise in order to advance the implementation of gender mainstreaming, but also to the need to enhance strategic capacities of women's groups to intervene. Liebert (2002) focused on the material incentives and the knowledge-based inducements, perceiving both as critical tools to supplement legal measures. She argued that the "knowledge-based communication strategies promise an alternative to legal compliance" (255). For her, knowledge-based communication constitutes "exchanges between national and regional decision-makers and organisations of civil society, such as women's organisations or trade unions" (254). Zippel echoes these arguments by showing that transnational expertise in particular represents a significant recourse, influencing not only actors' actions, but also solutions proposed by policy makers (Zippel 2004, 59).

To explain how women's groups in Poland engaged in the "translation" of the EU's history of gender-related policy making and how they made this knowledge available to a wider audience, we draw from the *boundary objects* concept introduced by Star and Griesemer (1989), which serve as an anchor or a bridge that facilitates and mediates between different social worlds. Their primary interest is in understanding how different actors with different viewpoints, located in different social worlds, can communicate across boundaries in order to contribute to a common goal. In their view, boundary objects can take numerous and different forms and therefore usually several systems of boundary objects operate. Boundary objects show flexibility as they are "plastic enough to adapt to local needs and the constraints of the several parties employing them, yet robust enough to maintain a common identity across sites" (1989, 393); they have different meanings for different people, but they also contain recognizable elements for those occupying other social worlds.

In our work, such a boundary object or medium is represented by *Kalendarium* (Calendar of Events), the regular, monthly publication of the Organization of Women's Initiatives (OŚKa)[3] in Warsaw, which was published between 1997 and 2005. OŚKa, as a national information center for women's organizations in Poland, served as a platform for exchange of ideas and information and as a place of meetings, seminars, and conferences where diverse groups of women and feminists met. Over the years OŚKa engaged in multiscale lobbying and mobilizing activities. We see *Kalendarium* as a knowledge-based communication strategy that has been created and used by women for women, and has been employed as a tool for political empowerment.[4] The information contained in *Kalendarium* was collected in two ways: organizations submitted information by fax or email directly to OŚKa, or staff members collected data, monthly, by calling all the women's groups that were registered in OŚKa's database (about five hundred). We have analyzed the contents of *Kalendarium* starting with the first issue in 1997 through those published in 2004. This period is of special interest for this research—given the high intensity of the EU negotiations with Poland and Poland's subsequent membership in the EU, we expect this time to be a highly formative period for women's political agency.

In addition, we draw on over one hundred interviews conducted during the collaborative Polish-Czech project (see note two). These narratives shed light on the formation process of women's political agency within the context of EU accession in Poland and the Czech Republic. In this paper we report the Polish portion of our findings. (Some of the findings from the Czech part of the study are reported in the chapter by Křížková and Hašková).

The Emergence of Women's Collective Agency in the Context of the EU Accession

Based on the analysis of *Kalendarium* (1997–2004) and collected narratives, we distinguish three phases of women's and feminist NGOs' engagement in the translation and production of knowledge about EU gender discourses during the accession period. Several contributors to this volume point to similar progressions in other countries, arguing that in order to understand the EU's impact on women, there is a need to distinguish between an accession period and a membership stage. They also pointed out that the enlargement process was not uniform and characterized by several stages (see Miethe and also Valiente). Our analysis not only reinforces this point, but also maintains that such a distinction needs to be made also when considering the accession period.

The three periods recognized through our analysis are: 1) *Introducing:* January 1997–September 1999; 2) *Informing:* October 1999–December 2001; and 3) *Engaging and Creating Partnerships:* January 2002–December 2004. While there are numerous ways to construct such distinctive periods, we were primarily guided by the changing intensity of Polish women's NGOs' responses to the progress of EU-Poland negotiations and Poland's subsequent admission to the EU, as well as to the noticeable shifts in state institutions' attitudes towards women's political subjecthood and gender equality in general. This point was underscored by Roth in the introduction to this volume, when she pointed out that the EU dismissal of the importance of gender concerns, while weak during negotiations, are especially not visible after the EU eastern enlargement.

Introducing: January 1997–September 1999

On 5 April 1994, Poland filed an application for membership in the European Union, and the process of harmonizing Polish law to the *acquis communautaire* began. Nevertheless, formal negotiations were not initiated until 1998, and negotiations on Chapter 13 ("Social Policy and Employment," the only place where gender concerns were located) did not start until 1999. It is clear that gender was marginalized from the beginning, because the application for membership in the EU—a rather complex and thorough document—did not mention women or make any reference to gender or gender equality (Mizielińska 2003).

For women, the preparation for EU membership began in 1996 when the Polish Labor Code of 1974 began to be reviewed and adjusted to European policy on equal opportunity in the workplace, in anticipation of the upcoming EU negotiations. Parallel to the EU negotiations, in 1997, after the Beijing conference[5], increased attention was focused on institutional mechanisms. This led to the establishment of the *Forum* of co-operation between the Office of the Governmental Plenipotentiary for Family and Women's Affairs and women's NGOs in Poland. *Forum* created a platform through which women's NGOs had input into the reviews of proposed changes in the Labor Code, thereby having the opportunity to provide legal opinions during this process.

While from the beginning the Polish government acknowledged that Poland did not meet EU equality standards, during the subsequent years it became clear that it was not too eager to introduce deeper changes. Rather, it did just the minimum of what was required. With the change to a mostly right-wing government in the fall of 1997, the attitudes of state officials became even more conservative. The new government's strong pro-family stand was behind the governmental decision to change the name of the Plenipotentiary for Family and Women's Affairs to the Plenipotentiary for Family Affairs, as well as the refusal to establish the Plenipotentiary for Equal Status of Women and Men, the title preferred by the EU (Mizielińska 2003).

What do we know about this period and women's strategies to become informed political subjects? Women's groups were aware of their growing power and visibility, and were the most mobilized social movement sector in Poland at that time. Women's NGOs hoped that the EU would bring significant changes to Polish equal opportunity law, but they had a very vague idea about what exactly EU accession would mean for women. An activist who at the time of the interview was leading an organization focusing on improving women's position in the labor market explained:

> We expected that something would happen, since we knew that in the EU NGOs have very different status, a different position vis-à-vis the state. We knew that they were not on the margins and that their voice was important. We also started to participate in various international events, where this voice was treated as important, [but] when I first heard about EU I had the feeling that I knew nothing (NPW2).[6]

Indeed, until 1997 there were few recognizable activities related to the EU on the part of women's and feminist groups. *Kalendarium* did not yet exist and even if there were some activities, they were conducted locally without connections to national events or other groups. The failure of Polish women's NGOs to enter negotiations and engage with the EU discourse on women and gender was parallel to the government's refusal to include NGOs in the negotiation process, and with the EU institutions being uninterested in cooperation with women's organizations in the candidate countries. The leader of a women's NGO that focuses on women's education recalled: "I don't have a feeling that we joined the negotiation process in the early stage. It happened without our participation, without our knowledge" (NPW8).

Women's NGOs wanted, however, to collaborate with women's groups from member states as they were hoping for supranational women's networks to become channels for contacts with EU institutions. The head of a reproductive rights organization reflected: "The need to cooperate came from us first, I mean from Polish NGOs. Earlier on we realized that women from the EU and aspiring member countries should cooperate, but they [EU women] were not ready yet. They thought that all laws were only for women from the EU. And then, probably for financial reasons, the openness from their side came" (NPW7). Yet, there was clearly a certain degree of mistrust and reluctance about what such cooperation might bring (see also Roth's introduction to this volume). What brought change was, among other factors, the EU requirement that groups from member states who wished to focus their activities on women's concerns in applicant countries had to have a partner from these countries. This combination of EU requirements with clear financial incentives created partnerships that led in many cases to effective collaborations across borders.

The analysis of the *Kalendarium* published during 1997–99 shows that at least ten women's organizations reported EU-related activities, with each of them organizing at least one or more events as described below. The first information regarding the EU and women appeared by the middle of 1997, when the first meetings about EU accession were organized. The first collective political actions that explicitly mentioned the accession process took place in December 1997, at which time letter writing to parliament and the prime minister was used as a lobbying mechanism (*Kalendarium* 1997, 13–14). Conferences (ten) and seminars/workshops (ten) emerged as the two main tools for collective political actions. These gatherings focused on the introduction of the European Union and discussions about different sets of rights protected by the EU Directives (29 percent of the entries). Introducing the meaning of the EU economic policies for women and explaining the basic facts about the accession process were the next two most important themes (21 percent each). The EU policies towards equality and equal treatment were initially of lower interest (17 percent) and only later did they emerge as a priority. Questioning what role women's and feminist NGOs should and could play vis-à-vis the EU represented the fourth distinguishable category (12 percent) (*Kalendarium* 1997–1999).

This sequence of topics and their appearance reflects the process of the "translation" of EU gender discourses. While many groups and their members were eager to gain new knowledge about the EU, this desire was nevertheless strongly shaped by the legacies of the past and the already visible negative consequences of the transformation period. Although women's rights were imposed on Polish women during the socialist period, some were also rapidly taken away after 1989, when the neoliberal economic regime was installed (e.g., women lost their reproductive and many of their social and economic rights). Women began to worry about losing their rights again, and became aware that nothing could be taken for granted: institutionally imposed, top-down rights could be easily dismantled and lost. The still existing mistrust of state institutions, a legacy of the past, overshadowed the possibility that the introduction of gender-focused policies and mechanisms could in fact be beneficial as it would create political opportunity structures that were missing previously.

Informing about the EU: October 1999–December 2001

The second stage, *informing*, was characterized by a greater flow of information between the EU and women's NGOs, and the greater propensity of women's groups to generate new information. This was no doubt caused by the increased speed of negotiations between the Polish government and the EU on the one hand, and the greater mobilization and engagement of women's groups on the other. Poland submitted the proposed Polish position regarding Chapter 13 ("Social Policy and Employment") at the end of May 1999; the formal negotiations began on 30 September 1999 and were closed in June 2001.

Along with the harmonization of the law, new terms such as *sex discrimination*, *indirect discrimination*, or *work of equal value* had to be defined, and concrete sanctions for employers had to be introduced. Initially the Polish government showed quite a strong resistance to any changes, claiming that certain legal protection already existed and proclaiming that some changes could be carried out only as long as they did not alter Polish "cultural practices," primarily understood as the leading role of Catholic Church and strong nationalistic sentiments (Graff 1999). With the advancement of negotiations it became clear, nevertheless, that the *acquis* had to be taken seriously. Despite movements on the legal front, EU negotiators noticed the weaknesses of the Polish system, such as the lack of a supporting institutional infrastructure or the mechanisms needed to collect gender-sensitive data.

Women's and feminist groups repeatedly tried to confront state resistance and persistently engaged in new mobilizations and collective agency formation practices—as in case of the Parliamentary Women's Group, which twice tried to introduce the equal status legislation prepared by feminists and academic legal experts and both times failed. Nevertheless, although still sporadically, women's NGOs began to engage more often in public debates and dialogue with other political actors. Similarly, while facing the misinformation provided by the state or its pure silence in regards to women's concerns, women's NGOs started to emerge as a source of information and knowledge. Finally, women's NGOs entered the transnational space and made an effort to initiate contacts with representatives of the EU as well as with women's organizations in the EU; such contacts would continue to intensify in the following years. The newly established contacts at the EU level, in fact, became political and strategic tools in lobbying the passive and uninterested (in gender practices) state.

Organizations also began to use the EU rhetorically. They hoped that by virtue of the EU's existence and the ongoing negotiation process, the EU would be able to exercise pressure on Polish institutions. Thanks to increasing funding coming from EU-based donors, and NGOs' more aggressive strategies of obtaining information, as recorded in *Kalendarium*, the greater number of conferences (sixteen) and meetings, seminars, and workshops (thirteen) began to address the possible effects that EU accession may have on women. In particular, they discussed concerns with the labor market (45 percent) and women's position in politics (35 percent). As *Kalendarium* also indicated, 2000 and 2001 witnessed three major information and publication initiatives: 1) the publication of all EU documents on equal rights translated by the Center for Women's Rights (CWR 2006), 2) the publication of the *EU Manual for Women* (OŚKa 2001), and 3) the Polish edition of *100 Words About Equality Between Women and Men* (KARAT Coalition 2006).

Does the greater intensity and diversity of actions imply an emergence of a stronger collective agency among women's NGOs and their greater political engagement? We believe that during that period such a shift began to become visible. Women's groups saw themselves as experts, capable of initiating numerous activities and lobbying actions. It is also worth noting that while during the first phase almost all events and activities were organized and sponsored by individual groups, without any visible collaboration (except for the Annual Conference of Organizations and Communities organized by OŚKa), the period of 1999–2001 indicates the beginning of new links and relationships between different actors, including Polish women's groups, political leaders, and/or governmental representatives of member states. Women's NGOs began to realize that they had to consolidate their efforts to become more effective in the public sphere. As one respondent working with an NGO that focuses its activities on women's economic rights put it: "Often there was too much information out there, and only in cooperation with other organizations was it possible to make sense of it. Such cooperation was a good experience for all of us, to cooperate with not only one, but two, three or more organizations" (NPW2).

What made the greater engagement of women's and feminist groups possible was the availability and greater access to European Union funds. Until 2000, Polish women's groups utilized funding obtained from the US (e.g., the Ford Foundation), internationally based donors such as UNDP, as well as Western European foundations such as the Friedrich Ebert or Heinrich Böll Foundations. Starting in 2000, NGOs could apply for EU financial support. During this period, technology became women's ally; most of the new contacts, alliances, and supranational coalitions were established in the cyberspace of the Internet and subsequently were used during lobbying efforts.

Informing, then, was the period of the consolidation of social forces and the redefinition of employed strategies. Similarly, as during the previous stage, women's and feminist organizations developed local networks of cooperation and information exchange, but during this period, women's NGOs were not only able to emerge as alternative sources of knowledge, they also became more effective than the government in reaching certain groups of people, particularly, in local communities.

As NGOs became more engaged in the public debate about the EU and about the implications of the EU accession for women, they started to develop their own agenda towards the European Union. This was undoubtedly necessary given that the Polish state had a rather ambivalent position towards women. One leader of a women's NGO working on improvement of women's position at the labor market stated: "I have a feeling that we had something to say, particularly in the case of the changes in the Labor Code. Our earlier action might have had some impact on the government; it made them think about some issues. It is debatable, however, to what extent they started to think under the pressure of the organizations, or was it rather that they read something in the EU documents" (NPW2).

Information and events recorded in *Kalendarium* indicate that the period from 1999 to 2001 was critical for the emergence of women's strengthened political agency. Indeed, after the parliamentary election in the fall of 2001, their efforts paid off: with the left-wing government in power and the re-establishment of the Office of the Plenipotentiary, the position of women's and feminist NGOs became more stabilized and even stronger.

Engaging and Creating Partnerships: January 2002–December 2004

The third period was unusually politically active, not only because it was governed by the left-wing government that was more sensitive to women's concerns, but also because it was marked by the European referendum (June 2003), Poland's accession to the EU (May 2004), and finally, the first for the accession countries, the European Parliamentary elections (June 2004).

Kalendarium's record of events and initiatives indicated that the plenipotentiary appointed by the leftist government was very keen on rebuilding links and collaborations with women's NGOs that had eroded under the previous right-wing government. Among the most significant aspects of the new image of the plenipotentiary were: 1) close co-operation with NGOs in order to develop and implement the second stage of the *National Plan of Action for Women*; 2) a nationwide campaign with the National Labor Inspectorate, focused on the dissemination of legal approaches to the equal treatment of women and men; 3) the initiation of a grant competition for NGOs-Equal Rights-Equal Opportunities; and 4) the introduction of changes in the way in which statistics are kept by the Ministry of Justice in order to include a new category of gender discrimination (*Kalendarium* 2002–2004; Mizielińska 2003). For women's NGOs, the cooperation with the plenipotentiary confirmed and stabilized their position as independent political actors, recognized by state institutions. A leader of a women's NGO focused on women's economic concerns recalled:

> It was very positive and we felt very much appreciated, we felt like we had something to say. We could discuss [issues] with the plenipotentiary and could convince her about different concerns. We had information coming from various channels: from Ministries, from the Office of the Plenipotentiary. . . . Now the channels of communication between the government and NGOs are becoming more open. . . . Through the plenipotentiary website we have unlimited access to all information, and we can further disseminate it (NPW2).

The newly emergent cooperation with the government initiated yet another important process: the involvement of the representatives of NGOs in institutionalized state and parliamentary politics. The realm of politics was no longer perceived as a separate world. Such an involvement with state and parliamentary institutions has special significance, since such collaborations would have not been possible only a few years ago given the deep ideological differences between the right-wing regime that was in power and women's political agenda.

The reinvigorated role that the plenipotentiary began to play, and the significantly greater political will on the part of the government to implement legislative changes, altered social relations and practices.[7] For women's and feminist NGOs, the recognition of their work by the state was perceived as the result of both their integrated efforts and the mediation of pressures from the European Union. An activist working with a network of women's NGOs described these effects in the following words: "There was a huge difference after 2002. First of all, they [the government] were aware that they had to consult on decisions with us, since this was a European Union requirement. Second, they had to institutionalize this consultation; so many political bodies were established to fulfill that requirement" (NPW9).

By 2002, a clear increase in the frequency and strength of collective actions undertaken by women's and feminist groups could also be observed, as groups were trying to become more active and visible by focusing on making actual interventions, rather than just passing on information. For example, they created transnational political spaces with a supranational lobbying umbrella organization, the European Women's Lobby (EWL) as well as with Women in Development Europe (WIDE, a network of women from Western Europe and developing countries) and ASTRA (a reproductive rights organization that includes women's organizations from Western and Eastern Europe). In 2002, NGOs from CEE countries, and Polish NGOs in collaboration with the EWL published the *Women's Guide to the European Union*. The Network of East West Women-Polska (NEWW-Polska), a Gdansk-based network of women from Eastern and Western Europe and the US, developed a website *Access News* (www.neww.org), which provided biweekly news about the EU, enlargement news, and the integration process. In 2003, Polish women's organizations began negotiations with the EWL about establishing the Polish Women's Lobby and joining the EWL. Although during negotiations, many women activists from Poland as well as the region raised criticisms of the process of representation currently practiced by EWL (the main concern was with existing EWL practices that may limit visibility of CEE women), for Polish women's NGOs this was a process of establishing themselves as political agents at the supranational European level. By entering umbrella organizations such as EWL, Polish groups established new alliances with other transnational political actors.

The great hopes for and initial appreciation of the role that the EU was perceived to play in the process of women's political identity formation became, particularly during the last period of negotiations, challenged by the emerging criticism towards the EU and its institutions (Grabowska 2006). Women started to be more pragmatic and less enthusiastic about the EU. The representative of an organization that focuses its activities on women's rights and international lobbying pointed out:

> We have established contacts with the EWL and WIDE. I have to admit that we had some doubts about the way they produced their materials on enlargement [materials produced by the EWL about the position of women in the candidates' countries]. But we Polish organizations had limited financial sources and difficulty in being able to react immediately to what was going on in the European Union, so they showed us what to do and set direction (NPW19).

Thus, the transnational cooperation not only began to be seen as an asset, but also became subject to greater scrutiny and evaluation through the newly enacted collective agency of Polish women's NGOs.

Although there were some signs of changes in the state's attitudes towards women's social and political positions, the majority of state institutions remained ambivalent. This was especially visible when, in an effort to secure the strong "yes" vote on the accession referendum, the Polish government entered into a deal with the Catholic Church: in return for silencing the efforts to change one of the most restrictive antiabortion laws in Europe, the Catholic Church offered to support the accession referendum and to actively campaign for a "yes" vote. This strategy of state-Church partnership was in clear conflict with the already mentioned states' effort to collaborate and engage with women's NGOs. Thus, the state reinforced its antiwomen position, leaving no doubt about its intentions to promote its own interests and utilize women's NGOs only when needed. For women's and feminist groups it was a great disappointment, as indicated by a leader of a women's rights organization: "Women's organizations were shocked, and we decided to present our position about what had happened. We prepared an open letter to the European Parliament, a letter that was available on the Internet, and was published in major media. This really worked" (NPW19). While the EU cannot regulate national abortion laws in member states, as a response to these letters, the European Parliament did pass a resolution supporting women's rights to choose (European Parliament 2002). At the same time, the Church attacked Plenipotentiary Jaruga Nowacka's efforts to introduce sexual education to schools, and the high-ranking Church official, Bishop Tadeusz Pieronek, called her "feminist cement that will not alter even if treated with acid" (NEWW-Polska).

What this period then indicates is how women's and feminist groups became visible as political agents in national and transnational political spaces. As reported in the *Kalendarium* and as evidenced in interviews, women's intense activity—due to their own efforts to inform and generate information about the EU, and also because of the support of the plenipotentiary and the European Union itself—enabled the creation of new political spaces that in turn opened up new possibilities for women's political engagement and partnerships. Women no doubt took advantage of their informed position and utilized it strategically vis-à-vis the state and other political actors. They became directly involved in EU generated activities. Building local, national, and transnational partnerships through engagement in political activism across geographical scales became a new tool for their political mobilization.

By repeatedly moving across scales, women's groups learned how to access and utilize diverse resources, and how to consolidate them in such a way that would allow them to be more effective in everyday collaborations with and resistances against national institutional structures. By engaging with the transnational expertise of the EU, they attempted to learn how to mediate sociopolitical struggles across scales, and through that process, produce the localized knowledge necessary for informed political actions. By crossing the boundaries of their nation-state, women leaders and women's groups created new political spaces that further empowered them in their struggles to gain access to public debates, to become visible actors, and to be able to influence governmental actions.

Locating Women's Political Subjecthood

Over the last ten years Poland has made a slow and, at least from the legal standpoint of view, certain progress in the area of equality between women and men. Many of the laws and standards introduced to the Polish public have been required by the European Union and implemented because of the EU's eastern enlargement. The EU thus played the role of the mediator between the often-reluctant national state and the growing women's movement in Poland; a trajectory that can be noted also in other CEE countries that have joined the EU (see in this volume contributions by Křížková and Hašková, and Kakucs and Pető). Since the EU provided women's NGOs with discursive and political tools as well as funding, to a certain degree the EU acted as a catalyst for the strengthening of the women's movement in Poland. The strategic utilization of the EU's supranational commitment to women as a tool to exercise pressure on the state and expose its shortcomings in the media began to represent a new political and spatial strategy that created the opportunity for women's engagement in public discourse and facilitated the women's movement's emergence as an important site for the production of alternative knowledge and politics.

As the case of the Polish women's movement indicates, relations between the EU and a national government were frequently mediated by a third party, in this case women's NGOs. Taking a pragmatic approach, many women activists perceived the struggle between the state and the EU as a dynamic that could be dislocated and strategically used for the benefit of women. In the opinion of a leader of an organization focused on reproductive rights:

Knowing that the European Union would not resolve certain problems for us, we nevertheless popularized the idea of the EU. We focused generally on the promotion of EU standards; in public we argued that they would oblige our state to change, even though we knew it would not be the case. . . . I think the European Union forced it [gender equality legislations] upon Poland itself. But we established our agenda in this process by being aware of what we knew and what we expected. We created the feeling that they [the government] could not fool with us and redefine our agenda (NPW7).

The European Union's enlargement process not only catalyzed the emergence of women's political subjectivities, but it also provided them with supranational space, within which the state's decisions could be questioned and challenged (Keck and Sikkink 1998). Thus, although in the upcoming period the Polish state will probably violate EU standards in the area of equal opportunities, women's groups will utilize this supranational site to argue against the government's decisions. The first such action has already been undertaken. When Poznań's government officials banned the gay and lesbian "Equality March" in November 2005, the organizers threatened to sue Poland in the European Court of Human Rights for not following EU equality standards, and eventually the government decision was overruled by the national court. More recently, during a meeting with Commissioner Spidla, a group of representatives from women's and minority groups demanded EU intervention into the Polish government's policies on women's and minority rights, pointing to fundamental discrepancies between the Polish state's and EU's understanding of equal opportunities (Feminoteka 2006).

Yet, as our data also indicated, it was and still is the Polish state itself that has remained the locus of politics on gender equality and women's positions in the public sphere. As the events that followed the October 2005 and later 2007 parliamentary elections have shown, while member states are required to meet EU standards of gender equality politics, the understanding and interpretation of these standards rests with state institutions. For example, despite the diminishing of the status and renaming of the Office of the Plenipotentiary of Equal Status, the Polish government argued that Poland still had an institution that supports gender equality even though the current office operates only at the level of a deputy minister. Once again, the right-wing state reinterpreted the meaning of equality, as it sees women located mostly within the private sphere and supports their traditional roles as mothers (for example, the proposed new law would drastically extend maternity leave) (Kula 2005).

Conclusions

The cartography of women's and feminist NGOs' changing position within the political landscape of Poland (during and after accession negotiations) has shown, despite many obstacles, a trajectory of women becoming political agents. By moving across scales, between the NGOs' local context and through transnational spaces, NGOs constructed new spatial and scalar relations that became tools in fostering their political mobilization. These strategies allow women's NGOs to question the masculine knowledge-production process and to demand greater visibility and inclusion. The movement across scales has also permitted them to actively engage in connecting different social worlds through continuous and an undetermined number of translations has been registered in *Kalendarium*.

The opening of the supranational scale of the EU or of the global political spaces of the UN is crucial for women's empowerment. They represent the sites that can be vigorously used as spaces for the mobilization and contestation of diverse strategies, as well as struggles that are transposed from the nation-state to the supranational level only to be brought back and strategically utilized to confront the resisting state "at home." The new links impacted relationships between the Polish state and interest groups and influenced the negotiations and bargaining between these actors. At the same time, however, the state retained the power and, as our analysis has shown, continually determined the placement of women's concerns in the political agenda. Thus, our analyses support the argument of the relevance of the state within the context of the new power relations between the EU and member states, and reinforce the point made by other contributors to this volume that the greatest gains are often made during the period of negotiations, prior to joining the EU. At the same time, women's collective agency, emerging from everyday practices that are embedded locally and transnationally as well as globally, which had already been strengthened through the accession period, can be expected to gain greater visibility as women's and feminist NGOs create new political spaces and confront their marginalization.

Notes

The research from which this paper benefited is part of a larger project directed by Joanna Regulska and funded by the National Science Foundation (grant No. BCS-0137954), with colleagues in the Czech Republic (Alena Křížková, Hana Hašková, Dagmar Lorenz-Meyer, and Lenka Simerská), Poland (Małgorzata Fuszara and Joanna Mizielińska), and the US (Magda Grabowska and Joanna Regulska). The project examined the process of EU eastern enlargement and explored the ways in which women in these accession countries have engaged as political actors in the construction of supranational political spaces, beyond the nation-state.

1. During the period of 2001–2005 we conducted over one hundred face-to-face interviews with leaders of women's NGOs, national politicians, and government officials in Poland and in the Czech Republic, and with the EU representatives in Brussels and EU-related women's NGOs. We have also analyzed state documents, EU documents, and have collected extensive materials from NGOs. In addition, four focus groups, two in each country, were conducted. The results will be published in a co-edited volume, *Shaping Women's Agenda and Public Discourses in the Enlarged Europe*.

2. Similarly Molyneux (1998) echoed these arguments by pointing out that integration of women's human rights into national and international political agendas was very much due to women's transnational collective organizing and networking.

3. OŚKa was restructured in 2006 and ceased to publish *Kalendarium*.

4. *Kalendarium* was a 45–50-page booklet, composed of nine sections: Events, Activities, Publications, OŚKa Library, Grants, Gender Studies, Advertisements, Women on the Internet, and Abroad. Each of these sections provided a basic set of descriptive information about past and future events and information about publications and grants available.

5. The preparation for the Beijing World women's conference was seen by many as first instance of Polish women's collective agency at the supranational level.

6. NWP2 refers to coding of the interviews and stands for Nongovernmental Women's Organization in Poland number 2 (the number reflects the alphabetical order of groups interviewed).

7. The governmental *Report on Poland's Institutional Adjustments to the Requirements of Membership in the EU* (2002), which was adopted by the Parliamentary Committee for the European Integration, indicates the shift in attitudes in at least three ways: 1) by emphasizing the role of NGOs, 2) by stressing the need to develop new institutional structures, and 3) by using new language (e.g., the word *gender*) or by adopting the EU language of equality of women and men.

References

Alvarez, Sonia E. 2000. Translating the Global: Effects of Transnational Organizing on Local Feminist Discourses and Practices in Latin America. *Meridians* 1 (1): 29–68.

Berger, Helge and Thomas Moutos. 2004. *Managing European Union Enlargement*. Cambridge and London: MIT Press.

Center for Women's Rights. 2006. http://www.cpk.org.pl/pl.php5/on/articles/cid/23 Accessed 21 December 2007.

Desai, Manisha. 2005. Transnationalism: The Face of Feminist Politics Post-Beijing. *International Social Science Journal* 57 (184): 319–67.

Ellina, Crystalla. 2003. *Promoting Women's Rights: Policies of Gender in the European Union*. New York: Routledge.

European Parliament. 2002. Resolution on the Violation of Women's Rights and EU International Relations, 2002/2286 (INI).

Feminoteka. 2006. Commissioner Spidla Listened to Women's NGOs. www.feminoteka.pl. Accessed 2 February 2006.

Fried, Susana M., ed. 1994. *The Indivisibility of Women's Human Rights: A Continuing Dialogue*. New Brunswick, NJ: Center for Women's Global Leadership.

Ghodsee, Kristen 2004. Feminism-by-Design: Emerging Capitalisms, Cultural Feminism, and Women's Nongovernmental Organizations in Postsocialist Eastern Europe. *Signs: Journal of Women in Culture and Society* 29 (4): 727–53.

Grabowska, Magda. 2006. Kobiety w Wyborach do Parlamentu Europejskiego. In *Polityka A Plec*, eds. A. Grzybek and J. Piotrowska, 123–45. Warsaw: Fundacja Im. Henricha Bolla

Graff, Agnieszka. 1999. Patriarchat po Seksmisji. *Gazeta Wyborcza*. 19–20 June 2003.

Herod, Andrew and Melissa W. Wright. 2002. Placing Scale: An Introduction. In *Geographies of Power: Placing Scale*, eds. Andrew Herod and Melissa W. Wright, 1–14. Oxford: Blackwell.

Hoskyns, Catherine.1996. *Integrating Gender: Women, Law and Politics in the European Union*. London: Verso.

Howitt, Richard. 2003. Scale. In *A Companion to Political Geography*, eds. John Agnew, Katharyne Mitchell, and Gearóid Ó. Tuathail, 138–57. Oxford: Blackwell.

OŚKA (Ośrodek Informacji Środowisk Kobiecych). 1997. *Kalendarium* (12): 13–14.

———. 2000. *Kalendarium* (6): 15.

———. 1997–2004. *Kalendarium*.

KARAT Coalition. www.karat.org. Accessed 15 January 2006.

Keck, Margaret E. and Kathryn Sikkink. 1998. *Activists Beyond Borders: Advocacy Networks in International Politics*. Ithaca, NY: Cornell University Press.

Kula, Magdalena. 2005. Równość płci od nowa. *Gazeta Wyborcza*. 18 November 2005, 7.

Liebert, Ulrike. 2002. Europeanising Gender Mainstreaming: Constraints and Opportunities in the Multilevel Euro-Polity. *Feminist Legal Studies* 10 (3): 241–56.

Marks, Gary and Marco R Steenbergen, eds. 2004. *European Integration and Political Conflict*, Cambridge: Cambridge University Press.

Marston, Sallie A., John Paul Jones III, and Keith Woodward. 2005. Human Geography without Scale. *Transactions of the Institute of British Geographers* 30 (4): 416–32.

Massey, Doreen. 2004. Geographies of responsibility. *Geografiska Annaler* 86: 5–18.

Merrill, Heather. 2004. Space Agents: Anti-racist Feminism and the Politics of Scale in Turin, Italy. *Gender, Culture and Place* 11 (2):189–204.

Mizielinska, Joanna. 2003. Polish State's Documents Analysis. Unpublished paper, Warsaw.

Molyneux, Maxine. 1998. Analyzing Women's Movements. *Development and Change* 29 (2): 219–45.

Network of East-West Women-Polska (NEWW-Polska). *Access News*. www.neww.org. Accessed 16 December 2005.

———. 2002. Letter to EU Authorities. *Access News*. 26 February. www.neww.org. Accessed 20 February 2006.

OŚKA. 2001. *EU Manual for Women*, Warsaw: OŚKA.

Pudrovska, Tetyana and Myra Marx Ferree. 2004. Global Activism in "Virtual Space": The European Women's Lobby in the Network of Transnational Women's NGOs on the Web. *Social Politics* 11 (1): 117–47.

Regulska, Joanna. 2000. Gendered Integration of Europe: New Boundaries of Exclusion. In *Gender in Transition in Eastern and Central Europe*, eds. Hildegard Maria Nickel and Gabriele Jähnert, 84–96, Berlin: Trafo-Verlag.

Siim, Birte and Bérengère Marques-Pereira. 2002. Representation, Agency and Empowerment. In *Contested Concepts in Gender and Social Politics*, eds. Barbara Hobson, Jane Lewis, and Birte Siim, 170–94. Cheltenham, UK: Edward Elgar.

Star, Susan Leigh and James R. Griesemer. 1989. Institutional Ecology, "Translations" and Boundary Objects: Amateurs and Professionals in Berkeley's Museum of Vertebrate Zoology 1907–39. *Social Studies of Science* 19 (3): 387–420.

Swyngedouw, Erik. 2000. Authoritarian Governance, Power and the Politics of Rescaling. *Environment and Planning D: Society and Space* 18: 63–76.

Walters, William and Jens Henrik Haahr. 2005. *Governing Europe: Discourse, Governmentality and European Integration*. New York: Routledge.

Woodward, Alison. 2001. Gender Mainstreaming in the European Policy: Innovation or Deception? Wissenschaftszentrum Berlin fur Sozialforschung, Discussion Paper FS 1 01–103, 2001.

Zippel, Kathrin. 2004. Transnational Advocacy Networks and Policy Cycles in the European Union: The Case of Sexual Harassment. *Social Politics: International Studies in Gender, State and Society* 11 (1): 57–85.

8

THE IMPACT OF EU ACCESSION ON THE PROMOTION OF WOMEN AND GENDER EQUALITY IN THE CZECH REPUBLIC

Hana Hašková and Alena Křížková

Introduction

In this chapter we evaluate the EU's impact on the promotion of gender equality and women's positions in the Czech Republic (CR) during the preparation for accession to the EU. We ask first how EU enlargement affected Czech women's civic groups, Czech politicians, and Czech state governmental bodies in their capacities and willingness to promote women and gender equality. Then we turn to role of the aforementioned actors in the promotion of women and gender equality in the Czech Republic during the EU accession process. Finally, we discuss whether EU enlargement led Czech women's civic groups to orientate themselves more towards supranational or national governmental bodies in their efforts to promote women and gender equality.

We argue that preparation for the CR's accession to the EU was the most important legitimizing force that helped to promote gender equality in the country. Furthermore, we argue that the attitudes of the EU and Czech governmental officials and politicians towards gender equality and women's positions during the period of EU eastern enlargement, together with changes in financial sources for Czech women's civic groups at that time, were the most important factors that shaped both the character of the promotion of women and gender equality in the country and the possibilities and obstacles women's civic groups faced in the promotion of their goals.

Czech women's civic groups are referred to as women's nongovernmental organizations (NGOs) and informal (nonregistered) women's civic groups and initiatives. Civic participation (and specifically women's civic organizing) is thus defined not only in terms of participation in formalized NGOs, which are commonly seen as representing civil society in the countries of Central and Eastern Europe (CEE) because they are the prevailing form of civic participation there (e.g., Hann 1996; Sloat 2005), but also in reference to informal (nonregistered) groups and initiatives.

The chapter is based on analyses of semi-structured expert interviews with Czech informal women's civic groups and NGOs, politicians, and officials from the Czech government, and representatives of the European commission and focus groups with representatives of the women's NGOs who have been previously interviewed, carried out between 2003 and 2005. [1]

Silence on Gender Equality During Socioeconomic Transformation (1989–97)

An emphasis on economic aspects and stress on the importance of economic changes—in particular in the transition to a market economy—resulted in the neglect and trivialization of the need to address inequalities in the position of men and women in society throughout the transformation period after 1989. No public discussion took place throughout the period of the transformation of Czech society on existing gender inequalities or on the need for gender equality measures and policies (Čermáková et al. 2000). The processes that occurred in Czech society over the course of the transformation period were primarily influenced by the economic reforms introduced into society and their acceptability within society (Machonin and Tuček 1996; Večerník 1998).

The only public discussion on gender inequalities was among newly created formally established or informal women's civic groups (including academic groups of women). In the first half of the 1990s, however, women's civic groups lacked experience, expertise, wider recognition, and contact with state bodies, politicians, and other social actors. The latter did not recognize gender equality as a political issue, and the Czech media and society in general were not gender sensitive (Osvaldová 2004; Čermáková et al. 2000). There appears to have been a rise in gender-conservatism at the beginning of the 1990s in the CEE region. This was shown in studies reflecting on the empowerment of male economic actors as citizens under the newly applied paradigm of the neoliberal market in the region, and on the negative effects on women in the region of the post-1989 withdrawal of social entitlements (e.g., Einhorn 2005). This was also well documented in statements made in the media and on the political stage in many CEECs. When the CR began encountering its first problems with unemployment, many politicians discussed abolishing the "mandatory work rule" and deploying the concept of freedom and freedom of choice in reference to the "voluntary" and "natural" return of women to the household and family responsibilities. Similar statements from this period included, for example, a claim that women should leave the labor market during periods of growing unemployment in order to make space for men, arguing that men are the "main breadwinners." Employers justified paying women lower salaries by citing a "man's obligation to feed his family" (Hašková 2005a). In addition to the absence of any wider social or political discussion of gender equality in the Czech Republic during the 1990s, there was also no formal foundation for cooperation between state governmental bodies and NGOs until 1998.

However, this situation changed over time. An important event occurred in the form of the Beijing World Conference on Women in 1995. As a result of this conference, the Platform for Action was created, and women's NGOs began to monitor governmental conformity with the document. In 1997 members of some women's NGOs and several women MPs in the Czech Social Democratic Party (ČSSD) and the Communist Party of Bohemia and Moravia (KSČM) initiated a discussion about gender inequalities in the Czech parliament. This led to the creation of the Department of Equality of Men and Women within the Ministry of Labor and Social Affairs (MLSA) in 1998. Furthermore, a program that serves to define governmental policy concerning gender equality and to evaluate the fulfillment of governmental policy concerning gender equality to date was adopted.

Thus the emerging debate about gender equality in the Czech Republic was strongly affected by three factors: the change in political regime (state orientation towards the neoliberal paradigm), some effects of the legacy of communism (generally widespread gender insensitivity in the country), and the Beijing conference, which initiated the first fruitful contacts between women politicians and women's civic groups in the country, followed by the establishment of the first Czech governmental programs and bodies focused on the promotion of gender equality, which were later on evaluated by the European Commission during the EU eastern enlargement.

Czech Women's Civic Organizing During Socioeconomic Transformation

In the civically and politically mobilized atmosphere of 1989 and the early 1990s, civic and political initiatives, groups, and organizations were created in all the countries of the former Eastern European bloc. According to Potůček (1997), approximately 20,000 civic associations were registered in 1992 in Czech society. Four years later, the number had reached 37,000 organizations, but dropped after a legislative amendment was introduced in 1997. Analyses of current women's organizations in the region have already reflected on the fact that women became more active in civic associations than they did in formal politics or large movements after the change in political regime (Gal and Kligman 2000a, 2000b; Kay 2000; Lang 1997). This was also evident in the significant decrease in the number of women representatives in the parliaments of all the CEECs after quotas for political participation were abolished and after the real decision-making power of parliaments increased (no longer being "puppet" parliaments) in the region at the beginning of the 1990s (Sloat 2004a, 2004b; Clavero and Galligan 2005). About seventy women's civic groups existed in the Czech Republic as early as the early 1990s. Like in other countries in the region, women's civic groups were founded as interest or self-help groups oriented around social problems, professional organizations, and branches of international organizations, and women's groups connected to political parties, churches, social movements, and the academic scene (Čermáková et al. 2000). In some cases they were founded by women who had emigrated from the country during the communist regime and returned after 1989. Many of the groups were supported on the basis of individual friendships with foreign feminists. Some were established as a result of pressure exerted by foreign/international organizations on similarly oriented organizations in the Czech Republic.

As in other countries, these groups have addressed a variety of issues, such as the situation of women in the labor market and the public sphere; violence against women and trafficking in women; reproductive rights; health and social services in (child) care; minority women's issues (e.g., Roma and lesbian women); environmental and ecofeminist issues; and issues of increasing gender sensitivity, awareness, and education among the public (Marksová-Tominová 1999; Sloat 2005).[2] Some have focused mainly on providing services to special groups of women (single mothers, victims of domestic violence, prostitutes, etc.) and thus substitute for the state where gaps exist in the provision of services. Others have focused especially on consciousness raising, education, promoting legislative changes, and lobbying in the area of gender equality.

Funding was derived through individual arrangements from private foundations; from bilateral development assistance from different countries in Western Europe, the US, and Canada; and also from international organizations such as the United Nations. Foreign and international foundations and organizations were the only significant funding bodies for Czech women's civic groups. Funding from these sources tended to be flexible: there was project funding, but also funding that could be used for the development of the organization itself. Furthermore, long-term, all-inclusive funding from foreign or international "parent organizations" like the Open Society Fund existed.

Since the beginning of the 1990s, women active in the newly created women's civic groups have distanced themselves from the Czech Women's Union, currently a women's NGO—a successor of a pre-1989 semi-state mass women's organization. Such semi-state mass women's organizations existed in all countries of the former Eastern European bloc. Furthermore, Czech feminists have been wary of Western feminists and feminisms. These women's groups included a wide range of topics, ideologies, and organizational structures. In the first half of the 1990s, there was no common issue that united them like the topic of abortion in Poland (Fuszara 2005). Instead their activities appeared as primarily fragmented and disjointed. There was, however, one important exception: as early as 1990, the Women's Council was established as an association of women's organizations and initiatives aimed at supporting full compliance with the Convention on the Elimination of All Forms of Discrimination against Women. However, in 1993 the council dissolved without having achieved any significant successes.

Some Czech women's civic groups co-created, joined, or developed long-term supportive or lobbyist networks with foreign and international women's organizations. Already in 1991, several representatives of Czech women's NGOs joined the Network of East-West Women, an organization supporting women's NGOs in postcommunist countries. In 1997, some of them also co-created and developed the Karat Coalition, an organization of women's NGOs from postcommunist countries lobbying at the supranational level for interests of women from this particular region.

The situation of women's civic organizing in the Czech Republic during the socioeconomic transformation thus was hugely affected by the change in the political regime (the general rise in the number of civic organizations and groups), by some effects of the legacy of communism (a lack of public support of civic groups), and by the enormous role that foreign and international donors and feminist activists played (personally, ideologically, and financially) in the development of women's civic organizations and groups in CEE.

The Impact of EU Enlargement on the Promotion of Gender Equality in Czech Politics (1998–2004)[3]

Those currently working on gender equality issues agree that if it had not been for the Czech Republic's preparation for accession to the EU, the issue of gender equality would never have received the amount of political and media attention that it has during the past several years. The arguments and positions maintained by the European Commission, which has clearly acknowledged the existence of discrimination based on gender, made it necessary for the issue of gender inequality to be addressed at the governmental level and for giving support to the goals of national women's NGOs (Zippel 2004).

The Czech Republic was among the countries that were criticized by the European Commission in its regular reports for inadequate progress in introducing gender legislation. Since the government considered it as one of the less-important conditions for the Czech Republic's accession to the EU, gender equality legislation was not enforced, positive action measures and positive discrimination policies were not implemented, and the transformational potential of gender mainstreaming[4] was not activated (Roth 2006). The state's window-dressing activities have been described in the following areas: Government gender equality bodies with limited responsibilities and frequently rotating, uneducated personnel emerged in patches and exhibited a minimum of activity. In addition, the interactions between the state and NGOs have been abusive and infrequent (Linková 2003; Pavlík 2004).

Up until 1999, among the institutions that were supposed to be responsible for gender equality policy, only the Department of Equality of Men and Women within MLSA existed. With regard to EU gender equality directives, the directive of equal treatment in the workplace was nowhere near being adequately implemented, and nothing like the burden of proof in sex discrimination cases existed at all. For example, no definition of direct or indirect discrimination or sexual harassment defined as sex discrimination in employment existed. In addition, it was necessary to further refine and introduce other new directives from the EU's equality *acquis* into Czech legislation.

The attitude of the Czech government towards the creation of legislation relating to the equality of men and women could be characterized as ambivalent. Its strategy was to mechanically adopt everything that constitutes a precondition for the Czech Republic's accession to the EU, but this was accompanied by its lack of interest in negotiating or creating any legislation in relation to the specific context or conditions of the Czech Republic, which would establish the need for specific legislation.

The attitude of politicians and public officials in the period of the Czech Republic's pre-accession negotiations on issues of gender equality was marked by a sense of disinterest in gender issues. It might be argued that this approach has been similar in relation to the implementation of other soft laws[5] (e.g., discrimination against the Roma population, or protection of the environment). However the state's attitude to and perception of the gender equality issues was more specific. Two closely related main factors differentiated gender equality issues from the other "soft laws issues." The first factor was the conviction that there is no need or even demand on the part of society for any substantial legislative measures addressing gender equality or for the development of relevant infrastructure, as gender equality is already established concretely in the constitution of the Czech Republic. The introduction of EU equality directives into the Czech legislation was usually perceived by Czech politicians, male and female, as a simple, technical task, required as one of the preconditions for accession, but otherwise unnecessary. The second factor was the emphasis on the negative experiences with egalitarian policies under the communist regime. These two factors resulted on the one hand in a lack of sufficient trust on the part of the public in the legislative changes that occurred in the area of gender equality, and on the other hand in a lack of steps to implement this legislation and the antidiscrimination measures and to put the new institutions into practice.

Thus, the EU eastern enlargement process brought about an increase in (or rather the emergence of) discussions on gender equality in Czech governmental and parliamentary structures. However, the knowledge and views of the EU and of Czech officials and politicians about the significance of gender equality politics resulted in the issue being discussed and evaluated formally, rather than substantially, in the pre-accession negotiations.

The Institutionalization of Gender Equality in the Czech Republic During the EU Enlargement Process

Throughout almost the entire pre-accession period, the work of the nongovernmental sector in the area of gender equality was essentially ignored by the government. In addition, the entire agenda for the negotiations over EU membership was placed in the hands of the Ministry of Foreign Affairs (MFA), including the public media campaign on joining the EU prior to the referendum on membership. Interviews with employees of the MFA revealed the catastrophic lack of knowledge as well as disinterest in gender issues. It was evident that some government officials did not even know about the basic government document on the issue of the equality of men and women, which the government had issued each year since 1998 and in which tasks for each ministry with regard to issues of gender equality are defined.

Despite the lack of interest and the purely formal approach of the government to issues of gender equality, by 2004 equality bodies had been established at the governmental level and most of the EU gender equality directives included in the EU equality *acquis* had been implemented into Czech legislation. Some of the directives were already reflected in the constitution of the Czechoslovak Socialist Republic, but the majority of the legislation had to be modified or newly introduced to ensure the establishment of gender equality—for example, in the case of maternity leave and the newly introduced parental leave. The highest-level body for the national policy of gender equality is the Government Council for Equal Opportunities for Women and Men (Council), established in October 2001. It is a permanent advisory body of the government and prepares proposals that promote and strive to achieve gender equality. The members of the Council include representatives of the government, women's NGOs, and experts, as well as representatives from trade unions and employers.

In May 2001 all ministries were charged to establish by January 2002 the equivalent of a full-time position to handle the agenda of gender equality. Additionally, the currently negotiated antidiscrimination law (that should unify a number of different antidiscrimination laws and establish an institutional body for monitoring and dealing with discrimination cases) had to be accepted and effectively applied.

However, the effective promotion of gender mainstreaming has been thwarted by numerous problems connected with the institutionalization of gender equality bodies in the CR. The problem is the centralization of these institutions in the capital city and concentration at the upper political level (the government ministries), and the fact that these institutions have no decision-making powers in the state apparatus or tools to efficiently enforce policies. At the regional level, institutional bodies for the promotion of gender mainstreaming have not yet been established. Governmental bodies, with the exception of the Council, did not include specialists in gender equality issues. Even in the case of the Department of the MLSA, which has been the governmental body coordinating activities in the area, none of its members (the leader of the department included) ever dealt with gender equality issues before their appointment to the MLSA. Furthermore, the harmonization of Czech laws with the EU equality *acquis* has only led to a marginal change in practice, which is reflected in the limited number of cases of discrimination based on sex officially recorded by Labor Bureaus and the courts. On top of this, none of these institutions has well-established information flows, and cooperation between them and other political and civic entities only occurs to a limited degree and is rigid in form and formal in character.

Thus, during the EU enlargement process gender equality policy was undervalued, and the structure of governmental equality bodies, whose objective is the promotion of gender mainstreaming in the Czech Republic, was ineffectively designed. The promotion of gender mainstreaming in the Czech Republic suffers especially from the limited authority of the newly established institutions, and the inadequate amount of knowledge of gender equality issues on the part of the representatives of these bodies. Furthermore, these institutions lack resources and personnel, are fragmented and communicate poorly with each other (compare similar situations discussed in this volume by Kakucs and Pető on Hungary and Regulska and Grabowska on Poland.)

However, our research also showed that the question of personnel and who is assigned to occupy particular functions is very important. Some politicians and officials assigned to gender equality issues, although they were previously not interested or qualified, became interested in promoting gender equality, becoming educated in this field, creating their own initiatives, and establishing ties with women's NGOs.

Although there was very limited cooperation between the components of state infrastructure and women's NGOs, representatives of NGOs admitted that through personal contacts it was possible to achieve their aims. Cooperation between several female politicians from the ranks of MPs from Social Democratic Party (ČSSD) and the Communist Party of Bohemia and Moravia (KSČM) and some NGOs occurred from the start of the accession negotiations period. One female MP from the ČSSD stated: "We basically started out from zero and essentially only thanks to enormous efforts and external pressure in particular from gender NGOs did the process slowly develop, including the Government Council [for Equal Opportunities for Men and Women] . . . so that we could say that this process of expansion helped get gender issues on the table."

It is evident that the above-cited politician considered partnership with women's NGOs an obvious and straightforward enough phenomenon that she used the term *we* when she spoke about their joint activities. The accession talks thus provided an opportunity structure not only for women's NGOs, but also for female politicians who, usually only at the instigation of these organizations, began to take an interest in the issue of gender equality.

However, the political actors who were supposed to address this issue demonstrated a lack of knowledge about and a lack of interest not only in these issues, but also in working with NGOs that had already been focusing on gender equality for a number of years. In this situation, when cooperation existed between women's NGOs and a handful of female politicians, it often took the form of an alliance against the formal stance of the government on gender equality issues, while it also established the first channels for women's NGOs to acquire an influence on decision-making processes.

The Impact of EU Enlargement on Czech Women's Civic Organizing[6]

Accession negotiations also had a profound impact on shaping the environment in which women's civic groups now operate in the CR. Newly created governmental bodies for the promotion of gender equality became potential partners for women's NGOs because the EU highlighted the importance of cooperation between them. Women's civic groups in the region have also used the existence of EU directives on gender equality to bolster their claims that their goals are important when lobbying the government for policy changes, and have used the argument that if the EU supports it, the government should support it as well. In effect, the governments of the EU candidate countries were forced to address in some form a number of the issues that women's civic groups in those countries had been raising since the early 1990s. Less attention has yet been devoted to the fact that the period of EU eastern enlargement also brought about a sharp decrease in the developmental funding of women's civic groups and increased their formalization.

Formalization meant that many women's civic groups were professionalized—that is, they became formally registered entities, with office space and staff with the expertise and skills that are required by the state or other donors—and they are supported and recognized by the state or other donors as experts on a particular issue. Furthermore, they became more project oriented, in that their activities consisted of conducting specific activities with clearly defined objectives, budgets, and timelines that are set by a donor, or within an unequal interaction between the donors and NGOs. In addition they became more reform oriented, in that they started to work to improve existing legal or institutional structures step-by-step, or to provide services that could be supported by the state and the EU, which are the main NGO donors in the era of EU accession. These trends have led to profound changes in terms of the existence, focus, strategies, partnerships, style of work, and organization of the activities of women's civic groups. On the one hand, these processes have also led to a strengthening of the impact that formalized women's NGOs have on legislative, institutional, and societal changes in specific areas of interest; on the other hand they resulted in a marginalization of women's informal civic groups and women's NGOs that focus on other areas of interest.

In the period of EU eastern enlargement, the EU and the state became the most important NGO donors in the CR, while foreign and international donors that acted in the country during the 1990s left the country as it moved into the EU sphere. This introduced an opportunity for obtaining large EU funding for gender equality projects, but also ushered in increased competition between different actors who depended on the same donors, along with new requirements that women's civic groups professionalize, focus on projects, and create extensive partnerships with actors outside the sphere of women's civic groups.

The professionalization and the project-based orientation of women's civic groups in the CR proceeded hand-in-hand with the process of orientation towards reform. An orientation towards reform meant that the professionalized and project-based women's NGOs and feminist activists (that became informal government advisors, members of the government advisory bodies on gender equality, the "tutors" of state officials in gender equality, or project coordinators and services providers acting with government or EU funds) work in an area designated by the state and the EU (the donors), and their activities are oriented towards achieving step-by-step reform to improve the existing legal and institutional structures. The relationship between the donors and women's civic groups is not equal. These donors decide who their expert NGOs are, and they have also the power to delineate the scope of topics, approaches, activities, and strategies of those who are dependent on their funding because there are no longer any other important donors in the region. The reform orientation of women's civic groups has resulted in a situation where women's NGOs act to improve the established institutional and legal structures. It also led to the marginalization of those women's civic groups that operate differently.

These are women's groups that focus on topics and strategies that lie outside mainstream topics (for example, ecofeminism and "natural" childbirth practices) and strategies (for example, radical criticism of governmental institutions rather than reforms of existing governmental structures, and small local initiatives rather than large projects) or that are engaged in activities and services of a different scope and character than the mainstream grants available today, which are now defined by the donors, that is, primarily the EU and the state. As a result, some women's civic groups, which were unwilling or unable to change their focus and strategies, have been shut out completely, while other NGOs have moved to become more involved in the issues, activities, and strategies that are supported and away from other issues.

The conditions attached to new funding bodies in the region have also encouraged changes in the partnerships of women's NGOs. The need to form extensive partnerships between disparate organizations and sectors was articulated in the region as one of the requirements for successfully applying for the new large amounts of EU project funds. One such example was a grant from the EU for a project on the issue of work/life balance that started in 2003. It was coordinated by the Czech Women's Union (CWU), a women's NGO that experienced strong opposition from Czech feminist groups during the 1990s. However, the structure of this grant was such that the coordinator had to be a professionalized entity and was required to contract a large number of partner organizations. Thanks to the formalized structure of this coordinating NGO, which has a number of permanent employees, additional funding, and property resources and therefore also the potential to successfully apply for and manage such large projects, the CWU was able to contract out tasks to many partner organizations in the academic, state, trade union, business, and NGO sectors. The partner NGOs contracted to work on specific tasks included even some who had declared a strong opposition to the CWU since the beginning of the 1990s, excluding it from umbrella women's organizations. The result is that women's NGOs in the region have begun to form partnerships with organizations in a variety of areas, focuses, and approaches, in ways they never would have done before. It is possible that this new funding situation in the region could serve to mandate cooperation across interests, with the goal of interconnecting different parts of the previously rather disjointed women's NGO scene and broadening responsibility for gender equality beyond just the domain of women's NGOs to society on the whole (employers, trade unions, media, and so on). The danger remains, however, that these partnerships have been created as only strategic, temporary, project-based partnerships, that they are not based on any mutual understanding, and thus, as the CWU puts it, without a productively close connection between them. This could lead to frustration on the part of the project partners involved and to limited expectations about the projects' outcomes. However, it could also cause organizations to know more about other organizations as partners and thus to make better project partner choices in the future.

While the CR was preparing for EU accession, the process of formalizing women's NGOs accelerated and came to affect more or less all women's NGOs in the country. But the image of an across-the-board formalization of women's NGOs in the region must be questioned, because also during the pre-accession period a small but nonetheless significant number of groups and initiatives increased their visibility in the region—little, unregistered, office-less, volunteer-based, occasionally active, creative, radical (not reformist), oriented towards campaign and protest activities (not project-oriented), operating on small budgets (with small resources based not on projects, but mainly on friendships, and obtained from the public through their public activities), and usually staffed with young women. It could be argued that these groups are still in the first stage of development (some women's NGOs that have recently become formalized started out in this way) and that they will start to formalize later on. However, there is one important difference between them and similar women's civic groups that started out in the first half of the 1990s: they explicitly reject the formalization trend, and bear signs of a new social movement. Even though they criticize formalized women's NGOs for being "over-formalized," depending on "window-dressing" for "abusive" government actors and collaborating with them, and for becoming increasingly distanced from the rest of the population by working in their offices on projects targeting issues and activities decided on by the donors instead of engaging in and supporting grassroots feminist activism, they also have many friends among women's NGOs, who allow them to use their office spaces, printers, and infrastructure for disseminating the materials of informal women's groups. A clear example of this kind of informal women's group in the CR is a group of anarcho-feminists active on an ad hoc basis. The existence of those informal campaign and protest-oriented women's civic groups in the CR contrasts with the predominant image of formalization of Czech women's nongovernmental groups. However, with the formalization of civil society groups and no tradition of public support for them, these informal groups are left at the margins of activities on women's rights and gender equality.

Supranational and National Opportunity Structures and Women's Networks

In the period prior to the Czech Republic's accession to the EU, representatives of women's NGOs saw one of the advantages of EU membership in the horizontal and vertical expansion of the political space. The optimism of some women's NGOs, however, was exaggerated, as became evident in the course of interviews with representatives of the European Commission that we conducted at the end of 2003 in Brussels. The EC directives are only general, and if a national government wants to avoid implementing them and instead introduces only formal legislative changes, the European Commission will not back any strategy of going around the national government and turning directly to

European bodies. Scholars of the eastern enlargement process point out that the integration of gender issues during the pre-accession period has been neglected and "the EU has failed to realize its influence in promoting gender awareness in CEEC" (Bretherton 2001, 75).

Even though the European Commission was not interested in intervening and altering relationships between actors at the national political level, officials of the EC were aware of the fact that gender equality issues were among the issues considerably neglected in the transformation of the Czech legislation. The approach of national politicians to EU policy and its individual spheres and their communication with them were very important for achieving the goals of the NGO sector, for example, with regard to gender equality issues. Therefore, if Czech women's NGOs want to attain reforms at the political level in the area of gender equality along the lines of EU directives, recommendations, and measures, they cannot just turn directly to the European Commission but must proceed through the national political level and find a politician who is willing to address these issues. However much circumventing national politics may appeal as an option when there are disinterest, technocratic procedures, and sometimes even a disputing of these issues on the side of Czech politicians and officials, this approach is not welcomed by the European Commission.

Foreign and supranational bodies have supported women's civic groups in the region of Central and Eastern Europe since the beginning of 1990s. However, the first supranational lobbyist network of women's NGOs in the region was the Karat Coalition, established in 1997. A representative of a well-established women's NGO, founded in the first half of the 1990s in Prague and focusing on raising gender sensitivity and awareness in Czech society, explained:

> We cooperated on establishing a network of women's organizations from Central and Eastern Europe, Karat. We got to know each other quite well during the years of co-operation, and so now we know each other and it is not like a situation in which you don't know your partner organizations. . . . But try to find a grant for that [to support the continuation of the lobbying organization]. . . . We [Karat Coalition] have a terrible problem with funding and this leads to a weakening of activities. We wanted to represent the region on different levels—the UN, Europe . . . in order to not be eaten by Western Europe . . . we have supranational experience, we have contacts, and I personally, with my experience, prefer intensive cooperation with organizations from postsocialist countries, because cooperation and mutual understanding is better. But there is a problem—the European women's lobby is an entrenched Western European organization that is connected to a good source of money [as an "expert body" of the EU] and they have the money and we have sh** again.

Somewhat later in the process of EU eastern enlargement, another important supranational body—the European Women's Lobby (EWL)—became a new, powerful actor on the scene, because with the accession to the EU, women's NGOs from the new member states obtained the right to become a member. However, Czech women's NGOs seemed united in their opinion that there were some bad sides to the powerful position that the EWL occupies. Not all of them felt that their interests were represented by the EWL, and they did not believe that they would be represented in the future even though the EWL uses the mechanism of a rotating presidency. Also some activists felt that the EWL did not address the EU enlargement process in its agenda up until shortly before the new member states joined the EU (Roth 2006).

Even though a sense of skepticism prevails, some Czech NGOs became EWL members. A representative of a well-established women's NGO focusing on raising gender sensitivity and awareness in Czech society that was founded in the first half of the 1990s in Prague explained:

> We also signed up for it [membership in the EWL]. . . . We are a bit skeptical about the organization, but we want to be members from the practical point of view. It is better to be in than to be out . . . one year ago the situation was such that they [the EWL] would admit some organizations we'd almost never heard of before, even though we have been working in the field for ten years. . . . This was a big impulse for us to get together and get to the EWL, in order to ensure that in the Czech representation of the EWL there would at least be organizations that have been active on these issues for several years. . . . We didn't want to let happen something that happened in some other countries—that some marginal organizations represent those countries.

Even though Czech women's NGOs have experience lobbying at the supranational level through the Karat Coalition, the EWL still seems too far removed from them. The powerful impact of EWL at the supranational level is evaluated positively, but it is still too remote in its concern for the situation in the region.

When it comes to lobbying, networking, and influencing policies and legislation, for Czech women's NGOs it seems more meaningful to concentrate on the national level, even though the government still lacks the political will and understanding to recognize their claims. But at the national level Czech women's NGOs have found their first governmental partners and have started to establish lobbying channels, and the national level seems to be closer to them and seems to have a more direct impact on Czech women's lives. Einhorn (2005) has pointed out that, at least recently, in the short to medium term the effects of lobbying supranational bodies like the EU or the UN must be seen as complementing rather than supplanting the nation-state's role in civic issues such as gender equality and women's issues.

Czech women's NGOs acknowledge the fact, studied and recognized by many scholars (e.g., Regulska 2002 cited in Einhorn 2005; Fraser 1997; True 2003), that transnational bodies are having an increasing impact on citizenship rights (such as gender equality) in individual nation-states in the era of globalization (and, in relation to recent development in the CEE region, the era of EU enlargement). However, the obstacles that Czech women activists seem to encounter at the national level due to lack of will on the part of Czech politicians and representatives of governmental bodies do not lead them to focus more on lobbying at the supranational level.

Conclusions

It is impossible to say whether and at what price gender equality and women's rights issues would have made progress at the political level in the Czech Republic if there had been no need for the country to harmonize its legislation and institutional structures on these issues with that of the EU as precondition for accession. However, it is clear that in a situation where political preference is clearly directed towards economic reforms, the process of the Czech Republic's accession to the EU considerably accelerated the assertion of gender equality as a political issue, even though the process of European integration was primarily focused on the strict evaluation of economic reforms and not as much on an evaluation of social reforms and their consequences.

The voices of women's NGOs that had been working on the issue of gender inequality for many years were only marginally acknowledged during the period of the Czech Republic's preparation for EU accession, and the entire process of promoting gender equality was substantially formalized by officials and politicians. Nevertheless, the emergence of an official institutional structure in the form of transposed EU equality directives and the establishment of government gender equality bodies helped create, with the tireless initiative of women's NGOs, an environment in which the potential of gender mainstreaming can be genuinely employed in the future.

While the Czech government officially accepted gender mainstreaming as the main tool for promoting gender equality, its horizontal (permeating all political processes and issues), procedural (requiring a gender-sensitive approach at all stages of policy making) and inclusive (encompassing the requirements, needs, and aspirations of women and men and thus based on a dialogue between government structures and civil society) dimensions have not yet been activated.

Similarly, under the influence of the accession negotiations, significant changes occurred on the part of civil society. Czech women's civic groups transformed rapidly during this period, in the sense of their orientation, how they operate, and their activities, strategies, and partners. These changes were ushered in by the increasing influence of the EU in the region. They were mainly brought about by the big change in funding, and also by the greater opportunities for influencing government decision-making processes owing to the formation of basic communication channels between governmental and women's nongovernmental sectors. On the one hand, the influence of women's NGOs on Czech government decision making was strengthened, though only within the framework of certain issues, while out-of-mainstream issues and the activity of nonformalized women's civic groups (some of which increased their visibility in reaction to processes of formalization of civic groups) became more marginalized. On the whole it can be said that the positive and negative impact of the processes whereby Czech women's NGOs were formalized, which were accelerated by the process of EU eastern enlargement, can be observed in the influence of Czech women's civic groups at the national and international levels. However, lobbying at the national level, despite the membership of these groups in multinational lobbying groups, continues to be their primary goal.

The analyses conducted on the functioning and development of state structures dealing with the promotion of gender equality in the Czech Republic, and their blind spots, reveal that to really employ the potential of gender mainstreaming and promote women and gender equality in the Czech Republic, it is essential that certain steps still lacking in the Czech Republic be taken. There is a need to develop an extensive web of gender mainstreaming infrastructure not only at the central level, but also regionally, and to ensure that the infrastructure is influential, stable, and well resourced (still lacking in 2007). There is also a need to strengthen civic dialogue and participation on the topic; to empower civil society as such; to promote gender awareness across the board; to introduce gender analysis techniques, and to create expertise in their use; and last but not least to ensure a gender-sensitive knowledge base (slowly improving up to 2007). Without the above-mentioned steps, the potential of gender mainstreaming opened up by the accession negotiations will not be activated and governmental and gender-sensitive nongovernmental structures of gender mainstreaming will continue to have no real influence on decision making and the real position of women in the country. Thus, gendering governmental as well as public structures and institutions as one of the processes of the democratization of society would not be achieved in such a situation.

Notes

1. The chapter is based on data and analyses that were collected and made under three international research projects: "Enlargement, Gender and Governance: The Civic and Political Participation and Representation of Women in EU Candidate Countries" project, coordinated by Yvonne Galligan (University of Belfast), and funded by the Fifth Framework Program of the European Commission (see www.qub.ac.uk/egg), "Constructing Supranational Political Spaces: The European Union, Eastern Enlargement and Women's Agency" project, coordinated by Joanna Regulska (Rutgers University), and funded by the United States National Science Foundation, and "Podpora společenské akceptace a efektivního prosazování genderové rovnosti ve veřejné sféře" project, coordinated by Marie Čermáková (Institute of Sociology, Academy of

Sciences of the Czech Republic), and funded by the Grant Agency of the Academy of Sciences of the Czech Republic. For more information on data, methodology, and analyses see Hašková and Křížková 2003; Kapusta-Pofahl et al. 2005; Hašková 2005b; and Hašková and Křížková 2006.

2. Interestingly, support for women in politics was not stressed by women's civic groups in CEE prior to the EU accession period. Furthermore, some issues, like the critique of the beauty industry and "beauty myth" or support for gender mainstreaming, so far have not become the main issue of any Czech women's civic groups even now.

3. Even though the Czech Republic officially applied for the accession to the EU in 1996, we define the EU accession period as the time period from 1998 to 2004, because during that time the EU accession negotiations were the most strengthened.

4. The EU defines gender mainstreaming according to the definition of the Council of Europe: "Gender mainstreaming is the (re)organisation, improvement, development and evaluation of policy processes so that a gender equality perspective is incorporated in all policies at all levels and at all stages, by all actors normally involved in policy-making" (Council of Europe 1998, 15). However, given the guidelines on how to develop and implement this policy strategy, there remains considerable ambiguity in this area (e.g., Einhorn 2005; Lorenz-Meyer 2003; Musilová 1999).

5. The term *soft law* refers to quasi-legal instruments that do not have any binding force, or whose binding force is somewhat weaker than the binding force of traditional law. They are politically but not legally binding. In the context of international law, the term *soft law* usually refers to agreements reached between parties (usually states) that do not amount to international law in the strictest sense. Soft law consists of non-treaty obligations, which are therefore nonenforceable. The term *soft law* is often used to describe various kinds of quasi-legal instruments of the European Community.

6. In this part of the text we draw on Kapusta-Pofahl et al. 2005 and Hašková 2005b.

References

Bretherton, Charlotte. 2001. Gender Mainstreaming and EU Enlargement: Swimming Against the Tide? *Journal of European Public Policy* 8 (1): 60–81.

Čermáková, Marie, Hana Hašková, Alena Křížková, Marcela Linková, Hana Maříková, and Martina Musilová. 2000. *Relations and Changes of Gender Differences in the Czech Society in the 90s.* Prague: Institute of Sociology of the Academy of Sciences of the Czech Republic.

Council of Europe. 1998. *Gender Mainstreaming: Conceptual Framework, Methodology and Presentation of Good Practices.* Strasbourg: Council of Europe.

Clavero, Sara, and Yvonne Galligan. 2005. "A Job in Politics Is Not for Women": Analysing Barriers to Women´s Political Representation in CEE. *Czech Sociological Review* 41 (6): 979–1004.

Einhorn, Barbara. 2005. Citizenship, Civil Society and Gender Mainstreaming: Contested Priorities in an Enlarging Europe. *Czech Sociological Review* 41 (6): 1023–40.

Fraser, Nancy. 1997. *Justice Interruptus: Critical Reflexions on the "Postsocialist" Condition.* New York and London: Routledge.

Fuszara, Malgorzata. 2005. Between Feminism and Catholic Church: Women's Movement in Poland. *Czech Sociological Review* 4 (6): 1057–76.

Gal, Susan, and Gail Kligman. 2000a. *The Politics of Gender after Socialism.* Princeton, NJ: Princeton University Press.

———, eds. 2000b. *Reproducing Gender: Politics, Publics, and Everyday Life after Socialism.* Princeton, NJ: Princeton University Press.

Hann, Chris. 1996. Introduction: Political Society and Civil Anthropology. In *Civil Society: Challenging Western Model*, eds. Chris Hann and Elizabeth Dunn, 1–26. London: Routledge.

Hašková, Hana. 2005a. Gender Roles, Family Policy and Family Behavior: Changing Czech Society in the European Context. In *Generations, Kinship and Care. Gendered Provisions of Social Security in Central Eastern Europe*, eds. Haldis Haukanes and Francise Pine, 23–52. Bergen: University of Bergen.

———. 2005b. Czech Women's Civic Organizing under State Socialist Regime, Socio-economic Transformation and EU Accession Eras. *Czech Sociological Review* 41 (6): 1077–110.

Hašková, Hana, and Alena Křížková, eds. 2003. *Women's Civic and Political Participation in the Czech Republic and the Role of European Union Gender Equality and Accession Policies*. Sociological Papers 03:09. Praha: Sociologický ústav AV ČR.

———. 2006. Rozhodčí a hráči: Vliv socio-ekonomické transformace a evropské intergrace na ženské občanské skupiny. In *Mnohohlasem. Vyjednávání ženských prostorů po roce 1989*, eds. Hana Hašková, Alena Křížková, and Marcela Linková, 81–102. Prague: Institute of Sociology, Academy of Sciences.

Kapusta-Pofahl, Karen, Hana Hašková, and Marta Kolářová. 2005. Only a Dead Fish Flows with the Stream: Subversive Voices, NGOization and Czech Women's Organizing. *The Anthropology of East Europe Review* 23 (1): 38–52.

Kay, Rebecca. 2000. *Russian Women and Their Organizations: Gender, Discrimination and Grassroots Women's Organizations, 1991–1996*. Basingstoke, UK: Macmillan.

Lang, Sabine. 1997. The NGOization of Feminism. In *Transitions, Environments, Translations: Feminisms in International Politics*, eds. Joan W. Scott, Cora Kaplan, and Debra Keates, 101–120. New York: Routledge.

Linková, Marcela. 2003. The Institutional Framework for Equal Opportunities Enforcement. In *Women's Civic and Political Participation in the Czech Republic and the Role of European Union Gender Equality and Accession Policies*, eds. Hana Hašková and Alena Křížková, 31–41. Sociological Papers 03/9, Institute of Sociology, Czech Academy of Sciences.

Lorenz-Meyer, Dagmar 2003. Policy Initiatives and Tools to Promote Women's Participation and Gender Equality in the Process of the Czech Republic's Accession to the European Union. In *Women's Civic and Political Participation in the Czech Republic and the Role of European Union Gender Equality and Accession Policies*, eds. Hana Hašková and Alena Křížková, 59–83. Sociological Papers 03/9, Institute of Sociology, Czech Academy of Sciences.

Machonin, Pavel, and Milan Tuček, eds. 1996. *Česká společnost v transformaci. K prom nám sociální struktury*. Prague: SLON.

Marksová-Tominová, Michaela 1999. *Formy ženských aktivit*. Praha: Gender Studies, o.p.s. Unpublished document.

Musilová, M. 1999. Equal Opportunity as a Matter of Public Interest. *Czech Sociological Review* 7 (2): 95–204.

Osvaldová, Barbora. 2004. *Česká média a feminismus*. Praha: Libri, Slon.

Pavlík, Petr, ed. 2004. *Stínová zpráva v oblasti rovného zacházení a rovných příležitostí žen a mužů*. Prague: Gender Studies, o.p.s.

Potůček, Martin. 1997. *Nejen trh*. Praha: Slon.

Roth, Silke. 2006. Sisterhood and Solidarity? Organizing for Gender Issues and Women's Equality in the Enlarged European Union. Paper presented at the Gender, Citizenship and Participation Conference, London School of Economics, 23–24 March 2006.

Sloat, Amanda. 2004a. Legislating for Equality: The Implementation of the EU Equality *Acquis* in Central and Eastern Europe. Jean Monet Working Papers 08/04. New York: New York School of Law.

———. 2004b. Where are the Women? Female Political Visibility in EU Accession States. *Transitions* XLIV-1: 45–58.

———. 2005. The Rebirth of Civil Society: The Growth of Women's NGOs in Central and Eastern Europe. *European Journal of Women's Studies* 12: 437–52.

True, Jacqui. 2003. *Gender, Globalization and Postsocialism: The Czech Republic after Communism.* New York, Chichester: Columbia University Press.

Večerník, Jiří, ed. 1998. *Zpráva o vývoji české společnosti 1989–1998.* Prague: Academia.

Zippel, Kathrin. 2004. Transnational Advocacy Networks and Policy Cycles in the European Union: The Case of Sexual Harassment. *Social Politics* 11 (1): 57–85.

9

THE IMPACT OF EU ACCESSION ON GENDER EQUALITY IN HUNGARY

ح

Noémi Kakucs and Andrea Pető

In 2005 and 2006, the Hungarian media were saturated with news of a sexual harassment case in which two individuals were involved from the newly founded Government Office for Equal Opportunities. The verdict passed in April 2006 stated that the defendant, a high-ranking, middle-aged male civil servant was not guilty of sexual harassment, as the plaintiff, a young female secretary, failed to prove the accusations, and the latter was sentenced to pay financial compensation for the moral damage caused. This is not the only case concerning sexual harassment in the country, but this case tells a lot about the paradoxes of how gender equality was institutionalized in Hungary. The irony of the case is that both parties were employed at the Government Office for Equal Opportunities, and that the plaintiff brought the case to the civil court and not to the Equal Treatment Authority (ETA), established purposely for the enforcement of the 2003 CXXV. Act on Equal Treatment and Promotion of Equal Opportunities. However, as critics of the act pointed out, without clear evidence it is almost impossible to prove sexual harassment whatever the location is. Moreover, as the low number of lawsuits (none of which regard sexual harassment) before the ETA show, there is little difference between the sentences passed by the ETA and the civil court (Rádi 2006, 116–18).[1]

As the small introductory story shows, there is a huge discrepancy between de jure and de facto implementation of gender equality in Hungary. Though it is difficult to assess the impact of the EU on decreasing gender inequalities in the lives of Hungarian women because the equality policies are aimed to produce long-term results and their immediate effect is minimal, this chapter examines the influence of the European Union in Hungary before and following the accession in May 2004. First, we provide an overview of various gender equality policies and their effectiveness, in particular gender mainstreaming (Beveridge et al. 2000; Booth and Bennet 2002), then we explain which framework the Hungarian government adopted and highlight the major developments of the Hungarian gender equality machinery since the 2004 EU accession. Finally, the chapter analyzes some of the different elements of strategic implementation of gender equality policy by focusing on changes in the labor market as well as civil society mobilization.

Achieving Gender Equality—An Overview of Strategies

The objectives of equal opportunities can be enacted in three ways: by modifying the constitution, through introducing the so-called equal opportunities law, or other laws and provisions (Silius 2000). However, as the cases of many countries show, formal equality before the law does not result in substantive equality between genders. Three approaches to gender equality that emerged during the development of equal opportunity policies in the EU can be identified: equal opportunity and treatment, positive action, and mainstreaming (Bacchi 1997, 2001; Booth and Bennett 2002; Rees 1998; Verloo 2001).

According to Booth and Bennett (2002, 433–5), the success of gender equality policies depends on the integrated application of equal opportunity polices, positive action, and gender mainstreaming. Though present in the European Commission's understanding of gender equality, the failure to articulate how the three perspectives complement each other resulted in misunderstanding and inconsistencies in gender equality policies (Booth and Bennett 2002, 435). The balance between the three perspectives is even more important in the newly enlarged EU context, because in new member states these perspectives might have developed unevenly or some of them might be totally missing. Only the EU could exert pressure on its member countries to equalize the imbalance of the perspectives. However, as the EU is primarily an economic unity, gender equality has been framed in terms of employment and social inclusion, and all equality policies, due to liberal ideology, are translated and reduced mainly into equal opportunities policy. But, as Sylvia Walby (2004) argued, one should not underestimate the complex ways the powers of the EU extend beyond the narrow economic scope and, through employment and social welfare regulations, initiate profound changes within gender regimes.[2]

The three approaches to gender equality mentioned above result in separate conceptual frameworks in policy making (Eveline and Bacchi 2005). To achieve

formal gender equality, first there is a need for firm equal opportunity and antidiscrimination regulations. However, as long as actual discriminatory structural barriers are not recognized and eliminated, enacting equal opportunities policies simply perpetuates inequalities rather than truly overcoming them. Therefore a new
strategy—gender mainstreaming—was introduced into policy making. Gender
mainstreaming is considered to have the potential to actually overcome inequality. However, it is often refuted on the ground of already existing gender equality
policies. As gender mainstreaming aims at long-term changes in gender regimes,
it requires high-level political commitment and comprehensive implementation
strategies, while the immediate results are not visible. Thus the analysis of the
process of institutionalization and implementation of gender mainstreaming has
become a great concern for feminist scholars (Bacchi 1997, 2001; Beveridge et
al. 2000; Booth and Bennett 2002; Eveline and Bacchi 2005; Pincus 2002; Rees
2005; Rubery 2002; Verloo 2001).

The commitment to gender equality and to gender mainstreaming is a political issue that very much depends on the political interests of parties and
governments, who are not necessarily prepared to meet the challenge of inves-
tigating the entire policy arena for compatibility with the objectives of gender
equality (Rubery 2002, 503). Introducing the gender equality perspective in
all policy areas implies the transformation of institutional structures and practices that perpetuate gender inequality. There are two tasks to be faced so that
gender mainstreaming as a strategy can be effectively implemented: first, the
necessary elements—such as resources, time, and organizational structures—of
the strategy need to be identified: second, thorough analysis is needed to describe the context that supports the mainstreaming strategy (Booth and Bennett 2002, 431).

To fuse the different gender mainstreaming strategies in the European context, Beveridge et al. (2000) demand a common theory to be adopted that over-
arches the various state practices. In their view, developmental theory serves as
a possible basis for the creation of a consistent theory or approach to gender
mainstreaming. Two approaches to gender mainstreaming are identified: an integrationist and an agenda-setting approach. While the integrationist approach
addresses gender issues within a set of policy paradigms, the agenda-setting approach aims at the transformation of already-existing policy agendas (Beveridge
et al. 2000, 388–91).

We get closer to the puzzle of explaining paradoxes of implementation of gender equality policies if we examine the different policy strategies and practices,
including gender mainstreaming, in the European context. As gender equality
policy in the EU was focusing on equal treatment and opportunities for women,
the accession of the CEE countries created a new situation. The institutionalization of gender mainstreaming in the EU-15 countries happened simultaneously
with the processes of eastern enlargement, and thus the horizontal expansion of

gender mainstreaming coincided with the horizontal expansion of the geopolitical boundaries of the EU. While gender mainstreaming was unevenly integrated in the old member states and in the wider European institutional structures[3], the accession of CEE countries created a challenge to gender equality policies, which in order to be effective have to be both vertically and horizontally integrated within these postsocialist democracies.

Adopting and Implementing Gender Mainstreaming in Hungary

The 2004 EU enlargement has brought significant challenges for both the old and the new member states regarding gender equality. The expansion introduced wider Europe to a new situation, that of dealing with countries that had experienced state socialism and statist feminism for several decades. Unlike the gradual and dynamic evolution of equal opportunity policies aiming to achieve de facto equality between women and men in the European Union[4], gender equality policies reappeared on the national political agendas of the Central Eastern European countries in the late 1990s only due to international pressure. In Hungary, similarly to other CEE countries[5] undergoing legal harmonization with EU legislation, the political parties were the main agents of top-down implementation, while they generally refused the idea of equal opportunities policy on the grounds of already-existing legal provisions. However, they could not openly oppose equal opportunities legislation, as the adoption of different UN conventions, especially the Convention on the Elimination of All Forms of Discrimination Against Women (CEDAW) and, more importantly, of EU provisions and directives had already made a significant impact (either directly or indirectly) on the legislation of these countries. Even though the normative power of the above-mentioned organizations was not coercive, and (as viewed by some critics) gender policies were considered to be of secondary importance in the EU accession negotiations, the failure to meet especially the EU standards might have resulted in specific economic restrictions and sanctions disadvantaging the disobeying parties (Böröcz and Sarkar 2005), a possible risk that none of accession countries wanted to undertake.

In the Hungarian legislation, there are antecedents of exercising the requirement of equal treatment and of promoting equal opportunities. Several major legal documents, such as the constitution[6], § 76 of the 1959/IV. Act about the Civil Code[7], § 5 of the 1992/XXII. Act about the Labor Code[8], or the 1998/XXIV. Act about the rights and equal opportunities of people living with disabilities contain normative provisions that are binding for persons, legal relations, and institutions under their scope. This means that the normative conception of law, which implies that it may advance the development of new, desirable attitudes, is not without antecedents. Thus, as the national legislation already contained provisions on equality, one would expect smooth institutional adjustment to the EU institutions and legislature. However, the above-mentioned gender-neutral policy frame in which the issue of gender was addressed together with issues of race, ethnicity, cultural differences, and disabilities obstructed the adoption of new policy measures that could tackle problems specific to gender. Thus, the EU integrationist approach was minimized in the Hungarian legislation.

Effective gender equality policies must be integrated, incorporating gender mainstreaming as strategy to take into consideration the relational nature of gender differences. However, the already-existing regulations on (gender) equality did not favor the introduction of the gender-sensitive policy in the Hungarian legislation. The introduction of the Joint Inclusion Memorandum (JIM) and the National Action Plan on Social Inclusion (NAP) in 2003 signaled the beginning of new policy processes. These documents were developed under tight EU guidance and were the most important documents regarding gender mainstreaming in Hungary. In these documents, gender mainstreaming was regarded as a horizontal principle and integrated within the larger social inclusion agenda.

The Joint Inclusion Memorandum, prepared in the framework of the accession process and signed with the European Commission in December 2003, outlined the main problems Hungary faced in terms of social exclusion and poverty and listed the tasks Hungary still had to complete in order to realize EU common social policy objectives in the country. It addressed the exclusionary effects of several social factors like poverty, ethnicity (with special emphasis on Roma), disability, gender, and, marginally, sexual orientation. Gender equality, though considered separately in a section of the document, appeared as a horizontal principle throughout all the chapters. It was argued that gender equality should be perceived as a comprehensive horizontal aim, which was above and between policy sectors. Referring to the strategy to be followed, the document argued, "addressing social exclusion needs a comprehensive approach, which mainstreams gender equality, integrates Roma in the society and provides equal opportunities for people with disabilities" (Joint Inclusion Memorandum 2003, 45). The National Action Plan on Social Inclusion (2004) addressed mainstreaming equal opportunity and social inclusion more generally, and within that mentioned more specifically, among other directives, "to take into account the women's perspective in every policy field" (National Action Plan 2004, 19).

Still within the framework of the social inclusion agenda, the National Development Plan I (NDP) was a document preparing the national policy machinery for spending EU structural funds in the period of 2004–06. Equal opportunity issues were translated by the NDP into questions related primarily to Roma, women (identifying subgroups of special needs), and the disabled by trying to articulate cross-sectional thinking. According to the implementation plans of the NDP, representatives of gender (women's) equality organizations were to be involved in the monitoring committees assigned to supervise the strategy formulation and operational activities of the five major program areas with EU funds on social and economic development of Hungary in 2004–06. In order to operationalize the equal opportunity principle, an equal opportunity guideline was developed for applicants and evaluators (Krizsán and Pap 2005, 34). The implementation of the National Development Plan was in progress in 2006 and has not yet been assessed, and at the time of writing it was too early to predict the impact of the EU Structural Funds on the lives of Hungarian women.

By 2006, two years after the accession, Hungary incorporated some elements of gender equality policy in the EU documents, but it did not adopt any strategic policy document to introduce gender mainstreaming. These policy documents marked the beginning of a process targeting long-term improvements in the situation of women. However, they also displayed the controversial position of gender equality issues on the Hungarian political agenda. As the State Audit Office Report argued (2006), the documents treated the issue of gender equality at a relatively high level of generality, without any detailed policies designing the adequate tools and instruments for implementing the policy objectives. These documents were adopted to comply with EU demands; however, they also revealed the discrepancies that resulted from lack of political will and commitment to the issue: no policy tools or systems of monitoring were developed, and the suggested policy aims did not address the real needs of Hungarian women.

Gender Equality Policies for Women without Feminist Participation?

In Hungary, the controversial relationship between the national government and civil society has a long tradition and is assumed to have long-lasting consequences. This is especially true in the case of the women's movement. Paradoxically, the typical entrepreneurs of "the East," the civil society activists and academics, who planned to create a bridge between EU norms and national-level legislation, were complaining about the gender-blind practices of their own governments, while the EU gender equality mechanisms, in the framework of antidiscriminatory legislation, were accepted by the same national political elite. This is even more striking if it is taken into consideration that scholarship on Eastern Europe in the early twenty-first century has emphasized that after the transition women's position in these societies was characterized by an alarming worsening—i.e., the position of women in the East converged to the position of women in the West as far as formal criteria of equality such as employment, participation in politics, and so on. For example, the number of women MPs in the first democratically elected Hungarian parliament in 1990 (7 percent) decreased dramatically in comparison with the "statist feminist" period (25 percent), and reached the same level as Great Britain in that year; the same tendency can be observed in the case of women's employment (see Pető 2003a, 2004).

The 2000 CEDAW Report on Hungary stated that while the number of NGOs increased radically after the political transition, the growth of the number of women's organizations slowed down considerably after the initial boom (Krizsán and Pap 2005, 14). It is important to note that following the transition there was no crucial issue that could have facilitated the emergence of a strong women's movement in Hungary (like the issue of abortion, which facilitated group forma-tion during the mid-1960s to 1970s among Western feminists, and still is a mobi-lizing force for women in Poland). This resulted in the weakening of access and influence within national policy making for women's organizations.

As Walby (2004) argues, the interaction between the three levels of gov-ernance involved in gender policies—global, regional, and national—deter-mines the success of implementing gender equality policies. Besides the inter-action of the different levels of governance, a successful gender equality policy would also require interaction and cooperation between governmental and nongovernmental actors, i.e., a balance between the expert-bureaucratic and participatory-democratic models of policy implementation. This could ideally be achieved only if both the representatives of the national government and women's NGOs cooperate in policy making. Hence, the prerequisite of suc-cessful implementation of gender equality policies is the existence of a strong feminist movement including state (femocrats) and non-state (independent) feminists and high-level participation of women in decision making at all lev-els of policy making.

However, in Hungary the implementation of gender equality policy was the task of specialized experts and administrators. As many policies were prepared on short deadlines, the national machinery might be blamed for excluding the representatives of civil society wishing to be involved. On the other hand, as the government had to produce visible results on short term, it is understandable that the time for procedural requirements and social debate was short. Thus, it can be claimed that both the governmental side and the NGO side operated retroactively rather than proactively with respect to crucial issues concerning women's rights. Therefore, even influential women's NGOs failed to make any significant contribution to the policy process beyond representing a critical voice. Ideally, for effective cooperation, both open policy-making processes and the professional competence of NGOs are required.

The Hungarian government in the past years followed the integrationist path, and since 2003 has founded (independently from the women's NGOs) sixteen local-level offices called Houses of Opportunity in major regional cities. These institutions were financed partly by the ministry and partly by municipal budgets, defining both the activities (consultations, trainings on labor market reintegra-tion) and the target groups these institutions address. This meant that the con-cept of equal opportunities was negotiated by these parties so that it could be integrated in the already-existing institutional frameworks.

Unfortunately, it is telling that some of the regional office reports simply omitted women's/gender issues from their platforms. Some restricted the inclusion of gender to the "Women in the Media" lecture series organized under the auspices of the ministry. The few regional offices that incorporated gender issues in their programs focused mainly on the issue of women's reintegration into the labor market by offering counseling and awareness-raising programs (House of Opportunity 2006). According to the official report (2006) on the operation of these institutions, gender-related inequalities were not addressed separately—rather, women were defined as a disadvantaged group along with children, the elderly, Roma, etc., thus simplifying the complex dimension of gender inequalities.

The Institutionalization of Gender Equality in Hungary

Setting up the national machinery, as the first strategic step of the implementation of gender equality, was accomplished relatively early in Hungary following the Beijing Declaration of 1995. At the end of that year, the Secretariat for Women's Policy (which was renamed the Equal Opportunity Secretariat in 1996) was established within the Ministry of Labor. The secretariat had predominantly consultative status, and in the first years it was considered a relatively "progressive and effective organ," though not capable of pursuing any gender mainstreaming tasks (Krizsán and Pap 2005, 12). In 1998, the newly elected conservative government changed the institutional status of the secretariat and integrated it at a relatively low institutional level in the Ministry of Social and Family Affairs. Following the government change in 2002, the secretariat was reorganized several times by the new socialist-liberal government. First, it was renamed the Directorate General for Equal Opportunities, and operated in the Ministry of Employment and Labor. Following its reorganization, the directorate was elevated to ministerial status and integrated into the new Government Office for Equal Opportunities established in 2003, which included equal opportunity policies on three main grounds: ethnicity, disability, and gender. The governmental restructuring in 2004 brought yet another change in the Hungarian women's policy machinery. The Government Office for Equal Opportunities was "downgraded" and integrated within the new Ministry of Youth, Social and Family Affairs and Equal Opportunities (ICSSZEM). From June 2004, this same ministry was responsible for social inclusion issues falling under the EU Social Agenda.

The continuous restructuring of the women's policy machinery in the Hungarian governance severely damaged its official function and scope of authority. It was integrated into ministries (Labor and Social Affairs) that were not "political," i.e., not backed by separate parliamentary act or law and therefore subjected to the will of the ruling governments (Jalusic and Antic 2000, 21–22). As the alterations in the position of women's policy machinery show, there was no direct correlation between the effectiveness of the machinery and its position in the institutional hierarchy. Instead, the policy access and influence of the machinery much depended on the personal commitment of various politicians responsible for this policy area.[9]

The elevation of the state machinery to the rank of governmental office accompanied a policy shift from gender equality policy focus to equal opportunity policies on all grounds. As a consequence, the policy frames referred to general equal opportunity concerns, with fewer statements made on gender issues specifically. At the same time, gender mainstreaming could rarely be considered present even at the rhetorical level in the key policy statements of the ministerial office. The tasks attributed to the directorate within mainstreaming were primarily the coordination of gender-related actions of different ministries in the fields of employment, social policy, education, and economic policy, and monitoring gender equality aspects of certain strategic policy documents.

The broad institutional umbrella was widened even further by its inclusion in the social inclusion agenda. The Ministry of Youth, Family and Social Affairs and Equal Opportunities was responsible for the promotion of social cohesion and for the implementation of the EU Social Agenda aiming at the modernization and development of the European social model. Even within this framework, the principle of gender equality was conceptualized as a horizontal principle in Hungarian policy making and not a separate target to be achieved. Consequently, as there was not any wide demand from the population for specific programs targeting women, gender issues were "mainstreamed"—included in the larger frame of social inclusion, which resulted in the marginalization of gender equality.

By 2006, it seemed that the shift brought the complete marginalization of gender equality issues in Hungary. Only one small department was dealing with gender equality issues under the supervision of a deputy state secretary in charge of strategic development and international affairs, not equal opportunities, unlike the departments on Roma policy and disabled policy (Krizsán and Pap 2005, 10). In October 2004, officially altogether nine people were responsible for the coordination and implementation of gender equality policy in Hungary, and the number of employees gradually decreased. From the start, the expertise in gender equality policy was not a prerequisite for the staff to be hired. The Report of the State Audit Office (2006) on the operation of the Ministry in 2005 highlighted the imbalance between the number of civil servants and experts, and warned that the small number of experts jeopardized the effective operation of the directorate. However, due to the lack of institutionalization of gender studies in Hungary[10] it is rather hypocritical to demand expertise.

The governmental restructuring following the parliamentary elections in 2006 brought the reorganization of the gender equality machinery within the Ministry of Social Affairs and Labor. Moreover, a new Gender Equality Council was established by the 1089/2006. (IX. 25.) Governmental Decree on the Establishment of the Gender Equality Council, replacing the inoperative Council of Women's Representation. This council was a consultative body with an increased number of civil society representatives and experts. Though the immediate impact of the reorganized gender machinery on women's lives was not yet visible, the governmental restructuring and the initial developments can be considered as a new opportunity window for women's NGOs to gain political access and policy influence on gender related issues.

Further Problems: The Three-legged Equality Stool

The implementation of gender equality policy covers a wide scope of policy making, as the gender equality perspective should be considered and introduced into all policy fields—the most important being the fields of political representation, employment, and public services. This logic does not fit in the structure of local administration, and because of this, we can see the resistance of state administrations throughout Europe. Employing certain rhetorical devices, it is easy to manipulate, "forget," postpone, and disregard the complex and intricate system of responsibilities and financial obligations. One way of resistance is the suspension or deferment of decision making, and questioning the actuality of the problem in question. In Hungary and its neighboring countries, the absence of the political legitimization of equal opportunities policy, as well as its weak institutionalization and poorly funded system, made this kind of "forgetting" very easy.

Achieving the *acquis*, Hungary satisfied the EU demands and achieved de jure fulfillment of all formal legal requirements relevant to equality (implicitly gender equality) imposed by the EU. However, Hungary did not adopt any strategic policy document to introduce gender mainstreaming. Instead some elements of gender equality policy were included in national legislation by modifying the already existing labor, social, and family codes during the accession process. The core element of gender equality policy in the Hungarian context, similar to the other member states, were equal opportunities and equal treatment in employment, and the major site of implementation was the labor market, the sphere where women are the most disadvantaged.

Several studies have been directed on labor market participation, with special focus on women, following the regime change and the impact of the European Union (Büködi 2005; Fodor 2004, 2005). According to these studies, the rate of employment fell dramatically and unemployment had spread by the early 1990s as a result of the political and economic changes. In 1993, the decrease in unemployment began, and favorable changes such as the expansion of the labor market began in 1997. In recent years, this positive trend stalled and showed growth again only in 2003.

The employment rate of men in Hungary, as in other countries, was tradition-ally higher than that of women. In 2003, 51 percent of women and 63 percent of men were employed (Büködi 2005, 16), and 45 percent of all employed were women (Krizsán and Pap 2005, 54). Women's participation in the service sector has been traditionally higher than men's: in 1992, 64 percent and in 2003, 74 percent of women in employment had a job in the service industry (Büködi 2005, 23). Women were over-represented in poorly paid state sector jobs such as health care and education.

Table 9.1 presents the wage disparities between women and men according to the data (1998–2003) of the Hungarian Central Statistical Office.

According to these results, the wage differential between women and men gradually decreased in recent years. However, despite women's overall higher level of education, in 2003, women's gross average income was 13 percent lower than that of men. Though not visible in this table, the gender pay gap varied ac-cording to the qualification requirements of various occupations. Women's wages were 90 percent of men's wages in case of the so-called simple jobs (which do not require qualification), while 70 percent in case of jobs requiring higher qualifica-tion (university or college degree). In positions of comparable income both in the private and in the state sector, women were paid on average some 13–14 percent less than men (Krizsán and Pap 2005, 49).

The statistical data on employment in the third period of 2005 show similar figures. Accordingly, women's employment rate decreased to 44 percent of all employed, which essentially means that only every second woman is economi-cally active[11] in Hungary. But it is important to note that the Hungarian number was the third worst average level of women's employment among the twenty-five EU member states. It should also be noted that the poor Hungarian score, i.e.

Table 9.1. Female Earnings as a Percentage of Male Earnings

Year	Gross earnings			Net earnings		
	Manual	Non-manual	Total	Manual	Non-manual	Total
1998	73	63	82	79	68	86
1999	72	61	81	77	66	84
2000	73	60	81	78	65	84
2001	74	61	81	79	65	85
2002	77	64	85	83	67	87
2003	78	66	88	84	71	90
2004	77	66	86	84	71	90

Source: HSCO, *Women and Men in Hungary 2004*, 124.

women's low employment rate, is partly due to the very low employment rate (11 percent) of women aged between fifty-five and sixty-four. In the last two years, the employment rate of both women and men has been rising, partly due to the higher retirement age for women and partly to the stricter rules on disability pensions (Büködi 2005, 16–17).

Two measures were introduced that indirectly fostered the closure of the gender pay gap: the introduction of the minimum wage and the 50 percent wage increase for those working in the public sector. These changes contributed considerably to the pay increases for women and the narrowing of the pay gap, as an increase in wages was introduced in sectors in which women were over-represented. Other ways of encouraging women's employment were the introduction of flexible working times and part-time and distant employment opportunities. In Hungary, however, in comparison with the EU-15, relatively few employees worked in flexible work arrangements: 22 percent compared to the 45 percent EU average. In 2003 only 6 percent of women employees in Hungary were employed part-time (Krizsán and Pap 2005, 44).

However, in order to at least approach the 60 percent of women's employment target of the Lisbon strategy, other institutional changes need to be introduced that could facilitate women's integration in the labor market. For full integration, equal opportunity policies are not enough; a gender-integrated approach is needed. In order to change the traditional pattern of the domestic division of labor, changes should be introduced in men's role as well; otherwise, gender equality remains a dream to be never fulfilled. The Act LXXXXIV. of 1998 (introduced in 1999) regarding parental leave permits both parents to apply for child-related benefits, whereas only mothers and single fathers were entitled to it. However, in 2006 there were still no provisions encouraging men to apply for parental leave (Monitoring the EU Accession 2002, 276), thus the percentage of applying fathers is very low. Therefore involvement of men in caring for children in practice remains symbolic. In fact, in 2003 only 6 percent of those who received childcare benefits, and about 1 percent of those who received a childcare allowance were men (National Action Plan 2004, 42). Another incentive for fathers to take on a greater share in family responsibilities is the right of fathers to have five days of work-time allowance upon the birth of the child. This provision serves the realization of a nontransferable leave available for fathers after the birth of a child. Besides this peculiar provision, other means should be introduced to encourage fathers to participate in family responsibilities (Krizsán and Pap 2005, 21).

Though the generosity of the Hungarian parental leave provisions (i.e., full-time leave until the child is three years old, with uniform social insurance benefits until the child is two years old and a lower, wage-based, allowance for the third year) is welcomed by many, the policy should be assessed and documented to avoid its ambivalent nature and to determine the extent the long parental allowance hinders women in returning to the labor market, particularly if not accompanied by the existence of flexible jobs. Generous parental leave provisions are beneficial only if accompanied with good institutional childcare arrangements to enable women to return to the labor market. But when these policies contradict each other, women's position becomes difficult. As the figures in the table 9.2 show, only two-thirds of women using parental leave returned to the labor market. Approximately half of those returning continued their careers at the original workplace, while a significant number of women started a career at a new workplace or became self-employed, which can be considered a disadvantage.

In order to avoid the entrapment caused by the prolonged absence of women from the labor market due to child rearing, changes have to be introduced in the childcare policy. Such a policy should not only focus on the payment of different forms of childcare benefits, but also on subsequent or parallel support for reintegration in the labor market. Furthermore, the increase in the availability of daycare would also contribute to the easier reintegration of women in the labor market.

If in Hungary the conditions of 2007 persist in the availability and affordability of childcare services, the targets set at the Barcelona summit with regard to childcare (i.e., providing childcare by 2010 to at least 90 percent of children aged between three years old and the mandatory school age and at least 33 percent of children under three years of age) will be difficult to meet. While the coverage for children below the age of three years old is below 10 percent, there is extensive coverage (90 percent) in kindergartens for the three to six age group. Moreover, there are wide regional disparities in access to childcare. The negative impact of the transition—that is, the closure of childcare institutions as a result of economic restructuring—was not compensated against. The responsibility of providing childcare facilities resides mainly with the central government, while the role of employers is barely visible. The growing deficit and the decrease in birth rates obstruct the creation of new childcare facilities, widening regional

Table 9.2. Trajectories of Former Childcare Benefit Recipients (in percent)

	1999	2002
Becomes housewife	12	17
Claims new maternity leave	16	12
Becomes unemployed	3	7
Becomes self-employed	2	3
Looks for new workplace	32	26
Returns to original workplace	35	3

Source: HSCO, *Women and Men in Hungary 2004*, 102.

disparities even further. According to the publication of the Central Statistical Office (KSH) the number of day nurseries in Hungary decreased by half between the years of 1990 and 2003 (CSO 2003, 177). In relation to this, in 2002 the main reason for the unsolved situation of childcare was seen as the lack of places in day nurseries (CSO with the Government Office for Equal Opportunities 2003, 96).

As this short overview on the Hungarian developments shows, Hungary adopted an integrationist approach to gender equality policies to be implemented through a top-down model. Promoted by the EU, the integrationist approach to gender mainstreaming promises to handle the complex issues of gender inequality through targeting women's employment in more effective ways. By the 2004 accession to the EU, Hungary committed itself to the promotion of gender equality. However, the question still remains how much the integrationist approach, if minimalized and limited to employment policy regulations, discloses or shades the inherently political character of the problem.

Conclusion

The accession of Hungary to the European Union created controversial feelings and expectations: lofty dreams of economic advancement and a greater influx of capital were mixed with deep apathy and strong anti-EU fears of inflation. The European Parliamentary elections in 2004 already signaled a gender-specific problem: women were more euro-skeptic than men, as 10 percent more women voted against joining the EU than men (Pető 2004). During elections, women voted for political values that ensured their equal access to goods, independent of gender differences. The appearance of gender equality in the norms and rights of EU member states has always been pushed through from above, and the key to their success was that the states played a major role in their formulation. In Hungary, both liberal and conservative parties showed a visceral disinclination to equal opportunities politics, as they expected the state to follow the patterns of statist feminism, the politics of pre-1989 Soviet-type emancipation, especially that aspect of it which focused on women's employment. The sociopolitical program that was identified with state tutelage and interference since 1990 has been dropped from the vocabulary of politics, and the parties have begun to voice the neoliberal idea that "smart people will get ahead." By now, in the narrow latitude of Hungarian economy the social impacts of this phenomenon have become enormous very fast.

In Hungary, the introduction of equal opportunities policy in all policy areas was a requirement of eligibility for EU accession. Under strong EU pressure, the process was initiated from the international level through legislative and institutional changes. During this process an integrationist approach was undertaken through an expert-bureaucratic model of implementation. There were changes in some policy areas with relevance for gender equality, such as policies concerning women's participation in the labor market, welfare benefits, domestic violence, prostitution, and abortion. However, by focusing on equal opportunities policies and distancing itself from any kind of positive action, the Hungarian national governance failed to include the three equality perspectives in its policies on gender equality. Through the integrationist approach, Hungary adopted and realized some level of institutionalization of women's policy machinery and some policy changes, and satisfied the minimum demands of EU. Gender mainstreaming was adopted at a rhetorical level in key policy documents, but in 2006, a comprehensive strategy included in all policy fields was still missing, and the principle of a women's perspective was subordinated to more important economic or social concerns. The governmental restructuring after the 2006 general elections can be viewed as an opportunity window for representatives of civil society to become involved in policy making. Gender mainstreaming as a strategy can facilitate cooperation between the parties. However, as long as there is no high-level mobilization and strong pressure from civil society and representatives of women's organizations, it is illusory to expect further developments.

Notes

1. For a discussion on sexual harassment in the EU, see the chapter by Kathrin Zippel in this volume.
2. For an extensive discussion on EU legislation on reconciliation of work and family life, see the chapter of Kimberly Morgan in this volume.
3. See for example Beveridge et al. (2000) on the uneven developments in Great Britain, and the analysis of Pollack and Hafner-Burton (2000) on the EU institutions.
4. For a discussion on the differences between the gender and employment regimes of old and new EU members, see the chapter by Angelika von Wahl in this volume.
5. See in this volume the chapters by Joanna Regulska and Magda Grabowska on Poland and by Hana Hašková and Alena Křížková on gender equality in the Czech republic.
6. Article 66 of the constitution states the following: (1) The Republic of Hungary shall ensure the equality of men and women in all civil, political, economic, social, and cultural rights. (2) In the Republic of Hungary mothers shall receive support and protection before and after the birth of the child, in accordance with separate regulations. (3) Separate regulations shall ensure the protection of women and youth in the workplace.
7. It prohibits discrimination against private persons on the grounds of gender, race, ancestry, national origin, or religion; violation of the freedom of conscience; any unlawful restriction of personal freedom; injury to body or health; and contempt for or insult to the honor, integrity, or human dignity of private persons shall be deemed as violations of inherent rights. This article is very useful in cases where the employer refuses to employ a woman owing to her gender.
8. (1) In connection with an employment relationship, no discrimination shall be practiced against employees on the basis of gender, age, race, national origin, religion, political views, or membership in organizations representing employees or activities connected therewith, as well

as any other circumstances not related to employment. Any differentiation clearly and directly required by the character or nature of the work shall not be construed as discrimination. (2) In the event of any dispute related to a violation of the prohibition on discrimination, the employer shall be required to prove that his actions did not violate the provisions of Paragraph (1). (3) Employers shall provide the opportunity to employees for advancement to higher positions without discrimination and solely on the basis of the length of employment, professional skills, experience, and performance.

9. During the 1998–2002 governmental term, the activities of the gender equality machinery were highly visible (e.g., an increased number of gender related publications and conferences), even though it was integrated at a low institutional rank in the Ministry of Family Affairs.

10. No accredited Gender Studies programs operate at the undergraduate level at public universities in Hungary. Except for the CEU Gender Studies MA and Ph.D. program, there are no graduate and postgraduate level courses. Furthermore, in 2006 the CEU Gender Studies Program was not yet accredited by the Hungarian Accreditation Committee. See Pető 2006.

11. Economically active person: employed and unemployed persons, entering the labor market (Women and Men in Hungary, 2004, 110).

References

Bacchi, Carol Lee. 1997. *The Politics of Affirmative Action: Women, Equality and Category Politics*. London, Thousand Oaks, New Delhi: Sage.

———. [1999] 2001. *Women, Policy and Politics: The Construction of Policy Problems*. London, Thousand Oaks, New Delhi: Sage.

Beveridge, Fiona, Sue Nott, and Kylie Stephen. 2000. Mainstreaming and the Engendering of Policymaking: A Means to an End? *Journal of European Public Policy* 7 (3): 385–405.

Booth, Christine, and Cinnamon Bennett. 2002. Gender Mainstreaming in the European Union: Towards a New Conception and Practice of Equal Opportunities? *The European Journal of Women's Studies* 9 (4): 430–46.

Böröcz, József and Mahua Sarkar. 2005. What is EU? *International Sociology* 20 (2): 153–73.

Büködi, Erzsébet. 2005. Women's Labour Market Participation and Use of Working Time. In *Changing Roles: Report on the Situation of Women and Men in Hungary 2005*, eds. Ildikó Nagy, Marietta Pongrácz, and István György Tóth, 15–43. Budapest: TARKI Social Research Institute [English language edition, 2006].

Hungarian Central Statistical Office (CSO). 2004. *Társadalmi helyzetkép 2003* . Budapest: Központi Statisztikai Hivatal.

———. 2005. *Women and Men in Hungary, 2004*. Budapest: Hungarian Central Statistical Office and Ministry of Youth, Family and Social Affairs and Equal Opportunities.

Hungarian Central Statistical Office (CSO) with the Government Office for Equal Opportunities. 2004. *Nők és férfiak Magyarországon, 2003*. Budapest: Központi Statisztikai Hivatal, Esélyegyenlőségi Kormányhivatal.

Eveline, Joan, and Carol Bacchi. 2005. What Are We Mainstreaming When We Mainstream Gender? *International Feminist Journal of Politics* 7 (4): 496–512.

Equal Opportunities for Women and Men. Monitoring Law and Practice in New Member States and Accession Countries of the European Union. Overview. 2005. Budapest, New York: Open Society Institute and Network Women's Program.

Fodor, Éva. 2004. The State Socialist Emancipation Project: Gender Inequality in Workplace Authority in Hungary and Austria. *Signs* 29 (3): 783–813.

————. 2005. Women at Work: The Status of Women in the Labour Markets of the Czech Republic, Hungary and Poland. Occasional Paper 3. United Nations Research Institute for Social Development. www.unrisd.org/publications/opgp3.

House of Opportunity 2006. National Equal Opportunities Network. 2006. Esélyek Háza 2006. Budapest: ICSSZEM. http://www.icsszem.hu/main.php?folderID=1105.

Hungarian Women's Lobby. 2003. Opinion and Critique of the Hungarian Women's Lobby Concerning the Draft Act on Equal Treatment and the Promotion of Equal Opportunities. November 28, 2003. http://habeascorpus.hu/allaspont/kritika/antidiszkr.2003.11.28.pdf.

Jalusic, Vlasta and Milica G. Antic. 2001. Women—Politics—Equal Opportunities. Prospects for Gender Equality Politics in Central and Eastern Europe. Ljubljana: Peace Institute.

Joint Inclusion Memorandum on Social Integration. 2003. Budapest: Hungarian Ministry of Health, Social and Family Affairs, 2003. http://www.icsszem.hu/main.php?folderID=1375&articleID=4960&ctag=articlelist&iid=1.

Krizsán, Andrea and Enikő Pap. 2005. Equal Opportunities for Women and Men. Monitoring Law and Practice in Hungary. Budapest, New York: Open Society Institute and Network Women's Program.

Monitoring the EU Accession Process: Equal Opportunities for Women and Men. 2002. Budapest, New York: Open Society Institute.

Committee to Combat Social Exclusion. 2004. National Action Plan on Social Inclusion: Hungary 2004–2006. Draft. http://www.icsszem.hu/main.php?folderID=1375&articleID=4961&ctag=articlelist&iid=1.

National Development Office. 2003. National Development Plan. Budapest: Nemzeti Fejlesztési Hivatal. http://www.nfh.hu/index2.htm?p=2&t=2&i=1777.

Pető, Andrea. 2003. "Angebot ohne Nachfrage." Ungarische Frauen als Bürgerinnen eines EU-Betrittslandes. In Europas Töchter. Traditionen, Erwartungen und Strategien von Frauenbewegungen in Europa, eds. Ingrid Miethe and Silke Roth, 183–203. Opladen, Germany: Leske + Budrich.

————. 2003a. European Integration: Politics of Opportunity for Hungarian Women? European Integration Studies 2 (2): 81–86.

————, ed. 2003b. Női esélyegyenlőség Európában. Nőtudományi tanulmányok és a munkaerőpiac kapcsolata Magyarországon. Budapest: Balassi.

————. 2004. European Enlargement and Gender. A Politics of Opportunity for Women in Countries with Statist Feminist Heritage. In Rechte erweitern? Die EU-Reform und der Erweiterungsprozess aus Geschlechterperspektive, ed. Birte Rodenberg. Berlin: Heinrich Böll Stiftung, NRO Frauen Forum, Frauennetzwerkstelle Geschlechtergerechtigkeit im Zuge der EU Erweiterung. Werkstattgeschichte 39: 73–83.

———— ed. 2006. Teaching Gender Studies in Hungary-Társadalmi nemek tanítása Magyarországon. Budapest, ISZCSEM.

Pincus, Ingrid. 2002. The Politics of Gender Equality: A Study of Implementation and Non-Implementation in Three Swedish Municipalities. Örebro Studies in Political Science 5. Örebro, Sweden: Örebro University.

Pollack, Mark A. and Emily Hafner-Burton. 2000. Mainstreaming Gender in the European Union? Journal of European Public Policy 7 (3): 432–56.

Rádi Antónia. 2006. Korpusz delikátesz: Vitatott zaklatási botrányok. HVG 28.15 (14 April 2006): 116–19.

Rees, Teresa. 1998. Mainstreaming Equality in the European Union: Education, Training and Labour Market Economy. New York: Routledge.

Rees, Teresa. 2005. Reflections on the Uneven Development of Gender Mainstreaming in Europe. International Feminist Journal of Politics 7 (4): 555–74.

Rubery, Jill. 2002. Gender Mainstreaming and Gender Equality in the EU: The Impact of the EU Employment Strategy. Industrial Relations Journal 33 (5): 500–22.

Secretariat for Equal Opportunities. 1998. Egyenlő Esélyek Titkársága. *Fundamentum* 4: 153–54.

Silius, Harriet. 2002. Women's Employment, Equal Opportunities and Women's Studies in Nine European Countries—A Summary. www.hull.ac.uk/ewsi.

State Audit Office. January 2006. Report on the Examination of the Operation of the Ministry of Youth, Family, Social Affairs and Equal Opportunities. http://www.asz.hu/ASZ/www.nsf.

Verloo, Mieke. 2001. Another Velvet Revolution? Gender Mainstreaming and the Politics of Implementation. IWM Working Papers No. 5/2001. Vienna: Institut für die Wissenschaften vom Menschen

Walby, Sylvia. 2004. The European Union and Gender Equality: Emergent Varieties of Gender Regime. *Social Politics: International Studies in Gender, State & Society* 11 (1): 4–29.

Part III

Inclusion and Exclusion in EU Equality Politics

10

Preparing for EU Membership

Gender Policies in Turkey

Gül Aldıkaçtı-Marshall

This chapter focuses on the implementation of the European Union's gender policy directives at the national law level in Turkey, and the role of Turkish feminist groups in this process. Turkey stands out as a unique case among the countries included in this volume, because Turkey is the only country that remains outside of the European Union (hereafter EU) despite the fact that its relationship with the European Economic Community dates back to 1963. A brief explanation of the history of Turkey's relationship with the EU is followed by a discussion of changes in civil and penal codes, labor law, and the constitution. The importance of EU-initiated "conditionality" in reframing women's issues is underscored. The final section examines the part secular-oriented Turkish feminist groups have been playing in these gender policy changes.

Most studies on the issue of the implementation of EU policies are largely about how member states converge or diverge from each other in implementing the provisions of the EU, and how each member state's internal structure influences the implementation (Risse et al. 2001; Duina 1999. See also Bulmer and Lequesne 2002 for a review of works on the implementation of EU requirements at the national level). What these studies ignore is how candidate countries for EU membership, such as Turkey, implement required criteria.

The gap in the literature can be attributed to the fact that, as Zielonka and Mair (2002) point out, the EU has increased its demands on candidates over time. Since the 1997 Luxembourg summit, all the candidate countries, including Turkey, have been obligated to inform the European Commission (the executive body of the EU) on developments in areas designated by the EU. The European Commission issues a regular report every year that evaluates the performance of the candidate country (Kıvılcım Forsman 2004). In the past, the European Commission has expected all member countries to implement EU provisions and directives, although in actuality the extent to which the directives were implemented varied among member states (Liebert 2003). As put forward by the Luxembourg summit, candidate countries are also currently required to implement a substantial number of directives before being admitted to the EU.

Hoskyns (1996, 116) calls attention to two integration levels of EU directives: "first, the incorporation of the terms of the Directive into national law, and second, their application on the ground and the achievement of practical outcomes." This chapter is primarily concerned with how Turkey has implemented EU directives on gender equality at the national law level and what types of roles the EU and the feminist groups in Turkey have played. I argue that the recent political environment in Turkey has created favorable conditions for feminist groups to influence the drafting process of laws. This inclusive political environment is the product of Turkey's quest to join the European Union.

The utilization of opportunities in the political arena by Turkish feminist groups is best explained by the theory of "political opportunity structures" (Meyer 2004; Meyer and Staggenborg 1996; McAdam 1982; Tilly 1978; Eisinger 1973). Following Gamson and Meyer (1996), who assert that the concept has become too broad and vague, I distinguish stable (long standing) and volatile (short term) as two types of opportunities on two ends of the political opportunity spectrum (Gamson and Meyer 1996, 281–282). In the Turkish case, two "stable political opportunity structures"—namely, worldviews and the cultural climate (Gamson and Meyer 1996, 281)—set the stage for the recent EU-oriented changes. By worldview I mean the Turkish elite's long-established position that Turkey should be part of Europe. This worldview has its roots in the reform period at the end of the Ottoman Empire, and gained momentum with Turkey's decision in the late 1980s to work toward joining the EU. Turkey's determination to enter the EU prompted the ruling elite to comply with the EU's pre-accession stipulations and created a cultural climate of reform in the late 1990s and early 2000s. Within this climate, Turkish feminist groups, which had consistently asked for changes in discriminatory laws since the beginning of the feminist movement in the early 1980s with limited success, began to pressure the Turkish state, insisting that Turkey comply with the EU's requirement for gender equality. The persistent worldview and the climate of reform led to policy changes and the coverage of these changes by the media. Specifically, these dynamic, "volatile opportunities" (Gamson and Meyer 1996, 281)—that is, policy changes and mass media access—presented Turkish feminists with an opportunity to participate in the current policy-making process.

As Meyer and Staggenborg (1996, 1634) stated, "social movements can influence policy, alter political alignments, and raise the public profile and salience
of particular issues." My research on feminist organizations' political activities
reveals that in regard to recent policy changes, Turkish feminist groups successfully shaped the public agenda, especially through press releases that were picked
up by the national media. They were successful in raising the importance of issues such as honor killings and virginity tests to the extent that not only did they
put pressure on parliament members, but they also drew the EU's attention to
these issues, which in turn pressured the Turkish state to make changes in law.
Feminist groups also monitored the proposal stage and decision-making process
of the new laws.

The involvement of feminists in the process of policy making and their focus on specific issues point to the relationship between political opportunity
structures and framing. Policy change brings about "possible reframing of issues"
(Gamson and Meyer 1996, 282). What we see in the Turkish case is a contention between a large majority of parliament members as institutional actors and
feminist groups as extrainstitutional actors over how to reframe gender specific
laws. This contention came about as a result of the EU's requirement that candidate countries align their laws with the laws of the EU before becoming full
members.

This chapter is based on a documentary analysis of official reports and new
laws. These documents include the regular reports of the European Commission
on Turkey from 1998 to 2005; Turkish government memos and the Justice Ministry's commission reports that cover old and revised civil and penal codes; and the
texts of revised labor law, civil and penal codes, as well as the constitution. I also
examined two reports that were published in 2003 and 2004 on the European
Union's gender policies and the state of gender policies in Turkey. These reports
were prepared by Aydın (2003) and Uysal (2004) with support from the Turkiye
İktisadi Kalkınma Vakfı (Turkish Economic Development Fund). I have looked
at the official documents to find out about the changes that happened in national
law. By amending its laws, the Turkish state has provided tools for the implementation of those laws at the ground level. However, these documents do not address the ground-level implementation of new policies. Moreover, despite these
significant changes, loopholes remain in laws addressing honor killings and virginity tests. These loopholes have been heavily criticized by Turkish feminists.

In addition to the above documents, I draw on internet sites of two major
feminist organizations, namely Uçan Süpürge (Flying Broom) in Ankara[1] and
Kadının İnsan Hakları-Yeni Çözümler Vakfı (Women for Women's Human
Rights/New Ways) in İstanbul.[2] Both of these organizations have been actively
involved in gender policy changes in recent years and have written about them
to inform other women around the country. The websites of the feminist activists
counterbalance the information presented by government documents by giving

activists' accounts of the events related to policy changes. They also offer some information about the application of new policies on the ground. Nevertheless, the websites are selective in their presentation of news about policy changes and tend to focus on the successes of activists.

History of Turkey's Relationship with the European Union

Turkey's relationship with the EU—or with the "European Community" as the EU was known before the Maastricht Treaty of 1991—goes back to the 1963 Ankara Treaty. Turkey officially applied for EU membership on 14 April 1987. Although the end of the Cold War initially reduced the geopolitical importance of Turkey for the EU in the late 1980s and let the EU turn towards Eastern Europe, the complete collapse of the Soviet regime increased Turkey's importance for the EU once again (Kramer 1996, 210). The Gulf crisis and the situation of the Central Asian states in the post–Cold War period provided Turkey with an opportunity to take on a larger role in regional and global stability. The scholar Müftüler-Bac explains the relationship between Turkey and Central Asian states as follows:

> The end of centralized Soviet power in Central Asia has given the present leaders an opportunity to develop stronger inter-regional relations and to initiate economic and political relations with the outside world. These states are located in a region where the emergence of stable governments would contribute positively to the balance of power in the post–Cold war era. Turkey, as a country which shares certain cultural ties with the region, can help these Central Asian republics to establish an inter-regional identity as well as serving as a guide in their quest for stability. It is expected that Turkey will become politically more important in regional and global politics because of its cultural and ethnic links with the large Turkic populations in a region undergoing profound political change (1997, 46).

Following the initial application for accession, the Copenhagen Summit of June 1993 linked Turkey's full membership to the adoption of a set of political criteria that would bring about sweeping changes in Turkey (Karluk 2003). Like in the cases of Eastern European countries, Turkey's status for EU membership should be considered within the enlargement process of the EU. Within this process, "the applicant states are confronted with the requirement to implement a set of conditions that are aimed at making them EU compatible. Their progress in meeting these conditions is subject to regular screening. Accession is meant to take place only once the applicants meet the envisaged targets" (Zielonka and Mair 2002, 4).

In December 1995, the European Parliament approved the customs union between the EU and Turkey. In the Helsinki Summit, which was held in December

1999, the EU officially recognized Turkey as a candidate for full membership (Karluk 2003). However, at the Copenhagen Summit in December 2002, unlike Estonia, Cyprus, Hungary, Latvia, Lithuania, Malta, the Slovak Republic, Poland, Slovenia, and the Czech Republic, Turkey did not receive a date to start negotiations for accession. The main reason given by the European Commission was that although Turkey had made considerable progress in meeting the European Commission's requirements, it had not yet fully satisfied the 1993 Copenhagen political criteria to uphold human rights and respect minorities. Turkey was criticized for not taking enough action against torture; control of the government by the military; imprisonment of activists, scholars, and journalists for expressing opinions against the state's interests; and failure to comply with the decisions of the European Human Rights Court (Karluk 2003, 794). The European Commission stated that it would re-examine Turkey's fulfillment of the political criteria in 2004.

The disappointing outcome of the 2002 summit left a group of Turkish bureaucrats and scholars suspecting that the EU was not assessing Turkey's performance objectively. The reason for this, according to some, was that Europeans have a long history of prejudice against Turks and Islam (Karluk 2003). Moreover, a close look at the EU's history reveals the inconsistent application of their democratic threshold. The literature on EU membership processes has established that Greece (and then Portugal and Spain) was brought into the union with the understanding that "membership would help consolidate democratic practice and anchor the country firmly in the Western alliance" (Markou et al. 2001, 218). Yet, Turkey was later denied membership primarily because of its democracy and human rights record. Furthermore, the EU itself was criticized by some scholars for being duplicitous, as it has used different criteria in judging human rights records of member countries and candidate countries (Williams 2004).

Despite their disappointment, in order to speed up the membership process and to show the EU that they were serious about accession, Turkish officials made substantial changes in law in the early 2000s. On 6 October 2004, Romano Prodi, president of the European Commission, recognized Turkey's efforts by announcing the opening of negotiations for Turkey's European membership (European Commission 2004a, 167). Finally, in December 2004 Turkey received the date of 3 October 2005 from the European Commission for the opening of accession negotiations, passing another milestone on the road to joining the EU.

The EU Criteria and Gender Policies in Turkey

In the current context of EU integration and Europeanization, gender equality is a "conditionality" to be fulfilled by candidate countries in order to be considered for EU membership (Schmid 2004; Williams 2004). In its regular progress reports on Turkey, the European Commission has included gender conditionality within the larger category of political rights, or in European Commission terms the "political criteria" that encompass the stability of institutions guaranteeing democracy, the rule of law, human rights, and respect for and protection of minorities.

As the European Commission gradually extended conditions for membership from the economic to the political and tied Turkey's membership to the fulfillment of the Copenhagen political criteria, Turkey found itself with no alternative but to implement the major EU directives, including directives on gender equality. Between 2001 and 2004, the Turkish parliament amended the civil code, penal code, and labor law. It also made major changes in the constitution.

The civil code from 1926 was amended on 22 November 2001. The coalition government of the time, headed by Bülent Ecevit, argued that the civil code that had been adapted from the Swiss civil code could not respond to modern Turkish society. The push to update the Turkish civil code was further justified by the argument that even Western European countries like Germany and Switzerland have changed their civil codes recently to keep up with contemporary circumstances in those societies (Başöz and Çakmakçı 2001, 736–37). Thus, in changing the civil code the Turkish government demonstrated its preference for following the example of other European countries.

The revised civil code inaugurated crucial changes for the betterment of women's status. For example, the legal age for marriage is eighteen for both sexes now whereas previously girls were allowed to marry at age fifteen and boys at age seventeen. In addition, the section that declared the husband to be the "head of the family" is omitted. Now husband and wife both have the legal authority to decide on matters such as where the couple lives and which schools children attend. One of the most important changes in the revised code addresses divorce rights. Women are now entitled to half of the assets gained by the couple during marriage (State Institute of Statistics 2003).

Despite criticism from some members of parliament for its hasty passage, the revised penal code, which was enacted on 26 September 2004 and took effect on 1 June 2005, made significant progress toward eliminating articles that discriminate against women (Yılmaz 2004). Government memos and commission reports leave little doubt that the most substantial reason behind the amendment of the penal code, as in the case of the civil code, was the EU criteria. In their meeting on 30 June 2004, the members of the commission of justice in parliament stated that the representatives of the EU have been pleased with their efforts (Yılmaz 2004, 720). Still, they also emphasized that the call for change is not only external, but also internal, recognizing demands from civil society initiatives, especially women's NGOs (Yılmaz 2004, 721).

One of the most important reforms of the penal code is the inclusion of sexual violence against women within the category of "crimes against an individual" instead of "crimes against society" (Özkan Kerestecioğlu 2004). This philosophical shift from property to individual agent opens the door for many specific articles to be extended, eliminated, or modified. Virginity examination of girls, which caused an outcry among feminist groups in Turkey and internationally, is covered by article 287 of the revised penal code. Although the fact that examinations are still allowed by court order establishes a large loophole, virginity examinations can no longer be requested by individuals such as principals of schools, directors of orphanages, and parents. Furthermore, in compliance with the EU's Equal Treatment Directive of 1976 (76/207/EEC), article 105 of the revised penal code brings penalties against people who sexually harass their co-workers. Some of the most important changes are contained in article 102 of the penal code. It extends the definition of rape, punishing rape within marriage with seven to twelve years in prison. The code also rules out the promise of marriage as a way of escaping the legal consequences of rape. Previously, a man who had raped a single woman or a teenager would receive little or no punishment if he accepted to marry her. Under the revised code, marriage no longer shields the man from the legal ramifications of rape. The issue of abortion in the case of rape is also addressed by the new version of the code. Women can terminate a pregnancy as late as twenty weeks if it happened as a result of rape.[3]

The issue of honor killing is also covered by the amended penal code. The old code allowed a judge to give a short sentence to a person, usually a man, who murdered a female relative if he claimed that he killed his relative because she dishonored the family with her behavior. International newspapers occasionally cover some of the more shocking cases in Turkey, Jordan, or other countries where these honor killings happen. In recent years the United Nations and Amnesty International have put the elimination of honor killings on their agendas. According to article 82 of the revised Turkish penal code, murder justified by "traditions and customs" will be punished by life in prison. Persons who motivate the killer will also receive heavy sentences (European Commission 2004a, 45). Moreover, persons who force the female member of the family to attempt suicide for supposedly dishonoring the family will receive two to five years of imprisonment. According to article 84, this sentence becomes four to ten years if the female member dies as a result of her attempt. Despite these welcome changes, the phrase "traditions and customs" does not include all honor killings and leaves room for a lighter sentence if "unjust provocation" can be demonstrated.

In addition to amending civil and penal codes, in compliance with the EU directives on providing gender equality at work, the parliament amended the labor law in 2003. Since then pregnant women have been able to take sixteen weeks of paid maternity leave and up to an additional six months without pay after the delivery.[4] If a worker goes to court claiming gender discrimination after being laid off, employers now have the burden of proof (Özkan Kerestecioğlu 2004).[5]

The constitution has also gone through some changes in recent years. The equality between women and men is expressed in several places in the new version. Article 10 of the constitution states that everyone is equal before the law. No distinction can be made on the basis of language, race, color, sex, political opinion, philosophical stand, or religion. The Turkish parliament recently made an important amendment to this article (ratified, 05/07/2005–5170/1). The paragraph states that "women and men have equal rights and the state has the responsibility to ensure the implementation of these rights." Concerning the institution of family, article 41, which asserts that "the family is the basis of Turkish society," now includes an important clarification (ratified, 10/03/2001–4709/17), stating that the family "is based on equality among partners."

The European Commission followed these changes in Turkish law closely. It also warned Turkey at every opportunity about what would happen if the EU directives were not implemented. In 2005 Joost Lagendijk, the head of the commission on Turkey in the European Parliament, expressed his and the parliament's disappointment with the stalled enactment of the revised penal code in the following statement: "They asked me in the European parliament why the enactment of it [the penal code] was delayed. I could not answer [because] I was not informed [by the Turkish officials]. This is a deficit [on the Turkish part]."[6]

An analysis of the European Commission's regular reports on Turkey's progress toward accession reveals specific issues on which the European Commission focuses when judging Turkey's progress in the area of gender equality. Until the enactment of the amended civil code, the regular reports emphasized the necessity for a change in civil code, especially the need for change in the article that designates men as the head of the family.[7] The reports brought up the issues of violence against women, particularly honor killings, as well as virginity examinations, women's illiteracy rate, and women's low employment rates.[8] They also stressed that labor law had to be amended.

The regular reports praised Turkey when amendments to laws were adopted, as the following quote illustrates: "The adoption of these reforms demonstrates the determination of the majority of Turkey's political leaders to move towards further alignment with the values and standards of the European Union" (European Commission 2002, 17). The 2004 regular report applauded Turkey for the major amendments, affirming the new penal code's condemnation of virginity examinations, honor killings, and sexual assaults, but stressed that "despite legal and practical initiatives to tackle the problem of discrimination and domestic violence this remains a major problem. Sustained efforts will be required to ensure that women take an equal place in society" (European Commission 2004a, 45).

Turkish feminist groups know that for Turkey much is riding on the fulfillment of the EU requirement, and they are using this to put their cause on the public agenda. In an interview with journalist Neşe Düzel that was published in the newspaper *Radikal* on 6 September 2004, and posted the same day on the Uçan Süpürge website, Selma Acuner, who is an academic and a member of

Kadın Adayları Destekleme ve Eğitme Derneği (Association for Supporting and Training Women Candidates), a women's NGO that works to increase women's participation in elections as candidates, emphasized that

> We are going to ask the prime minister whether his party wants Turkey to be an EU member. Turkey has to fulfill the political criteria to begin the accession negotiations. One of the criteria is the equality between women and men and [the amendment of] Turkish penal code that would provide this equality. The equality between women and men is a serious matter that can hinder Turkey's membership. It is as significant as the Cyprus issue. About ten days ago, the European Commission repeated this [providing gender equality] as a condition and stated that 'women's rights are still a problem in Turkey.' If adultery becomes a punishable crime and virginity exams are allowed, the door is left open for honor killings to continue, and if the latest amendment to the penal code is enacted, the EU might never give us a date to start the negotiations.[9]

The above quote points to the significance of women's involvement in policy changes. The following section will cover this issue.

Turkish Feminist Groups and Gender Policies in Turkey

The European Commission's pressure on the Turkish government to implement the 1993 Copenhagen Criteria forced Turkey to work on changing its gender policies, creating a window of opportunity for feminist activists to accelerate their program and become more visible as political constituents in civil society. Feminist groups, the majority of which are secular, used various tactics, from signed petitions and fax campaigns to press releases and visitations to political party leaders and parliament members, to affect the amendment process (Özkan Kerestecioğlu 2004).

Twelve days before the ratification of the penal code, members of about eighty women's organizations around the country came together with banners to walk to parliament. They demanded that virginity controls be criminalized and adultery not be punished by law. These women were allowed to enter parliament thanks to the efforts of some senators from the center-left Cumhuriyet Halk Partisi (Republican People's Party).[10] The Istanbul University Women's Studies Program led a petition campaign that gathered 119,000 signatures to change the civil code (Özkan Kerestecioğlu 2004, 81). One of the major influences of feminist groups was in regard to divorce rights in the civil code. When parliamentary members of the Islamist-oriented Fazilet Partisi (Virtue Party) and the Milliyetçi Hareket Partisi (Nationalist Party), part of the coalition government at the time, decided to omit from the discussions the article on divorce rights that gave women the right to half the assets gained in marriage, representatives from approximately forty-five women's organizations visited parliament members who were opposing the article and persuaded them to include it in the amended code.[11]

Women's NGOs established TCK Kadın Platformu (the Women's Penal Code Forum) to monitor the amendment process of the penal code and published the report "Kadın bakış açısından TCK (The Penal Code from Women's Perspective)."[12] This report that focused on issues of rape, honor killing, virginity examination, sexual assault at the work place, and sexual assault against children, was made public through a press release and also sent to the justice commission of parliament responsible for drafting the penal code, despite the fact that the commission did not ask feminist groups for their views.[13]

Feminist groups that are members of the Women's Penal Code Forum regularly monitored the developments in the parliament and made an effort to initiate a relationship with the justice commission on the penal code. They have benefited from access to a friendly secular-oriented media. In their press release, they stated that

> We as women's groups who know that this law has a lot to do with protecting women's right to live, watched the process [parliamentary discussions on the penal code] closely. We made written suggestions [to the justice commission of the parliament] to reform the articles, which ignore women as human beings and individuals, so that they guarantee women's human rights. We have had a positive relationship with the justice commission since the penal code proposal came to the parliament. . . . We as women and as women's organizations guarantee that we will defend these legal achievements for which we long struggled. We let the public know that starting from the ratification of the version of the penal code, we will make every effort to ensure that the new laws are learned, implemented, and used.[14]

Staying true to their pledge, a group of women in Ankara organized a large meeting in a five-star Hilton hotel two days after the penal code was ratified. According to Uçan Süpürge, the meeting brought in about four hundred people including activists, politicians, academics, and representatives of the embassies of European countries. It highlighted what women had achieved through the amended penal code and what still needed to be done.[15] Moreover, posters, CDs, and a booklet about the penal code were distributed to women in various cities around Turkey.[16] These actions of the feminist NGOs in Ankara show that feminist organizations consider informing women about the changes in laws to be their responsibility.

Feminists in their support for amendments associated with EU criteria encountered the patriotic sensitivities of some Turks, which have begun to boil over as a result of the government's push for EU membership. A vocal faction of Turks strongly believes that the EU is changing the structure of Turkey, telling Turkey what to do, and diminishing its sovereignty. Feminist organizations, like some members of parliament, consistently argue that the changes in laws are not primarily due to the requirements of the EU, but rather the demands of civil society organizations.[17] Thus, internal demand and need for change have been the dominant discourse some parliament members and feminists have employed against nationalistic discourse.

Feminist groups have considered the improvements in laws to be an important development. For example, they have praised the shift in the categorization of sexual violence against women in the penal code and interpreted this new framing to be the recognition of women as individuals rather than the property of family or society (Özkan Kerestecioğlu 2004). However, through their websites and press releases they have pointed out that much still needs to be changed in the penal and civil codes. Regarding the penal code, for instance, the Women's Penal Code Forum listed their most pressing concerns as follows: 1) Virginity exams should be banned under any circumstances. Virginity exams without the woman's consent should be punished by law; 2) Discrimination on the basis of sexual orientation should be defined as a crime and should be treated in the same way as the discrimination cases based on language, religion, sex, and so on; 3) The article that forbids the sexual relationship among young people between the ages of fifteen and eighteen should be eliminated; 4) Women should be able to have an abortion up to twelve weeks into pregnancy; and 5) Honor killings should be categorized as deliberate murder. The word "customs" as a motive for murder should be replaced by the word "honor" so that there is no room for an interpretation of the law that would reduce the punishment.[18] Whether these demands will eventually become law remains to be seen.

The divorce right in the revised civil code that covers assets obtained after 1 January 2002 has also been criticized by numerous feminist organizations, who argue that the date limit will exclude many women, especially housewives who were married before this date and now do not have their own assets. In 2003, feminist groups mounted a petition campaign called *Kadına karşı ekonomik şiddete hayır* (No to economic violence against women) and collected 35,000 signatures to send to the parliament (Özkan Kerestecioğlu 2004, 82).

The feminist focus has been in line with the European Commission's position to enforce the laws on the ground. There are signs that the new laws are starting to be taken seriously in Turkey, in part thanks to feminist efforts. There have been discrimination cases in courts in recent years, a number of them being ruled in favor of the plaintiff. For example, a female lawyer won a sexual harassment case against her co-worker.[19] Another case is indicative of how hiring policies are being forced to be more egalitarian: One of the state institutions that discriminated against women engineers in its hiring policy was publicly criticized by İstanbul Kadın Kuruluşları Birliği (the Istanbul Union of Women's Organizations) and İstanbul Barosu Kadın Hakları Komisyonu (the Istanbul Bar Women's Rights Commission) after the enactment of the labor code and article 10 of the constitution. These two women's organizations called on the Association of Geologists to sue the General Directorate of Mineral Research and Exploration.[20] One day later, the Associations of Geologists, Mechanical Engineers, Electronic Engineers, Cartography and Cadastral Engineers, and Geophysics Engineers publicly denounced the government institutions' policy on hiring and called the policy "sex discrimination in engineering."[21] The Union of Turkish Engineers and Architects went to the Council of the State and sued the state institution for its hiring policy, winning the case.[22]

However, these developments have been accompanied by reports that pointed to the overall slowness of implementation at the ground level (European Commission 2005a; European Parliament 2005). In its 2005 report on Turkey, the European Commission stated: "There has been little progress regarding women's rights, although the entry into the force of the Penal Code delivers some important improvements, as reported last year" (2005a, 32).

In addition to tracking and demanding the implementation of the amended laws, feminist groups are putting new issues such as women's political participation on the public agenda. They are focusing on the implementation of article 10 of the constitution and lobbying to change the election system. Regarding elections, their aim is to establish a quota system that would legally require at least 30 percent representation for women in political parties and in the elections (Özkan Kerestecioğlu 2004). This emphasis on quotas parallels the EU's stand on "positive action" that was made public by the 1997 Amsterdam Treaty. The EU encourages states to take measures to increase the number of women in areas where they are traditionally underrepresented. Being aware of this policy and of Turkey's pledge to review the Political Parties Act in its National Program for the Adoption of the *Acquis*-2001, women's groups in Turkey continue to pressure the state to change the Political Parties Act with increasing gender equality in mind.[23]

Conclusions

The implementation of the stipulations of the EU in the area of gender policy in Turkey shows the power of the EU to affect the internal structure of candidate countries. Gender policy changes, as part of the general political criteria regarding human rights, have been brought to the table by the EU as a conditionality, setting the stage for the EU to evaluate Turkey's performance on a political, as well as economic level. So far, the EU has been using the political criteria as a reason for delaying Turkey's membership, and has signaled that in the future it may halt the membership process solely on the basis of political criteria (European Commission 2005b).

These stipulations, mostly welcomed by Turkish feminist groups, have created a climate of reform in Turkey in which institutional actors of parliament and feminist groups have contested each other over the reframing of women's issues on a legal level. Although parliament members have had more power in this contest, feminist groups have been able to elbow some of their demands into the debate. Specific ally opportunities for policy change and media access allowed feminists to be persistent and vocal in their demands.

Turkish feminists have seen the reframing of crimes against women as crimes against individuals rather than crimes against society as a significant development. However, they have criticized the legal loopholes regarding issues such as virginity examinations, honor killings, consensual sex among youth, and sexual orientation. Moreover, they have been working to change the Political Parties Act so that more women participate in politics. The contention between the politicians in power, many of whom have been male, and feminist groups over reframing women's issues is an ongoing process.

Policy change had allowed feminists to be involved in policy making, and now it is permitting them to monitor the implementation of the policies on the ground. Turkey has been giving conflicting signals regarding the ground-level application of amended laws. There have been cases that point to the eagerness of Turkish courts to implement the new laws. Yet at the same time, violence against women continues to be a major problem. These conflicting signals have been heavily criticized by the EU, which insists that making changes at the national level is not enough. It wants to see ground level application (European Commission 2005, 2004b, 2004c). This insistence on ground-level application, especially in Turkey's case, suggests a new direction in the EU's attitude toward assessing the human rights records of candidates.

As Gamson and Meyer (1996, 276) emphasized, "like the concept of frame, opportunity balances elements of structure and agency. . . . Opportunities open the way for political action, but movements also make opportunities." Turkish feminists who have used the opportunity of policy making are now constructing new alliances both inside and outside of parliament. Feminist groups' efforts to form new alliances, combined with the EU's insistence on allowing NGO's to participate in governmental decision making, promises to provide feminists with a stronger voice in future debates on social policy in Turkey.

Notes

1. http://www.ucansupurge.org.
2. http://www.kadinininsanhaklari.org.
3. Uçan Süpürge, "Yeni TCK Kadınlara Neler Getiriyor (What Does the New TCK Bring Women en)," 24 September 2004, www.ucansupurge.org (accessed 11 September 2005).
4. 1992 EU Directive on safety and health at work of pregnant workers and workers who have recently given birth or are breast feeding (92/95/EEC) allows for fourteen weeks of paid maternity leave (Ellina 2003, 51).

5. According to the 1997 Directive regulating the burden of proof in cases of sex discrimination (97/80/EC), a plaintiff can go to the court "under the 'presumption of discrimination' and transfers the burden of proof to the employer, who must show that no discrimination took place" (Ellina 2003, 52).

6. Uçan Süpürge, "Kadına Dayak Avrupa'da Hayal Kırıklığı Yarattı (Battering of Woman Caused Disappointment in Europe)," 5 April 2005, www.ucansupurge.org (accessed 11 September 2005).

7. See the regular reports on Turkey's progress toward accession between 2000 and 2005, as well as the progress reports of 1999 and 1998. http://europa.eu.int/comm/enlargement/turkey/docs. htm.

8. Women's illiteracy rate in 2000 was 19.4% (Directorate General on the Status and problems of Women 2004). According to 2005 statistics, women's employment rate in Turkey is 22.3% (http://wwwtuik.gov.tr/PreIstatistikTablo.do?istab_id=446), significantly below the EU average of 56% (http://epp.eurostat.ec.eupa.eu/).

9. Uçan Süpürge, "Yasayla, Flörtü de Yasaklıyorlar (Flirting is being Forbidden by Law)," 6 September 2004, www.ucansupurge.org (accessed 11 September 2005). The issue of adultery created turmoil between the EC and the current Islamic-oriented conservative government. Although adultery had been deleted from the penal code for men in 1996 and for women in 1998, the current government attempted to make it a punishable crime again. The European Commission, European Parliament, and Turkish feminist groups strongly opposed the proposal of the government. Claudia Roth, a member of the German parliament, stated that punishing adultery is incompatible with what Europe stands for and it gives an impression that the Turkish government wants *sharia*, the Islamic Canon (Uçan Süpürge, "Roth: Zinaya Hapis Cezası Şeriat Kokuyor (Roth: Criminalization of Adultery Smells like Sharia)," 14 September 2004, www. ucansupurge.org [accessed 11 September 2005]).

10. Uçan Süpürge, "Kadınlar Meclise Yürüdü (Women Marched on Parliament)," 14 September 2005, www.ucansupurge.org (accessed 11 September 2005).

11. Kadının İnsan Hakları ve Yeni Çözümler Vakfı, "Son Dakika Atağı (Last Minute Effort)," 20 March 2001 (first published by the newspaper *Akşam* on 20 March 2001), www.kadininsanhaklari.org (accessed 30 November 2004).

12. Although initially a number of women's organizations mobilized under the Women's Penal Code Forum, on 1 April 2005, some organizations from Ankara established another forum to monitor the changes in the penal code. The lists of the original Women's Penal Code Forum and Ankara Women's Penal Code Forum reveal that some organizations remained as members of both forums (see Uçan Süpürge, "İşimiz Bitmedi, Sekiz Madde Daha Var (We are Not Done Yet, There are Eight More Items)," 11 June 2005, www.ucansupurge.org [accessed 11 September 2005] for the list of original Women's Penal Code Forum. For the list of Ankara Women's Penal Code Forum, see Uçan Süpürge, "TCK İçin Mücadeleye Devam (Struggle for TCK Continues)," 3 June 2005, www.ucansupurge.org [accessed 11 September 2005]).

13. "Kadının İnsan Hakları ve Yeni Çözümler Vakfı, "Kadın Bakış Açısından Türk Ceza Kanunu (Turkish Penal Code from Woman's Perspective)," 4 June 2003 (first published by the newspaper *Cumhuriyet* on 4 June 2004), www.kadininsanhaklari.org (accessed 30 November 2004).

14. Uçan Süpürge, "Kadınlar Meslis'teydi (Women were at Parliament)," 24 September 2004, www. ucansupurge.org (accessed 9 November 2005).

15. Uçan Süpürge, "TCK İçin Mücadeleye Devam (Struggle for TCK Continues)," 3 June 2005; and "TCK için Mücadeleye Devam Ediyoruz! (We continue to Struggle for TCK)," 11 June 2005, www.ucansupurge.org (accessed 11 September 2005).

16. For an in-depth view of the activities done in each city see www.ucansupurge.org.

17. For an example see the interview with one of the founders of the Women for Women's Human Rights at http//www.wwhr.org/?id=778 (accessed 19 November 2004).

18. Uçan Süpürge, "İşimiz Bitmedi, Sekiz Madde Daha Var (We are Not Done Yet, There are Eight More Items)," 11 June 2005, www.ucansupurge.org (accessed 11 September 2005).
19. Uçan Süpürge, "Şahitsiz Taciz Cezasız Kalmadı (Sexual Harassment without a Witness did not Remain Unpenalized)," 10 August 2004, www.ucansupurge.org (accessed 11 September 2005).
20. Uçan Süpürge, "Yasalarda Eşitlik Var, Uygulamada Yok (Equality is in Laws, But not in Practice)," 19 November 2004, www.ucansupurge.org (accessed 11 September 2005).
21. Uçan Süpürge, "Ayrımcılığa Kınama (Condemning Discrimination)," 20 November 2004, www.ucansupurge.org (accessed 11 September 2005).
22. Uçan Süpürge, Danıstay Ayrıma 'Dur' Dedi (The Council of State Said No to Discrimination), 30 April 2005, www.ucansupurge.org (accessed 11 September 2005).
23. See Highlights of the National Programme. Available from http://europa.eu.int/comm/enlargement/turkey/docs.htm).

References

Aydın, Senem. 2003. *Avrupa Birliği'nde Kadın Hakları ve Türkiye*. İstanbul: İktisadi Kalkıma Vakfı Yayını.

Başöz, Lütfü and Ramazan Çakmakçı. 2001. *Yeni Türk Medeni Kanunu*. İstanbul: Legal Yayıncılık.

Bulmer, Simon and Christian Lequesne. 2002. "New Perspectives on EU-Member State Relationships." *Research in Question* 4: 2–35. http//www.ceri-sciences-po.org/publica/qdr.htm.

Directorate General on the Status and Problems of Women. 2004. *İstatistiklerle Kadının Durumu*. Ankara.

Duina, Francesco G. 1999. *Harmonizing Europe: Nation-states within the Common Market*. Albany, NY: State University of New York Press.

Ellina, Chrystalla. 2003. *Promoting Women's Rights: The Politics of Gender in the European Union*. New York and London: Routledge.

Eisinger, Peter. 1973. The Conditions of Protest Behavior in American Cities. *American Political Science Review* 67 (1): 11–28.

European Commission. 2002. Regular Report on Turkey's Progress towards Accession. October SEC(2002) 1412. http://europa.eu.int/comm/enlargement/turkey/docs.htm.

———. 2004a. Regular Report on Turkey's Progress towards Accession. October SEC(2004) 1201. http://europa.eu.int/comm/enlargement/turkey/docs.htm.

———. 2004b. Issues arising from Turkey's Membership Perspective. Commission Staff Working Document. SEC(2004) 1202. http://europa.eu.int/comm/enlargement/report_2004/pdf/issues_paper_en.pdf.

———. 2004c. Recommendation of the European Commission on Turkey's progress towards Accession. Communication from the Commission to the Council and the European Parliament. SEC(2004) 656. http://europa.eu.int/comm/enlargement/report_2004/pdf/tr_recommandation_en.pdf).

———. 2005a. Turkey 2005 Progress Report. November SEC(2005) 1426. http://europa.eu.int/comm/enlargement/turkey/docs.htm.

———. 2005b. Negotiating Framework for Turkey: Principles Governing the Negotiations. http://europa.eu.int/comm/enlargement/turkey/docs.htm.

European Parliament. 2005. Report on the Role of Women in Turkey in Social, Economic, Political life. A6–0175/2005. http://www.europarl.eu.int/activities/expert/committees/reporys.do?committee=1250&language=EN.

Gamson, A. William and David S. Meyer. 1996. Framing Political Opportunity. In *Comparative Perspectives on Social Movements*, eds. Doug McAdam, John D. McCarthy, and Mayer N. Zald, 275–90. New York: Cambridge University Press.

Hoskyns, Catherine. 1996. *Integrating Gender: Women, Law, and Politics in the European Union*. London and New York: Verso.

Karluk, Rıdvan. 2003. *Avrupa Birliği ve Türkiye*. İstanbul: Beta Basım.

Kıvılcım Forsman, Zeynep. 2004. Türkiye'nin Avrupa Birliği Üyeliği'nin Ön Koşulu Olarak Kadın Hakları. In *Türkiye'de ve Avrupa Birliği'nde Kadının Konumu: Kazanımlar, Sorunlar, Umutlar*, eds. Fatmagül Berktay et al., 139–63. İstanbul: KA-DER Yayınları.

Kramer, Heinz. 1996. Turkey and the European Union: A Multi-Dimensional Relationship with Hazy Perspectives. In *Turkey between East and West: New Challenges for a Rising Regional Power*, eds. Vojtech Mastny and R. Craig Nation, 203–232. Boulder, CO: Westview Press.

Liebert, Ulrike. ed. 2003. *Gendering Europeanisation*. Brussels: P.I.E.-Peter Lang.

Markou, Cristos, George Nakos, and Nikolaos Zahariadis. 2001. Greece: A European Paradox. In *The European Union and the Member States: Cooperation, Coordination, and Compromise*, eds. Eleanor E. Zeff and Ellen B. Pirro, 217–33. Boulder, CO: Lynne Rienner Publishers.

McAdam, Doug. 1982. *Political Process and the Development of Black Insurgency*. Chicago: University of Chicago Press.

Meyer, David. 2004. Protest and Political Opportunities. *Annual Review of Sociology* 30: 125–45.

Meyer, David and Suzanne Staggenborg. 1996. Movements, Countermovements, and the Structure of Political Opportunity. *The American Journal of Sociology* 101 (6): 1628–60.

Müftüler-Bac, Meltem. 1997. *Turkey's Relations with a Changing Europe*. Manchester, UK: Manchester University Press.

Özkan Kerestecioğlu, İnci. 2004. Türkiye'de Kadının Toplumsal Konumu: Kazanımlar ve Sorunlar. In *Türkiye'de ve Avrupa Birliği'nde Kadının Konumu: Kazanımlar, Sorunlar, Umutlar*, eds. Fatmagül Berktay et al, 35–54. İstanbul: KA-DER Yayınları.

Risse, Thomas et al. 2001. Europeanization and Domestic Change: Introduction. In *Transforming Europe: Europeanization and Domestic Change*, eds. Maria Green Cowles et al., 1–20. Ithaca, NY: Cornell University Press.

State Institute of Statistics. 2003. Women's Rights in Turkey. Women Information Network in Turkey. http://www.die.gov.tr/tkba/English_TKBA/kadin_haklari.htm.

Schmid, Dorothee. 2004. The Use of Conditionality in Support of Political, Economic and Social Rights: Unveiling the Euro-Mediterranean Partnership's True Hierarchy of Objectives? *Mediterranean Politics* 9 (3): 396–421.

Tilly, Charles. 1978. *From Mobilization to Revolution*. Reading, MA: Addison-Wesley.

Uysal, Taylan. 2004. *Ayrımcılıkla Mücadele: Kadın-Erkek Eşitliği Programları*. İstanbul: İktisadi Kalkınma Vakfı Yayını.

Williams, Andrew. 2004. *EU Human Rights Policies: A Study in Irony*. New York: Oxford University Press.

Yılmaz Zekeriya. 2004. *Gerekçe ve Tutanaklarla Yeni Türk Ceza Kanunu*. Ankara: SeçkinYayıncılık.

Zielonka, Jan and Peter Mair. 2002. Introduction: Diversity and Adaptation in the Enlarged European Union. In *The Enlarged European Union: Diversity and Adaptation*, eds. Peter Mair and Jan Zielonka, 1–18. London and Portland, OR: Frank Cass Publishers.

11

Gender and Ethnic Minority Claims in Swedish and EU Frames

Sites of Multilevel Political Opportunities and Boundary Making

Zenia Hellgren and Barbara Hobson

A Multidimensional Research Agenda

Over the last decades, social groups and social movements have challenged the false universalism in the frames of citizenship and membership that has shaded out particularized experiences and identities, including gender, ethnicity/race, sexual preference, disability, and religious beliefs (Hobson 2003a; Fraser 2003; Honneth 1995). One of the most interesting phenomena of our era is that these dialogues around citizenship and exclusion are occurring more and more in transnational arenas. The EU has been a key actor supporting nongovernmental organizations and transnational networks to promote citizenship claims and rights. EU institutions, treaties, laws, and courts have been venues for challenging discrimination based upon gender, sexual preference, ethnicity/nationality, and religion.

Whereas some scholars analyzing the effect of transnational venues on frameworks of citizenship argue for the decreasing importance of the national context for claims making (Smith et al. 1997; Soysal 1994), others maintain the persistence of national embeddedness, specifically in gender and ethnic/migrant claims making and political struggles (Koopmans et al. 2005; Liebert 2003). In this article we seek to contextualize this discussion and to make the case that how EU law and policy norms (known as *soft law*) get translated into national settings reflects distinctive processes involving *which groups, which issues, and which political configurations.* We concentrate on one societal context, Sweden, and use two case studies of gendered claims and ethnic minority/immigrant claims, in order to be able to map these differences, and to analyze the mechanisms underlying the complex play of national and transnational actors and institutions. We use concepts from social movement theorizing, boundary making, and brokering:[1]

(1) We have defined boundary making as the processes by which certain individuals and groups (as well as certain types of claims) are privileged in discourse and policy: who gets recognized also shapes what claims can be made and vice versa (Hobson 2003a; Hobson et al. 2007).

(2) We define brokering in a multilevel governance context as the pursuit of allies who bridge policy domains, increasing the power resources of social groups to negotiate with and/or put pressure on their national governments.[2]

When we build in the transnational level, boundary-making processes appear more complex and multilayered. New research questions emerge:

(1) Transnational arenas offer new political opportunities for groups not recognized in national settings. They also provide new brokering partners, increasing the power resources of groups to broker with their national governments. *How does the brokering with transnational actors and institutions affect the agendas of groups, their strategies and alliances?*

(2) Not only new claimants, but also new claims are given legitimacy, particularly in the European context in which the EU law supersedes national law. From this perspective we can imagine boundary-making processes occurring on the institutional level. *How are transnational frameworks mediated by and translated into national institutions: made into law, interpreted by courts, and implemented by bureaucracies?*

(3) In light of the growing tendency of the EU away from hard law to soft law—toward a more norm-constructing role—it is necessary to consider the ways in which discourses and the framing of citizenship at the EU level can open up or close off political opportunities at the national level. This logically leads us into a discussion of the translation process itself. *Which citizenship frames are compatible or contested at the EU level and appear contentious in a specific national context, and how does this reflect boundary-making processes?*

We focus on several competing EU frames, including the social versus the market, and individual discrimination/equal treatment versus positive action (the latter a remedy acknowledging discrimination of the social group). These are contentious arenas on both the EU and member state level. In our analyses of the Swedish case, we also highlight discursive frames that are highly relevant to our case; for example, the EU agendas encouraging civil society and diversity, which have not had much play in the highly institutionalized forms of Swedish politics. Finally, in comparing ethnic and gender groups in Sweden, we are able to make visible what Bell (2002) calls the hierarchies of equality in EU law in terms of rights and remedies for discrimination, involving gender and ethnicity. These exist at the EU level, but are even more pronounced in Swedish politics and policy making as gendered claims have been privileged and recognized long before Sweden's entry into the EU. Only fairly recently have ethnic discrimination issues emerged on the Swedish agenda. The EU Directives' implementation in Swedish law in 1999, and subsequent expansion in 2003 and 2005, played a key role for an increased focus on ethnic discrimination. The EU has been a catalyst for various antiracist groups, offering them new political opportunities and leverage.

In the first section, we consider how gender and ethnic discrimination are lodged in EU law and policy and their varied layers of institutionalization. We provide a general discussion of leverage politics in a multilevel governance framework. Here we present a model illustrating the different levels of political opportunity between EU and national contexts and boundary-making processes that occur in the translation of contested EU discursive frames. Then we turn to our two case studies of ethnic and gender politics in Sweden, considering how EU venues—institutions, discourses, and actors (transnational networks)—have shaped the strategies of feminist and antiracist movements, two movements positioned differently in Swedish political life.

Emergence of Antidiscrimination and Gender Equality in the EU

Gender dimensions are more embedded and institutionalized in EU law than are those relating to ethnic minorities and immigrants. Gender equality claims have greater legitimacy, having been inscribed in the original treaty since 1950, and EU case law on gender equality has been built up over the last three decades with a prolific number of cases (see von Wahl in this volume). Not only questions involving direct discrimination in the labor market in terms of pay, recruitment, and pensions, but also laws addressing indirect discrimination, including part-time work and labor market protections and rights for motherhood and for parental leave are enshrined in EU law (Hervey and O'Keefe 1996; McGlynn 2001). Moreover, issues that lie outside the EU market framing of rights have become part of the EU agenda, such as domestic violence and trafficking (Carson 2004). Gender mainstreaming to achieve gender equality appears in Amsterdam

Treaty documents; it has been implemented in many member states (Daly 2006). In contrast, directives against ethnic discrimination are a recent phenomena,[3] and no "ethnic mainstreaming" comparable to gender mainstreaming has been legitimized, even as a part of EU soft law.

In both gender and ethnic antidiscrimination law, concerns over EU legitimacy and competence played a role in the expansion of European law and policy in these areas. Gender equality law inserted as Article 13 in the Treaty of Rome lay dormant for nearly two decades. Women's mobilization and specific feminist actors put the pressure on for equal pay laws to be applied (Hoskyns 1996), which resulted in the well-known Defrenne cases No. 1 and 2.[4] Directives addressing ethnic/racial discrimination reflect both the growing importance of organized civil society in Europe through antiracist mobilization from below and the intense lobbying and legal expertise of the European movement coalition, the Starting Line Group, which formulated laws that were later implemented (Bell 2002). In addition, the directives addressing ethnic discrimination can be seen as a response to the emergence of racist and xenophobic movements in Europe (Hobson et al. 2007). Furthermore, whereas the European Women's Lobby is one of the most well-financed and well-organized networks at the European level, the European Network Against Racism (ENAR) is relatively new and lacks the organization and funding of the more institutionalized EWL (Cullen 2004).

In the EU framework, there are privileged forms of claims making: those lodged in the market integration frame most often trump those that concern social dimensions of European policy. This is evident when competing claims exist. As Schierup et al. (2006, 50) maintain, the EU antidiscrimination directives are part of the "embedded neoliberalism" in which the EU's new social model constructs social exclusion within a framework of neoliberal consensus. This consensus does not question the very rules of the game, or address the mechanisms behind inequality.

There are also privileged claimants and claims within the social frame: Gender issues and women's groups have broader areas of claims making than ethnic/immigrant groups, and have the most access to EU justice and rights. This shapes the translation process, but it does not necessarily determine the outcome of claims. Variations in member states exist, reflecting differences in gender logics and dimensions of membership, referred to as *integrationist regimes* (Soysal 1994). Moreover, mobilized actors may or may not use EU venues. Finally, specific events, political configurations, and power brokering in societies influence the power resources of different groups.

Multilevel Governance and Boundary Making

The research on the EU, citizenship and inclusion, and multilevel governance tends to look in terms of flows upward or downward—policy moving from one level to another, up to the transnational, down to the local or regional (Mahon et al. 2006). Within the EU frame of multilevel governance and social movements involving recognition of gender and ethnicity, we need to think in dynamic terms, considering what kind of leverage groups have to pressure their governments for policy change (brokerage) and how these policies are translated into specific institutional settings (boundary-making processes).

Keck and Sikkink (1998) provide us with one model of leverage politics in the boomerang effect: movement actors leapfrog their national governments and find allies in transnational networks and organizations or support from other nation-states, who create moral leverage on their recalcitrant governments to follow norms and standards accepted by international communities concerned with human rights. Keck and Sikkink provide important insights on how transnational advocacy networks operate and the importance of brokering partners for placing contentious issues on a national agenda. Nevertheless, their model does not offer much purchase on the access and influence of networks in the European context. Nor does it allow us to reveal the multilayered role of the EU in law, policy, and norm construction. Finally, their boomerang pattern of supranational players and nation-states does not capture the processes that shape the translation and implementation of supranational ideas and policy into national contexts. These are not only dependent upon courts and ministries and administrative bodies, but also upon discourses and the framing of claims.

In her analysis of how EU measures on sexual harassment have been mediated and translated into national policy contexts, Zippel (2004 and in this volume) proposes another, more apt metaphor of the ping-pong. This metaphor highlights the fact that policy decisions are not lodged at a single level, but tend to be bounced back and forth between levels and between different actors in ping-pong fashion. This metaphor reflects the importance of mobilization of constituencies for the implementation of EU law both beneath and beyond the nation-state. Helferrich and Kolb (2001) describe this process as multilevel coordination, in their analyses of women's movements' successes in altering the Amsterdam Treaty to include positive action.

Still, the ping-pong model does not allow us to analyze the processes by which some claims get recognized but others do not (Hobson 2003a). Mark Bell (2002) in his study of antidiscrimination law in the EU speaks of tensions and divergences when analyzing the market and social frames in EU law, which suggest the dimensions of institutional compatibility as well as contestation around EU frames. In order to incorporate boundary making between different institutional levels and the role of social movements responding to EU policy and discursive opportunities and constraints, we have constructed a simple model that reflects (1) the strength and weakness of movement actors' political opportunities, and (2) how boundary-making processes operate in the translation of EU venues into national frameworks (see Figure 11.1).

EU frames that are easily fitted in the national legal and institutional context are the most difficult to challenge, as they require groups with power resources and strong brokering partners to contest both their own governments and EU legitimacy. Mobilized groups are better able to create contentious politics with EU political opportunities, both EU law and discourse, even when they run counter to national citizenship frames and ideologies. There are numerous cases of gendered groups that have challenged governments when there has been a lack of compatibility with national ideologies and citizenship frames. Hobson's study (2003b) of gender equality directives in Ireland reveal how social movement actors had to overcome their government's resistance and used EU brokering partners. Other studies of enlargement countries' weak compliance to EU gender equality law and policies (see chapters on Poland, the Czech Republic, and Hungary in this volume) reveal how oppositional actors (church and conservative political parties)

Actors in Dialogue	Contested Discursive EU Frames	Institutions Nat'l, Supra-nat'l
Social Movement orgs (nat'l, trans-nat'l) Political Parties Govt bureaucrats (Ministers; Ombudsmen, Femocrats) NGOs, Church groups	Market vs. Social Equal Treatment/ Positive Action— structural inequality Immigration inside vs. outside European Borders Free flow of labor/services vs. Collective agreements	EU Court/National Courts EU Law/National Law EU soft law (codes of good practice) / Nat'l protocols/Nat'l govt commissions
Boundary Making		
Privileged Actors with Strong Brokering Partners	Discursive Resources	Compliance/ non-implementation Compliance/ implementation Institutional Change

Figure 11.1. Boundary Making and Translation Processes

are the privileged actors (see Regulska and Grabowska in this volume and Gal and Kligman 2000). In both these cases, boundary-making mechanisms operate in terms of how the laws are fitted into national institutional context and the discourse in which they are embedded (see Figure 11.1).

There are rare examples in which groups bring issues onto the supranational European level that are incompatible with EU frames (outside their competence), but strongly supported and legitimated in national governments. This was true of trafficking, which was mainly a Swedish initiative. Here again, boundary-making processes operate on the discursive level (see Figure11.1), as feminist groups employ discursive resources that fit with EU frames: in this case, migration framework. Another example was the ways in which feminist groups linked domestic violence to its harmful effects on women's ability to function as workers. Finally, bringing issues on the rights of (irregular) immigrants from outside EU borders has been blocked at the EU level and has been difficult to mobilize around in most member states. This is shown in our discussion of the Swedish case.

The Swedish Case

Sweden is an interesting case in which to analyze these processes of mediation and translation. Sweden appears as a EU-skeptic country in light of Eurobarometer studies and its overwhelming rejection of the Monetary Union. A brief overview of the Eurobarometer reveals that, for instance, in 2004, 33 percent of Swedes compared to a 17 percent European average considered the EU "a bad thing," 59 percent of Swedes compared to 35 percent of Europeans believe that their country has "not benefited" from EU membership, and 32 percent of Swedes compared to 14 percent of Europeans would be "very relieved" if the union broke down (Eurobarometer 2004; 2001). However, Swedish citizens appear to be among the most positive toward enlargement of the EU. Moreover, Sweden is a complier country, quickly implementing EU law and regulations. The Swedish presidency in 2001 was one of the most active in promoting European agendas, particularly around gender equality (Towns 2002). During the last years, the president of the European Women's Lobby has been a Swede. In contrast to its visible role in promoting gender equality on the European scene, Sweden has not been in the vanguard of antiracist/ethnic minority agendas on its own turf or in Europe.

As is true of the EU level, in Sweden gender equality is far more embedded in law and institutional bureaucracies than polices for equality and justice toward ethnic minority groups. Gender and ethnic mobilized groups are differently situated in the polity in terms of representation in ministries, parliamentary seats, and policy-making bureaucracies. This shapes the ways in which they perceive the EU as a resource for increasing their power resources and brokering with governments. The former have sought voice and influence within Swedish political parties; each party has its own women's organization. These structures have inhibited coalitions across party lines and the development of autonomous women's movements to push radical agendas from outside institutional structures (Eduards 1991; Hobson 2003a). The latter, ethnic groups, have been represented through immigrant nongovernmental organizations and civil society organizations (Soysal 1994; Hellgren 2005). Women's political identity formation has a long history dating back to suffrage and, more importantly, the flowering of cross-class women's organizations in the 1930s (Hobson and Lindholm 1997; Hobson 2003b). The mobilization of different immigrant groups against ethnic discrimination is a more recent phenomenon in Sweden. A broad mobilization of different ethnic groups against discrimination has occurred in the early twenty-first century, after the implementation of EU laws.

Swedish ethnic and antiracist mobilizing groups have tended to view the EU as a source of political opportunity, while women's groups have tended to view the EU as a threat to gender equality gains. Considering our two cases, we can see both incentives and disincentives to use EU venues. Our point of departure in the comparison of the two cases is that path dependencies and political cultures play a role in shaping the EU impact on gender and ethnic politics.

Gendered Claims: Swedish and EU Frames

Characterizing integrationist women's politics in Sweden, Hobson has used the term *institutionalized feminism* (Hobson 2003b). In this framework[5], the key players are found in governmental ministries, equality commissions, and other government bureaucracies.[6] They have become the privileged speakers for women's interests, which has resulted in a less diverse women's movement; immigrant women lack a political presence in this institutionalized feminist model. Since the 1990s, women's mobilization has lead to a dramatic increase in women's political representation, which in the 2006 election was at 47 percent.

Swedish women were less favorable than men to EU membership, as seen in the gender gap in original voting for membership, which widened to 10 percent in the vote against the EMU.[7] In the debates around membership in 1994, women in the "no" campaign highlighted the democratic deficit in the EU, that women would risk losing voice and influence in the Swedish political arena. Furthermore, they argued that membership in the EU posed a threat to the social and economic rights that Swedish women had achieved over the past decades. As they saw it, pressures for convergence in policies would result in a race to the bottom, a minimalist welfare state (Gröning 1993). Moreover they maintained that dominant countries in the EU, such as Germany, that support a traditional familialist model would seek to imprint their male breadwinner model into Swedish society (Gröning 1993). This of course did not happen, and in fact, EU gender equality law and discourse has moved more toward the Swedish model: an individualized benefit system, a dual-earner family norm and discourse on work/life balance and policies that allow for the reconciliation of employment and family responsibilities (Hobson et al. 2007).

However, the discourses on work/life balance and family/reconciliation policies run parallel with neoliberal ones, including self-sufficiency and making work pay (Lewis 2006). Both Swedish and European women's groups see these two strains of EU policy making as reflections of the incoherence in the EU between social goals and its goals for productivity and competitiveness (European Commission 2002, 2003; Interview EWL president 2005). The latter, goals for productivity and competitiveness, have received a higher priority in the EU than social goals for reconciling family and employment. Still, reconciliation polices have gained some ground in the 1990s, the parental leave directive being a notable example. Work/life balance and family/reconciliation polices are arenas in which Swedish feminists and the Swedish government have been key actors. This was evident during Swedish EU presidency.

Political Opportunity

When one thinks of the political opportunities of social movement actors in the context of the EU, it is usually understood in terms of what kinds of leverage transnational venues make available to influence national or regional governments. This is the path of the boomerang effect (Keck and Sikkink 1998). Yet in the case of Swedish feminists the reverse is true. It is in the trans-European arena that Swedish feminists have been most active, while they have not taken advantage of opportunities to leverage their own government, even when an EU Court ruling on equal pay offered them such a possibility.

Exporting the Swedish Model

Although Swedish feminists have not used the EU as a forum for importing new agendas and policies in Sweden, some feminists have nevertheless pursued EU venues in order to export Swedish models of gender equality, and more recently, Swedish agendas on prostitution. In the beginning of the twenty-first century, these Swedish feminists see themselves as shapers of a new Europe and rather than viewing enlargement as a threat to gender equality gains made in EU, they perceive it instead as an opportunity for introducing gender equality norms in these countries, and for integrating women's organizations in these countries into European forums for political learning and strategizing (interviews, Eva Fagor and Kristi: see also Winberg and Hjelm-Wallín 2003).

When Sweden assumed the presidency of the Council of Ministers of the EU 2001, the notion of Swedish gender equality policy as an export to be emulated by other EU member states became official policy. At the outset of the launching of the presidency, the then minister of gender equality, Margareta Winberg, announced her ambition to introduce Swedish policies of daycare and the individualized taxation and social security to those societies organized around a household wage that privileged a single male breadwinner family (Göteborgsposten, 24 January 2001 and Towns 2002, 158). Gender equality became a defining characteristic of the Swedish presidency through seminars and the photo exhibition of gender equality that was on display in the European council for its duration (Towns 2002). Though it is difficult to export agendas on the European level that are outside EU competence, Swedish feminists were instrumental in having issues, such as prostitution, embedded in the concept of Social Europe, legitimated by EU documents and discourse.

Feminist mobilization around prostitution politics in Sweden dates back to the 1970s, when government commissions wrestled with the expansion and visibility of the organized prostitution economy and their perception that this was the result of the wave of immigration from southern Europe. Once again, in the 1990s prostitution politics were pushed from below, and then channeled through parliament by femocrats and feminists in different political parties (Hobson 2003b). Whereas the first wave resulted in tougher laws against pimping, the second mobilization produced a law criminalizing the customer.

Sweden has been one of the main proponents of abolitionism in current European debates on prostitution. The Swedish Eurocommissioner Anita Gradin was a key policy entrepreneur, setting up the first EU conference on trafficking in Vienna in 1996 and initiating the STOP and DAPHNE programs for funding projects on violence against women. Swedish women were key players in moving the European Women's Lobby toward an abolitionist position. Prior to the Beijing Conference, the EWL did not have a position on prostitution and trafficking. After Sweden joined the EWL, the lobby moved toward an abolitionist position: whereas at first there seemed to be support in the lobby for decoupling trafficking from prostitution, by 1998 the EWL position shifted toward resolutions condemning prostitution and trafficking (Outshoorn 2005). One can see the influence of Swedish debates in the second resolution in 2001, which called on members to lobby their national states and push for client criminalization. This position had considerable support in the Committee of Women's Rights in the EU parliament.

From the perspective of boundary making and framing, their success appears comprehensible. Prostitution policy is understood as outside the competence of the EU (as all criminal law is a national jurisdiction). Nevertheless, the growing concern over trafficking (Joint Action of the Council of Ministers on trafficking 1997) has led to a coupling of prostitution politics to migration politics, clearly embedded in EU law and policy. The Council of Ministers Framework on Combating Trafficking in Human Beings in 2001, which replaces earlier measures, does not mention prostitution in seeking a common policy against illegal migration, however it is implicit and has resulted in soft law, requiring member states to outlaw trafficking to protect victims of trafficking (Outshoorn 2005). Alongside the compatibility of this social concern with the market and flow of persons, in many European countries there was a disquiet concerning enlargement. In this context, trafficking and prostitution have been linked to the flow of migrants from enlargement countries to the 15 Western European States (Kligman and Limoncelli 2005).

Compatible/Incompatible Frames: Which are Contested?

Before Sweden entered the EU, the principle of work for equal value was not part of antidiscrimination law (Eklund 1996). This legal principle has the potential to open up new types of gendered claims around pay equity, which were lodged in collective bargaining agreements.

Upon Sweden's entry in the EU, the Swedish gender equality ombudsmen seized upon an opportunity to apply the EU directive on equal pay for work of equal value in a case involving midwives and technicians employed at the municipal hospital at Örebro. The case was sent back twice from the European Union Court for review (case C-236/98); each time the Swedish Labor Court argued that the pay differential was based on market demands and held fast to the principle of collective agreements, claiming that to apply the principle of equal pay would undermine collective bargaining agreements (Case A 153/95). The composition of the Swedish Labor Court embodies the very corporatist framework that has locked out gendered claims in the past; the judges include politicians, employers, and union representatives. Unions have been one of the strongest antagonists toward creating pay equity schemes, seeing them as state interference in collective bargaining.

To bring the case back to the EU again, a very costly affair, would have entailed the mobilization of women's collectives in Sweden and/or the enlistment of other European women's networks to create pressure from the EU level. The first equal pay cases (Defrenne No. 1 and 2)[8] resulted in the mobilization of women across Europe, and the first ruling against quotas and positive action (the Kalanke case, (C-450/93)) produced a multilevel coordination of mobilized women's groups that was crucial for the incorporation of an article legitimating proactive measures in the Amsterdam Treaty (Helferrich and Kolb 2001). The Örebro case did not have the same symbolic importance for transnational lobbies and networks. Moreover, in contrast to feminists in the Irish Women's Council who went to Brussels to broker to pressure their government to implement the first equal pay directive there (Hobson 2003b), Swedish women did not turn to EU or transnational lobbies to challenge their government's intransigence in the equal pay for work of equal value case.

One could interpret the unwillingness of feminist groups to press this case as a reflection of their EU-skepticism, but this explanation does not do justice to the complexities in the matter. Instead we would like to suggest that our model is a more useful lens for analyzing political opportunities and contested politics in light of compatible and incompatible frames. First, this principle of an equal pay instrument to redress inequalities challenges a basic tenet institutionalized in the longue durée of Swedish social democracy (collective agreements supersede all others). Strong opposition to this principle of wage setting came from all three social partners: employers, unions, and the government itself, which was the employer in this case.

There is irony in this case, in that the central argument made by the Swedish government/employer was that the difference in wages was justified by market demand. However, Sweden has been held up as the paradigm example of prioritizing social protections over market ones (Esping-Andersen 1990). In contrast, in this particular case, the market argumentation is one highly validated in the EU, but the EU court actually did not accept it as a compelling reason for the gendered inequalities in pay between the technicians and midwives.

Compatibility

Mainstreaming appears highly compatible with gender equality policy frameworks in Sweden. Within an international comparative study, Sweden is noted as an active complier (Daly 2006). In Sweden, the institutional and organizational structures for administering mainstreaming already existed: policymaking elites and gender experts (femocrats) scattered throughout the bureaucracy. In Sweden, gender mainstreaming has been integrated into technical and administrative monitoring systems; however, it is not seen as threatening nor has its transformative potential been actualized. An example of this is the yearly gender equality plans that all workplaces have to send to the government. There is no law or administrative procedure to enforce their implementation; they are a paper trail that rarely results in significant change.

Whereas some scholars argue for the transformative possibilities in mainstreaming gender (Rees 1998; Squires 2005), others see mainstreaming as technocratic, depoliticizing gender, and undermining the basis of proactive policies (Stragitaki 2005). Mainstreaming is based upon a premise that gender-distinctive strategies marginalize and ghettoize gender equality strategies. In effect, it assumes an integrationist strategy, that applying pressure from within will reach all administrative and policymaking structures. Those who promote the idea that gender mainstreaming has the potential for a transformative agenda acknowledge that it is highly dependent upon active groups in civil society, those outside the system who can articulate gender and create pressure for systematic change (Jahan 1995; Squires 2005). However, in Sweden, with its highly institutionalized feminist organizations and structures for administering and evaluating gender equality policies, it is unlikely that mobilization and contentious politics around gender mainstreaming will occur. Rather, the thrust of feminist politics has been aimed toward another EU frame, positive action and quotas, which are contested at the EU level and at the Swedish national level.

Incompatibility/Contestation

In Sweden, feminist groups have viewed positive action and quotas as key strategies for challenging long-standing discriminatory practice and for placing women in positions of decision making. Though quotas have been part of the Norwegian gender equality plans (Leira 2002), in Sweden there has been strong resistance. In policy discourse and the media, quotas are presented as coercive/undemocratic as well as a form of reverse discrimination.[9] On the European level, quotas also have been contested, beginning with the well-known Kalanke case (C-450/93), which viewed quotas as antithetical to EU aims for equality of opportunity, not equality of results. Positive action is accepted as a measure for increasing positions of the underrepresented sex, but it cannot be automatic.

One of the most celebrated cases on positive action in Sweden reached the EU Court for deliberation. It involved quotas in academia. Addressing embarrassingly low numbers of female professors in a society noted by the UN as the most gender equal in the world, Carl Tham, the then minister of education in 1995, proposed a one-time creation of twenty female professorships. The case bears his name in popular parlance, the Tham professor case. One instance, involving the appointment of a female professorship in Chemistry, was sent directly to the EU Court for deliberation (C-407/98). As it had in the Kalanke case, the court stated that quotas went further than EU law allowed.

Positive action to achieve gender balance is not outside the confines of Swedish policy making. In fact, in the political field gender parity has been achieved through informal and voluntary measures: by alternating women and men on voting lists. The measure called "every other seat for women" (*varannan damernas*). This was not represented as confrontational or as women competing for men's seats, but rather as a measure to enhance Swedish democracy. The name itself was a metaphor that harkened back to Swedish traditional culture, in which women could ask men to dance, every other dance. When positive action was applied to the academy, special rights were cast as undemocratic and challenging core values of merit and competence for one's job, and running counter to Swedish legal norms of equal treatment (Törnqvist 2006).

In this instance oppositional groups to positive action were able to use the EU as a legal and discursive resource. Quotas were against EU law, and they represented unequal treatment and reverse discrimination. Though this case had no effect on the other professorships, its symbolic impact dampened the possibilities for feminist groups for claims for positive action in the future.[10]

The Civil Dialogue and Diversity:
EU Frames Inserted into the Swedish Context

The EU has opened up a new civil dialogue, involving nongovernmental organizations and associations of civil society, in its recognition and funding of transnational networks and local and regional groups. This represents a more democratic paradigm than the corporatist model through social partners (Williams and Roseneill 2004; Greenwald 2003).

Sweden has been cast as a society in which grassroots feminist movements have had little political space (Gelb 1989). Though a feminist civil society grew in the 1990s (Hobson 2003b), for the most part, feminist politics are channeled through parties and well-placed femocrats in institutions. It is noteworthy that the first umbrella organization of women's groups representing different NGOs was the Swedish Women's Lobby (SKL), which is an affiliate of the European Women's Lobby. This organization was launched by femocrats within the Social Democrat government after the UN Women's Conference in Beijing (1995) and was a top-down initiative, a reflection of the hegemony of institutionalized feminism. It also reveals how boundary-making processes discipline unruly members and discourses. From the beginning, the organization had women representatives from all political parties and was totally dependent upon government funding. So when members of the SKL board criticized the government for its weak stance on gender equality in the EU Constitution, women from different parties left the organization and funds were cut.

Immigrant women's organizations were integrated into a feminist organization for the first time with the establishment of the SKL. This civil society import opened up the possibility for more diversity in gender claims. However, their inclusion in this network has not resulted in a general transversal feminist political agenda. Women from these immigrant organizations claim that their perspectives and issues are often submerged in debates on gender equality.[11] Gender equality is not understood in terms of intersectionality, representing gender-immigrant-class issues (Mulinari 2001).

The dilemma for immigrant women's organizations in the current politics of gender and ethnicity (interview RIFFI, 2005) is that they have little voice in the political processes in Sweden either on immigrant or gender issues: Politicians contact men's immigrant organizations when they are interested in immigrant questions, and these groups have received substantial funding. Swedish women's groups are contacted in the media about gender equality issues. Swedish immigrant women's groups are asked to speak about honor related violence (HRV), including honor killings or girls kidnapped and forced into marriage, cases sensationalized in the media that cast immigrants as unable to integrate into Swedish society. However these groups are involved in many grassroots issues of their constituencies, in addition to shelters and support networks for HRV victims (Interview RIFFI 2007).

Struggles for ethnic equality in Sweden and the EU

In comparison with feminist organizations who have visibility and voice in Swedish politics, ethnic minority and immigrant groups in Sweden represent a group with less recognition and less power. For their struggles against nonrecognition and discrimination, the transnational level is an important dimension. The emergence of EU antidiscrimination directives has been crucial for Swedish debates and policy surrounding ethnic discrimination, and has been a catalyst for antidiscrimination mobilization. When analyzing such activism, we can see more directly the ways in which boundary-making processes and brokering partners reveal the opportunities and constraints in what claims can be made and who is making them.

Ethnic Minorities and Immigrant Groups in Swedish Society

Until recently, immigrant and ethnic organizations mainly focused on the political situation in their respective "homelands" and/or functioned as sociocultural communities. Over the past decade, there has been a shift towards a more active interest in obtaining political influence in Swedish society. However, dependency on state funding has tended to hamper ethnic organizations from political participation and privileged their functioning as service entities for minorities (Aytar 2004).

Immigrant organizations in Sweden were largely formed on the basis of ethnic or national identity as a part of the 1970s multiculturalist immigration policies. Some research has interpreted the politics surrounding these organizational structures as a governmental means to depoliticize and culturalize ethnic minorities' activities, preventing a trans-ethnic formulation of immigrants' collective interests (Schierup 1991; Södergran 2000).

There is a strong consensus in Swedish society for the ideals of the respect of human rights. For instance, according to the Eurobarometer 2001, 60 percent of the Swedes, compared with 47 percent of Europeans, thought the EU should prioritize the work against discrimination based on gender or race (Eurobarometer 2001). Positioning itself as moral leader in international politics on human rights, Swedish governments tend to be sensitive to international criticism. This can provide groups with discursive resources to use the politics of embarrassment, but it can also hamper antiracist groups' ability to make visible the extent of ethnic discrimination in Swedish society (Carson 2005). This points to what Carson and Burns (2006) have defined as a *Swedish paradox*: the boundary between an official discourse on tolerance and intolerant practices, by which a broad recognition of such practices is obstructed.

The EU as Political Opportunity

In contrast to most feminist groups in Sweden, ethnic and antidiscrimination organizations tend to view the EU as a source of political opportunity. It should however be noted that actors within antidiscrimination organizations tend to be more well informed about EU laws, and use these laws in their practical work more than organizations representing specific ethnic groups.[12]

Over the last decades in Sweden, the legal possibilities to act against ethnic discrimination have increased significantly. The Swedish Ombudsman Against Ethnic Discrimination (DO) was founded in 1984, but there was little activity involving ethnic discrimination in that office until 1999, when a weak Swedish antidiscrimination law was modified to adapt to the EU law. The Racial Equality Directive led to further expansions in the law in 2003 and 2005, so that ethnic discrimination would apply to discrimination covering a range of social areas besides the labor market. Not only did the law ease the burden of proof for the person discriminated against, but required that those guilty of discrimination should pay an indemnity (SFS 2005, 480; www.do.se). These opportunities for redressing ethnic discrimination spawned dramatic increases in grassroots activity and a flowering of new organizations and networks.

The EU has promoted a new civil dialogue in its recognition and funding of transnational networks and local and regional groups, for example, the Europewide antidiscrimination networks that serve as an inspiration for actors on the national level. Several Swedish actors are involved in European networks on different organizational levels, the most famous one being the European Network Against Racism (ENAR). Both mainstream NGOs and ethnic organizations in Sweden actively take part in European networks, where antidiscrimination is a central concern. Representatives from the National Integration Office (DO) and the recently founded national network of antidiscrimination bureaus perform study trips to other European countries to learn from their experiences of antidiscrimination work, and occasionally invite international lecturers to Sweden. Swedish NGOs and social groups acknowledge the importance of a strong civil society as the basis for greater independence vis-à-vis the state. In 2003, a national Center Against Racism incorporating over 100 NGOs organizations was founded. The center, which became one of the most vocal actors within the Swedish mobilization against racism and ethnic discrimination, was initially planned to be a governmental institution. However, this was challenged by a network of civil society organizations, including ENAR and the Afro-Swedes

(*Afrosvenskarnas riksförbund*), who insisted that the center should be independent. EU law and civil society discourse were enabling for these groups, who claimed that it gave them more leverage with the Swedish state (interview, Center Against Racism 2005).

When considering EU opportunities for ethnic and immigrant groups, one must, however, keep in mind the limited scope of the EU directives on antidiscrimination. Furthermore, agendas that are not compatible with the overall framework of the EU are not likely to be supported. The EU mainframe of unequal treatment and the focus on direct discrimination shades out the possibilities for introducing broader frameworks that address the structural features of discrimination. From this perspective, the translation processes from the EU context into national contexts reveals tensions between market and social, and individual and structural remedies, and in the Swedish case, the contestation around the free flow of labor—a core EU principle that is in conflict with the principles of solidarity embedded in workers' job security and wages, which are discussed in the following sections. The overall EU framework, Schierup et al. claim, allows for more liberal (labor) immigration policies as a means to undercut welfare states and labor unions—a coupling that under unfortunate circumstances easily fuels xenophobic agendas and nationalist protectionism (Schierup et al. 2006, 35–37).

Divergent Perspectives on Ethnic Discrimination: Institutional and Discursive Boundary Making

The current debates on ethnic discrimination reveal how boundary making operates on both institutional and discursive levels, defining which explanations and which measures against discrimination are considered acceptable, and which are not. Within the limits of the EU antidiscrimination framework, discrimination is framed as individualized unequal treatment. The EU seemingly increases leverage for groups mobilizing against ethnic discrimination, but agendas are only legitimized as long as they do not question the individualist logic of EU market integration policies; there is no possibility for group action. The crucial question is then what measures can be implemented when laws to protect the individual are not enough in practice. Bell claims that the antidiscrimination directives contain the potential for a shift from a market integration to a social citizenship frame for antidiscrimination if they are interpreted this way, but simultaneously states that the directives are silent on measures such as quotas or positive action (Bell 2002, 191–202).

The EU antidiscrimination law, based on equal treatment, has been easily fitted into Swedish legal framing of discrimination. Antidiscrimination lawyers at DO, however, claim that the knowledge of these laws is low among both employers and people exposed to ethnic discrimination, and that the laws remain weak as long as there is no established case law. Out of fourteen cases concerning discrimination in hiring, in only one case did the court find ethnic discrimination (Carlson 2007). In most cases, the lawyers agree that ethnic discrimination is very difficult to prove, as word often stands against word in such cases. More importantly, the focus on individual cases does not permit the recognition of systematic and pervasive discrimination.

Equal Treatment and Structural Discrimination

Many movement and institutional actors in Sweden acknowledge the limitations of legal remedies for addressing ethnic discrimination, which focus on individual cases and do not reach structural and hidden discrimination. These dimensions are outside the scope of EU law. However, discourse and remedies addressing structural features of discrimination are not outside the boundaries of Swedish policy making. For instance, structural analyses of gender inequality appeared in a government commission in the 1990s on the unequal gendered distribution of power and economic resources (SOU 1997).

Within the context of social democracy, acceptance of structural explanations has a long history in relation to class inequalities. This explains the assignment of two governmental commissions on power, integration, and structural discrimination (www.sou.gov.se/maktintdiskrim; www.sou.gov.se/strukturell). Yet, describing Swedish society in terms of ethnic power hierarchies appears to be strongly contentious. This aspect of one of the commission reports has been criticized by government actors, the media, unions, and employers (Dagens Nyheter 9/7 2006; Svenska Dagbladet 20/8 and 29/9 2006). The head of this commission study, Masoud Kamali, concluded that ethnic discrimination is embedded in the structures of Swedish society and emphasizes the need of socioeconomic redistribution, as ethnic minorities often are at the bottom strata of society. Taking a position that focuses on equality of outcomes, he recommended controversial measures, including positive action (Integrationens svarta bok 2006). Even before the commission report was finished, leaders of both employers' organizations and unions unanimously said "no" to positive action for immigrants in an open letter published in Sweden's main daily Dagens Nyheter (DN 23/2 2006).

Given the contention around positive action in the Swedish public debate and the lack of any EU hard or soft law advocating positive action toward ethnic discrimination, it is not surprising that there has only been one Swedish example of the application of this principle: an attempt to use quotas to redress the low proportion of immigrants in higher education. In 2004, the Law Department at Uppsala University introduced a policy to reserve 10 percent of the places in the educational programs for applicants with immigrant background. A case challenging this action (NJA 2006) was brought to court by two ethnically Swedish women with higher grade point averages than the applicants with immigrant backgrounds. The university lost the case on the grounds that it violated the principle of equal treatment in Swedish law. In the media and even on the website of the Stockholm Law School, the Swedish women were cast victims of *ethnic discrimination*. The Swedish court awarded them SEK 75,000 each as compensation. This case appears to close the door for measures for quotas or positive action against ethnic misrepresentation in Sweden.

A Backlash for Ethnic Minority Struggles

The optimism that followed the implementation of EU directives a few years ago has seemingly turned into a more pessimistic attitude among antidiscrimination actors. There are several indicators of a backlash for the antidiscrimination and immigrants' rights struggle in Sweden. With the new conservative government that won the elections in September 2006, the structural discourse appears to have less political space and legitimacy. New boundary-making mechanisms are emerging in terms of who is heard and what can be claimed. Masoud Kamali is seen as a controversial figure, as are his findings and conclusions. He has been critical of all political parties in Sweden. Not to be forgotten is that he was appointed by the previous Social Democratic government to lead the antidiscrimination investigations and has fewer channels to put forward his arguments in the current government. The current minister of integration Nyamko Sabuni, herself an immigrant with Congolese roots, has profiled herself as a "hardcore liberal" who strongly rejects any multiculturalist policies or positive action measures. One of her first actions as Minister of Equality and Integration was to cut the funding for the Center Against Racism by 2008.

Another sign of a shift towards a less tolerant climate is that the anti-immigration party *Sverigedemokraterna* (Sweden Democrats) gained mandates in several communalities particularly across the south of the country. In one communality, Landskrona, the party gained more than 22 percent of the votes. The party has tried to camouflage its overtly racist arguments by casting itself as a protector of the welfare state, playing on the fear that increased immigration will result in a dismantling of the welfare state.

Conflicting Frames and European Borders:
The Free Flow of Labor and the Swedish People's Home

The Swedish universalist framework of citizenship, embodied in the metaphor of the People's Home, has been built around the assumption that inclusionary citizenship embraces the principles of solidarity and social rights. Within this context, the EU core principle of the free flow of labor appears incompatible not only with the Swedish model of welfare benefits and the standards and working conditions, but also with the Swedish narratives of membership and inclusionary citizenship.

Undocumented workers or workers from the enlargement countries who are willing to work for wages below collectively bargained wage agreements are viewed as undermining the fabric of Swedish society. The first case challenging the EU goal of free competition among workers across Europe has emerged in Sweden and involves Latvian construction workers hired by a municipality for about half of Swedish wages (LO 2005). The Swedish construction workers' union Byggnads proclaimed a blockade of the Latvian company and demanded that the Latvian workers be paid a Swedish wage, which their Latvian employer was not willing to accept. The Swedish labor court supported Byggnads' right to obstruct the delivery of goods, but the case was taken to the European Union Court in January 2007. Byggnads' actions were upheld by the EU Court; they were declared not to collide with EU principles of free movement (www.svt. se, 24.5.2007). Several countries from the EU-15 submitted briefs in support of Sweden in this case. Finally, on December 18 2007, the EU Court declared Byggnads' actions had violated the EU principles of freedom of movement of services within the union (Dagens Nyheter 19.12.2007). This case may constitute one of the most important test cases in the EU, as it addresses collective bargaining models and market integration politics. The new Swedish Conservative government has claimed that they will encourage labor immigration, but also declared that they support Byggnads in the Latvian case, clearly an indication of the consensus around the collective bargaining principle. Beyond the Latvian case, the response to undocumented workers reflects a deeper contested terrain in Sweden and Europe, embracing the rationale and basic foundations of the EU: defining the borders of Europe.

Discrimination Inside and Outside European Borders: How Immigrant Organizations View "Fortress Europe"

The boundary making in EU law and discourse limits the scope of claims making involving immigrant groups from outside "Fortress Europe." These boundaries are drawn at different levels: through the way integration and immigration were bifurcated at the institutional level, and through the very way European borders are defined.

In Sweden, there has been a readiness and receptivity to implement European antidiscrimination directives, alongside restricted immigration and asylum policies (Brochmann 1999). Some movement actors try to break these boundaries by discursively linking the fields together, but the critique of immigration policies in the Swedish context has, in contrast to other European countries, largely been limited to refugees' rights. Irregular immigration is still a marginal, though according to some NGOs (www.lakareutangranser.se) growing, phenomenon in

Sweden. Hjarnø (2003, 127) explains this fact by the democratic tradition of the Swedish labor market, based on agreements between labor unions and employers, which make it extremely difficult to hire undocumented workers. Whereas the Swedish labor unions view irregular immigrants as undermining the Swedish labor movement, in southern European countries such as Spain, NGOs and labor unions support the "economic refugees'" right to escape misery in their countries of origin. The Spanish government has approved several major amnesties for irregular immigrants over the last years (Izquierdo 2005). In Sweden, this potentially more radical part of the antiracist agenda is largely absent.

Swedish antidiscrimination activists nevertheless maintain that there are discrepancies between EU antidiscrimination policies legitimizing ethnic minorities' claims making within the European borders, and the Schengen treaty's restrictive immigration and asylum policies are seen to be at odds with universal human rights principles. They emphasize the importance of adapting a global and not merely European perspective, and raise issues regarding European trade regulations that can discriminate against third world countries by perpetuating the unequal distribution of the world's resources. For them, this is global discrimination. Similar to Bell's (2002, 67) analysis, the NGO Caritas, a salient antidiscrimination advocate, and the Center Against Racism underscore that the negative image of immigrants and asylum-seekers that European politicians and mass media often present increases the Swedish majority's skepticism against ethnic minorities in general and therefore obstructs antidiscrimination work (interviews, Caritas and Center Against Racism 2005). These activists claim that the political field of immigration and asylum practices cannot be decoupled from integration and antidiscrimination aims.

> In Europe, they want to integrate those who are here, but not let anyone else in. It is a matter of understanding that poverty causes immigration and refugee waves, and the solution is combating poverty, not closing borders. Discrimination is embedded in a power structure with its roots in colonialism. You can discriminate also through international trade practices (Mkyabela Sabuni, interview 2005).

These actors lobby against strict immigration and asylum policies at the EU level, but at the same time they embrace the EU as an arena to combat discrimination and racism. For example Caritas' European network sought to block the EU sanctions against airlines and transport companies that accidentally transport undocumented migrants into European territory (interview, Caritas 2005). Yet they have used EU resources to combat discrimination at the national level.

The divergent discourses on immigration and ethnic minorities reflect major tensions around citizenship in contemporary Europe, as well as boundaries between insiders and outsiders on different arenas. Movement actors contest current practices and divisions between immigration and integration policies.

Unlike other European countries, there is virtually no advocacy for the rights of undocumented immigrants in Sweden. "Fortress Europe" is instead targeted within the antidiscrimination framework.

Concluding Discussion

At the beginning of this chapter, we raised several questions that address how transnational arenas can shape the political opportunities and agendas of social movement actors. The EU has been able to provide legal and discursive resources. Our analyses of gender and ethnic groups in one specific context, Sweden, illustrate that whether and how these resources are utilized is very much dependent on how different actors are situated in the national polity. For antidiscrimination groups, the EU has been a source of leverage politics, a brokering partner for making claims on the Swedish state. For feminist groups, the EU has been a platform for exporting Swedish agendas. Civil society has been a discursive resource for ethnic antidiscrimination groups, enabling them to affirm their rights for an independent organization. But lacking any power resources or an institutional base has left them vulnerable to shifting political winds and to backlash.

Our two cases also highlight the fact that EU frameworks open new opportunities for leverage politics, while closing off others. The EU decision on gender positive action delegitimized a contested form of claims making in Sweden and gave its antagonists another trump card. For ethnic groups, integration and antidiscrimination frameworks have given them legal leverage—pressuring the Swedish government for tougher laws against direct discrimination—but has endowed them with few remedies to implement them or reach the structural features of ethnic discrimination.

What Bell (2002) affirms as hierarchies of equality at the EU level is highly visible in the two struggles in Sweden: ethnic antidiscrimination and gender equality. The former have only recently found any recognition in Swedish debate. Antidiscrimination activists cannot draw on any EU case law considering positive action. Some EU documents suggest the possibility that mainstreaming ethnicity will be part of the EU agenda. The EU has encouraged this by seeking to bring together under one rubric of discrimination different forms of nonrecognition and exclusion in the wording of the charter of fundamental rights and the Constitution. Also in many countries, including Sweden, the offices of the ombudsman for equality now encompass gender, ethnicity, and sexual preference. Despite these administrative and discourse shifts, gendered claims remain privileged over ethnic antidiscrimination ones in most EU member states (Bell 2002). Hence our study reinforces the position of those who underscore the continuing importance of the national context for recognition struggles (Koopmans et al. 2005).

Finally, the tensions within EU frames surrounding the market and social, and the boundaries restricting insiders and outsides in Europe (Figure 11.1) are replayed in the Swedish context in distinctive ways. An intolerance toward overt racism and a liberal citizenship policy sit alongside a total lack of recognition and punitive policy toward undocumented immigrants. There is no political space for antidiscrimination groups to address discrimination with a global perspective. The tensions surrounding the Latvian workers' case in Sweden, involving the EU market frame of the free flow of labor and services, brings to the surface some of the deepest conflicts around social rights and migration rights. Sweden has one of the most open policies toward migrants from the EU enlargement countries, but clearly the acceptance of migrants assumes that their presence will not affect core institutions in the Swedish welfare state (the privileged position of collective agreements) or the discursive universe of solidarity.

Notes

1. Both these mechanisms are described more fully in Hobson 2003a.
2. The idea of brokerage has a long and rich tradition within the literature on network theory. It was applied to social movement theory in McAdam et al. (2001), though in a much less specified way.
3. The Antidiscrimination Directives refer to Article 13 in the Amsterdam treaty from 1997, which prohibited discrimination based on gender, race, ethnicity, physical disability, religion, or sexual preference, and the Racial Equality Directive 2000/43 that implemented the principle of equal treatment between persons irrespective of racial or ethnic origin.
4. Case 80/70 1971 no 1; Case 43/75 no 2.
5. Some scholars have seen the Swedish case as an exemplar of femocracy (Bergqvist 1999).
6. Researchers of women in politics, using the term gender machinery, analyze the myriad institutional forms of women's participation and influence in government administrative bureaucracies (Mazur 2001).
7. A survey of the Statistical Central Bureau (SCB) showed that among women the "yes" vote was 38; the "no" vote 60; and "blank" 2. For men the equivalent figures are: 49, 49, and 2 . "The EU-preferences in November and the Referendum on the Euro": SCB 61 SM 0302.
8. Case 80/70 1971 no 1; Case 43/75 no 2.
9. Legal challenges have been made to gender quotas and more recently to quotas for minorities. This is discussed later in the chapter.
10. It may have had some influence on the Swedish court's summary ruling against a quota system initiated by Uppsala to increase the number of immigrants in law school, as discussed in the following section.
11. The following discussion is based upon interviews with representatives from immigrant women's organization done by Zenia Hellgren.
12. The large Assyrian community in Sweden, however, constitutes an exception. They have a well-organized national association as well as international networks; they work actively with both antidiscrimination issues and a wide range of other areas (Interview, Assyriska 2005).

References

Aytar, Osman. 2004. Kommunikation på olika villkor—om samrådet mellan invandrarorganisationerna och svenska staten. In *Föreningsliv, makt och integration*. DS 2004, 49.

Bell, Mark. 2002. *Anti-Discrimination Law and the European Union*. Oxford: Oxford University Press.

Bergqvist, Christina, ed. 1999. *Equal Democracies? Gender in the Nordic Countries*. Oslo: Scandinavian University Press.

Brochmann, Grete. 1999. Controlling Immigration in Europe. In *Mechanisms of Immigration Control—A Comparative Analysis of European Regulation Policies*, eds. Grete Brochmann and Tomas Hammar, 297–335. Oxford and New York: Berg.

Carlson, Laura. 2007. Searching for Equality: Sex Discrimination, Parental Leave and the Swedish Model with Comparisions to the EU, UK and US Law. PhD Dissertation, Department of Law, Stockholm: Justis Förlag.

Carson, Marcus. 2004. From Common Market to Social Europe? Paradigm Shift and Institutional Change in European Union Policy on Food, Asbestos and Chemicals, and Gender Equality. Stockholm Studies in Sociology, PhD, Stockholm University. Stockholm: Alqvist & Wicksell.

———. 2005. Combating Racism and Discrimination/Promoting Minority Culture. Report from the EU project CIVGOV, WP2.

Carson, Marcus and Tom R. Burns, 2006. A Swedish Paradox: The Politics of Racism and Xenophobia in the Good Society. Report Submitted to Government Commission on Power, Integration and Structural Discrimination.

Cullen, Pauline P. 2004. Coalition and Cooperation within the Platform of Social NGOs. In *Coalitions Across Borders: Transnational Protest and the Neo-Liberal Order*, eds. Jackie Smith and Joe Bandy, 71–94. Lanham, MD: Rowman and Littlefield, 2004.

Daly, Mary. 2006. Gender Mainstreaming in Theory and Practice. *Social Politics* 12 (3): 433–50.

Eduards, Maud. 1991. Toward a Third Way: Women's Politics and Welfare Policies in Sweden. *Social Research* 58 (3): 677–705.

Eklund, Ronnie. 1996. The Swedish Case—The Promised Land of Sex Equality? In *Sex Equality Law in the European Union*, eds. Tamara Hervey and David O'Keefe, 337–56. New York: John Wiley and Sons.

Esping-Andersen, Gøsta. 1990. *The Three Worlds of Welfare Capitalism*, Princeton, NJ: Princeton University Press.

Eurobarometer, 2001, 2004, http://ec.europa.eu/public_opinion

European Commission. 2000. Directive 2000/43/EC. Implementing the Principle of Equal Treatment Irrespective of Racial or Ethnic Origin. (Race Equality Directive). Brussels.

———. 2002. Increasing Labour Force Participation and Promoting Active Ageing. Brussels: COM, 9 Final.

———. 2003. Scoreboard on Implementing the Social Policy Agenda, Brussels: COM, 57 final.

Fraser, Nancy. 2003. Rethinking Recognition: Overcoming Displacement and Reification in Cultural Politics. In *Recognition Struggles and Social Movements: Contested Identities, Agency and Power*, ed. Barbara Hobson, 21–34. Cambridge: Cambridge University Press.

Gal, Susan, and Gail Kligman. 2000. *The Politics of Gender after Socialism: A Comparative-Historical Essay*. Princeton, NJ: Princeton University Press.

Gelb, Joyce. 1989. *Feminism and Politics: A Comparative Perspective*. Berkeley, CA: University of California Press.

Greenwald, Justin. 2003. *Interest Representation in the European Union*, 2nd ed. Basingstoke, UK: Palgrave.

Gröning, Lotte. 1993. *I mörkret blir alla katter grå*. Stockholm: Tiden.

Helferrich, Barbara and Felix Kolb. 2001. Multilevel Action Coordination in European Contentious Politics: The Case of the European Women's Lobby. In *Contentious Europeans: Protests and Politics in an Emerging Polity*, eds. Doug Imig and Sydney Tarrow, 143–161. Lanham, MD: Rowman & Littlefields.

Hellgren, Zenia. 2005. Overcoming the Discrepancy between EU Anti-discrimination Directives and Persisting Discrimination at the National Level. Report from the EU project CIVGOV, WP 3.

Hervey, Tamara and David O'Keefe, eds. 1996. *Sex Equality Law in the European Union*. Chichester, UK: Wiley.

Hjarnø, Jan. 2003. *Illegal Immigrants and Developments in Employment in the Labor Markets of the EU*. Aldershot, UK and Burlington, VT: Ashgate.

Hobson, Barbara. 2003a. Introduction. In *Recognition Struggles and Social Movements*, ed. Barbara Hobson, 1–20. Cambridge: Cambridge University Press.

———. 2003b. Recognition Struggles in Universalistic and Gender Distinctive Frames: Sweden and Ireland. In *Recognition Struggles and Social Movements*, ed. Barbara Hobson, 64–92. Cambridge: Cambridge University Press.

Hobson, Barbara, Marcus Carson, and Rebecca Lawrence. Forthcoming. Recognition Struggles in Transnational Arenas: Negotiating Identities and Framing Citizenship. *Critical Review of International Social and Political Philosophy* Special Issue: Gender and Diversity.

Hobson, Barbara and Marika Lindholm. 1997. Women's Collectivities, Power Resources and the Making of Welfare States. *Theory and Society* 26: 475–508.

Honneth, Axel. 1995. *Struggle for Recognition: The Moral Grammar of Social Conflicts*. Cambridge, UK: Polity Press.

Hoskyns. Catherine. 1996. *Integrating Gender: Women, Law, and Politics in the European Community*. London: Verso.

Integrationens svarta bok. 2006. Agenda för jämlikhet och social sammanhållning SOU 2006: 79.

Izquierdo, Antonio. 2005. La inmigración irregular en el cambio del milenio: una panorámica a la luz de las regularizaciones y de los contingentes anuales de trabajadores extranjeros en España. In *Integraciones diferenciadas: migraciones en Cataluña, Galicia y Andalucía*, eds. Carlota Solé and Antonio Izquierdo, 73–88. Barcelona: Anthropos.

Jahan, Rounaq. 1995. *The Elusive Agenda: Mainstreaming Women in Development*. London: Zed Books.

Joint Action. 1997. *Joint Action of 24 February, Concerning Action to Combat Trafficking in Human Beings and Sexual Exploitation of Women.*) 97/154/JHA, 1997.

Jämställdhetsombudsmannen, Lena Svenaeus mot Örebro läns landsting. *Arbetsdomstolens Domar*, Vol. 1, 1996: Judgment no. 41/96. Case no. A 153–195.

Keck, Margaret and Kathryn Sikkink. 1998. *Activists beyond Borders: Advocacy Networks in International Politics*. Ithaca, NY: Cornell University Press.

Kligman, Gail and Stephanie Limoncelli. 2005. Trafficking Women after Socialism: To, Through and From Eastern Europe. *Social Politics* 12 (1): 118–40.

Koopmans, Ruud, Paul Statham, Marco Giugni, and Florence Passy. 2005. *Contested Citizenship—Immigration and Cultural Diversity in Europe*. Minneapolis, MN and London: University of Minnesota Press.

Leira, Arnlaug. 2002. *Working Parents and the Welfare State: Family Change and Policy Reform in Scandinavia*. Cambridge: Cambridge University Press.

Lewis, Jane. 2006. Work/Family Reconciliation Equal Opportunities and Social Policies: The Interpretation of Policy Trajectories at the EU Level and the Meaning of Gender Equality. *Journal of European Public Policy* 13 (3): 420–37.

Liebert, Ulrike, ed. 2003. *Gendering Europeansation*. Bruxelles: P.I.E—Peter Lang.

Mahon, Rianne, Caroline Andrew, and Robert Johnson. 2006. Policy Analysis in an Era of Globalisation: Capturing Spatial Dimensions and Scalar Strategies. In *Critical Policy Studies*, eds. Michael Orsini and Miriam Smith, 41–64. Vancouver: University of British Columbia Press.

Mazur, Amy G. 2001. *State Feminism, Women's Movements, and Job Training: Making Democracies Work in the Global Economy*. New York: Routledge.

McAdam, Doug, Sidney Tarrow, and Charles Tilly. 2001. *Dynamics of Contention*. Cambridge: Cambridge University Press.

McGlynn, Claire. 2001. The Europeanization of Family Law. *Child and Family Law Quarterly* 13.

Mulinari, Diana. 2001. Race/Ethnicity in a Nordic Context: A Reflection from the Swedish Borderlands. In *Svensk Genusforskning i Världen*, ed. Anna Johansson, 6–27. Göteborg: Nationella sekretariet för genusförskning.

Outshoorn, Joyce. 2005. The Political Debates on Prostitution and Trafficking of Women. *Social Politics* 12: 141–55.

Rees, Teresa. 1998. *Mainstreaming Equality in the European Union*. London: Routledge.

Schierup, Carl-Ulrik. 1991. The Ethnic Tower of Babel. In *Paradoxes of Multiculturalism*, eds. Aleksandra Ålund and Carl-Ulrik Schierup, 113–35. Aldershot: Avebury.

Schierup, Carl-Ulrik, Peo Hansen, and Stephen Castles. 2006. *Migration, Citizenship and the European Welfare State. A European Dilemma*. Oxford: Oxford University Press.

SFS 2005: 480. Swedish Antidiscrimination law.

Smith, Jackie, Charles Chatfield, and Ron Pagnucco. 1997. Social Movements and World Politics. A Theoretical Framework. In *Transnational Social Movements and Global Politics: Solidarity Beyond the State*, eds. Jackie Smith, Charles Chatfield, and Ron Pagnucco, 59–77. Syracuse, NY: Syracuse University Press.

Södergran, Lena. 2000 Svensk invandrar- och integrationspolitik—en fråga om jämlikhet, demokrati och mänskliga rättigheter. Umeå, Sweden: Umeå Universitet, doctoral dissertation, 2000.

Soysal Nhoglu, Yasemin. 1994. *Limits of Citizenship—Migrants and Postnational Membership in Europe*. Chicago: The University of Chicago Press.

Squires, Judith. 2005. Is Mainstreaming Transformative? Theorising Mainstreaming in the Context of Diversity and Deliberation. *Social Politics* 12 (3): 366–89.

Statens offentliga utredningar (SOU). 1997. Rapport till Utredningen om fördelning av ekonomisk makt och ekonomiska resurser mellan kvinnor och män: numbers 83, 87, 113, 117, 135.

Stragitaki, Maria. 2005. Gender Mainstreaming vs. Positive Action. An Ongoing Conflict in EU Gender Equality Policy. *European Journal of Women's Studies* 12 (2): 165–86.

Törnquist, Maria. 2006. *Könspolitik på gränsen: Debatterna om varannan damernas och Thamprofessurena*. Stockholm: Arkiv Förlag.

Towns, Ann. 2002. Paradoxes of (In) equality—Something is Rotten in the Gender Equal State of Sweden. *Cooperation and Conflict: Journal of the Nordic International Studies Association* 37 (2): 157–79.

Williams, Fiona and Roseneil, Sasha. 2004. Public Values of Parenting and Partnering: Voluntary Organizations and Welfare Politics in New Labour's Britain. *Social Politics* 11 (2): 181–216.

Winberg, Margareta. and Hjelm-Wallín, Lena. 2003. Our Contribution Gives Results. Debatt, *Göteborgsposten* 6:2, 4:2, 5:2

Zippel, Kathrin. 2004. Transnational Advocacy Networks and Policy Cycles in the European Union: The Case of Sexual Harassment. *Social Politics* 11 (1): 57–85.

12

FRAMING EQUALITY

*The Politics of Race, Class, and Gender in the
US, Germany, and the Expanding European Union*

Myra Marx Ferree

The European Union is an unprecedented effort to reshape political relations within as well as across national boundaries, and formulates a certain ideal for a modern, democratic member state. Moreover, as the contributions in this volume attest, to an unparalleled degree the EU's endorsement of gender equality as a fundamental value is part of this ideal, and the EU demands (at least discursively) that its member states embrace this principle. However, as the case studies show, the degree of actual translation of this principle into practice on the ground varies considerably across countries, depending on factors such as the stance of the national governments or local political mobilizations.

This chapter moves beyond the specifics of the individual case studies to suggest some of the underlying political values engaged both by the EU and by these locally mobilized interests. I suggest that the hybridity of the EU model incorporates two competing senses of transnationalism: an orientation to neoliberalism and economic competitiveness on the global level, and a specific regional claim to the distinctive success of "Europe" as a model of modernity and social progress.

Given the tension between these two orientations—liberalism and social democracy—manifest in so many of the chapters in this volume, the contrast between the ways that gender has been understood and women incorporated into the polity in Germany and the United States is especially illuminating. The German version of the "European social model" that is seen as a sign of regional success is by no means the norm—indeed, as Miethe points out, the West German model that has become hegemonic in unified Germany is itself under pressure as a laggard in comparison to other EU member states in the crucial dimensions of modernity that gender relations represent. Nonetheless, it expresses certain social democratic principles that are more significant in Europe than those of classical liberalism, and reflects how class relations have played an important role in shaping European feminist movements and state policy. The United States is a helpful model to understand because it embraces a relatively pure form of liberalism as a political standard, and has a history of struggling with the accommodation of racial and ethnic differences within its understanding of citizenship, an issue that is new but pressing in Europe, as the chapter by Hobson and Hellgren makes clear.

My argument is that the EU's own approach to gender equity can be understood as a mixture of these principles as well as of innovative ideas brought in from global feminist mobilizations (Hobson 2003; Verloo 2005). After discussing the normative dimension of politics in general and then exploring the implications of these two models in their own contexts, the paper addresses their specific integration in EU policy models. The conclusion steps back from the specific case studies of this volume to consider in general terms how the hybridity of the EU explains both the potential problems for women and the genuine hope for transformative change in gender relations that this enormous political project carries.

The Significance of Political Norms and Frames

The EU expansion to twenty-seven nations—the widening of its scope—and the more extensive involvement of the EU in matters of daily importance to individual citizens—the deepening of its reach—has made what was already a large and difficult political matter of European integration even more challenging. Both the widening and the deepening of the competences of the EU have taken it away from the original intent of its founders, as a narrow economic compact among nation-states, and have created something new. This new EU is not a nation or a state. Moreover, it is highly problematic to equate the EU with "Europe" as there are non-member states (such as Switzerland) that are certainly core parts of whatever one imagines Europe to be, and other states that are being considered for membership (e.g., Turkey, see Aldıkaçtı-Marshall in this volume) where the definition of being "European" is contested. Nonetheless, the attention paid to "Europe" as a whole increasingly is focused on the EU as such, whether as a partner entity in international relations or as a new transnational type of entity whose practices are important for changing citizenship expectations and identities across both sides of the old East/West boundary of the political imaginary. It is this latter imagined community that I consider the "new Europe" being produced in and through the existence and expansion of the EU.

As the previous chapters have shown, this new Europe is shaped already by the Treaty of Amsterdam, which elevated the equal treatment of women and men to the status of a defining principle for the EU. The significance of this principle as such was further reinforced by its use in shaping the accession process, and a poor reflection is necessarily cast on the older member states by their failure to realize standards they claimed were of central importance to a European identity in regard to new members. Directives emphasize the principle of state responsibility for making women citizens on the same basis as men, and specific treaty clauses affirm women's equal rights and commit the EU to resist and reject gender discrimination (Cichowski 2002; Walby 2004).

These clauses and directives would not exist without women's active lobbying (Cichowski 2002; Stratigaki 2004), but their enforcement and elaboration in specific instances—sexual harassment and gender mainstreaming policies, goals for women's employment and the provision of childcare, antidiscrimination law—also demand an engaged and active women's rights policy community, as the chapters of this volume have amply documented. But the meaning of gender equity is itself a contested ideal. Historically, as well as today, feminist mobilizations have drawn upon sometimes-conflicting discourses of sameness and difference, equality and autonomy, rights and needs, parity of representation in decision making and particular accommodation in policy outcomes to shape their political claims. The normative meaning of gender equity in the EU itself is still open to interpretation, and will be formed by the processes of contention that this book describes.

This is not a wholly new process. The shape of feminist claims making has been formed historically by the opportunities and obstacles with which women have contended in trying to become fully empowered citizens in democratic states (Hobson 2003). These particular structures of opportunity are not merely given by institutional features of states such as party dominance, centralization and state capacity, or welfare regime type, although all of these play important roles. Rather, these institutional features are themselves constructed in the same long-term historical development that has formed gender relations in a particular state in a specific way (Offen 2000; Gerhard 2001). Gender is thus not a side issue brought into the gender-neutral mechanisms of state action, but gender relations are part of the making of democracies from their beginnings and are today part of the construction of the EU as a new system for making European citizens.

Most of the previous chapters have focused on the nationally specific institutional features of both states and feminist movements to explain the process by which the EU comes to have its particular influence. This is only half the picture;

in addition to institutions, normative understandings of citizenship and states inform national and EU politics. Understanding how gender is incorporated in political thought and principles of democratic action as well as in the formal institutions of states draws analytic attention to how political norms function. This normative quality of politics is expressed in how issues and entities are framed.

In this approach to the political process, framing means the process of saying what a political problem is, whose needs are to be addressed, and what kinds of solutions are imaginable (Stone 2002, Snow and Benford 1988). Such frames are closely related to the organizational structures and interests that become institutionalized (Ferree 2003). Politics is done with words, but they are not *mere* words.

Framing is an *interactive* process by which actors with agendas encounter specific discursive opportunities in the form of institutionalized texts (Ferree et al. 2002). Framing has elements of both agency and structure, and is both enabling and constraining. Active "framing work"—what feminists, unions, politicians, and others actually do to give meaning to an issue—combines with the more passive sense of a "framework" as the institutionalized scaffolding of language imbedded in court decisions and other key texts that produces the effective meaning of a concept such as gender.

Comparative analysis reveals much about how the institutional structure of policy language and the ongoing struggles of particular groups to define issues combine to create different meanings for concepts in different contexts (Ferree, 2003). Such path-dependent frames both limit and empower political actors, making different strategies more or less feasible. The concept of gender has different connotations in how citizenship is understood in the US than in Europe, and these differences also change the feasibility of certain types of politics, as the following analysis attempts to show.

As a legacy of nineteenth- and twentieth-century feminist mobilizations, gender equality has effectively become part of what defines any country or policy as "modern." This is an important gain, and it is on this shared vision of modernity that contemporary gender politics normatively rests in many parts of the world, making it part of "development." To see how the frameworks of states and the framing work of movements intersect, it is useful to look at two contrasting cases, Germany and the US.

The German Model of Gendered Citizenship

Germany is like many EU member states in that the discursive institutional context for understanding gender has been shaped by class struggle rather than by racial privilege. Germany's liberal revolution failed in 1848, and the bourgeois individual as a politically empowered citizen never became central to German political thought. Instead, the conflict between capital and labor in Germany made it the home of the world's strongest socialist party at the end of the nineteenth century, the center of socialist internationalism that took hold by the beginning of the twentieth century, and offered even Christian conservatives a practical justification for the welfare state as a means of moderating political tensions and economic inequalities. This also left an important mark on gender relations in German conceptions of citizenship and democracy (Allen 1991; Gerhard 2001).

Although, in comparison with much of Europe, Germany was more often subjected to authoritarian governments, beginning with the repression of socialism and of all political associations of women in the Prussian state at the turn of the previous century, it is similar in that the struggle against social injustice was historically tied to the struggle against political repression and authoritarianism (compare for example, Valiente's chapter on Spain). From the latter part of the nineteenth century forward, gender was framed as "like class" in demanding voice for the disenfranchised, as well as making economic support for the "socially vulnerable" a shared premise for all political actors from left to right of the political spectrum.

Unlike class, race in Germany was defined as being about who could belong to the nation and enjoy any rights of citizenship. In this it was similar to other countries in Europe that were defining state boundaries in ethnic terms, as a single "nation" or people. Jewish "otherness" also implied an exclusion from citizenship until, in shocking fashion, Germany under Hitler took exclusion of the "other" to the extreme of genocide. Since "race" means the Holocaust, not subordination within the nation, the ability to see gender as in any way like race is limited (Balibar and Wallerstein1991; Lutz 2006).

In the aftermath of World War II, each of the resultant two German states took class politics in different directions. Yet in each newly defined nation-state, class and its relationship to gender was a core part of the political arrangements deliberately being constructed. The ideal worker, the "natural" family, and good work-family politics were defined in Cold War terms as opposing images of ideal state-citizenship relations in East and West (Ferree 1995b). The "social market economy" of the West and a breadwinner-housewife marriage were institutionalized via active state policies (Moeller 1993). The GDR economy and the mother-centered family were both directed through active politics as well (Ferree 1993). This institutionalization of an active welfare state that is intended to align state-family-market relations with an international political order dichotomously shaped by the Cold War characterizes all European countries after WWII. It is a core aspect of modern gender relations, albeit one that is currently in a state of change (Jenson and Saint-Martin 2003, and Miethe in this volume).

Within this framework of political development, class was the analogy that worked for gender in Germany, both before and during its separation into two different states. Drawing on socialist theory, the working class was framed as a social collectivity defined by its relation to production, not by the biological characteristics of individual members, and it won entitlement to have the state respond to needs expressed by a political party on its behalf. Inequalities among citizens were defined from the nineteenth century on as socioeconomic, rather than racialized as biological. Women's status was defined by their relation to the system of reproduction rather than production. Thus the framing of women as mothers was as a *social relation* rather than as a difference among individuals.

In the West German Basic Law of 1949, for example, the principle that women and men are politically equal was explicitly affirmed (in Paragraph 2, Article 3), but this was consistently interpreted as allowing unequal pay, gender-exclusive opportunities, and family authority based on a supposedly functional difference between men and women. Both the left and the right attacked what they perceived as the "equal rights" version of feminism and agreed that as mothers, women were entitled to the active protection and support of the state, just as workers and employers are also entitled to be treated as groups for the purposes of state-led social policy (Moeller 1993).

In the German model, citizens are framed as members of the nation in the context of a socioeconomic relation based on gender. Therefore the way the active state draws a line between the "public" matters of production and the "private" relations of family and reproduction is critiqued by feminists as core to the subordination of women (Gerhard 2001). Bringing the private relations of families into the public realm of state intervention—whether in confronting violence or supporting mothers—is critical to European gender politics, which is built on the analogy of class politics as a mobilization to make the state responsible for its citizens, rather than leaving them to the mercy of "private" exploitation. The instrumental uses of gender by the state to protect male power are contrasted with feminist, emancipatory ones. But neither type of gender politics is seen as separate from how the state works to address profoundly *social* relations, which both class and gender are understood to be.

The US Framework of Gendered Citizenship

The United States is well known as a polity institutionalized along lines of liberal individualism. The claims of classical political liberalism—individualism, self-determination, independence—were institutionalized in the founding documents of the US, which also allowed racist slavery and the domination and virtual extermination of native peoples. For American feminists, organizing a movement to claim women's rights as citizens has always demanded some choices about how to relate to the political struggle over racialized citizenship, since American nation building has depended in critical ways on the social construction of race as an essentialized form of group difference. The institutionalized practice of importing slaves, the territorial expansion of the United States that brought in new groups of people already living in these places, and the voluntary immigration of ethnically diverse individuals were all means of expanding the nation.

But the definition of who became an American, and on what basis, has always been a process of inclusion on racially unequal terms (Glenn 2002). Rather than a nation-state built on the imagined homogeneity of its people and the defense of its borders against the "other," as typical of Europe, the racial order of the US has relied on the inclusion but also the subordination of multiple "others" (Collins 2001). The legality of subordination revolves around the legitimacy of claims to political rights. Since discourses that justify and challenge racialized differences in status in terms of the prevailing liberal discourse of rights form the master frame for American politics, thinking about race has always offered American feminists an analogy for understanding their own inclusion and subordination.

The race analogy enters into American thinking about gender and citizenship in four different ways. First, there is the narrowly political struggle over who within the nation is actually a citizen with rights, rather than a political subject and dependent. Women and members of racialized groups are framed as similar in that they are constructed as dependents, and thus not fully rights-bearing individuals (Fraser and Gordon 1994). Second, because the Declaration of Independence claims that it is "self-evident" and "natural" in how people are "endowed by their Creator" that they should have rights, American movements struggle with the idea of "nature" and "natural difference" as justifications for inequality. Were it not for their "difference," construed as biological, women and racialized minorities could have equal rights, and so equality and difference are placed in opposition: to claim equality is to deny difference and vice versa (Gamson 1995; Vogel 1993).

Third, difference and subordination become packaged together as defining a "natural" hierarchy of merit in the relations of production. Both women and racial minorities are framed as "disadvantaged" by their group membership, and as less able to achieve in what is framed as an inherently fair and yet hierarchical system of competitive capitalism. Thus, affirmative action is understood as an intervention to help those less able to help themselves, and readily extended to other forms of physical or mental "disability" (Bacchi 1996).

Finally, of course, American women and members of racialized groups have worked together for their rights and have been joint beneficiaries of equal rights politics, from the Civil Rights Act of 1964 to various executive orders promoting the increase of "underrepresented groups" in science, sports, and education in general, to court decisions that make gender increasingly a "suspect classification" like race (Lens 2003). Compared to other countries, American antidiscrimination law is strong, broad, and enforceable.

Comparing Frameworks between the US and Europe

The framework for gender institutionalized in the US is not only liberal in its core premises, it privileges a metaphor of gender being like race. Seen as a form of second-class citizenship, both gender and race subordinations are effectively challenged by framing that denies the extent and natural basis of any difference from the normative (white male) citizen. A transformative politics of gender is thus one that undercuts the importance of group membership for politics and attempts to help disadvantaged individuals achieve their (presumably biologically given) full potential.

Such a model works very poorly in Germany. Since the racial "other" has been outside the system of citizenship rather than in a specific subordinated position within it, the analogy of gender with race is not particularly helpful to German feminists, or most other Europeans either.[1] However, this absence of resonance may change as the pressure for redefining citizenship in multiethnic terms becomes more pressing in Europe (Snow and Corigall-Brown 2005; and Hobson and Hellgren in this volume).

By contrast, seeing gender as like class is extremely fruitful in Germany, and in most European states with traditions of social democracy. The gender-class analogy is most problematic in the postsocialist states of Eastern Europe for the same reasons, where socialism as a principle was heavily discredited by its association with repressive authoritarianism, and the analogy often functions to create guilt by association for feminist policy making.[2] Organizing women to be a group *for* themselves as well as *in* themselves in the given relations of production and reproduction is a logical strategy that raises little concern about essentializing natural difference, since "women" are like "workers" in being understood as positions in social relations, not so much types of persons. Making claims for social entitlements for mothers, and for women's power and self-determination in the relations of reproduction, means a struggle to direct state policy to meet the needs women collectively define.

Especially in Western Europe, feminists can use the class analogy to buttress claims for political power on the basis of parity in representation. Because the member states of the EU were historically neither democratic nor liberal, political demands for representation have always demanded struggle, and socialist parties were the loudest and leading voice. Leaders of socialist parties claimed the right to speak on behalf of all oppressed people. However, the institutionalized left, in challenging state authoritarianism, typically did not open a space for multiple independent critiques. Often, leftist parties defined a single dimension of opposition and sometimes represented it in authoritarian ways. But the unity of the working class as a framework for voicing political opposition also successfully constructed group unity and interest representation as a political demand rather than an appeal to biological similarity. Because the typical European framework for claims of social inequality is class conflict, women's mobilization as a group, when perceived as like class, offers a model of group mobilization that legitimates it, especially in the democratic West, as the logical consequence of a shared social position and a prerequisite for reshaping the state.

This framework also imposes institutional challenges for feminists. Group needs can be spoken of as legitimate political demands, but class-based mobilizations are far better institutionalized than those of gender and tend to drive organizing into this single left-right dimension. Parties of the left define themselves as able to speak and act for women. The use and misuse of women's organizations, when women were "instrumentalized" to achieve the party's goals, made autonomy an important issue for feminists in Germany in the 1960s and in the postsocialist 1990s (Ferree 1987, 1996). In both the postsocialist and social democratic states of Europe today, the quality of relationships with the left, with institutionalized political parties, and with labor unions remain key issues for feminist mobilization, while these are more marginal issues in US gender politics.[3]

To sum up, the framework institutionalized for understanding social inequality in Europe has been historically defined by class, and is only now coming to terms with including racial/ethnic diversity and combating the problems of "second-class" citizenship (see chapter by Hobson/Hellgren in this volume). When they have been able to take class as a legitimate metaphor for gender subordination, European feminists have challenged the boundaries of public and private and brought the inequalities of private families under the challenging scrutiny once reserved for the inequalities produced by private enterprise (consider the Spanish law demanding equal participation in housework by men that Valiente discusses). "Social inclusion," formerly understood solely as a matter of addressing economic marginalization, is reframed as also implying some means to mitigate the costs of motherhood (Morgan 2006 and this volume). European feminists have thus created a powerful politics of critique, advocacy, and representation.

By seeing gender as like class, the active role of the state in regulating and reshaping family relations is defined as a legitimate intervention against inequality. The social organization of reproduction in childcare leaves and subsidies, abortion and contraception laws, and affirmative action policies directed at mothers have been increasingly institutionalized.

As this comparison shows, both race-based and class-based gender politics work, but in different ways. The race-based gender politics of the US works against confounding the characteristics of individuals with those of the group and uses state power to allow women more freedom to make "unexpected," counter-stereotypical choices, whether in the market or the family. The class-based gender politics of Germany works against social hierarchies and uses state power to insure that women's conformity to gender-based expectations in balancing work and family does not generate too much inequality in outcomes.

In Germany, where the framework of the welfare state situates women as a special group with distinctive interests, feminists have used the analogy of class to claim legitimate representation for women in politics (Stetson and Mazur 1995). Thus there are women charged with representing women's affairs in every city, town, and state government (Ferree 1995a). Ministries for women that are supposed to represent women's political interests exist at the state and federal level, and in 2004 women held 46 percent of all ministerial-level positions and are now coming close to half of all elected members of parliament. Germany's most recent federal chancellor, the top political position, is a conservative woman. (Ferree 2006)

Throughout Western Europe, with the class analogy for gender relations, "gender democracy" is seen as a new parallel to "social democracy," and quotas to advance parity of political representation are legitimate (Freedman 2004; Lovecy 2000). Lacking this group-centered discourse, the US falls well behind most European countries in its share of women in elected office. In the 2004 US Congress, women are just under 15 percent of the representatives (15% and 14% respectively in the Senate and House) and women hold only 25 percent of state-level executive roles. Political roles are understood as solely individual achievements, and the obstacles to women winning the financial and organizational support for top offices are still formidable.

Because both liberal and social democratic frameworks for gender have already been challenged and modified by feminists—not only in this current wave of mobilization, but from the earliest stages of democratic state formation—the institutional politics of gender today present embedded opportunities on which activists can continue to build, as well as obstacles that still need to be addressed in each system. Full citizenship for women remains a goal rather than an achievement in either case, but the available tools for the necessary activist framing work also differ.

The Hybrid EU Political Model of Gender

The European Union offers a still-developing field of political action for feminist framing work. Formed initially as a mere common market, the EU began from classical liberal principles of competition and a limited role for the state. Yet the initial member states of the EU embraced the goal of a "social market economy" that would apply social democratic principles of regulating private enterprise to ensure the common good and actively reduce inequality. Pushed and pulled between such frameworks, the EU is potentially open to US-style liberal antidiscrimination politics that would invoke a race analogy, as well as to more typically European class-style gender politics that privilege women's self-representation in politics, foster active support for balancing work and family, and legitimate targeting benefits to mothers no less than to "workers" on the basis of their social needs.

The EU's own gender politics have already shown signs of accommodating both approaches. Feminist activists working within the framework of the EU have increasingly taken a dual-action approach (Zippel 2006 and this volume). The hybridity of the EU as a novel form of governance, linking both national and transnational decision makers, may be especially suitable to a politics of gender that defines citizenship simultaneously in more than one framework, as Wahl also argues in this volume. Yet the hybridity of the EU model represents not only an opportunity for progress, but also a range of possible new obstacles for women who wish to claim full citizenship rights.

Social actors engaged in these definition struggles include social movements, interest groups, states and parties, and the media. When talking about gender at the EU level, the actors who have voice are the European Commission and its diverse executive offices, the European Women's Lobby as a commission-funded umbrella organization of national European women's organizations, the member states who enter into or reject treaties, and the European Court of Justice, which decides on the applicability of EU law and mediates conflicts between national law and EU mandates (Cichowski 2002). Although all these actors have legitimate voice, the amount of authority these voices carry is obviously very different. The framing of gender emerging at the EU level as articulated by these various actors reflects the hybridity of the frameworks available to them, challenges old frameworks, and to the varying degree that the voices are authoritative, also begins to institutionalize the new ones. Table 12.1 presents a summary of this hybrid model.

In this table, the two primary dimensions are the non-gender-specific institutional *framework* for policy making (either predominantly liberal or social democratic principles) and the gender-specific analogy made with either race or class in the *framing work* done by engaged social actors. In each cell, the emphasized aspects of gender relations are summarized and the terms that can be used discursively to most effect are in each case highlighted. The positive and negative interactions between the institutionalized frame for equality and the active framing of gender in analogy to race or class can thus be examined more closely. I highlight first the concordant cells in the upper left (liberal/race) and lower right (socialist/class) and then the discrepant ones in the lower left (liberal/class) and upper right (socialist/race).

In the top-left cell, in liberal market-led structures that define the EU's formal competences, the race metaphor provides a supportive opportunity structure for talking about diversity as a goal. In this context it is both efficient and appropriate to extend the language of rights to encompass respect for "individual differences"—which is what race and gender are conceptualized as being—and thus to dismantle group stereotypes and strive for an open process. Thus it is not surprising that there is a great deal of talk in EU circles about diversity, including

Table 12.1. The Interactions of Institutional Frameworks and Activist Framing Shaping EU Gender Politics

	Institutionalized framework for political decision making	
Active framing of gender politics:	Liberal framework	Social democratic framework
Ideas and terms privileged by analogy with race	Individual difference and rights, group stereotypes block individual choice, distort markets, focus on changing private industry	Secondary (and divisive) group differences, redistribution-led politics for all citizens, but only for citizens
	"diversity"	"social inclusion"
	"diversity management"	"borders/exclusion"
Ideas and terms privileged by analogy to class	Market-based hierarchy based on achievement, production-led politics fosters winners and losers inside the system	Party-based representation, autonomous voice of group represents needs electorally and in administrative office, focus on changing government practices
	"competition"	"parity"
	"merit"	"gender mainstreaming"

borrowing the idea of "managing diversity" from the US, as Alison Woodward (2004) has shown. Her many pictures illustrate forcefully how widely the image of gender and race diversity is institutionalized in EU materials.

This language and imagery redefines gender equality as something good for both individual citizens and for the corporate bottom line, but it says little about social justice. Adaptation to a "changing workforce" and to "global competition" makes valuing diversity a tool for increasing corporate profitability by better fitting competition into actual market conditions, rather than a matter of citizenship and rights (Edelman, Fuller and Mara-Dritta 2001).

The second productive and powerful framing draws on the synergy between the social democratic framework of member states and the discourses of class for framing women's special needs for both protection and representation, as depicted in the lower right-hand cell of table 12.1. As positions in production and reproduction, gender and class constitute formative social relations that entitle women and the working class to claim particular rights. Institutionalizing rules for gender parity within legislatures, commissions, and courts can be legitimated as part of how women claim their own voice in the EU system. Unlike the classic social democratic parties as representatives of workers' special interests, women are expected to represent themselves within the various mass parties as well as autonomously as a group in relation to EU administrative decision making.

The European Commission's funding for the European Women's Lobby (EWL) reflects the definition of women as a group with special collective interests whose representation as such lends legitimacy the EU system as a whole (Cichowki 2002). The EWL is made up of quite mainstream groups with modest and often stereotypical goals, but is accorded policy influence in "representing women" (Williams 2003). Additionally, the resonance of the class analogy with the institutional politics of gender at the member-state level provides a useful tool at the EU level, since EU-level gender equity advocates can use their gains at the national level to pressure the EU decision makers to respond to women's claims, as well as vice-versa, in a continuing ping-pong game (Zippel 2004).

Such political effectiveness in pushing particular policies "on behalf of women" may be diluted, many feminists fear, if gender mainstreaming places the authority for deciding what is in the interests of women in the hands of bureaucrats insensitive to the ramifications of gender in women's lives (Verloo 2005). Yet a very considerable advantage to gender mainstreaming is that by treating not just persons but policies and objects as gendered, every issue can be considered for its impact on both women and men (Roth 2004). The institutionalization of "gender training" as part of the mainstreaming process can be seen as institutional-level consciousness-raising work on the implications of gender. Developing gender mainstreaming in a way that respects the feminist knowledge base about gender relations in designing programs preserves the transformative mission of feminist advocacy politics. Although encouraging the diffusion of responsibility of working for gender equity throughout the state is no simple task, the EU's official endorsement of gender mainstreaming is a rhetoric that opens a door for party and pressure group activity within the system, and as these chapters have demonstrated, many but not all national feminist movements have seized these opportunities.

Invoking a class analogy is also productive for women political activists within the EU, because it unsettles the identification of systems of oppression with defense of the interests of the presumably male industrial worker. Not only are such workers an ever-smaller share of the labor force, but the use of class and gender claims has expanded domain of concern from the shop floor to a broader range of family, community, and social issues. The classic "social inclusion" language of social democracy is being more often extended to "new risk groups" like single mothers, poorly educated minority women, and part-time workers (Jenson and Saint-Martin 2003). New issues are also being promoted as economic in nature. For example, networks formed around specific issues such as sexual harassment and domestic violence are successfully framing these issues as costs to employers in the loss of women's productivity, and thus as warranting EU intervention (Walby 2004). Women have emerged within the EU as self-representing political actors to an unprecedented degree, and while there is still a considerable distance to go to achieve parity or truly mainstream attention to gender equity in policy making, the strides taken in just a few decades are impressive.

Turning now to the discrepant cells, the framing of gender as like class will have less positive resonance in relation to the EU's own liberal framework, as the lower-left cell of table 12.1 indicates. Institutionally framing economic competition and individual merit as the principles that underlie women's position, once all discrimination is cleared away, leaves no place to acknowledge children except as a "choice" and makes the disadvantages childrearing brings seem individual consequences of a personal decision, rather than structural features of a system. Since liberal political principles accept the legitimacy of market-based hierarchies among individuals and groups on the grounds of differences in achievement, the language of competition and merit tends to make workplace inequalities seem to follow "naturally" from the gender division of labor outside the workplace and therefore "fair" (Verloo 2003). Since an even more fundamental goal than gender equity for the EU is to support the market and its supposed efficiency, interventions in gender systems that are framed as not about enhancing competition are seen as illegitimately bringing in "less qualified" people as workers or students. Because this is a "market-led" model, all private inequalities of gender, like those of class, remain silent forces, difficult to name critically and thus largely outside the bounds of public or state-led remediation.

The discrepant combination of talking about gender by analogy with race in a social democratic discursive framework is depicted in the upper-right cell of table 12.1. Insofar as the EU attempts to deal with ethnic diversity at all, it does so in encouraging open borders and social equality for its citizens, but allows this state-led policy framework to exclude from concern those who are positioned outside the borders of the "community" and without attention to the processes of racialization that create "second-class citizens" within the EU (Knocke 2000; Agustin 2004). Because the EU member states have long construed race and ethnicity as being a "secondary contradiction" and divisive element, any discussion of group loyalties and of socioeconomic differences by ethnic or religious membership has been intentionally suppressed. In such a context, calling attention to race unleashes unspoken animosities; political parties that make it an issue are, with reason, seen as frightening. To talk in racial terms is to talk about exclusion.

Such racialized language is available for gender politics when it allows the speaker to highlight "the other," the "non-European," as the wellspring of patriarchy. In this discourse, the way to eradicate patriarchal institutions is to forbid them legally and thus exclude them from the domain of citizenship. Many EU member states have attempted to do just this by focusing on wearing a headscarf as a distinctive symbol of "private," religiously based patriarchy and then excluding the veiled women from various citizen rights in employment, education, or politics. By attempting to drive patriarchal relations of "the other" out of the public sphere, these policies make their own patriarchal practices invisible, defining "European women" as simultaneously "white," "liberated" and "privileged" in contrast to the other (Agustin 2004).

Tying race and gender together, by framing those "outside" the EU as less modern and thus less equal in their gender relations than those "inside" Europe, leads to absurdities such as the denigration of the newer members of the EU from Central and Eastern Europe as inherently more "backward" and less modern in their gender relations than the older member states, as Eva Fodor (2005) has tellingly demonstrated in her comparison of the language applied to Eastern and Western European issues for women in UN and EU documents. By objective measures of education, employment, and family power, women in the accession states experience more gender equity than their West European counterparts, but the framing device of backwardness allows the discussions of the status of women to revolve not around women's real social position, but the perceived level of "Europeanness," operationally defined as the variable levels of EU citizenship among the member states.

Conclusions

The implications of this analysis for the prospects for gender equality in the hybrid model of the EU suggest caution, but not cynicism. As in the US, the market orientation of the EU creates a productive synergy between liberalism and use of the race analogy, encouraging not merely the depoliticizing language of "diversity," but a raft of strong antidiscrimination measures embedded in law and embraced by "private" industry. Activists using antidiscrimination laws and policies can bring in authentically competitive mechanisms to institutions like universities that have operated like exclusionary good old boys' clubs. Formal tests and open searches could be good for women candidates, who have shown in systems like the US that they can indeed compete with men. Women activists have also used the heritage of social democracy effectively to pressure EU governance structures to strive for parity of representation in electoral and party politics as well as for gender mainstreaming and interest group representation in administrative decision making. Feminist advocacy networks at the EU level have been empowered, even as grassroots service projects in member states have faced ever more severe budget cuts.

The challenge is to resist the threats to women's equality and autonomy posed, on the one hand, by the class-based language of competition and merit as explaining away the costs of unpaid carework socially assigned to women, and, on the other hand, the race-based language of exclusion and "othering" that makes patriarchy in Europe someone else's problem. For example, migrant groups and women's groups can cooperate to support associations of migrant women in making claims for social inclusion (as Hobson and Hellgren in this volume and Williams 2003 suggest). The use of gender relations as an indication of modernity can even be framed as a challenge from new, postsocialist member states to the older members to finally modernize their gender relations (Roth 2004).

While the hybridity of the EU structure offers a potentially valuable "ping-pong effect" between national and transnational actors (Zippel 2004), the complexity of the new discursive space thus opened up includes significant dangers as well. Women, especially mothers, can appear in the more neoliberal discourse of the EU as "uncompetitive" and as less valuable. The scaling back of the welfare state that the EU has encouraged in the name of market efficiency poses a great danger to social inclusion as a policy goal. Because unmarried mothers are disproportionately poor and dependent on state assistance, this turn toward a neoliberal institutional framework will jeopardize their actual well being as well as making it harder to frame effective opposition to such policies. Framing all women as vulnerable victims—whether as unmarried mothers, trafficked sexual commodities, targets of domestic violence, or subjects of any other real risk—is also a dangerously disempowering discourse.

Women's strong representation in political parties and government offices is a tremendous political resource, but it does not overcome the limits of party discipline nor necessarily give women equal voice with men in shaping the agenda of the party as a whole. Moreover, the bureaucratic, top-down decision making that characterizes EU policy making lessens the role of electoral accountability and competition for women voters. Gender mainstreaming could become an administrative fig leaf over the absence of actual policy pressure for gender equity (Verloo 2005), just as the presence of prominent women in positions of political power can disguise the continued underrepresentation of women in positions of economic power.

However, the hybridity that the EU represents in relation to gender, race, and class has possibilities. A liberal and narrowly economic definition of citizenship does not exist in hegemonic position, as in the US, but is being integrated with the social and democratic aspirations of the European states that are its members. This could present new opportunities for gender politics. The terrain of the EU could be as promising as its potential suggests, or as dangerous as the sum of its risks. As the EU both widens in scope and deepens in its reach into more and more areas of policy, the actual outcomes for women may well depend on the vigor and effectiveness with which organized efforts to frame gender equity issues develop. Because the EU still has the status of an experiment in the making, the energetic use of effective frames by feminist advocacy networks may well turn out to the key factor explaining whether the more optimistic or the more pessimistic scenario prevails.

Notes

1. Despite recent changes not only in Germany, but also throughout Europe, more readily offering immigrants citizenship, an institutionalized "second-class citizenship" by racial/ethnic origins that characterizes the US is not (yet) a part of the European experience.

2. The complexity this introduces into feminist organizing in unified Germany, trying to develop appeals to both sides of the German experience, is something I have dealt with in other papers. See for example, Ferree 1993 and 1995b.

3. Insofar as feminism has become identified with the Democratic Party in the US, this is likely to change. But such partisan alignment is relatively recent in the US, and the Democratic Party is still far from being a "left" party in European terms.

References

Agustin, Laura Maria. 2004. At Home in the Street: Questioning the Desire to Help and Save. In *Controlling Sex: The Regulation of Intimacy and Identity*, eds. Elizabeth Bernstein and Laurie Shaffner, 67–82. New York: Routledge.

Allen, Ann Taylor. 1991. *Feminism and Motherhood in Germany 1800–1914*. New Brunswick, NJ: Rutgers University Press.

Bacchi, Carol. 1996. *The Politics of Affirmative Action: Women, Equality and Category Politics*. Thousand Oaks: Sage Publications.

Balibar, Etienne and Immanuel Wallerstein. 1991. *Race, Nation, Class: Ambiguous Identities*. New York: Verso.

Cichowski, Rachel. 2002. "No Discrimination Whatsoever": Women's Transnational Activism and the Evolution of EU Sex Equality Policy. In *Women's Activism and Globalization: Linking Local Struggles and Transnational Politics*, eds. Nancy Naples and Manisha Desai, 220–38. New York: Routledge.

Collins, Patricia Hill. 2001. Like One of the Family: Race, Ethnicity and the Paradox of US National Identity. *Ethnic & Racial Studies* 24 (1): 3–28.

Edelman, Lauren, Sally Riggs Fuller, and Iona Mara-Drita. 2001. Diversity Rhetoric and the Managerialization of Law. *American Journal of Sociology* 106 (6): 1589–1641.

Ferree, Myra Marx. 1987. Equality and Autonomy: Feminist Politics in the United States and West Germany. In *The Women's Movements of Western Europe and the United States*, eds. Mary Katzenstein and Carol McClurg Mueller, 172–95. Philadelphia: Temple University Press.

———. 1993. The Rise and Fall of Mommy Politics: Feminism and Unification in (East) Germany. *Feminist Studies* 19 (1): 89–115.

———. 1995a. Making Equality: The Women's Affairs Officers of the Federal Republic of Germany. In *Comparative State Feminism*, eds. Dorothy Stetson and Amy Mazur, 95–113. Thousand Oaks: Sage Publications.

———. 1995b. Patriarchies and Feminisms: The Two Women's Movements of Unified Germany. *Social Politics* 2 (1): 10–24.

———. 1996. Institutionalization, Identities and the Political Participation of Women in the New Federal States of Germany In *Women and Postcommunism, Research on Russia and Eastern Europe*, eds. Mehta Spencer and Barbara Wejnert (eds). Greenwich, CT: JAI Press, 17–32.

———. 2003. Resonance and Radicalism: Feminist Abortion Discourses in Germany and the United States. *American Journal of Sociology* 109 (2): 304–44.

———. 2006. Angela Merkel: What Does it Mean to Run as a Woman? *German Politics and Society* 24 (1): 93–107.

Ferree, Myra Marx, William A. Gamson, Jürgen Gerhards, and Dieter Rucht. 2002. *Shaping Abortion Discourse: Democracy and Public Sphere in Germany and United States*. New York: Cambridge University Press.

Fodor, Eva. 2005. Really So Different? A Comparison of Discourses on Working Women in East and West Europe. Paper presented at conference on Gender Politics and the EU, University of Pennsylvania, February.

Fraser, Nancy and Linda Gordon. 1994. On the Genealogy of Dependency: Tracing a Keyword of the US Welfare State. *Signs* 19 (2): 309–36.

Freedman, Jane. 2004. Increasing Women's Political Representation: The Limits of Constitutional Reform. *West European Politics* 27 (1): 104–23.

Gamson, Josh. 1995. Must Identity Politics Self-destruct? A Queer Dilemma. *Social Problems* 42 (3): 390–407.

Gerhard, Ute. 2001. *Debating Women's Equality: Toward a Feminist Theory of Law from a European Perspective*. New Brunswick, NJ: Rutgers University Press.

Glenn, Evelyn Nakano. 2002. *Unequal Freedom: How Race and Gender Shaped American Citizenship and Labor*. Cambridge: Harvard University Press.

Hobson, Barbara. 2003. Recognition Struggles in Universalistic and Gender Distinctive Frames: Sweden and Ireland. In *Recognition Struggles and Social Movements: Contested Identities, Agency and Power*, ed. Barbara Hobson, 64–92. New York: Cambridge University Press.

Jenson, Jane and D. Saint-Martin. 2003. New Routes to Social Cohesion? Citizenship and the Social Investment State. *Canadian Journal Of Sociology-Cahiers Canadiens De Sociologie* 28 (1): 77–99.

Knocke, Wuokko. 2000. Migrant and Ethnic Minority Women: The Effects of Gender Neutral Language in the EU. *Gender and Citizenship in Transition*, ed. Barbara Hobson, 139–55. New York: Routledge.

Lens, Vicki. 2003. Reading Between the Lines: Analyzing the Supreme Court's Views on Gender Discrimination. *Social Science Review* 77 (1): 25–50.

Lovecy, Jill. 2000. "Citoyennes a part entiere?" The Constitutionalization of Gendered Citizenship in France and the Parity Reforms of 1999–2000. *Government and Opposition* 35 (4): 439–62.

Lutz, Helga. 2006. Doing Gender and Doing Ethnicity: Intersectionality in the Debate on Social Inequalities. Paper presented at conference, Re-visioning the Future: Perspectives on Gender Studies, Braunschweig, Germany, 4–6 May.

Moeller, Robert. 1993. *Protecting Motherhood: Women and the Family in Postwar West Germany*. Berkeley, CA: University of California Press.

Morgan, Kimberly. 2006. *Working Mothers and the Welfare State. Religion and the Politics of Work-Family Policies in Western Europe and the United States*. Palo Alto, CA: Stanford University Press.

Offen, Karen. 2000. *European Feminisms, 1700–1950: A Political History*. Palo Alto, CA: Stanford University Press.

Roth, Silke. 2004. One Step Forwards, One Step Backwards: The Impact of EU Policy on Gender Relations in Central and Eastern Europe. *Transitions/Revue des Pays de l'Est* 44 (1): 15–28.

Snow, David and Robert Benford. 1988. Ideology, Frame Resonance and Participant Mobilization. In *From Structure to Action: Comparative Social Movement Research across Cultures*, eds. Bert Klandermans, Hans-Peter Kriesi, and Sidney Tarrow, 197–217. Greenwich, CT: JAI Press.

Snow, David and Cathrin Corrigall-Brown. 2005. Falling on Deaf Ears: Confronting the Prospect of Non-Resonant Frames. In *Rhyming Hope and History: Activists, Academics and Social Movement Scholarship*, eds. David Croteau, William Hoynes, and Charlotte Ryan, 221–38. Minneapolis, MN: University of Minnesota Press.

Stetson, Dorothy McBride and Amy Mazur. 1995. *Comparative State Feminism*. Thousand Oaks, CA: Sage.

Stone, Deborah. [1988] 2002. *Policy Paradox and Political Reason: The Art of Political Decision-Making*. New York: Norton.

Stratigaki, Maria. 2004. The Cooptation of Gender Concepts in EU Policies: The Case of "Reconciliation of Work and Family." *Social Politics* 11 (1): 30–56.

Verloo, Mieke. 2003. Reflections on the Dutch Case in Gender Mainstreaming. In *Observatoria. Gender-Mainstreaming- Eine Strategie zur Verringerung der Einkommensdifferenzen zwischen Frauen und Männer?*, eds. Hannah Steiner and Itta Tetschert, 125–39. Vienna: Netzwerk Oesterreichischer Frauen- und Mädchenberatungsstellen.

———. 2005. Studying Gender Equality in Europe. *European Studies Newsletter of the Council for European Studies* 34 (3/4): 1–3.

Vogel, Lise. 1993. *Mothers on the Job: Maternity Policy in the US Workplace*. New Brunswick, NJ: Rutgers University Press.

Walby, Sylvia. 2004. The European Union and Gender Equality: Emergent Varieties of Gender Regime. *Social Politics* 11 (1): 4–29.

Williams, Fiona. 2003. Contesting "Race" and Gender in the European Union: A Multi-layered Recognition Struggle for Voice and Visibility. In *Recognition Struggles and Social Movements: Contested Identities, Agency and Power*, ed. Barbara Hobson, 121–44. New York: Cambridge University Press.

Woodward, Alison. 2004. Images of Diversity. Paper presented at conference on Gender Mainstreaming, University of Leeds, UK. April.

Zippel, Kathrin. 2004. Transnational Advocacy Networks and Policy Cycles in the European Union: The Case of Sexual Harassment. *Social Politics* 11 (1): 57–85

———. 2006. *The Politics of Sexual Harassment: A Comparative Study of the United States, the European Union and Germany*. New York: Cambridge University Press

LIST OF CONTRIBUTORS

Gül Aldıkaçtı-Marshall is Assistant Professor in the Department of Sociology at the University of Louisville. She received her doctorate in sociology from the University of Pennsylvania in 2001. Her research and teaching interests are in the areas of gender, social movements, social policy, and the mass media. Currently she is analyzing the dynamics of national and transnational activism of feminists whose advocacy efforts are shaping gender policies in Turkey.

Pauline P. Cullen is Assistant Professor of Sociology at Dickinson College in Pennsylvania. She completed her doctorate in Sociology from the State University of New York at Stony Brook in 2003. Her research and publications have examined the transnational dimensions of social movements, international organizations, welfare states, and globalization, in particular, mobilization by nongovernmental organizations for political action on social rights around the institutions of the European Union. She is the author of "Obstacles to Transnational Cooperation in the European Social Policy Platform," in *Negotiating Differences and Unity in Transnational Struggles Against Neo-Liberalism*, edited by Jackie Smith and Joe Bandy, Rowman and Littlefield 2004, "Coalitions Working for Social Justice," in *Forging Radical Alliances Across Difference: Coalition Politics for the New Millennium*, edited by Jill Bystydzienski and Steve Schacht, Rowman and Littlefield, 2001, and "Coalitions Working for Social Justice— Transnational NGOs and International Governance," in *Contemporary Justice Review Journal* 2, 2 (1999).

Myra Marx Ferree is Martindale Bascom Professor of Sociology and Director of the Center for German and European Studies at the University of Wisconsin–Madison. She is a long-time student of the women's movements, co-author of

Shaping Abortion Discourse: Democracy and the Public Sphere in Germany and the US (Cambridge 2002) and co-editor of *Global Feminism: Women's Activism, Organizing and Human Rights* (New York University Press 2006). She is currently writing a book on transformations of German feminism, tentatively titled *Sisterhood since the Sixties* (Stanford 2009). Her other work in progress includes a new project on transnational feminist identities and web-networks. The 3rd edition of *Controversy and Coalition: The New Feminist Movement* (co- authored with Beth Hess, Routledge 2000) on the US women's movement includes a new introduction focusing on international feminism.

Magda Grabowska is a PhD candidate at the Women and Gender Studies Department at Rutgers University (ABD February 2005). In 2000 she graduated from the Sociology Department at Warsaw University, and in 2001 entered the PhD program in WGS at Rutgers University. She worked in OSKa (Women's Information Center) in Warsaw, and is the co-founder of the informal women group "Sisterhood Street." She is the author of reports on the functioning of the antiabortion law in Poland (*Attitudes of Rural Women toward Reproduction Issues*, 2000) and articles and pamphlets on the European Union and women in Poland (*On the way to the European Union. A guide not only for women*, 2002).

Hana Hašková is a PhD candidate in sociology at Charles University in Prague. Since 1999 she has worked in the Gender Sociology Department at the Institute of Sociology of the Academy of Sciences of the Czech Republic, and since 2002 she has taught courses on Gender and Family at Charles University. Her research focus is on gender, reproduction, and women's civic participation. Since 2002, she has been a coordinator and principal investigator of a Czech research team in the international research project Enlargement, Gender and Governance, funded by the EC. She has been also a coordinator and principal investigator of two national research projects on childbirth practices and discourses, and childless and childfree identities. She has also participated in other research projects, including an international research project Constructing Supranational Political Spaces, funded by the NSF.

Zenia Hellgren is an advanced PhD candidate in sociology at Stockholm University specializing in migration, ethnic relations and political theory. Her dissertation addresses the boundaries of social membership and focuses on immigrant claims-making in Sweden and Spain. She contributed to several book projects and to *Arena*, a Swedish review for cultural and political debate. Her recent publications include "The myth of the multicultural society. Theoretical perspectives on multiculturalism" in *Migration and ethnicity—perspectives on a multicultural Sweden*, ed. Mehrdad Darvishpour (in Sweden) and "The limits of solidarity. Irregular immigrants and apathetic refugee children in the Swedish welfare state" in *The Struggle of "paperless" immigrants and the Extension of Citizenship: a Global Perspective*, eds. Liliana Suárez Navaz, Raquel Macià, and Angela Moreno (in Spanish).

Barbara Hobson, Professor of Sociology, holds a chair in Sociology with a specialization in Comparative Gender Studies at Stockholm University. She has published numerous articles and books on gender and welfare states concerning themes of gender and citizenship, men and social politics, and social movements and gender diversity in welfare states, including *Recognition and Social Movements: Contested Identities, Agency and Power* (Cambridge University Press, 2003), *Making Men into Fathers: Men, Masculinities and the Social Politics of Fatherhood* (Cambridge University Press, 2002), *Gender and Citizenship in Transition* (MacMillan 2000) Her current ESF project involves large scale study of gender, capabilities, and agency across European societies. She is a founder and a current editor of the journal *Social Politics: International Studies of Gender, State, and Society* (Oxford University Press).

Noémi Kakucs holds a Masters degree (2006) in Gender Studies from the Central European University in Budapest. Her research interests include anti-discrimination policy (especially on the grounds of race, ethnicity, and gender), implementation and equal opportunity policies, gender equity policies (in particular gender mainstreaming) in Central and Eastern Europe. Her recent publications include "Women in European Societies: Societal justice East and West" in *Movements, Migrants, Marginalisation.* "Challenges of Societal and Political Participation" in *Eastern Europe and the Enlarged EU*, edited by Sabine Fischer, Heiko Pleis and Hans-Henning Schröder (Bremen: Research Centre for Eastern European Studies 2007).

Alena Křížková is senior researcher in the Gender & Sociology Department at the Institute of Sociology, AS CR. In 2007 she received her PhD. in sociology from the Faculty of Social Sciences, Charles University in Prague. She deals with gender relations in the labor market, in organizations, management, and entrepreneurship, and with issues concerning civic and political participation of women in relation to the Czech Republics' membership in the EU. She has been coordinator of the Czech team on the project Constructing Supranational Political Spaces: The European Union, Eastern Enlargement, and Women's Agency, funded by the NSF , and participated on the project Enlargement, Gender and Governance, funded by the EC. Křížková is the co-author of *Management of Gender Relations, Position of Women and Men in Organization* (published in Czech in 2004), *Sexualized Reality of the Working Relations* (published in Czech in 2006), and co-editor of *In Multiple Voices: Negotiating Women's Spaces after 1989* (published in Czech with English abstracts in 2006). She provides expertise to the

European Commission on a regular basis as a member of a Network of Experts on Gender Equality in Employment and Social Inclusion.

Ingrid Miethe is Professor for Pedagogics at the Protestant University of Applied Sciences in Darmstadt. She was born and raised in East Germany and received her PhD in Political Science from the Freie Universität Berlin. Her books include *Frauen in der DDR Opposition* [in German] (1999), and *Biographies and the division of Europe: experience, action, and change on the 'Eastern side'* (edited with Roswitha Breckner and Devorah Kalekin-Fishman) (2000) and *Bildung und Soziale Ungleichheit in der DDR* (Barbara Budrich Verlay 2007). Her book, *Europas Töchter: Traditionen, Erwartungen und Strategien von Frauenbewegungen in Europa* (edited with Silke Roth) (2003), focuses on the implications of EU expansion for women and women's movements.

Kimberly J. Morgan is Assistant Professor of Political Science at George Washington University, and was previously a participant in the Robert Wood Johnson Foundation's Scholars in Health Policy Research program at Yale University. Her research and teaching interests include childcare and parental leave, health policy, taxation, and more broadly, the politics of the welfare state. Her articles have appeared in *World Politics*, *Comparative Politics*, *Politics and Society*, *Social Politics*, and the *Journal of Policy History*. She is the author of *Working Mothers and the Welfare State: Religion and the Politics of Work-Family Policies in Western Europe and the United States* (Stanford University Press 2006).

Andrea Pető is Associate Professor at the Department of Gender Studies at the Central European University, and an Associate Professor at University of Miskolc, where she directs the Equal Opportunity and Gender Studies Center. Presently she is working on transitional justice, gender, and the Holocaust. She has published extensively on gender and politics in Eastern Europe and is the author of numerous articles and edited volumes in several languages (English, Russian, German, Croatian, Serbian, Bulgarian, Georgian, Hungarian, Italian, and French). Her publications include *Women in Hungarian Politics 1945–1951* (Columbia University Press/East European Monograph 2003) and a monograph exploring gender and conservatism: *Napasszonyok és Holdkisasszonyok. A mai magyar konzervatív női politizálás alaktana*, (Women of Sun and Girls of Moon. Morphology of Contemporary Hungarian Women Doing Politics [2003]).

Joanna Regulska is Professor of Women's and Gender Studies and Geography and the Director of the International Programs, School of Arts and Sciences at Rutgers University. She is the founder and director since 1989 of the Local Democracy Partnership (formerly Local Democracy in Poland) Program, Rutgers University. Most of her research and teaching concentrates on women's agency, political activism, grassroots mobilization and construction of women's political spaces. She has also conducted extensive work on the impacts of political and economic restructuring on the process of democratization, citizens' participation and decentralization in Central and Eastern Europe. Most recently she has edited and co-edited with Jasmina Lukić and Darja Zaviršek *Women and Citizenship in Central and East Europe* (Ashgate 2006), *Women's Activism in Public Sphere* (Wydawnictwo OSKA, 1999), *Being Active* (Wydawnictwo OSKA, 1998) and *Informational Policy at the Local Level* (1995, 2nd edition 1997). Currently she is working on two co-edited volumes: *Cooperation or Conflict? State, The European Union and Women* (in Polish) with Magda Grabowska, Małgorzata Fuszara, Joanna Mizielińska and *Reinventing Gender of Europe* with Bonnie Smith.

Silke Roth is Senior Lecturer in the Division of Sociology and Social Policy at the University of Southampton, United Kingdom. Her areas of teaching and research include gender, social movements, biographical methods, and transnational nongovernmental organizations. She is the author of *Building Movement Bridges: The Coalition of Labor Union Women.* (Greenwood/Praeger 2003), and has edited several volumes on women's movements, nongovernmental organizations, and transnational careers.

Celia Valiente is Associate Professor at the Department of Political Science and Sociology of the Universidad Carlos III de Madrid, Spain. Her current research is on public policy and social movements in Spain from a gender perspective. She is the author with Monica Threlfall and Christine Cousins of *Gendering Spanish Democracy* (2005). Her articles were published in *Gender and Society, European Journal of Political Research, Politics and Gender,* and *South European Society and Politics.*

Angelika von Wahl is Associate Professor of Political Science at San Francisco State University. Her comparative research focuses on Western Europe and the United States, the European Union, welfare state politics, labor markets, social mobilization, and gender. She is also currently working on a comparative research project on human rights abuse and reparations in Germany, Japan, and the US. She is the author of *Equal Employment Regimes: Equal Employment Opportunities for Women in Germany and the USA* [in German] (Leske + Budrich 1999) and co-editor of *Gender and Politics* (Leske + Budrich 1999). Recent articles were published in *Social Politics, West European Politics* and *WZB–Jahrbuch.*

Kathrin Zippel is Associate Professor of Sociology at Northeastern University and affiliated with the Minda de Gunzburg Center for European Studies at Harvard University. She has received her doctorate from the University of Wisconsin–Madison (2000). Her general areas of interest include political sociology and gender with specific research interests in social movements, (welfare) states, the law, the social dimension of the European Integration process, and globalization. Her articles have appeared in *Social Politics*, *The Review of Policy Research*, and the *Forschungsjournal Neue Soziale Bewegungen*. She is the author of *The Politics of Sexual Harassment: A Comparative Study of the United States and the European Union* (Cambridge University Press 2006).

INDEX

Printed in the United States
144755LV00006B/57/P